CW00621555

VINTAGE TALES

By The Same Author

Books on Wine and Kindred Subjects

The Gourmet's Companion (edited, with introduction)
The Compleat Imbiber: Nos 1–12 (edited, 1956–71)
Morton Shand's A Book of French Wines (revised and edited)
In a Glass Lightly
Lafite: The Story of Château Lafite-Rothschild
Mouton-Rothschild: The Wine, the Family, the Museum
Bollinger
Cognac
Wine with Food (with Elizabeth Ray)
The Wines of Italy
The Wines of France
The Wines of Germany
The Complete Book of Spirits and Liqueurs
The St Michael Guide to Wine
Ray on Wine
Lickerish Limericks, with filthy pictures by Charles Mozley
The New Book of Italian Wines

& sponsored works on
Ruffino Chianti, Warre's Port, the Bartons of Langoa and Léoville, etc.

Books on Other Subjects

Scenes and Characters from Surtees
Algiers to Austria: 78 Division in the Second World War
The Pageant of London
Merry England
Regiment of the Line: The Story of the Lancashire Fusiliers
Best Murder Stories (edited, with introduction)

VINTAGE TALES

AN ANTHOLOGY OF WINE AND OTHER INTOXICATIONS

EDITED BY

CYRIL RAY

CENTURY PUBLISHING
LONDON

To Charles Mozley
Old friend and good companion

EDITOR'S NOTE

Most of the pieces here assembled come from collections that I
edited in the past: *The Gourmet's Companion* (1963) and the
twelve volumes of *The Compleat Imbiber* (1956-71) except for no.
3, a new edition of which is on the way. All are now out of print.
Among those pieces that I thought deserved another airing are
some that I specially commissioned for the *Imbiber* and that have
appeared nowhere else.

C.R.

Compilation Copyright © Cyril Ray 1984

All rights reserved

First published in Great Britain in 1984
by Century Publishing Co. Ltd,
Portland House,
12-13 Greek Street, London W1V 5LE

Design and production arrangements by David Edwards

British Library Cataloguing in Publication Data
Vintage tales.
    1. Drinking customs—Anecdotes, facetiae, satire, etc.
I. Ray, Cyril
394.1′3   GT2880
ISBN 0 7126 0255 0

Typeset, printed and bound in Great Britain by
Butler & Tanner Ltd, Frome, Somerset

Contents

[5]

CONTENTS

All these things here collected are not mine,
But divers grapes make but one sort of wine;
So I from many learned authors took
The various matters printed in this book.
What's not mine own by me shall not be father'd.
The most part I in fifty years have gather'd;
Some things are very good, pick out the best,
Good wits compiled them, and I wrote the rest.

John Taylor the Water Poet
from MISCELLANIES, 1652

Introduction

WYNFORD VAUGHAN-THOMAS

In his collection of *Vintage Tales*, Cyril Ray invites us to a literary wine-tasting of choice vintages from the cellars of those classic anthologies he edited, from the late 50s to the early 70s, under the title of *The Compleat Imbiber*. I have a set of them on my shelves and how well they still read! What a pleasure it is to take them down, at the end of a hard day, and turn over the beautifully printed pages! Every volume offers the savour of an era of wine-drinking and wine-writing the like of which we will not see again. Those were the days when vintners almost felt it their privilege as well as their duty to give writers, artists and even poets a splendid run for their money. *The Compleat Imbiber* was laid out by designers of the quality of Charles Hasler and employed every eye-catching device known to the printers of the period. Splendid drawings and old photographs were scattered through the pages with a lavish hand. And all for twenty-five pre-inflation shillings! No, it would not be possible today. That it was possible even in the 60s was surely due to the editorial skill

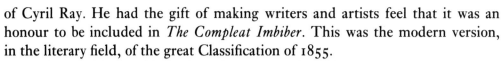
of Cyril Ray. He had the gift of making writers and artists feel that it was an honour to be included in *The Compleat Imbiber*. This was the modern version, in the literary field, of the great Classification of 1855.

Cyril Ray claims, with justice, that a great deal of rubbish has been written about wine. He is particularly hard on that somewhat florid, 'baroque' style of wine writing that flourished between the wars – the period that began with the publication of George Saintsbury's *Notes on a Cellar Book* and included such oenological eulogies as Maurice Healy's *Stay Me with Flagons*. Of course I agree with him, but I do so with regret and a certain feeling of guilt. How can I desert such old friends as Morton Shand or Warner Allen, for it was through their books that I took my first tentative steps in the complex and difficult art of wine appreciation? I revelled in their classical quotations, and their fine writing seemed to me to distil the very aroma of a great vintage. When all was said and done, where else, at the time I was growing up, was I to find the key to the glories that lay in the glass? Certainly not in that least vinously inclined tract of the whole surface of the earth – South Wales.

I was brought up in a country and in an age when Teetotalism reigned unrestrained. Was not St David himself, our patron saint, known as 'Dewi Ddyfrwr' – David the Waterdrinker? G.K. Chesterton hit the nail on the head, or drew the cork out of the bottle, when he sang, 'You can't get wine at a PSA, or chapel, or Eisteddfod.' Even in my early youth, young men leaving for London to become drapers or milkmen – the certain passport to wealth for Welshmen at the turn of the century – were presented in chapel with a little red book entitled 'Y Gwr Ifanc Oddicatref' – the Young Man away from Home. The earnest author, John Angell Jones, gave a hair-raising account of all the temptations that lay in wait for the innocent in the Big City. Unfortunately he gave precise instructions where all these delights lay, from the cigar divans of the Haymarket and the gardens at Cremorne to the wine-taverns in Holborn. The new arrivals made straight for them and were never seen in Wales again. I suppose that my equivalent of John Angell Jones was Morton Shand.

Fortunately for me, our home was a happy oasis in this teetotal desert. My father enjoyed a glass of wine but, an impecunious musician, he could not afford to lay down noble vintages. His notes were never 'Notes from a Cellar Book'. We drank an acceptable table wine, supplied by the local wine merchant. I do remember one occasion, however, when we were invited to sample greater things. My rich Uncle Arthur arrived with what he described as 'an exceptional bottle'. It certainly was! Of all things, it was a hock that had been produced in Wales.

Introduction

Towards the end of the nineteenth century, the Marquess of Bute, one of the richest men in Britain, had a romantic dream. He had restored an ancient Welsh stronghold known as Castell Coch, the Red Castle, on a hillside near Cardiff. His architect was the celebrated William Burges, who peppered the building with pointed turrets until it looked like a Rhineland Schloss. All that was now required was a vineyard at its foot. When you have unlimited money you can realise the impossible dream. Soon the vineyard was in production. You can picture the grapes ripening happily, and the Welsh vignerons singing – in four part harmony, of course – as they tended the vines before going to choir practice in the chapel.

The wines were duly placed on the London market and appeared on Messrs Hatch, Mansfield's list as 'Welsh Wines; Canary Brand'. The catalogue was coy about their quality, simply stating that 'although these wines cannot be said to possess that delicate aroma and flavour of the best foreign wines, they are eminently wholesome and honest.' Fair enough! No fine writing here à la Maurice Healy or Morton Shand. *Punch* was not so kind. It declared that it took four men to drink one bottle of the wine – the drinker himself, two to hold him down, and one to pour it down his throat.

We knew nothing of this when Uncle Arthur uncorked his bottle of Château Cardiff. It happened a long time ago, and I cannot remember what Lord Bute's wine actually tasted like. Indeed, I didn't care, for I felt, instinctively, that this was an 'occasion' – a moment to be savoured to the full. I still have that feeling whenever a really great and rare bottle is opened, even when age may have caused its glory to fade. I feel that I am privileged to be present when the product of all that skill, care and knowledge is decanted. I lift liquid history in my glass and ... but stop: Hold on! I am on the verge of falling headlong into that prohibited, florid phraseology of the nineteen-twenties. Warner Allen salutes me as a brother; Maurice Healy lifts his glass to me across the years.

Yet I cannot help thinking that great wine – really great wine – needs and even cries out for poetry. Unfortunately, the great poets are not altogether reliable when it comes to wine. Look at Keats ... Surely that glorious second verse of the *Ode to a Nightingale* is the perfect expression of the glory of a great wine 'tasting of Flora and the country green'; a delicious draught

> '*Full of the true, the blushful Hippocrene,*
> *With beaded bubbles winking at the brim,*
> *And purple-stained mouth...*'

Excellent, magical, we said – until we bought the *Compleat Imbiber* for 1967. In it, Marghanita Laski got her analytical mind to work on Keats's poem and pointed out the problems. Keats, we know, was a claret-lover, but what sort of claret was it that reminded him of 'Provençal' song and not of Bordeaux? Furthermore, what great claret has all those beaded bubbles and gives you a purple-stained mouth?

Marghanita reminds us that, in Keats's day, the term 'claret' had a wider geographical connotation. Keats was a poor man. He and his friends never had the money to buy the notable Bordeaux vintages. He probably bought his wine from his local wine-merchant who advertised his wines as 'claret type'! What the merchant actually sold to Keats may have been a Portuguese wine, which would certainly have bubbled and may have left not only a purple stain but a hang-over as well.

Ah, well, we must not look to the well-known names when it comes to Wine and Poetry. In *Vintage Tales*, Cyril Ray has rightly included his own witty vinous perambulation among the poets, and his survey confirms my suspicion that the Big Boys are not to be trusted when it comes to the accurate celebration of the glory of wine. The lesser poets do better and the frivolous ones best of all. This volume is pleasantly salted with the sort of verse that goes extremely well as the port circulates. In the closing pages, however, Cyril Ray has printed a serious poem by the one poet who was not renowned for his discriminating taste in wine, although he could make moving use of it in metaphor and symbolism.

Dylan Thomas was my fellow townsman and we shared many a glass together in Swansea, although I remember that his own glass was rarely filled with the produce of the grape. He was devoted to that warm, weak, brown ale that was sloshed around the more obscure pubs of Swansea and points west. I can, however, recall one occasion when we did share a bottle of wine together in a remarkable hostelry known as Number Ten. Anything farther removed from Downing Street it was hard to imagine. The Swansea Number Ten was a wonderful piece of architectural knitting from the nineteen-hundreds. It had a balcony where you could take a discreet sherry with the ladies, little separate compartments where you could talk long after closing hours, a collection on the walls of drawings by the *Punch* artist Bert Thomas (born in Swansea) and, most surprising attraction of all, a huge stuffed bear presiding over the bar. That bear gave the place a surrealist touch that was just up Dylan's street. He assured me that the old bear had once been the most prominent public figure in the town, accustomed to perform a dance with his keeper outside the main railway-station. He was thus the first impression the newly arrived traveller received of Swansea. There came a day, however, when the bear, no doubt fed up with the continual late arrival of the London train, turned on his keeper and hugged him to death.

He was immediately shot: 'the fate of all true artists,' said Dylan. The proprietor of Number Ten was deeply moved by the bear's sad fate. He had him stuffed and gave him a permanent home in the bar. This was, he felt, the least he could do for someone who had done so much for Swansea.

The old bear cast a kindly eye on us as I poured out the wine. I had just been paid unexpectedly for an article and I felt I could stand Dylan a bottle of champagne, since, as usual, he had no money at all. He drank his portion in a series of quick gulps, and then turned to me with a smile and asked for a large whisky 'just to take the taste away'.

At least he didn't deal with my champagne in the way he dealt with the magnificent port at a certain Oxford college. Dylan had rejected the wines offered at High Table in favour of a series of pints of ale. At last, the superb port was served, which, far more than its learning, was the college's real claim to fame. Dylan simply lifted his glass of port, looked at it, tipped it happily into his pint of beer and drank the lot.

Dylan's treatment of the college's greatest treasure cannot be excused but can be understood. The bounty of Nature and human ingenuity have combined to create a bewildering variety of drinks to make glad the heart of man. Cyril Ray has done well gently to remind those of us who are devoted to wine that there are other palates to be considered. Whisky, stout and other popular beverages therefore appear in these pages. And I found, during many visits to Burgundy, that even the *negoçiants* who deal with the greatest wines of the Côte d'Or were prepared to concede the merits of the great malts.

In truth, there is no accounting for taste, and distinguished men have peculiar habits when it comes to wine. I remember talking to an old waiter in a restaurant on the Champs-Élysées that had been patronised by James Joyce. Apparently there came a time when the creator of *Ulysses* was sternly forbidden to touch alcohol, and his wife enforced the ban. 'Ah,' said the waiter, 'it was a sad thing to see a great artist deprived of his inspiration and so I took steps to help. I arranged for a little secret store.' With pride, he showed it to me. It was the cistern of the gentleman's lavatory, where, when the great man made a necessary retirement, he found a beautifully cooled bottle of his favourite wine – a Fendant from Switzerland. Now I have nothing against Swiss wines. But how sad to go to such lengths to get Fendant in the capital of the country that produces the glories of Burgundy and Bordeaux!

I was saved from cultivating a taste for Fendant by the luck of growing up in the decade between the wars, and then laying down my cellar in the period that immediately followed the peace of 1945. Nature hurried to heal the wounds of war with a succession of great vintage years. In addition, prices had not yet

hit astronomic heights. Writers – even poets – had not yet been driven for their drink into the arms of the giant self-service store. There were still good local wine-merchants ready to make noble bottles possible, and great men from the previous decades who had known George Saintsbury and had heard Belloc recite his *Heroic Ode in Praise of Wine*. Cyril Ray salutes Raymond Postgate as his master: I do the same for André Simon. André it was who introduced me, among many other things, to the unusual charm of old vintage champagne, and took me on memorable tours of Burgundy and Bordeaux. He always had trouble with my name, and always introduced me as 'Vineyard Vaughan-Thomas'. What wine lover could wish for a better title?

Yes, this was the time of great men introducing us to great wine at not such great prices – the perfect recipe for a Golden Age of Wine-Writing. From its best vintages, Cyril Ray has compiled this most attractive of literary wine-lists.

A Little of What You Fancy...

CYRIL RAY

A great deal of rubbish is written about wine. I do not refer merely to such adventures of the soul among masterpieces as once were charted for the dons and the doctors, the St James's Street clubmen and the learned judges who, until a generation or so ago, largely composed the wine-buying classes - charted by literary gents confident that every historical allusion would be picked up and that no classical tag would need translation.

It was almost a century ago that Meredith wrote, in *The Egoist*, that:

Of all our venerable British of the two Isles professing a suckling attachment to an ancient port-wine, lawyer, doctor, squire, rosy admiral, city merchant, the classic scholar is he whose blood is most nuptial to the webbed bottle. The reason must be, that he is full of the old poets. He has their spirit to sing with, and the best that Time has done on earth to feed it. He may also perceive a resemblance in the wine to the studious mind, which is the obverse of our mortality, and throws off acids and crusty particles in the piling of the years until it is fulgent by clarity. Port hymns to his conservatism. It is magical: at one sip he is off swimming in the purple flood of the ever youthful antique.

'Purple flood' is the phrase indeed for many such a passage as Morton Shand's on claret, written in the 1920s (and I quote only a part of it):

> To compare the magnificent harmony of a fine Bordeaux to a flight of alexandrines is to pay it a doubtful compliment ... for the genius of no great wine is less emphatic, declamatory or monotonous. Grandeur it has, and in high degree, but I find the 'scansion' of Bordeaux, if scansion there must be, ranges from the Horatian to the Miltonic, from the rippling lyrics of Herrick to the sway and surge of Swinburne in the infinite variety of its scope; the 'rhythm' of its incarnadine burden, the lilt of splendid majesty, never the din of rant drowning the creaking of the buskins...

Or Maurice Healy, opining just before the Second World War that Clos de Vougeot would 'probably regard Chambertin with the air that Marie Antoinette might have adopted towards Mirabeau; it would acknowledge the ancient blood of Romanée-Conti, without quite according the salute due to Royalty; to Richebourg it would behave as Mrs Thrale towards Dr Johnson.'

That sort of writing about wine can be defended, and has had its defenders.

Warner Allen (a classical scholar, as predicated by Meredith) excused himself in the 1950s for having been guilty, a quarter of a century before, of comparing a Pichon-Longueville 1899 with a Mouton of the same vintage in these terms:

'It had not quite the character of the Mouton nor its depth and showed more of the superficiality of the silken fop, but it was a courtier clothed in velvet with a finesse that left the enchanting memory of a dashing cavalier. Like Cyrano de Bergerac, it had *panache*, a plume in its hat.'

He had been doing his best, he explained, 'to communicate to someone who is as fascinated as I am by the elusively delicate sensations produced by such a wine some idea of what that particular wine meant to me'.

Note, though, that whereas in the 1920s he had written that passage about *panache*, himself with *panache*, by the 1950s he felt obliged, if not to apologise, at any rate to explain what he now describes as 'indulging in a purple patch'.

For by the time his *Through the Wine Glass* appeared, in 1954, Raymond Postgate's *The Plain Man's Guide to Wine*, which had first appeared in 1951 (from the same publisher, interestingly enough), was already in its third impression. It gave the death-blow to the baroque style of writing about wine, and it is still, happily, in print.

Postgate, whose pupil I like to consider myself to have been, for I admired him more than anyone who has ever written about wine – a better classical

scholar than Warner Allen, but one who believed that scholarship was not to be shown off but to be shared, and a Socialist who believed that so should be the good things of life – permitted himself no flight more fanciful than that sauternes should be taken 'in the right company – which is a plump, pretty and rather greedy young woman', and then only after he had specified precisely with what dishes, immediately going on to explain that the wine in itself is syrupy but that fruit takes the edge off the sweetness, and then, in the simplest terms, what makes it sweet.

This is, indeed, plain writing for the plain man – commonsense about wine expressed in a commonsensible way.

"*One Chateauneuf du Pape '64,*
One Bourgogne Passetoutgrain '47,
Two Beaujolais Brouilly '59,
One Bordeaux Cotes de Bourg '64." *Punch*, 2 November 1966

Since Postgate's time, though, quite another sort of nonsense has come, not so much to be written (though it *is* sometimes written), but to a much greater extent talked, believed, and even *feared* about wine.

It is based on various closely related assumptions such as that there is some *mystery* about wine; that only men (and men rather than women) with a special, God-given, sense of taste can appreciate and understand it; that such-and-such a wine *must* be served with such-and-such a dish, at such-and-such a temperature; and that it is a breach of decorum to serve at any time and in any circumstances anything but the finest wine with a famous name, usually French or German.

Not only is this nonsense, but it is more harmful nonsense than the fancy fine writing that I made mock of in the opening paragraphs of this chapter. That, at any rate, conveyed or attempted to convey enjoyment.

The new nonsense inhibits enjoyment by raising such questions as, 'Am I doing the right thing?' 'Will my host (or my guest) despise me?' 'Am I enjoying this wine as much as I ought to enjoy it?'

(I suspect that for many people sex is not as much fun as it was before there were so many handbooks about it. I recently read somewhere that the tit-and-*tochas* magazines have driven more men to the psychiatrist's couch than to the whore's boudoir: they have been made to worry about their performance . . .)

The truth is – or the truths are – that:

There is no mystery about wine. It is the fermented juice of freshly gathered grapes – one of the oldest beverages known to man, one of the most natural and one of the most wholesome.

It is not meant to be a status symbol, but to be enjoyed, and anyone can enjoy it who can enjoy a glass of beer or a glass of lemonade; a slice of roast beef or a plate of fish and chips; a peach or an oyster.

Our sense of taste tells us how to savour such things; our sense of taste tells us how to savour a glass of wine. If it doesn't, don't drink it.

And whence, may I ask, comes the notion that women are less capable than men of appreciating and understanding wine? They ought to be – and potentially are – if anything, more capable. In this country, at any rate, men seem to be more heavily afflicted with bronchial and respiratory ailments than their wives and daughters, and these are afflictions that damage or diminish the sense of smell – and a sense of smell plays a large part in any consideration or appreciation of wine.

Women can choose or match a scent or a soap or a toilet-water more promptly and more surely than a man, just as they can taste a sauce or a soup in preparing dinner or say, more decisively than any man not professionally engaged, that this cushion clashes with those curtains, or that such a scarf would never do with such a frock.

A sense of smell, a sense of taste, and an eye for colour – most women have all these, to at least as great a degree as any man.

What they have lacked until our own time has been experience, because the economic and the social pattern of life in wine-drinking households has left women financially dependent on fathers or husbands, to whom it has fallen, therefore, to choose and to buy, to cellar and to serve the family's wines.

Now, at last, in this country, or so the statisticians say, more wine is bought

by women than by men – thanks to the bulk shipping of cheap, branded wines and to the growth of supermarkets and self-service stores. The hand that reaches for the cornflakes brings home the burgundy. Splendid!

Perhaps this easy availability of sound, cheap wine will put an end to the apologies offered by nervous hosts for not serving a château-bottled claret or a late-gathered hock, where they would never apologise – why should they? – for not serving caviar, or smoked salmon, or pâté de foie gras, or oysters.

The pattern of wine-drinking in this country was laid down over the past couple of centuries by a leisured and learned – at any rate, moneyed – middle class when French, German, Spanish and Portuguese wine-growers lived simply and cheaply. The British wine-drinker was spoiled.

Now, we must get used to the fact that good wine is grown in North Africa and South America, as well as in Western Europe, and that swagger wines that have now reached an economic price are for swagger occasions.

How odd, meanwhile, that a host will apologise humbly for a perfectly respectable Chilean Cabernet or Yugoslav Traminer, whose wife, with a gracious smile, and not a hint of an apology, is serving frozen peas and bottled 'salad cream'.

To enjoy wine, as I have already suggested, what is needed is a sense of smell, a sense of taste and an eye for colour.

All else is experience and personal preference.

We all know the difference in taste and texture not only between fish and meat, but between mutton and beef, and between herring and halibut, because we have learned about food by eating it.

(And sympathise, I beg you, with the wretched wine-writer trying to explain the difference between claret and burgundy, or between hock and sauternes, by imagining yourself putting into words, to someone who has never eaten meat, the difference between the taste of beef and the taste of mutton . . .)

Just as we learn about food by eating it, so we learn about wine by drinking it – not by reading about it: not even in books by me . . .

And just as some people prefer beef to mutton, so some will prefer burgundy, say, to claret.

It is a purely subjective choice: there is no moral judgement involved and no nice point of etiquette. My wife likes her beef underdone: I like the outside slice. She would choose a 1967 or a 1969 claret, because she likes her red wines to have a little crispness, a little edge, to them: I would choose a 1962, or even a very much older one, for I like them soft, and full-blown.

[19]

(Some men like eighteen-year-old girls, some prefer thirty-five-year-old women...)

Neither of us is right, neither wrong.

So there are no rules about the drinking and serving of wine such as might have been brought down by Moses, or laid down by the more recently late Miss Mitford.

But as people have been drinking wine for thousands of years, the very types we know today for many hundreds, there is a certain amount of accumulated wisdom available – no, not wisdom perhaps, but accumulated experience – that is worth consulting before one goes one's own way.

Just as we know without trying, thanks to folk-memory, that mustard goes well with roast beef but less well with baked apples, that bacon and eggs is a more palatable combination than kippers and strawberry jam, so our ancestors tell us that red wine with fish leaves a sort of metallic taste in the mouth, and that white wine is more refreshing if served approximately cellar-cool, whereas red wine shows off its fragrance and its fruitiness at room temperature. But there is no reason why we should not try for ourselves and, if we disagree with our great-grandfathers, drink our white wine tepid, our red wine with lumps of ice in it, and wash down *sole Normande* with vintage port.

The only law there is about wine-drinking is that of the Abbey of Thélème – *Fay Ce Que Vouldras.* Or, to translate Rabelais's French into Marie Lloyd's English, a little of what you fancy does you good. . . .

Every anthology of English verse bears witness that Browning iced his claret and that Thackeray drank burgundy with bouillabaisse. Keats wrote in a letter of his liking for 'claret cool out of a cellar a mile deep', and sweet ratafia biscuits to go with it.

In our own time, John Christie not only had the taste to create Glyndebourne but the self-confidence to insist that only German wines should be served there – and only the sweetest at that. And Baron Philippe de Rothschild, at Château Mouton, where he makes what many people, including myself, regard as one of the greatest red wines of the world, and what some others, including Baron Philippe, regard as *the* greatest, drinks the great, sweet Château d'Yquem after dinner so heavily chilled that it has slivers of solid ice in the glass, which must drive the Marquis de Lur Saluces, who makes it, to tremble with rage...

I do not suggest that you follow the example either of the late Mr Christie or of Baron Philippe – merely to bear them in mind when you read our words on wine with food as reminders that nothing that we say – or that anyone else says – about how or where or when to drink this wine or that needs to be paid any attention to at all. . . .

A Little of What You Fancy

Only that when a particular wine and a particular dish and a particular person – as it might be you, dear reader – do hit it off, time and place and loved one all together then, as a forgotten poet, Eric Chilman, sang to his lady:

> Do I recall the night we met,
>   With both our hearts *en feu*?
> As if I ever could forget,
>   Dear *Cordon Bleu*!
>
> A lover's moon was in the sky.
>   We dined alone, we twain.
> *Sole Véronique* was partnered by
>   A still Champagne.
>
> You wore a bandeau on your hair,
>   And with the *Coq au Vin*
> Produced a magnum old and rare
>   Of Chambertin.
>
> Château d'Yquem, a last surprise,
>   Was climax, crown and seal.
> I might forget your lovely eyes,
>   But not that meal.

from WINE WITH FOOD, 1975

[21]

First Faltering Steps

EVELYN WAUGH

In my childhood wine was a rare treat; an adult privilege to which I was admitted on special occasions. At my school there was no taboo against drinking (as there was against tobacco). Housemasters occasionally made a mild grog or cup for senior boys. I remember being embarrassed when one Ascension Day (a whole holiday) my companion got very drunk on liqueurs at a neighbouring hotel. It was at the University that I took to drink, discovering in a crude way the contrasting pleasures of intoxication and discrimination. Of the two, for many years, I preferred the former.

I think that my generation at Oxford, 1921–24, was the last to preserve more or less intact the social habits of the nineteenth century. The ex-service men of the First War had gone down. Undergraduate motor-cars were very few. Women were not seen except in Eights Week. Oxford was still essentially a market-town surrounded by fields. It was rare for a man to go down for a night

during term. The generation after ours cherished closer links with London. Girls drove up; men drove down. Cocktail shakers rattled, gramophones discoursed jazz. The Cowley works enveloped the city. But in my day our lives were bounded by the University. For a brief Indian summer we led lives very much like our fathers'.

In the matter of drink, beer was the staple. I speak of undergraduates of average means. There were a few rich men who drank great quantities of champagne and whisky; a few poor men who were reputed to drink cocoa. The average man, of whom I was one, spent £100 a term and went down £300 in debt. Luncheon was served in our rooms with jugs of beer. Beer was always drunk in Hall. At my college there was the custom of 'sconcing' when a breach of decorum, such as mentioning a woman's name or quoting from a foreign tongue, was fined by the provision of beer for the table. At one time I used to drink a tankard of beer for breakfast, but I was alone in that. It was drawn and served without demur. The Dean of my college drank very heavily and was often to be seen feeling his way round the quad in his transit from Common Room to his rooms. There were occasions such as bump-suppers and 'smokers' when whole colleges were given up to bacchanalia. In my first year there was a 'freshers' blind' when we all got drunk on wines and spirits and most of us were sick. Some white colonials got obstreperous and the custom was given up. All drinks were procurable at the buttery but the bursar scrutinised our weekly battels and was liable to remonstrate with a man whose consumption seemed excessive. My friends and I had accounts with wine merchants in the town, relying on the buttery for beer and excellent mild claret, which was the normal beverage at club meetings held in undergraduate rooms. No one whom I knew ever had a bottle of gin in his rooms. I remember only one man being sent down from my college for drunkenness and that not his own; late at night he hospitably passed tumblers of whisky out of his ground-floor window to a friend in the lane, who was picked up insensible by the police. I always thought it a harsh sentence. The poor fellow had come three thousand miles from the United States to imbibe European culture.

There were six or seven clubs with their own premises; some, like the Grid, highly respectable, others, Hogarthian drinking dens. The most notable of the dens was named the Hypocrites, in picturesque Tudor rooms over a bicycle shop in St Aldates (now of course demolished). There the most popular drink was red Burgundy drunk from earthenware tankards. A standing house rule was: 'Gentlemen may prance but not dance.' The oddest of these clubs with premises was the New Reform at the corner of the Cornmarket on Ship Street. This was subsidised by Lloyd George in the belief that it would be a nursery for earnest young Liberals. It became a happy centre of anarchy and debauch. Habits of extravagance grew and in my last year we drank a good deal of champagne in mid-morning at the New Reform and scoffed from the windows at the gowned figures hurrying from lecture to lecture. There was a vogue for whisky and crumpets at tea-time in the Union. I think it is no exaggeration to say that, in my last year, I and most of my friends were drunk three or four times a week, quite gravely drunk, sometimes requiring to be undressed and put to bed, but more often clowning exuberantly and, it seemed to us, very funnily. We were never pugnacious or seriously destructive. It took very little to inebriate at that age and high spirits made us behave more flamboyantly than our state of intoxication really warranted. Not many of us have become drunkards.

We were not discriminating. In a novel I once gave a description of two undergraduates sampling a cellar of claret.* I never had that experience at that age. Indeed I do not think that at twenty I could distinguish with any certainty between claret and burgundy. Port was another matter. The tradition of port drinking lingered. Many of the colleges had ample bins of fine vintages of which undergraduates were allowed a strictly limited share. Port we drank with reverence and learned to appreciate. The 1904s were then at their prime, or, at any rate, in excellent condition. We were not ashamed (nor am I now) to relish sweet wine. Yquem had, of course, a unique reputation. Starting to drink it in a mood of ostentation, I was led to the other white Bordeaux. Tokay was then procurable and much relished. Bristol Milk, and a dark sherry named Brown Bang were also favourites. We tried anything we could lay hands on, but table-wines were the least of our interests. We drank them conventionally at luncheon and dinner parties but waited eagerly for the heavier and headier concomitants of dessert.

Nowadays, I am told, men privately drink milk and, when they entertain, do so to entice girls. It is tedious for the young to be constantly reminded what much finer fellows their fathers were and what a much more enjoyable time we had. But there you are; we were and we did.

© *From* THE COMPLEAT IMBIBER 6, 1963

*See 'Yes, I Think So ...' p. 323.

Buzzings of a Far-flung Bar Fly

James Cameron

When I began to serve my time as an itinerant bagman of letters in foreign lands I resolved, being sensitive to the opinion of others and also rather hard up, to drink only the wine of the country; everyone told me it was not only economical but the smart thing. In consequence I have probably consumed over the years more fine varied bad drink than most people. The wine of the country is an okay enough proposition until you get to places like Senegal, for example, where it is made by the tribal ladies masticating the grain and spitting it into a pot to ferment later. I think this is the only beverage in the world to which I have had access that I have not drunk at all, let alone to excess.

I do not as a rule hold with travellers' tales of food and drink, and I listen to them with impatience. Most of them are concerned with the natural values and comparative excellences of this drink or that; I have spent too much time in places where one was lucky to get a drink at all. I have little scholarship in the niceties of alcohol, but much in the business of hard pursuit. My standards are exacting, but not high.

One of my earliest rules of thumb concerned South African brandy, for instance; I was told to drink it only in the Transvaal, since there – because it is manufactured in the Cape – one could be sure that it was at least twenty-four hours old. I have had much pleasure and refreshment from Siamese gin and Bulgarian burgundy and American champagne and something they distil in Tunis from *dates*, of which no one will give you more than two – unless they themselves have had more than two, of course, when they will give you all you want, and their wife.

Pretensions like these are easily exposed, to be sure; nevertheless I reckon to have acquired a moderately pretty palate for indifferent drink. In fact I cannot at the moment think of any intoxicant in the world (apart from that stuff in Senegal) that I do not enjoy, and will take as much as I can get hold of. I have drunk Russian *kvass* in Tashkent and Tibetan *chang* in Sikkim, and Anatolian *raki* and Mexican *tequila* and Indonesian *schnapps*, and nasty though they are they were good enough for me at the time. I once even learned a trick by which one can affect to tell one kind of Japanese *saké* from another, which is a piece of bogus *bushido* if ever I heard of one.

I am therefore not an exquisitely discriminating imbiber, and on the whole an inconsiderable oenophil (if that *really* is the word). I was brought up in a wine country, and dosed with pinard as a toddler, but that develops lust rather than character, as Mendès-France was always insisting. I have, however, a rather delicate feeling for the wines from the steep hillsides of the Upper Nile, of which I know quite a bit. Lest anyone should think I am joking about this, and that there are no Egyptian vineyards, let me say that only the other day I was given a half-case by a friend of mine whose business it is to promote Anglo-Egyptian relations, and if he thinks this is the way to do it, who am I to argue? It has a decorative label which says it is called Omar Khayyám, and a very nice unpretentious little Omar Khayyám it is. I sometimes wonder who drinks it, since it must rarely come here, and in Egypt the poor cannot afford the one and fourpence a bottle it costs, and the rich, as everywhere else these days, drink only *eskosh ouiski*. Still, the half-case saw me over a difficult weekend, and *Vive* it, say I.

It will be apparent, then, that I cannot finesse about drink with any conviction, and when in the company of scholarly drinkers I must resort to gamesmanship. I may not know a good wine from a marvellous wine, but I can tell a real stinker – not that it stops me drinking it; still, I can tell. I also know where the best rum in the world is made. So do all sorts of people, but I say

the Seychelles, because nobody thinks of that. It goes very well with tortoise-meat. I am not lying. In Uganda I have drunk hot lager beer with fried locusts; rather like scampi, because the legs fall off. I can go on like this for ever, without straying from the literal truth. I am unknown to every good *sommelier* in Europe, but I have an Addict's Pass for the Permit Room in Bombay, and what is more, I know where there is a bar in the Vatican.

Everyone goes on about Famous Bars. These tales are spread by newspaper-men and the like, and indeed it is a fact that in most places there is one pub to which these people gravitate, for the mutual dissemination of rumours and the endless repetitive bull of the trade. It is not necessarily the best pub in town, but it chances to be the correct place, nobody knows why – the Crillon in Paris, the Cockpit in Singapore, the Grocer's in Athens, Blake's in New York, the Ledra in Nicosia, the Cosmopolitan in Cairo. I think it has something to do with getting credit. Some time after Suez I managed to go back to Cairo and found the back of the Cosmopolitan bar ranged with scores of glasses stuffed with correspondents' chits, to the value of several hundred pounds, some of them years old. The barman was philosophical about them – things would settle down, the reporters would return one day and pay their bills. Or if they didn't, he said, somebody would; and he gave me my own bundle, totalling eleven and a half pounds. I wonder who had put away all that drink.

There is a Longest Bar In The World in some six or seven cities of my acquaintance. I suppose the most famous – and for all I know the longest – was in Shanghai. It exists no more, untimely quenched by the flood of history. I think I was one of its very last customers – long after the brave days of the Settlement and the Concession, of the oriental empire of the Jardine Mathesons and the Sassoons, the *taipans* and the *compradores*; of the sweet life for some, and thirty thousand starved corpses picked from the gutters every year. This was not long after the Revolution, and somehow I came down from the dedicated Communist austerities of Peking to the phantoms of international Shanghai. I found the old Cathay Hotel mysteriously renamed the King Kong – and I also found the old Long Bar, still, astonishingly, in business. It must have been the only real bar left in all China. It looked like Wembley week after the exhibition closed. Two sombre Czechs and an interpreter in the regulation blue boiler-suit crouched morosely in the dusty shadows; that was all. They told me the place was to be converted into an annexe of the Youth Pioneers' Committee Hall, and by now it has been.

Do not imagine that all China was as unconvivial. I did some immensely rewarding gastronomical researches in Peking, but I shall not weary you with their conclusions, as they are very intricate. Once I had a dinner party with which I wished to cut a bit of a dash, since my guests were men of some moment in the hierarchy, albeit they all dressed like engine-drivers. I chose the best and most expensive restaurant in the city, which in China is done by seeking out the one with the most dishevelled and ruinous exterior. The Chinese observe the rule that the worth of an eating-house is assessed by the unpretentious squalor of its appearance, on the sound principle that the better the food, the more eagerly will its avid customers have knocked the place about. By the same analogy, the innkeepers contend with each other in finding humble and deprecating names for their establishments – 'The Contemptible Place of Wang Tsei-Teng', 'The Mean Table of the East Market', and so on. There is always lively competition for the name 'The Worst Restaurant In Town'. The superb place to which I was enviously recommended was called 'The Restaurant Into Which One Would Not Take A Dog'.

I will not go into the incomparable excellence of the meal, except to say that its thirty-two courses were built around the unchallengeable basis of the *chao ya-tze*, the famous lacquered duck, and that we drank three gallons of *huang-chou*, the rice wine which is served hot from small porcelain cups, and which has very little therapeutic quality. The Chinese compensate for the blandness of their table drinking by the almost lethal ferocity of their liquor, *mao-t'ai*, which is made from sorghum and is carried about in stone flasks because, I imagine, it would dissolve anything else. We took a certain quantity of this too because, vile though it is, I greatly enjoy it. The meal lasted most of the night and cost me nearly two hundred and forty thousand dollars. At that time the Chinese rate was sixty-nine thousand dollars to the pound; the bill was therefore, for twelve people, some three pounds ten. Still, I was on expenses.

After as much miscellaneous consumption as I have had to do in the course of my duties, one develops a recondite interest in the vagaries of the stuff itself. Just as you can now buy European *saké* – made, I believe, in Holland – so, of course, you can buy Japanese Scotch. Some of it is worse than others. I remember after the war, when our problems were sore, a friend of mine in India produced, with a cruel laugh, a bottle of whisky made in Yokohama. The label was a Union Jack with a superimposed picture of St Paul's, which read: 'PUREST SCOTCH WHISKY, BREWED AT BUCKINGHAM PALACE UNDER THE PERSONAL SUPERVISION OF H.M. KING GEORGE VI'.

This was a very low-comedy bottle, but the interesting double-bluff about it was that inside was, in fact, a very good whisky; indeed it was an outstanding Speyside single-malt that my friend kept in this terrible bottle so that he would not have to give any to his friends. In fact they implored him not to do so. They drank Solon gin while he supped his whisky, making wry faces; thus he

gained a reputation for an engaging whimsicality without being thought mean.

So much for the big world. When my time came not long ago to leave the hurly-burly of Grub Street for the tormenting anxieties of an independent literary life, I felt a brief urge for limbo, and set up for a while in the west of Ireland. The village was not a place of very complex diversion. There were indeed only the customary two forms of relaxation from toil, and as one of them was out of the question for me in the circumstances, there remained only drinking. In west Ireland this is taken seriously enough, God knows, though by any standards it is more copious than exotic.

Still, I did find one final variant on this great and catholic theme. The only things the village had to offer to the world were lobsters and crayfish of unusual quality; through the commerce in these a close identification had grown with the buying-port in France. The French boats came and went continually, introducing all manner of new values. We got plenty of wine, for instance. Nobody thought much of it. We also got plenty of Pernod. This was different; the fisherfolk took to it enthusiastically; they drank it in a large glass – fifty-fifty, Guinness and Pernod.

And then there was the time in Baluchistan, where they drink only . . .

© *from* THE COMPLEAT IMBIBER 4, 1961

To Cynthia,
not to have him choose

P. M. Hubbard

Drink to me only with thine eyes at first,
And I will suitably respond with mine.
Gazing, we get myopia at the worst,
And when by gazing we can raise a thirst,
Cynthia, I'll ask for wine.

We do our passion wrong to leave it thus
Pledged to perpetual splendour on its own.
Love has its own intrinsic impetus
Which flags by fits and makes a void in us
We dare not leave alone.

To Cynthia

Wine seals these sad interstices of mind
With its own warmth. Wine builds its bridge above
The hollow darkness love can leave behind.
Wine is, to one who has both loved and wined,
A better bet than love.

But sweetest Cynthia, need we parcel up
What should conjointly cast a double spell?
Must love be lost because we sit and sup?
I do not mind a kiss within the cup
If there be wine as well.

Good wine refines what is already gold
And gilds the lack of what we have not got.
Good wine enhances half-a-hundredfold
My joy in life, and will when I am old,
Which love, alas, will not.

Therefore, sweet Cynthia, having once to live,
I find in wine too dear a thing to lose.
Love me, if you have any love to give,
But hold me to no hard alternative
For fear of what I choose.

© *from* THE COMPLEAT IMBIBER 2, 1957

In Moderation

ANGUS WILSON

I'm an old man now – eighty-two next birthday. There aren't many left of the crowd I used to knock around with. Most of them either did themselves too well or coddled themselves like a lot of old women; either way is fatal. In fact the only chap that's left from the old days of Romano's and the Café Royal (when it *was* the Café Royal) is Copperdyke – 'Grouser' Copperdyke. It would be Copperdyke; for of all the miserable old so-and-so's that the Almighty for some strange fancy of His own chose to put breath into, Copperdyke's the one to give you a pain in the neck. Always has done, always will. I meet him now and then at the club. Always comes bellyaching up to me, nobody else'll listen to him. Not that they're much of a crowd nowadays anyhow; not a man among them; not a real man. The last time I saw him he started on about Death – Death! I ask you.

'We shan't be spared much longer now, Murdoch,' he said, 'and it can't be too soon for me.'

'I can well understand that,' I said; 'if I'd had to go around with your dismal chivvy I'd have prayed for release long ago.' I don't tolerate fools gladly, never have; and in any case I kicked Copperdyke round the school cloisters as long ago as '89, so there's no point in mincing words with the blighter now.

'But if you think,' I went on, 'that *I'm* ready to shuffle off this mortal coil – to plagiarise from one Bill Shakespeare – you've got another guess coming. I'm good for another ten years or more. At the least,' I added, just to make the point quite clear.

'Ah, well,' he said in that bleating voice of his, like an old nannygoat's, 'we none of us know our hour. But do you ever think, Murdoch, what's in store for us? We haven't exactly led exemplary lives.' Well, that did start me laughing. If 'Grouser' Copperdyke so much as has half a glass of whisky he's under the table; he doesn't know one end of a horse from another; and as to women, he used to think himself a hell of a 'blood' if he winked at a barmaid, and if she winked back you couldn't see him for dust. So, if he hasn't led an exemplary life ...

Anyway, I'm not taking the trouble to write all this down just to tell you about Copperdyke. As a matter of fact, he's got nothing to do with it; but when you get to my age you'll find you tend to stray from the subject a bit. Not that you won't be lucky if your faculties are as good as·mine. I don't want to boast, but, as I say, I'm eighty-two. No, Copperdyke wouldn't interest anybody, but what he said started me thinking about myself and what I suppose you might call my philosophy of life. I haven't done a lot of thinking; I haven't had the time. I've done a bit of everything else though, and in the course of it I've knocked around a good deal and known a good number of men and women of all kinds; and I've formed a few conclusions. The principal of them is, I suppose, that if you want to get the best out of life, don't have any doubts about yourself. That's where all the trouble comes from, as you'll see when I tell you about my great-nephews. When I see a man who's afraid to enjoy himself, or a man that makes a beast of himself for that matter, I can tell the reason straight away: they're not sure of themselves, they're frightened of life.

I'm not a religious man; my old father was a parson and I saw a good deal too much of that as a kid. But if old Copperdyke's right and there is a Last Trump and all the rest of it, I'm not too worried about myself, because if the Recording Angel's anything like the sportsman he should be, he's likely to say, 'Well, Billy Murdoch, you certainly haven't been a plaster-cast saint, but I will say this for you – you've never been afraid of life.' And I never have; and that's why I've enjoyed it – with moderation.

Now, my brother Ted was a teetotaller and he was dead before he was fifty.

His son Joe drank himself to death about the same age. As to *his* sons, my great-nephews, well, you'll hear about them. And here I am, eighty-two, and some afternoons (I won't say mornings) I feel more like twenty-two. And moderation's done it. I can sit down to a partridge or a grouse now with a bottle of Beaune or Macon; and none the worse for it. In fact, all the better. Not that I haven't had my ups and downs. What did Kipling say? 'If you can walk with kings nor lose the common touch.' I don't know about 'the common touch'; as I say, my father was a parson, and my mother's people were country gentry. But I walked with kings all right; at least, with one of them. He was HRH then, but it comes to the same thing. Yes, I've been racing and played baccarat with Edward VII when he was Prince of Wales. That was when I was up. Many years later, in 1913 to be exact, I had a spot of trouble over a cheque and then I dined for six months at His Majesty's expense under rather different conditions. That was when I was down. And I've had plenty of in-betweens.

In my old age I've managed to make things pretty comfortable for myself. People talk about wars being dreadful things; and so they are, of course. But you'll never stop them, that's what I always tell people. Man's a fighting animal. And I've always believed in looking on the best side of things. Of course, this last war was a tame affair. I spent most of it in a hotel in the Highlands. They fed us shockingly, but I got a bit of shooting and a rubber of bridge in the evening. But the Great War was altogether a different matter. As I told you, I'd had a spot of trouble in '13 and I was a bit down on my uppers when it broke out. But I've never known anything quite like the spirit of it – Forgive and Forget was the order of the day. I'm not a sentimentalist, but it cured me of any tendency to cynicism that misfortune may have bred in me. I was pretty near over-age when it started, and recent experiences had left me a bit groggy, so there was no opportunity of competing with the young chaps in the active field. And in any case there was some damned red tape at that stage which stood in the way of my getting a commission – 'must be of proven character' or some such tommy-rot. I will say that one or two of my pals at the War Office were as sick about it as I was, and raised hell about it, but they couldn't get past 'my spot of trouble', it was too recent. But everyone was as decent as they could be; said what a damned shame it was, and so on. And they found me a place in Harry Mungo's outfit – outfit's the right word; we were responsible for supply of uniforms. Nobody had expected the showdown and we were as unprepared as we could be. I never knew a chap I liked as much as Harry – wonderful business brain and a real sportsman. He made things hum and soon had the stuff pouring out. As the saying went then – 'That's the stuff to give the troops'. He and I were as thick as – well, as thick as you can be. Later on they gave us all commissions. I ended up a major, but, of course, I never used the rank after the war, although a lot of frightful counter-jumpers did.

Well, Harry came out at the end of the war with quite a packet in the bank. They made him Lord Eiderdown. He was as pleased as a kid with a new toy, but, poor chap, he never had much time to play with it. He had a stroke four months after the armistice – strain and worry, of course; if ever the Germans killed a man without putting a bullet through him, that man was Harry Mungo. Florrie, that was his missus, was in a terrible way. They'd no kids, nothing to console her. And between you and me, she was no happier for having the title. A fish out of water. She'd been Florrie Riggs that had doled me out many a brandy and soda in the Empire Bar in the old days. But if she wasn't a lady by birth, she had a lady's heart – as big as a bullock's – would give you the dress off her back if anyone pitched her a hard tale. And there were plenty of all sorts only too eager to sponge on Flora, Lady Eiderdown. It's a funny thing how intuition can tell you something. Old Harry had died too suddenly to have a word with me before he went on. But I somehow knew as sure as God made little apples that he'd wanted to say something, and what he'd wanted to say was, 'Billy, take care of my old Dutch.' No more than that, but I could almost hear him saying it.

Well, there she was surrounded by a crowd of twisters and spongers, so I married her. Of course, it was a bit late in the day for the straight-and-narrow as far as I was concerned, and Harry had spoilt her, so we had our little rough-and-tumbles. I was at Monte trying out a new system, when she passed over in '27. But as I've said, whatever her faults, she had a big heart and she left me all she had. Of course, with death duties and income tax and what not, it isn't what it was. And the fact that the bookmakers have had it all their own way for the last fifteen years hasn't helped. But still, I'm comfortable and a man whom people take trouble with, as I knew when I was re-elected to the club, despite the little affair of '13. And so it should be when you get to my age. Not a lot of bowing and scraping, you know, but people properly attentive when you choose to tell a yarn, which I often do. Respect in moderation, like everything else.

That's where we come to my great-nephews, who are the real subject of this little moral tale. And about time too, you'll probably say. Bertram and Reggie – ghastly names – and a ghastly pair of outsiders to carry them. Neither of the 'boys' – that's what they're called in the family, although they won't see forty again – has any more idea of the art of living than a Hottentot; and I'm probably libelling a perfectly respectable race of savages in saying that. They've always been unsure of themselves; afraid of life. As a result, they've gone to two equally unpleasant extremes. Bertram's as miserable and mean a little blighter as you'll find in a month of wet Sundays; Reggie's a showy sort of bounder with the mistaken idea that making a splash is the mark of a gentleman. I've said they're afraid of life; well, that's putting it mildly; they're afraid of everything - especially me.

But they won't leave me alone. To hear the way they and their wives squabble over who's to give me Christmas dinner you'd think I was the dearest object to their lives. And so I suppose I am - in prospect. 'You'll come to us, Uncle Billy, for a quiet little family dinner? You always find it so noisy up at Reggie's.' 'Uncle Bill'll be with us this year, won't you? You like a bit of fun, like the rest of us. They tell me it's like a funeral wake down at Bertram's.' Up and down, you see, because Bertram lives at Wimbledon and Reggie at Hendon - God-forsaken holes, both of them! You can tell the sort of ghastly suburban lives they lead simply from that. Well, I've put a stop to it this year. My last little visits to Ivydene (Bertram's) and 642 Plumpeach Court (Reggie's) set them back enough so that even their lack of pride won't allow them to 'forgive' me for at least another year.

The invitations arrived the same week to bid me welcome home. I'd just been to Le Touquet for a month - a favourite spot of mine. As I said to my man Bartlett (he looks after my clothes, drives the car, etc. His old woman cooks me the odd meal at home - makes an almost perfect steak-and-oyster pie, a thing you can't get in any of these damned restaurants nowadays), as I said to him, 'What a perfect welcome, I don't think.' (I'm very fond of Harry Tate's old sayings.)

Well, first it was Wimbledon. Ivydene's one of those old Victorian houses - well-built in its own way, but must be kept really warm. Hilda (that's Bertram's wife - long, anaemic, horse-faced woman with no dress sense) keeps it just above zero. Not a comfortable chair in the place - all little rumfteyfoo things that would break under anyone who's had a proper meal. But they don't have proper meals there.

It seemed there were to be guests - Sir George and Lady Duckberry. 'Such nice people, Uncle Bill, he's on the board of Bertram's firm.' Well, I saw how it was to be - killing three birds with one stone: please rich great-uncle, impress boss with rich great-uncle, show off to rich great-uncle by producing boss. All right, I thought, as I sat drinking a thimbleful of grocer's sherry, we'll see.

Of course the show started as soon as the Duckberrys arrived. Pompous ass, he was, and she was one of those gushing women full of the local Women's Conservative Association and what the dear Duchess said when she reviewed the Girl Guides.

In Moderation

'How did Bartlett find traffic this evening, Uncle Bill?' Bertram asked. And just to rub it home Hilda said, 'Uncle Bill has the most marvellous chauffeur. A real Cockney character. Been with him for years.' Then we went at it – how did I find Le Touquet? Was I going to Bermuda again this winter? and so and so on. Well, if there'd been any decent drink about and a little more of it, I might have felt warmer to human foibles, but as it was I froze in every sense of the word. I might have been a hundred, shrunk into myself, an old, old man. 'Ah,' I said, or 'Hm', or 'Oh'. Part of the time I didn't hear the questions, couldn't remember Bartlett's name, and once or twice when Lady Duckberry was looking my way I made a sort of senile face just to put her mind off duchesses for a bit. And all the time I kept looking surprised, as though I'd never heard of Bermuda or Le Touquet. Bertram and Hilda didn't know whether to be worried at the exhibition or pleased to see how quickly I was likely to hop this planet and leave them the filthy lucre. But Sir George and his lady had no doubts; they thought that since I'd never heard of Bermuda, Bertram was simply putting on a show.

I was beginning to feel that I'd gone too far when we sat down to the meal, but then I knew I hadn't: tomato soup just to cover the bottom of the plate; something Hilda called *au gratin*, and what was under the cheese only an inspector of nuisances could have told; a stringy old fowl with bullet peas; and a ghastly mixture of custard, old cake and those damned cherries from bottles; *one* bottle of inferior, lukewarm Barsac. I was just in the mood when Bertram, after leaving me to senile silence for a bit, decided to have one more go. Lady Duckberry had just told us how personally upset she'd been by the announcement that there were to be no more presentations at Court, but how she hoped that now her little girl might have a chance of meeting the Queen at a smaller, more intimate gathering.

'Ah,' said Bertram, 'what would the older generation have said about "no debs"? Queen Victoria or even Edward VII? He was a great stickler for form, was he not, Uncle, despite his gay life?'

That was the signal for Hilda to whisper a loud aside to old Duckberry, 'Uncle Bill knew Edward VII personally.' Sir George swelled his face up at me as though I was one of the performing monkeys at the Zoo; and his good lady gave me a splendid display of all her teeth. 'Ah!' he said pompously, and 'Really?' she gushed. But if Bertram and Hilda thought I was going to entertain their guests on grocer's sherry and one glass of Barsac they were sadly mistaken.

'Ah,' I said solemnly. 'Maybe.'

'Maybe what?' asked Sir George, as a man of authority used to a straight answer.

'Maybe he would have approved, maybe he wouldn't,' I said.

'Oh!' said Lady Duckberry in a disappointed tone. 'He must have been such a fascinating man. Do tell us about him, Mr Murdoch.'

Then I looked at Bertram as though he'd put me into a tight corner.

'I'm afraid the stories of my youth, Lady Duckberry,' I said, 'are rather of the smoking-room variety.' And I looked as pompous as her old man.

She won't see fifty-five again, but she whinnied like a young filly who's been given her mouth.

'Oh, I don't think you need mind about that. We women of today are used to hearing the most shocking stories.'

Then I looked as though I'd been asleep since '05, like Rip Van Winkle (charming musical piece there was about that, by the way, in the days when there *was* musical comedy) come to life.

'Oh,' I said, 'I'm sorry to hear it. That's all I can say.' I looked as sour and dry as the Barsac we'd all drunk. 'I may be out of date but I like personally to know whether I'm talking to a lady or a whore.' I didn't say any more and when the coffee came I looked at the bluish liquid and said I had to be toddling, and would they ask Bartlett to bring round the car. I can't stick meanness, and I can't be expected to talk if I'm not properly fed.

Of course, it was all quite different up at Reggie's. He lives in one of those beastly chromium-plated flats furnished like the things cinema managers call the foyer. Reggie's wife Ethel has a voice like a corncrake, dresses as loudly as her voice, and is that thing I most abominate, 'mutton dressed up lamb fashion'. When you go to Bertram's you feel you're paying a visit to the tomb; when you go to Reggie's it's like the Parrot House. Bertram's so afraid you'll get something out of him, he locks up the silver; Reggie's so afraid he won't get something out of you, that he tries to get you drunk. He's never sure of himself, Reggie, unless everyone's half-seas-over on a lot of filthy cocktails he mixed himself. Ethel wouldn't know how to give a dinner, so she doesn't try; anyhow it doesn't matter, because you couldn't taste anything after all that muck in your inside.

If I hadn't been to Bertram's I wouldn't have gone up to Hendon – I never go to cocktail parties, I've too much respect for my palate – but I wasn't going to have Bertram saying I'd favoured him. They'd draw conclusions about my will.

There was a terrible crowd there – painted-up old hags and a lot of counter-jumpers who'd rob a blind woman of her apples. Ethel always kisses me. Filthy habit, unless it's a pretty girl. I took my glass of poison into a corner, pushed one of those damned indoor plants that make their flat like a conservatory out of the way and sat down. For a good while I kept intruders away by putting in my eye-glass and barking whenever they came near. Anyway, they were screaming far too much to notice me.

Then suddenly Reggie brought some blighter up to me – fearful-looking fellow with a blue chin. 'I want you to meet Rawston Morris, Uncle, he's one of the best.' I felt like ordering one of the worst, but all I said was, 'How d'ye do?' It turned out that the chap called himself a company promoter. Well, as Reggie runs a bucket shop, I put two and two together pretty quickly. They talked a shocking lot of nonsense about the state of the country and the market and one thing and another. I didn't listen, but said 'Ah' and 'You don't altogether surprise me'. Every now and again Reggie said 'Have another' and I said 'No'. One had given me the belly-ache already. Then it turned out they'd got what Mr Morris called 'a little inside knowledge' and they were 'prepared to let me in on the ground floor'. Shocking taste talking business like that at a party, anyway.

I think Ethel noticed my look, for she came up and said, 'You've got a far-away look in your eye, Uncle Bill.' Then she gave me a little scream. 'I know what it is,' she cried; 'it's your new Edwardian hairstyle, Connie. That's Mrs Morris, Uncle. I bet she's set you dreaming on all your lady-loves, hasn't she? Uncle Bill was a regular masher when he was young.' Well, that put the lid on it. I looked at Mrs Morris through my eye-glass – she was as skinny as her husband was gross. 'As a matter of fact,' I said, 'with no wish to be other than gallant, I have to confess that it was your husband that was bringing the past back to me. By the way he speaks and the turn of his head I'd swear it was old Smiler Thompson.'

'Oh,' she said, 'and who was that?'

'A chap I knew in the Scrubs,' I told her, and then I started to tell them about Smiler Thompson, what a nice sort of cove he was, and what a business head he had, and how he'd got there. But Ethel and Reggie started up such a chatter that I don't think they heard this end of the story. Well, they shouldn't give an old man such strong drinks, it's bound to loosen his tongue.

So I shan't be going to either of my great-nephews for Christmas. I'm sitting down quite quietly with Mr and Mrs Bartlett – after all, Christmas knows no rank – we're not having a turkey, we're having a grouse each and a sole Colbert to start with; no Christmas pudding; it doesn't do at my age, but Mrs B. makes a fine *crème brulée* and that's an old-fashioned sweet you don't seem to get today; and an excellent Stilton to follow. A dry Amontillado; a bottle of Niersteiner; a couple of bottles of Beaune; cognac for Bartlett and me and a glass of Marsala for Mrs B. Everything in moderation.

© *from* THE COMPLEAT IMBIBER 2, 1958

[39]

Bottle Doggerel

ROSEMARY BAZLEY

Try counting bottles
Instead of counting sheep,
And the right kind of bottles
Will send you to sleep.

High bottles, low bottles,
Heady have-a-go bottles,
Cannot-say-no bottles,
Row upon row;
Slim-hipped shandy bottles,
Thin-lipped dandy bottles,
Rip-roaring brandy bottles,
Every one aglow;

Bottle Doggerel

Well-worn whisky bottles,
Bilious Bay of Biscay bottles,
Russian very risky bottles,
Peppermint or port;
Wasp-waist loose bottles,
Stiff-necked puce bottles,
Lurid lemon-juice bottles,
Any shape or sort;

Lightly-coloured red bottles,
Slightly swollen-head bottles,
Carry-you-to-bed bottles,
Try them for yourself;

Cloudy bottles, clear bottles,
Greasy, queasy, queer bottles,
Better bitter beer bottles,
All along the shelf;

Try counting bottles
Instead of counting sheep,
For the right kind of bottles
Will send you to sleep.

 from A WINE AND FOOD BEDSIDE BOOK, 1972

St Cobden and St Cripps

RAYMOND POSTGATE

It is an interesting and significant fact that the two statesmen to whom sensible wine-drinkers owe most – in the strict sense of financial debt – are eminent figures of what is called 'the Left'. They are also both named Richard. Richard Cobden, by negotiating a commercial treaty with France in the year 1860, pulled down the duty on French table wines from 12s. to 2s. a dozen bottles. Richard Stafford Cripps in 1949, of his own volition and with no treaty, cut the duty on table wines from 25s. a gallon to 13s. A gallon contains six bottles, so we have still a long way to go to get back to Cobden's day, even allowing that his shilling was worth five of ours; nevertheless, Cripps's cut was an enormous slash in the right area.

What exactly is meant by 'the Left' is another matter; I am inclined to think that it hasn't any meaning at all now. I find pundits far more Brahminical than I am describing as 'on the extreme Left' supporters of the Stalinist programme of despotic denial of any personal liberty and of total ownership of all wealth by the controlling oligarchy. This, I thought, was considered rather over-con-servative in the days of Merodach-Baladan, King of Babylon, who held firmly to this policy, until he died suddenly of a highly convenient stroke. He was succeeded, after a little milling around, by Sennacherib, the Assyrian Emperor, who had all the charm, tolerance and vigour of Mr Krushchev, and almost exactly the same social policy.

As a historian, I say that none of this makes sense. 'On the Left' in fact has nowadays nothing but a geographical meaning; it means no more than the sergeant's 'By the right – *number!*' But between 1789, when the phrase was invented during the French Revolution, and 1934, when Stalin made nonsense of it, to be 'on the Left' did have a perceptible meaning. It meant to be more in favour of liberty and of equality than the other party, and until it was found that these two objects might not always coincide it was a useful measuring-stick and a political litmus paper. Used so, it is fair to say that both Richards were 'on the Left' in their day; and it is an interesting oddity of historical writing that 'the Right', that is, the Conservatives in that period, nevertheless nobbled in the long run the credit of being the true friends of sensible drinking. I think this probably originated from the Conservative Party's Beer Act, which allowed anybody at all to brew, and as a result of which the sovereign people, as Sidney Smith said, was either reeling or sprawling until it was repealed. Still, whatever be the reason, I would like my friends who still like to think of themselves as 'on the Left' to consider the history of Cobden and Cripps and fall into line behind those two great leaders.

The earlier and, at this date, the less lovable Richard set out on his enterprise in the autumn of 1859 when he was MP for Rochdale. He went to Hawarden and collected the blessing of the Chancellor of the Exchequer, Mr Gladstone, who afterwards included in his 1860 Budget the reduction of duties he nego-tiated. But his interest in pushing through the treaty with France which led to the sensational changes was not gastronomic, or oenophilic. He liked his wine well enough, as any sensible Victorian did, and from the beginning had announced his hope of 'greatly reducing' the duty on wine. But his aim was political; it was to use the wine trade to reduce the danger of war.

On both sides of the Channel, Napoleon III and Lord Palmerston were permitting the most nonsensical and dangerous meetings and propaganda, de-manding war about nothing in particular. 'Get the two nations into debt with each other' was Cobden's recipe to end this. Bring free trade about between France and England – or as near free as might be – and there would be a solid phalanx of merchants and employers in both countries who would make sure that the hot air remained hot air. He saw no possible flaw in his argument. He

was quite convinced that merchants and manufacturers were the only people that mattered, or had any real power. All his political calculations were always based on such simple reasoning. 'If every Chinaman would buy only one cotton night-cap a year from us,' he quoted approvingly, a 20% rise in Manchester sales would result and most problems would be settled. He was also an internationalist in principle, of course, but his internationalism was the rather chilling kind that dislikes all nations impartially. He wrote to his chief French correspondent in the middle of his campaign, 'Every Frenchman I know, except my friend Monsieur Chevalier, is very deficient in moral courage.' As for the British, they were 'the most aggressive, quarrelsome, warlike and bloody nation under the sun'. These verdicts were delivered before his treaty was concluded; it is not recorded whether he considered its operation did, as he hoped, moderate British ferocity and improve French moral fibre. Certainly, the two nations snarled at each other rather less. Also, the imports of French wines rose from 250,000 gallons to 4,500,000 gallons, and the price of cheap claret fell to 1s. 6d. a bottle. (Champagne could be got at 3s. 6d., but it was not very nice.) Mr Gladstone, who regularly had the most curious good luck in politics, collected all the popularity for this change, and the new cheap wine was called 'Gladstone Claret'.

Stafford Cripps I knew personally. I met him first some twenty-five years or more ago, when he was a very different person from the 'Austere Chancellor' that the nation knew in the late 40s. For one thing, he was round-faced and excitable, with large tortoiseshell-rimmed glasses; for another, he had plenty of hair; for a third, he had almost no common sense at all. In all three respects he changed round to the opposite in later life. His face became thin and ascetic, his glasses rimless and schoolmasterly, his hair turned white, sparse and wispy, and he acquired a fair amount of political horse-sense. He still could be emotional – his voice on the radio showed that – but in later days he was never excitable. His speeches could be vehement, but it was a controlled vehemence. Behind it all he was cool, even cold; there was ice behind the fire.

In the 30s, however, his vehemence was not controlled. He was determined to be 'on the extreme Left', and made speeches which he would have regretted afterwards if he hadn't forgotten them. He glared at what seemed to be his opposite number.

> *Whose was the face that launched a thousand ships?*
> *Sir Oswald Mosley's or Sir Stafford Cripps'?*

asked a Fleet Street poet. He had but one characteristic that he carried forward to his second period – he didn't listen to other people's opinions. He relied, not

wholly unnaturally, on his own inordinately powerful mind and his store of information and experience, which was nothing like as great, of course, as it was a decade later. He was perfectly willing and even anxious to hear facts from anyone; to them, he would listen with the greatest attention. But to opinions or advice he would listen no more than a punched-card computer does. In fairness, I ought to add that at this period there was one exception to this rule – the leader of the Labour Party, George Lansbury. Lansbury was a much older man, an equally earnest Christian, and his mentor in Socialism; Cripps deferred to him, for the last and probably the first time in his life. But it was an effort. Lansbury used to have to say to him: 'Stafford, you have not heard what I said. You have not been listening,' and then Cripps would leash back his strong mind, which was already miles ahead, drawing deductions which were quite often false though logical; he would say: 'I am sorry, GL. Please repeat what you said,' and listen with a rigid attention and despite what was almost a physical strain, for he was a profoundly good man and knew that spiritual pride is a sin.

In the intervening years, before his 1949 Budget, he learned a good deal – indeed a great deal – by experience, in Russia, India and at home. But I think that, typically, he learned most from things, not people. I remember meeting him suddenly in Millbank – about 1942, I suppose. Anyway, it was when he had made a failure of being Leader of the House of Commons (what a crazy appointment!) and had been appointed Minister of Aircraft Production. His face was radiant, and even had a good colour (though that may have been the setting sun on it); he seemed to be walking aimlessly for his own pleasure. This was so unusual that I stopped and asked him outright how he found his new job.

'Ray,' he said, 'I have never enjoyed anything so much in my life. I have never before got my hands upon a really big machine. I am controlling things and making things; I am organising. What I am learning every week astounds me.' He extricated himself from me then with the greatest courtesy and skill; I realised then that there was another thing he had learned which he once didn't know. I had a fresh demonstration of this some while later when he was President of the Board of Trade and sent for me officially; he wanted to know certain things about (I think) the furniture trade. He hardly questioned me; he just directed my remarks with an imperceptible bridle. Within five minutes he had all the information that was in my mind; he had cleared out my brain as neatly and swiftly as a fishmonger eviscerates a crab; and I was outside his door.

These qualities made him the great Chancellor that he was in the post-war years. If he had been less skilled, less well-informed, less swift and brilliant, and above all less determined, we should never have made the recovery that we did. If the nation, including his own party, had known what the truth was in 1945, it would have been reduced to a screeching terror. The task before us was just impossible, in ordinary economic terms. This is no place to go into it in detail, but the rough outline is that there were fifty million people on an island which could support twenty-five million, and they had no reserves, damned little productive capacity and a fabulous list of debts. By *laissez-faire* economics, therefore, every other person ought to have died of starvation.

It was as part of the process of guiding us through this period of privation that Cripps reduced so dramatically the price of wine. On the face of it, a very odd thing to do; there were puritans and 'blue-noses' enough to point that out. Nor was Cripps the person you would expect to do it; he was a vegetarian and a teetotaller. (This was not a matter of principle, though; his stomach was very weak and literally could not tolerate meat or wine.) His action was due to two of the characteristics I have mentioned. First was his refusal to listen to anyone else's opinions. The outcries from the puritans and prohibitionists were merely bellowings of opinions. No facts were contained in them that he didn't know already, and he therefore did not hear them. It is a soothing recollection to recall how totally he ignored them; he did not even answer. The second was his swift deduction from facts. Financially, he saw that the existing tax was so high that to cut it in half would actually bring more revenue in. The imports would rise more than enough to compensate for the cut. Therefore, the change was a saving. Economically, he saw that revival of Western Europe must be treated as a whole. Wine was the one staple of which France had a considerable surplus. Therefore, arrangements must be made for this surplus to be profitably con-

sumed – that is to say, exchanged for goods which we might be able to offer. These considerations were facts. The cry, 'You are encouraging luxury expenditure in a time of austerity', contained no facts. All the nouns in that sentence were metaphors; they conveyed nothing but opinions. Therefore, Cripps did not consider them.

Up to this moment my study has been addressed equally to Socialists, Conservatives, Liberals and idiots (I use the word in the Greek sense of course). From here on I am writing with Socialists particularly in view, and I would ask others to look in as it were from outside, observing if they choose the odd behaviour of the animals in the cage, or if they prefer walking to some other part of the zoo, where they will find their own friends cracking nuts, and perhaps waiting to drink port with them. I hope that Liberals, at least, will stay, for though Cobden is farther away than Cripps, he is still on my side.

The reasons why both Liberal and Labour politicians and voters have often allowed themselves to become the enemies of decent drinking are, as is usual in this country, to be found in history. As I said, the Beer Act of the 1830s may have been the beginning of it, but the decisive steps were taken in the 1870s. Those two very skilful players, Gladstone and Disraeli, were making moves against each other which were as carefully calculated as in chess. For reasons that are too complicated to explain here, Disraeli 'played' the publicans and Gladstone moved up the Nonconformists as a riposte. This won an election, but it didn't end with that. The two party leaders had done an unwise thing – they had each taken an organised 'interest' into their party, and they would never get rid of it again. Henceforward, the beer influence and the dissenting influence glared at each other from opposite camps, and sniped without ceasing.

The Labour movement inherited this feud from the Radicals – not unnaturally, because it found what it called 'the beer barons' pretty steadily supporting the Conservatives. Moreover, there were many areas then where anybody might want to see the gin-palaces shut down, out of simple revulsion at what went on there. But in taking the feud over thus thoughtlessly, the pioneers were being untrue to their own principles. Drunkenness was an effect, not a cause, of capitalism, as they proclaimed from every platform. Men and women drank themselves silly because life was intolerable. Let them have decent houses, healthy cities and countryside, parks and hospitals, a living wage, and reasonable leisure; then the problem of drunkenness would be three-quarters settled. For fifty years they, and we, have been agitating to get those things, but now that we have them – or at any rate some of them – we still are subject to the instinctive revulsions of the days of Keir Hardie. Or some of us are, at least, and some others pretend to be.

Now this simply will not do. Dear friends, the fundamental object of the Labour movement has always been a freer and a better life for the people as a whole. I am told that this is also true of the Liberal movement. To stop people taking good drink when and how they please, so long as they do not make a nuisance of themselves, is thus contrary to our principles. It is not an extension of freedom; it is an invasion of it. If the drink is bad, let the vendors be punished; if the drinkers misuse it, let them be punished. But we must not interfere with drinking itself. The freedom to drink may be abused, you say. Certainly it may. All freedom may be abused. Freedom to write books may result in the writing of very bad books, some of which will be vulgar, too. Freedom of the press may produce some utterly brainless and vicious papers. Painters will paint ghastly pictures which will be purchased by town councillors and royalty, and architects will build monstrously ugly masterpieces which nobody can avoid seeing. But we shall not for that reason close down the press, forbid any book-publishing except by the Oxford University Press under licence, and put all painters and architects in a pen. That is the policy of Sennacherib, and I don't know what it's turning up again for.

The true policy for us all was laid down by a man who was strictly abstemious and morally head and shoulders above the ordinary politicians of his day; I have quoted him before – George Lansbury. When he was First Commissioner of Works, he was denounced by a body called the 'London Free Church Federation' for allowing the Tilt Yard Restaurant at Hampton Court to sell wines, beers and spirits. He told them in reply: 'I should regard it as an impertinence on my part to attempt to impose total abstinence on other persons on the ground that I am an abstainer. Arrangements should be made so that people should be able to consume beer and spirits in healthful and happy circumstances.' He told the Free Churchmen to turn their energies to seeing that there were plenty of drinking places to which people would bring their whole families. The advice shocked them so much that for once they fell silent.

The meeting will now close, as it is opening time.

© *from* THE COMPLEAT IMBIBER 2, 1958

Bottling the Bookies

BRIAN ST PIERRE

Wine-drinking is more subjective than horse-racing and nearly as subjective as love, but the gamble is less: you get something for your money no matter what you pick.

A. J. LIEBLING

Too long ago, I was a young man just out of the Army, and went to a racetrack for the first time in my life. At the age when you hate to admit ignorance of anything, I quietly plunked my money down on whatever horse's name appealed to me.

When I told a horseplayer friend, he archly informed me of the First Commandment of Horseplaying: 'Never bet on a horse because you like its name.'

Knowing no other system and possessed of a budding grip on reality, I soon abandoned my dreams of making a killing playing the ponies. There are many better ways of letting money slip through your fingers, I discovered, one of which was wine – enough of a sporting proposition in itself.

But, not smart enough to let well enough alone, newly enamoured and showing off, one day last year I found myself 'instructing' a young lady on the Sport of Kings at a local racetrack. It turned out that she'd learned to read by skimming through the pages of *Racing Form*.

I became a desperate backslider. A horse named Port Wine's Girl was running, a filly, sired by Port Wine. I furtively placed a bet on her and she, quite flamboyantly, won. Later in the day, a horse named Wood and Wine ran, won and rescued my fortune. It quite properly scared me; gamblers go broke when they think they've found a system.

I consulted my friend, Society Jack, not because he's seen as many tracks as Willie Shoemaker, but because he wouldn't laugh or, more importantly, tell anyone else. (He is also a beer drinker and wouldn't know enough to steal my system – see how you get?)

'That's nothing new,' he said immediately. 'Ever hear of André Kostelanetz?'

'Sure, of course,' I said with some indignation. 'He was a symphony-orchestra conductor.'

'He was also quite a horseplayer,' Jack replied acidly. (To him what a fellow does away from the track is his own business.) 'He once spent a whole meet at Del Mar betting on horses with musical names, and made a bundle.'

I took it as a sign, of course.

Sometimes it was easy. Degustation gave me a taste of victory straight away. Champagne Sheila and Champagne Shower went flat from time to time, but bubbled up often enough. Import Wine was also inconsistent, just barely a winner. Chablis, on the other hand, had a lot of class and finished well. Vintage Proof seemed like a bit out of reach, but returned $79 on my over-cautious $2.

There were slow days, and stretching the system didn't work: Bold Press, Barwhine and Heresmudinyoureye may still be in search of the finish line, for all I know. Grape Juice never fermented. I thought of Dick Arrowood's Sonoma château and tried to get by with San Jean, but it was no go. Friuli did not travel well most times.

Other days I tried parlays, seeking further horizons. Port Wine's Girl did not match up with Sharp Cheddar, which was a nasty surprise, but I was relieved when Chablis and Petite Filet didn't make it, having suspected all along that the owner meant steak instead of sole.

Lovely Wine was lovely indeed, but The Wine Merchant lurked below the bottom line; Sherry's Boy was obviously named after a showgirl and not a fino, and Port Aglow a harbour rather than an after-dinner condition.

Brand names did prove to be reliable, as is so often said in the trade. Windsor, Gold Seal and Chalone delivered again and again: Life imitating Art.

Needless to say, with enough winners I became more outgoing; Society Jack accepted his fate stoically – not many horses have beer names.

I confessed my secret to the lady, a mistake I will never repeat. My only consolation was that I had an ace up my sleeve.

The next day, *la belle dame sans merci* giggled over *Racing Form*. She is, as my mother used to say, something of a high flyer, and brandished the *Form* around, chortling, 'I think I'll try your system and bet on Gin and Tux – that's my style, first-class cabin all the way!' The horse didn't come in, I am happy to record.

At last, my ace was up: Pete's Sirah. I could be reaching, but etymology seemed to be on my side. If the owner meant 'sir', he surely would have used the Elizabethan 'sirrah'. It could only be a nice play on the wine-grape, I told myself a dozen times while waiting in line to bet.

I prayed as the horses left the starting gate but Pete's Sirah was true to type – he uncorked well, opened up immediately (even aggressively), dithered a little in the middle, but came through with a very lasting, hearty finish. (The price was right, too.)

I retired on the spot. Systems go flat, and the wise man retires from the field with honour intact, especially if he has acquired the wherewithal to replenish his wine cellar.

My equine wine education wasn't over, however.

I told an erudite friend of my experience, and he referred me to the oddest horse-and-wine story of all. In James Joyce's *Ulysses*, which chronicles a day – 16 June 1904 – in the life of a motley crew of Dublin Irishmen, Leopold Bloom tries to get a bet on the Gold Cup at Ascot and fails. After 632 pages of Joycean prose, he finally discovers how it came out.

This really is what the result was: The winner was Throwaway, a long shot. The second horse, also paying a good price, was named Zinfandel.

Shades of Agoston Haraszthy! The grape of California had only acquired its proper name, after some variant spellings, perhaps twenty or so years before – and the horse was English.

Through Cyril Ray, I put the question to Lord Howard de Walden, whose grandfather had owned the horse. Alas, the animal had been bought from a Colonel H. McCalmont, already named Zinfandel, and no one has the foggiest notion how or why. Perhaps the colonel was well-travelled and an amateur of wine; perhaps it was merely the wine that was well-travelled. We'll never know.

But I do wish I'd been there with my system.

Do you know what the pound was worth in those days?

A Good Appetite

A. J. LIEBLING

The Proust *madeleine* phenomenon is now as firmly established in folklore as Newton's apple or Watt's steam kettle. The man ate a tea biscuit, the taste evoked memories, he wrote a book. This is capable of expression by the formula TMB, for Taste > Memory > Book. Some time ago, when I began to read a book called *The Food of France* by Waverley Root, I had an inverse experience: BMT, for Book > Memory > Taste. Happily, the tastes that *The Food of France* recreated for me – small birds, stewed rabbit, stuffed tripe, Côte Rôtie, and Tavel – were more robust than that of the *madeleine*, which Larousse defines as 'a light cake made with sugar, flour, lemon juice, brandy, and eggs'. (The quantity of brandy in a *madeleine* would not furnish a gnat with an alcohol rub.) In the light of what Proust wrote with so mild a stimulus, is it the world's loss that he did not have a heartier appetite. On a dozen Gardiners Island oysters, a bowl of clam chowder, a peck of steamers, some bay scallops, three sautéed soft-shelled crabs, a few ears of fresh-picked corn, a thin swordfish steak

of generous area, a pair of lobsters, and a Long Island duck, he might have written a masterpiece.

The primary requisite for writing well about food is a good appetite. Without this, it is impossible to accumulate, within the allotted span, enough experience of eating to have anything worth setting down. Each day brings only two opportunities for field work, and they are not to be wasted minimising the intake of cholesterol. They are indispensable, like a prizefighter's hours on the road. (I have read that the late French professional gourmand Maurice Curnonsky ate but one meal a day – dinner. But that was late in his life, and I have always suspected his attainments anyway; so many mediocre witticisms are attributed to him that he could not have had much time for eating.) A good appetite gives an eater room to turn around in. For example, a nonprofessional eater I know went to the Restaurant Pierre, in the place Gaillon, a couple of years ago, his mind set on a sensibly light meal: a dozen, or possibly eighteen, oysters, and a thick chunk of steak topped with beef marrow, which M. Pierre calls a *Délice de la Villette* – the equivalent of a 'Stockyards' Delight'. But as he arrived, he heard M. Pierre say to his headwaiter, 'Here comes Monsieur L. Those two portions of *cassoulet* that are left – put them aside for him.' A *cassoulet* is a substantial dish, of a complexity precluding its discussion here (Mr Root devotes three pages to the great controversy over what it should contain.) M. Pierre is the most amiable of restaurateurs, who prides himself on knowing in advance what his friends will like. A client of limited appetite would be obliged either to forgo his steak or to hurt M. Pierre's feelings. Monsieur L., however, was in no difficulty. He ate the two *cassoulets*, as was his normal practice; if he had consumed only one, his host would have feared that it wasn't up to standard. He then enjoyed his steak. The oysters offered no problem, since they present no bulk.

In the heroic age before the First World War, there were men and women who ate, in addition to a whacking lunch and a glorious dinner, a voluminous *souper* after the theatre or the other amusements of the evening. I have known some of the survivors, octogenarians of unblemished appetite and unfailing good humour – spry, wry, and free of the ulcers that come from worrying about a balanced diet – but they have had no emulators in France since the doctors there discovered the existence of the human liver. From that time on, French life has been built to an increasing extent around that organ, and a niggling caution has replaced the old recklessness; the liver was the seat of the Maginot mentality. One of the last of the great around-the-clock gastronomes of France was Yves Mirande, a small, merry author of farces and musical-comedy books. In 1955, Mirande celebrated his eightieth birthday with a speech before the curtain of the Théâtre Antoine, in the management of which he was associated with Mme B., a protégée of his, forty years younger than himself. But the theatre was only half of his life. In addition, M. Mirande was an unofficial director of a restaurant on the Saint-Augustin, which he had founded for another protégée, also forty years younger than himself; this was Mme G., a Gasconne and a magnificent cook. In the restaurant on the rue Saint-Augustin, M. Mirande would dazzle his juniors, French and American, by dispatching a lunch of raw Bayonne ham and fresh figs, a hot sausage in crust, spindles of filleted pike in a rich rose *sauce Nantua*, a leg of lamb larded with anchovies, artichokes on a pedestal of foie gras, and four or five kinds of cheese, with a good bottle of Bordeaux and one of champagne, after which he would call for the Armagnac and remind Madame to have ready for dinner the larks and ortolans she had promised him, with a few *langoustes* and a turbot – and, of course, a fine *civet* made from the *marcassin*, or young wild boar, that the lover of the leading lady in his current production had sent up from his estate in the Sologne. 'And while I think of it,' I once heard him say, 'we haven't had any woodcock for days, or truffles baked in the ashes, and the cellar is becoming a disgrace – no more 34s and hardly any 37s. Last week, I had to offer my publisher a bottle that was far too good for him, simply because there was nothing between the insulting and the superlative.'

M. Mirande had to his credit a hundred produced plays, including a number of great Paris hits, but he had just written his first book for print, so he said 'my publisher' in a special mock-impressive tone. 'An informal sketch for my definitive autobiography,' he would say of this production. The informal sketch, which I cherish, begins with the most important decision in Mirande's life. He was almost seventeen and living in the small Breton port of Lannion – his offstage family name was Le Querrec – when his father, a retired naval officer, said to him, 'It is time to decide your future career. Which will it be, the Navy or the Church?' No other choice was conceivable in Lannion. At dawn, Yves ran away to Paris.

There, he had read a thousand times, all the famous wits and cocottes frequented the tables in front of the Café Napolitain, on the boulevard des Capucines. He presented himself at the café at nine the next morning – late in the day for Lannion – and found that the place had not yet opened. Soon he became a newspaperman. It was a newspaper era as cynically animated as the corresponding period of the Bennett-Pulitzer-Hearst competition in New York, and in his second or third job he worked for a press lord who was as notional and niggardly as most press lords are; the publisher insisted that his reporters be well turned out, but did not pay them salaries that permitted cab fares when it rained. Mirande lived near the fashionable Montmartre cemetery and solved his rainy-day pants-crease problem by crashing funeral parties as they broke up and riding, gratis, in the carriages returning to the centre of town. Early in his career, he became personal secretary to Clemenceau and then to Briand, but the gay theatre attracted him more than politics, and he made the second great decision of his life after one of his political patrons had caused him to be appointed *sous-préfet* in a provincial city. A *sous-préfet* is the administrator of one of the districts into which each of the ninety *départements* of France is divided, and a young *sous-préfet* is often headed for a precocious rise to high positions of state. Mirande, attired in the magnificent uniform that was then *de rigueur*, went to his 'capital', spent one night there, and then ran off to Paris again to direct a one-act farce. Nevertheless, his connections with the serious world remained cordial. In the restaurant on the rue Saint-Augustin, he introduced me to Colette, by that time a national glory of letters.

The regimen fabricated by Mirande's culinary protégée, Mme G., maintained him *en pleine forme*. When I first met him, in the restaurant, during the summer of the Liberation, he was a sprightly sixty-nine. In the spring of 1955, when we renewed a friendship that had begun in admiration of each other's appetite, he was as good as ever. On the occasion of our reunion, we began with a *truite au bleu* – a live trout simply done to death in hot water, like a Roman emperor in his bath. It was served up doused with enough melted butter to thrombose a regiment of Paul Dudley Whites, and accompanied, as was right, by an Alsatian wine – a Lacrimae Sanctae Odiliae, which once contributed slightly to my education. Long ago, when I was very young, I took out a woman in Strasbourg and, wishing to impress her with my knowledge of local customs, ordered a bottle of Ste Odile. I was making the same mistake as if I had taken out a girl in Boston and offered her baked beans. 'How quaint!' the woman in Strasbourg said. 'I haven't drunk that for years.' She excused herself to go to the telephone, and never came back.

After the trout, Mirande and I had two meat courses, since we could not decide in advance which we preferred. We had a magnificent *daube provençale*, because we were faithful to *la cuisine bourgeoise*, and then *pintadous* – young guinea hens, simply and tenderly roasted – with the first asparagus of the year, to show our fidelity to *la cuisine classique*. We had clarets with both courses – a Pétrus with the *daube*, a Cheval Blanc with the guineas. Mirande said that his doctor had discounselled Burgundies. It was the first time in our acquaintance that I had heard him admit he had a doctor, but I was reassured when he drank a bottle and a half of Krug after luncheon. We had three bottles between us – one to our loves, one to our countries, and one for symmetry, the last being on the house.

Mirande was a small, alert man with the face of a Celtic terrier – salient eyebrows and an up-turned nose. He looked like an intelligent Lloyd George. That summer, in association with Mme B., his theatrical protégée, he planned to produce a new play of Sartre's. His mind kept young by the theatre of Mme B., his metabolism protected by the restaurant of Mme G., Mirande seemed fortified against all eventualities for at least another twenty years. Then, perhaps, he would have to recruit new protégées. The Sunday following our reunion, I encountered him at Longchamp, a racecourse where the restaurant does not face the horses, and diners can keep first things first. There he sat, radiant, surrounded by celebrities and champagne buckets, sending out a relay team of commissionaires to bet for him on the successive tips that the proprietors of stables were ravished to furnish him between races. He was the embodiment of a happy man. (I myself had a nice thing at 27-1.)

The first alteration in Mirande's fortunes affected me so directly that I did not at once sense its gravity for him. Six weeks later, I was again in Paris. (That year, I was shuttling frequently between there and London.) I was alone on the evening I arrived, and looked forward to a pleasant dinner at Mme G's, which was within two hundred metres of the hotel, in the square Louvois, where I always stop. Madame's was more than a place to eat, although one ate superbly there. Arriving, I would have a bit of talk with the proprietress, then with the waitresses – Germaine and Lucienne – who had composed the original staff. Waiters had been added as the house prospered, but they were of less marked personality. Madame was a bosomy woman – voluble, tawny, with a big nose and lank black hair – who made one think of a Saracen. (The Saracens reached Gascony in the eighth century.) Her conversation was a chronicle of letters and the theatre – as good as a subscription to *Figaro Littéraire*, but more advanced. It was somewhere between the avantgarde and the main body, but within hailing distance of both and enriched with the names of the great people who had been in recently – M. Cocteau, Gene Kelly, la Comtesse de Vogüé. It was always well to give an appearance of listening, lest she someday fail to save for you the last order of larks *en brochette* and bestow them on a more attentive customer. With Germaine and Lucienne, whom I had known when we were all younger, in 1939, the year of the *drôle de guerre*, flirtation was now perfunctory, but the *carte du jour* was still the serious topic – for example, how the fat Belgian industrialist from Tournai had reacted to the *caille vendangeuse*, or quail potted with fresh grapes. 'You know the man,' Germaine would say. 'If it isn't dazzling, he takes only two portions. But when he has three, then you can say to yourself...' She and Lucienne looked alike – compact little women, with high foreheads and cheekbones and solid, muscular legs, who walked like *chas-*

seurs à pied, a hundred and thirty steps to the minute. In 1939, and again in 1944, Germaine had been a brunette and Lucienne a blonde, but in 1955 Germaine had become a blonde too, and I found it hard to tell them apart.

Among my fellow customers at Mme G.'s I was always likely to see some friend out of the past. It is a risk to make an engagement for an entire evening with somebody you haven't seen for years. This is particularly true in France now. The almost embarrassingly pro-American acquaintance of the Liberation may be by now a Communist Party-line hack; the idealistic young Resistance journalist may have become an editorial writer for the reactionary newspaper of a textile magnate. The Vichy apologist you met in Washington in 1941, who called de Gaulle a traitor and the creation of the British Intelligence Service, may now tell you that the General is the best thing ever, while the fellow you knew as a de Gaulle aide in London may now compare him to Sulla destroying the Roman Republic. As for the women, who is to say which of them has resisted the years? But in a good restaurant that all have frequented, you are likely to meet any of them again, for good restaurants are not so many nowadays that a Frenchman will permanently desert one – unless, of course, he is broke, and in that case it would depress you to learn of his misfortunes. If you happen to encounter your old friends when they are already established at their tables, you have the opportunity to greet them cordially and to size them up. If you still like them, you can make a further engagement.

On the ghastly evening I speak of – a beautiful one in June – I perceived no change in the undistinguished exterior of Mme G.'s restaurant. The name – something like Prospéria – was the same, and since the plate-glass windows were backed with scrim, it was impossible to see inside. Nor, indeed, did I notice any difference when I first entered. The bar, the tables, the banquettes covered with leatherette, the simple décor of mirrors and pink marble slabs were the same. The premises had been a business employees' bar-and-café before Mme G., succeeding a long string of obscure proprietors, made it illustrious. She had changed the fare and the clientele but not the cadre. There are hundreds of identical fronts and interiors in Paris, turned out by some mass producer in the late 20s. I might have been warned by the fact that the room was empty, but it was only eight o'clock and still light outdoors. I had come unusually early because I was so hungry. A man whom I did not recognise came to meet me, rubbing his hands and hailing me as an old aquaintance. I thought he might be a waiter who had served me. (The waiters, as I have said, were not the marked personalities of the place.) He had me at a table before I sensed the trap.

'Madame goes well?' I asked politely.

'No, Madame is lightly ill,' he said, with what I now realise was a guilty air.

He presented me with a *carte du jour* written in the familiar purple ink on the familiar wide sheet of paper with the name and telephone number of the restaurant at the top. The content of the menu, however, had become Italianised, the spelling had deteriorated, and the prices had diminished to a point where it would be a miracle if the food continued distinguished.

'Madame still conducts the restaurant?' I asked sharply.

I could now see that he was a Piedmontese of the most evasive description. From rubbing his hands he had switched to twisting them.

'Not exactly,' he said, 'but we make the same cuisine.'

I could not descry anything in the smudged ink but misspelled noodles and unorthographical *'escaloppinis'*; Italians writing French by ear produce a regression to an unknown ancestor of both languages.

'Try us,' my man pleaded, and, like a fool, I did. I was hungry. Forty minutes later, I stamped out into the street as purple as an aubergine with rage. The minestrone had been cabbage scraps in greasy water. I had chosen *côtes d'agneau* as the safest item in the mediocre catalogue that the Prospéria's prospectus of bliss had turned into overnight. They had been cut from a tired Alpine billy goat and seared in machine oil, and the haricots verts with which they were served resembled decomposed whiskers from a theatrical costume beard.

'The same cuisine?' I thundered as I flung my money on the falsified *addition* that I was too angry to verify. 'You take me for a jackass!'

I am sure that as soon as I turned my back the scoundrel nodded. The restaurant has changed hands at least once since then.

In the morning, I telephoned Mirande. He confirmed the disaster. Mme G., ill, had closed the restaurant. Worse, she had sold the lease and the good will, and had definitely retired.

'What is the matter with her?' I asked in a tone appropriate to fatal disease.

'I think it was trying to read Simone de Beauvoir,' he said 'A syncope.'

Mme G. still lives, but Mirande is dead. When I met him in Paris the following November, his appearance gave no hint of decline. It was the season for his sable-lined overcoat *à l'impresario*, and a hat that was a furry cross between a pork pie and a homburg. Since the restaurant on the rue Saint-Augustin no longer existed, I had invited him to lunch with me at a very small place called the Gratin Dauphinois, on the rue Chabanais, directly across from the building that once housed the most celebrated sporting house in Paris. The rue Chabanais is a short street that runs from the Square Louvois to the rue des Petits Champs – perhaps a hundred yards – but before the reform wave stimulated by a Municipal Councillor named Marthe Richard at the end of the Second World War, the name Chabanais had a cachet all its own. Mme Richard will go down in history as the Carry Nation of sex. Now the house is closed, and the premises are devoted to some low commercial purpose. The walls of the midget Gratin Dauphinois are hung with cartoons that have a nostalgic reference to the past glories of the street.

Mirande, when he arrived, crackled with jokes about the locale. He taunted me with being a criminal who haunts the scene of his misdeeds. The fare at the Gratin is robust, as it is in Dauphiné, but it did not daunt Mirande. The wine card, similarly, is limited to the strong, rough wines of Arbois and the like, with a couple of Burgundies for clients who want to show off. There are no clarets; the proprietor hasn't heard of them. There are, of course, a few champagnes, for wedding parties or anniversaries, so Mirande, with Burgundies discounselled by his doctor, decided on champagne throughout the meal. This was a *drôle* combination with the mountain food, but I had forgotten about the lack of claret when I invited him.

We ordered a couple of dozen *escargots en pots de chambre* to begin with. These are snails baked and served, for the client's convenience, in individual earthenware crocks, instead of being forced back into shells. The snail, of course, has to be taken out of his shell to be prepared for cooking. The shell he is forced back into may not be his own. There is thus not even a sentimental justification for his reincarceration. The frankness of the service *en pot* does not improve the preparation of the snail, nor does it detract from it, but it does facilitate and accelerate his consumption. (The notion that the shell proves the snail's authenticity, like the head left on a woodcock, is invalid, as even a suburban housewife knows nowadays; you can buy a tin of snail shells in a supermarket and fill them with a mixture of nutted cream cheese and chopped olives.)

Mirande finished his dozen first, meticulously swabbing out the garlicky butter in each *pot* with a bit of bread that was fitted to the bore of the crock as precisely as a bullet to a rifle barrel. Tearing bread like that takes practice. We had emptied the first bottle of champagne when he placed his right hand delicately on the point of his waistcoat farthest removed from his spinal column.

'*Liebling*,' he said, 'I am not well.'

It was like the moment when I first saw Joe Louis draped on the ropes. A great pity filled my heart. '*Maitre*,' I said, 'I will take you home.'

The dismayed *patronne* waved to her husband in the kitchen (he could see her through the opening he pushed the dishes through) to suspend the preparation of the *gendarme de Morteau* – the great smoked sausage in its tough skin – that we had proposed to follow the snails with. ('Short and broad in shape, it is made of pure pork and … is likely to be accompanied … by hot potato salad.' – Root, p 217.) We had decided to substitute for the *pommes à l'huile* the *gratin dauphinois* itself. ('Thinly sliced potatoes are moistened with boiled milk and beaten egg, seasoned with salt, pepper, and nutmeg, and mixed with grated cheese, of the Gruyère type. The potatoes are then put into an earthenware dish which has been rubbed with garlic and then buttered, spotted with little dabs of butter, and sprinkled with more grated cheese. It is then cooked slowly in not too hot an oven.' – Root, p 228.) After that, we were going to have a fowl in cream with *morilles* – wild black mushrooms of the mountains. We abandoned all.

I led Mirande into the street and hailed a taxi.

'I am not well, *Liebling*,' he said. 'I grow old.'

He lived far from the restaurant, beyond the place de l'Etoile, in the Paris of the successful. From time to time on the way, he would say, 'It is nothing. You must excuse me. I am not well.'

The apartment house in which he and Mme B. lived resembled one of the chic modern museums of the quarter, with entrance gained through a maze of garden patches sheathed in glass. Successsive metal grilles swung open before us as I pushed buttons that Mirande indicated – in these modern palaces there are no visible flunkies – until we reached an elevator that smoothly shot us upward to his apartment, which was rather larger in area than the Square Louvois. The décor, with basalt columns and floors covered with the skin of jumbo Siberian tigers – a special strain force-fed to supply old-style movie stars – reminded me of the sets for *Belphégor*, a French serial of silent days that I enjoyed when I was a student at the Sorbonne in 1926. (It was, I think, about an ancient Egyptian high priest who came to life and set up bachelor quarters in Paris in the style of the Temple of Karnak.) Three or four maids rushed to relieve Mirande of his sable-lined coat, his hat, and his cane topped with the horn of an albino chamois. I helped him to a divan on which two Theda Baras could have defended their honour simultaneously against two villains of the silents without either couple's getting in the other's way. Most of the horizontal surfaces in the room were covered with sculpture and most of the vertical ones with large paintings. In pain though he was, Mirande called my attention to these works of art.

'All the sculptures are by Renoir,' he said. 'It was his hobby. And all the paintings are by Maillol. It was *his* hobby. If it were the other way around, I would be one of the richest chaps in France. Both men were my friends. But then, one doesn't give one's friends one's bread and butter. And after all, it's less banal as it is.'

After a minute, he asked me to help him to his bedroom, which was in a wing of the apartment all his own. When we got there, one of the maids came in and took his shoes off.

'I am in good hands now, *Liebling*,' he said. 'Farewell until next time. It is nothing.'

I telephoned the next noon, and he said that his doctor, who was a fool, insisted that he was ill.

Again I left Paris, and when I returned, late the following January, I neglected Mirande. A Father William is a comforting companion for the middle-aged – he reminds you that the best is yet to be and that there's a dance in the old dame yet – but a sick old man is discouraging. My conscience stirred when I read in a gossip column in *France-Dimanche* that Toto Mirande was convalescing nicely and was devouring caviar at a great rate – with champagne, of course. (I had never thought of Mirande as Toto, which is baby slang for 'little kid', but from then on I never referred to him in any other way; I didn't want anybody to think I wasn't in the know.) So the next day I sent him a pound of fresh caviar from Kaspia, in the place de la Madeleine. It was the kind of medication I approved of.

I received a note from Mirande by tube next morning, reproaching me for spoiling him. He was going better, he wrote, and would telephone in a day or two to make an appointment for a return bout. When he called, he said that the idiotic doctor would not yet permit him to go out to a restaurant, and he invited me, instead, to a family dinner at Mme B.'s. 'Only a few old friends, and not the cuisine I hope to give you at Maxim's next time,' he said. 'But one makes out.'

On the appointed evening, I arrived early – or on time, which amounts to the same thing – *chez* Mme B.; you take taxis when you can get them in Paris at the rush hours. The handsome quarter overlooking the Seine above the Trocadéro is so dull that when my taxi deposited me before my host's door, I had no inclination to stroll to kill time. It is like Park Avenue or the near North Side of Chicago. So I was the first or second guest to arrive, and Mme B.'s fourteen-year-old daughter, by a past marriage, received me in the Belphégor room, apologising because her mother was still with Toto – she called him that. She need not have told me, for at that moment I heard Madame, who is famous for her determined voice, storming at an unmistakable someone: 'You go too far, Toto. It's disgusting. People all over Paris are kind enough to send you caviar, and because you call it monotonous, you throw it at the maid! If you think servants are easy to come by ...'

When they entered the room a few minutes later, my old friend was all smiles. 'How did you know I adore caviar to such a point?' he asked me. But I was worried because of what I had heard; the Mirande I remembered would never have been irritated by the obligation to eat a few extra kilos of fresh caviar. The little girl, who hoped I had not heard, embraced Toto. 'Don't be angry with *Maman!*' she implored him.

My fellow guests included the youngish new wife of an old former Premier, who was unavoidably detained in Lille at a congress of the party he now headed; it mustered four deputies, of whom two formed a Left Wing and two a Right Wing. ('If they had elected a fifth at the last election, or if, by good luck, one had been defeated, they could afford the luxury of a Centre,' Mirande told me

in identifying the lady. '*C'est malheureux*, a party without a Centre. It limits the possibilities of manoeuvre.') There was also an amiable couple in their advanced sixties or beginning seventies, of whom the husband was the grand manitou of Veuve Clicquot champagne. Mirande introduced them by their right name, which I forget, and during the rest of the evening addressed them as M. and Mme Cliquot. There was a forceful, black-haired man from the Midi, in the youth of middle age – square-shouldered, stocky, decisive, blatantly virile – who, I was told, managed Mme B.'s vinicultural enterprises in Provence. There were two guests of less decided individuality, whom I barely remember, and filling out the party were the young girl – shy, carefully unsophisticated and unadorned – Mme B., Mirande, and me. Mme B. had a strong triangular face on a strong triangular base – a strong chin, high cheekbones, and a wide, strong jaw, but full of stormy good nature. She was a woman who, if he had been a man, would have wanted to be called Honest John. She had a high colour and an iron handgrip, and repeatedly affirmed that there was no affectation about her, that she was *sans façon*, that she called her shots as she saw them. 'I won't apologise,' she said to me. 'I know you're a great feeder, like Toto here, but I won't offer you the sort of menu he used to get in that restaurant you know of, where he ruined his plumbing. Oh, that woman! I used to be so jealous. I can offer only a simple home dinner.' And she waved us towards a marble table about twenty-two feet long. Unfortunately for me, she meant it. The dinner began with a kidney-and-mushroom mince served in a giant popover – the kind of thing you might get at a literary hotel in New York. The inner side of the pastry had the feeling of a baby's palm, in the true tearoom tradition.

'It is savoury but healthy,' Madame said firmly, setting an example by taking a large second helping before starting the dish on its second round. Mirande regarded the untouched doughy fabric on his plate with diaphanously veiled horror, but he had an excuse in the state of his health. 'It's still a little rich for me, darling,' he murmured. The others, including me, delivered salvos of compliments. I do not squander my moral courage on minor crises. M. Clicquot said, 'Impossible to obtain anything like this *chez* Lapérouse!' Mme Clicquot said, 'Not even at the Tour d'Argent!'

'And what do you think of my little wine?' Mme B. asked M. Clicquot. 'I'm so anxious for your professional opinion – as a rival producer, you know.'

The wine was a thin *rosé* in an Art Nouveau bottle with a label that was a triumph of lithography; it had spires and monks and troubadours and blondes in wimples on it, and the name of the *cru* was spelled out in letters with Gothic curlicues and pennons. The name was something like Château Guillaume d'Aquitaine, *grand vin*.

'What a madly gay little wine, my dear!' M. Clicquot said, repressing, but not soon enough, a grimace of pain.

'One would say a Tavel of a good year,' I cried, 'if one were a complete bloody fool.' I did not say the second clause aloud.

My old friend looked at me with new respect. He was discovering in me a capacity for hypocrisy that he had never credited me with before.

The main course was a shoulder of mutton with white beans – the poor relation of a gigot, and an excellent dish in its way, when not too dry. This was.

For the second wine, the man from the Midi proudly produced a red, in a bottle without a label, which he offered to M. Clicquot with the air of a tomcat bringing a field mouse to its master's feet. 'Tell me what you think of this,' he said as he filled the champagne man's glass.

M. Clicquot – a veteran of such challenges, I could well imagine – held the glass against the light, dramatically inhaled the bouquet, and then drank, after a slight stiffening of the features that indicated to me that he knew what he was in for. Having emptied half the glass, he deliberated.

'It has a lovely colour,' he said.

'But what is it? What is it?' the man from the Midi insisted.

'There are things about it that remind me of a Beaujolais,' M. Clicquot said (he must have meant that it was wet), 'but on the whole I should compare it to a Bordeaux' (without doubt unfavourably).

Mme B.'s agent was beside himself with triumph. 'Not one or the other!' he crowed. 'It's from the *domaine* – the Château Guillaume d'Aquitaine!'

The admirable M. Clicquot professed astonishment, and I, when I had emptied a glass, said that there would be a vast market for the wine in America if it could be properly presented. 'Unfortunately,' I said, 'the cost of advertising ...' and I rolled my eyes skyward.

'Ah, yes,' Mme B. cried sadly. 'The cost of advertising!'

I caught Mirande looking at me again, and thought of the Pétrus and the Cheval Blanc of our last meal together *chez* Mme G. He drank a glass of the red. After all, he wasn't going to die of thirst.

For dessert, we had a simple fruit tart with milk – just the thing for an invalid's stomach, although Mirande didn't eat it.

M. Clicquot retrieved the evening, oenologically, by producing two bottles of a wine 'impossible to find in the cellars of any restaurant in France' – Veuve Clicquot '19. There is at present a great to-do among wine merchants in France and the United States about young wines, and an accompanying tendency to cry down the 'legend' of the old. For that matter, hardware clerks, when you ask for a can opener with a wooden handle that is thick enough to give a grip and long enough for leverage, try to sell you complicated mechanical folderols. The motivation in both cases is the same – simple greed. To deal in wines of varied ages requires judgement, the sum of experience and flair. It involves the risk of money, because every lot of wine, like every human being, has a life span, and it is this that the good vintner must estimate. His object should be to sell his wine at its moment of maximum value – to the drinker as well as the merchant. The vintner who handles only young wines is like an insurance company that will write policies only on children; the unqualified dealer wants to risk nothing and at the same time to avoid tying up his money. The client misled by brochures warning him off clarets and champagnes that are over ten years old and assuring him that Beaujolais should be drunk green will miss the major pleasures of wine drinking. To deal wisely in wines and merely to sell them are things as different as being an expert in ancient coins and selling Indian-head pennies over a souvenir counter.

Despite these convictions of mine about wine, I should never have tried a thirty-seven-year-old champagne on the recommendation of a lesser authority than the blessed M. Clicquot. It is the oldest by far that I have ever drunk. (H. Warner Allen, in *The Wines of France*, published circa 1924, which is my personal wine bible, says, 'In the matter of age, champagne is a capricious wine. As a general rule, it has passed its best between fifteen and twenty, yet a bottle thirty years old may prove excellent, though all its fellows may be quite un-drinkable.' He cites Saintsbury's note that 'a Perrier Jouet of 1857 was still majestical in 1884', adding, 'And all wine-drinkers know of such amazing dis-coveries.' Mr Root, whose book is not a foolish panegyric of everthing French, is hard on champagne, in my opinion. He falls into a critical error more common among writers less intelligent: he attacks it for not being something else. Because its excellences are not those of Burgundy or Bordeaux, he underrates the pe-culiar qualities it does not share with them, as one who would chide Dickens for not being Stendhal, or Marciano for not being Benny Leonard.)

The Veuve Clicquot '19 was tart without brashness – a refined but effective understatement of younger champagnes, which run too much to rhetoric, at best. Even so, the force was all there, to judge from the two glasses that were a shade more than my share. The wine still had a discreet *cordon* – the ring of bubbles that forms inside the glass – and it had developed the colour known as 'partridge eye'. I have never seen a partridge's eye, because the bird, unlike woodcock, is served without the head, but the colour the term indicates is that of serous blood or a maple leaf on the turn.

'How nice it was, life in 1919, eh, M. Clicquot?' Mirande said as he sipped his second glass.

After we had finished M. Clicquot's offering, we played a game called lying poker for table stakes, each player being allowed a capital of five hundred francs, not to be replenished under any circumstances. When Mme B. had won everybody's five hundred francs, the party broke up. Mirande promised me that he would be up and about soon, and would show me how men revelled in the heroic days of *la belle époque*, but I had a feeling that the bell was cracked.

I left Paris and came back to it seven times during the next year, but never saw him. Once, being in his quarter in the company of a remarkably pretty

woman, I called him up, simply because I knew he would like to look at her, but he was too tired. I forget when I last talked to him on the telephone. During the next winter, while I was away in Egypt or Jordan or some place where French papers don't circulate, he died, and I did not learn of it until I returned to Europe.

When Mirande first faltered, in the rue Chabanais, I had failed to correlate cause and effect. I had even felt a certain selfish alarm. If eating well was beginning to affect Mirande at eighty, I thought, I had better begin taking in sail. After all, I was only thirty years his junior. But after the dinner at Mme B.,'s, and in the light of subsequent reflection, I saw that what had undermined his constitution was Mme G.'s defection from the restaurant business. For years, he had been able to escape Mme B.'s solicitude for his health by lunching and dining in the restaurant of Mme G., the sight of whom Mme B. could not support. Entranced by Mme G.'s magnificent food, he had continued to live 'like a cock in a pie' – eating as well, and very nearly as much, as when he was thirty. The organs of the interior – never very intelligent, in spite of what the psychosomatic quacks say – received each day the amount of pleasure to which they were accustomed, and never marked the passage of time; it was the indispensable roadwork of the prizefighter. When Mme G., good soul, retired, moderation began its fatal inroads on his resistance. My old friend's appetite, insufficiently stimulated, started to loaf – the insidious result, no doubt, of the advice of the doctor whose existence he had revealed to me by that slip of the tongue about why he no longer drank Burgundy. Mirande commenced, perhaps, by omitting the fish course after the oysters, or the oysters before the fish, then began neglecting his cheeses and skipping the second bottle of wine on odd Wednesdays. What he called his pipes ('*ma tuyauterie*'), being insufficiently exercised, lost their tone, like the leg muscles of a retired champion. When, in his kindly effort to please me, he challenged the *escargots en pots de chambre*, he was like an old fighter who tries a comeback without training for it. That, however, was only the revelation of the rot that had already taken place. What always happens happened. The damage was done, but it could so easily have been averted had he been warned against the fatal trap of abstinence.

© *from* BETWEEN MEALS, 1963

Cadenza

J. K. Huysmans

Each and every liqueur, in his opinion, corresponded in taste with the sound of a particular instrument. Dry curaçao, for instance, was like the clarinet with its piercing, velvety note; kümmel like the oboe with its sonorous, nasal timbre; crème de menthe and anisette like the flute, at once sweet and tart, soft and shrill. Then to complete the orchestra there was kirsch, blowing a wild trumpet blast; gin and whisky raising the roof of the mouth with the blare of their cornets and trombones; marc-brandy matching the tubas with its deafening din; while peals of thunder came from the cymbal and the bass drum, which arak and mastic were banging and beating with all their might.

He considered that this analogy could be pushed still further and that string quartets might play under the palatal arch, with the violin represented by an old brandy, choice and heady, biting and delicate; with the viola simulated by rum, which was stronger, heavier, and quieter; with vespetro as poignant, drawn-out, sad, and tender as a violoncello; and with the double-bass a fine old

bitter, full-bodied, solid, and dark. One might even form a quintet, if this were thought desirable, by adding a fifth instrument, the harp, imitated to near perfection by the vibrant savour, the clear, sharp, silvery note of dry cumin.

The similarity did not end there, for the music of liqueurs had its own scheme of interrelated tones; thus, to quote only one example, Benedictine represents, so to speak, the minor key corresponding to the major key of those alcohols which wine-merchant's scores indicate by the name of green Chartreuse.

Once these principles had been established, and thanks to a series of erudite experiments, he had been able to perform upon his tongue silent melodies and mute funeral marches; to hear inside his mouth crème-de-menthe solos and rum-and-vespetro duets.

He even succeeded in transferring specific pieces of music to his palate, following the composer step by step, rendering his intentions, his effects, his shades of expression, by mixing or contrasting related liqueurs, by subtle approximations and cunning combinations.

At other times he would compose melodies of his own, executing pastorals with the sweet blackcurrant liqueur that filled his throat with the warbling song of a nightingale; or with the delicious cacaochouva that hummed sugary bergerets like the *Romances of Estelle* and the '*Ah! vous dirai-je, maman*', of olden days.

But tonight Des Esseintes had no wish to listen to the taste of music; he confined himself to removing one note from the keyboard of his organ, carrying off a tiny cup which he had filled with genuine Irish whiskey.

He settled down in his armchair again and slowly sipped this fermented spirit of oats and barley, a pungent odour of creosote spreading through his mouth.

from A REBOURS, 1882
© (Robert Baldick's translation)

One for the High Road

PATRICK CAMPBELL

A lthough my formative years were beset by many dangers, hair-raising in retrospect, like the possibility of marriage to a badminton player called Gwen with a dental plate, or my near capture by a mackintosh and sports goods business, I am glad to be able to state that at no time was I ever menaced by teetotalism.

It would be untrue to say that my father sold his clothes and the furniture to buy drink, but there is no doubt that drink was always splashing about the home in ample measure.

I was nine when I ran head-on into my first gin and mixed. Mary, the parlour maid, came into the pantry with a tray of glasses. I was in the pantry waiting for Mary, but immediately transferred my attention to the glasses when I saw that one of them was full.

It was difficult to see how such an accident could have happened. The people who came to my father's house on Sunday evenings were always prepared,

failing any other nutriment, to suck the varnish off the doors. It was, therefore, with a sense of gratitude to Providence that I raised this unexpectedly flowing bowl to my lips.

For a few moments I felt superbly happy, powerfully adult. Then retribution followed swiftly, but in those few moments of liberation I was able to perceive that this was going to be the stuff for me. Realising my limitations, however, I left it alone for the next five or six years until, at fifteen, I shot down a flagon of Australian Burgundy, retailing then at the competitive price of 5s. This formal initiation took place during a dance in an hotel and had the effect of illuminating the occasion beyond anything I had as yet experienced.

I was engaged at the ball in some fast hip-shifting with the stately consort of a Dutch diplomat. She was a big woman, strapped into white satin, and must have been at least twice my age. I'd brought off a number of Latin-American impromptus as we rocketed round the corner past the band and now, with the straight before us, I threw myself into the feather step, a matter, as I recall it, of doubling the tempo and hanging on tight. The diplomat's wife, shaken by the in-and-out work on the corners, was unable to take the strain. I hadn't feathered more than a couple of times when I realised we'd overreached ourselves. I had the opportunity, however, to issue a word of warning. 'Look out, Mother,' I cried, 'we're going down!'

It might have been better for her if she'd let herself go, too, but foolishly she broke away, leaving me to crash to the ground alone. As I went down I took the front of her dress and a rope of pearls with me. Peeled them off from neck to waistline as clean as a banana.

It took her a little time to appreciate what had happened, but when she found out she made up for the delay. I've never seen such a burst of speed from a heavy woman, as she lit out for the ladies' cloaks. For myself, bruised but still gay, I returned to our table and put the iron back into my system with the heel of the flagon.

Next morning I awoke with difficulty, and then, by a reflex action, scratched among last night's finery to see if any currency had survived. The first thing I found was a dozen oysters, shelled, in the hip pocket of my dress trousers. It was this, coming on top of the stripping of the diplomat's paramour, that set my feet, as it were, on the bar-rail for life. I was learning, at the comparatively early age of fifteen, that under certain stimuli there is absolutely no means of telling what's going to happen next.

I recall some specific instances.

I had been at Wicklow Regatta - an event of highly concentrated social activity that lasts for four days, if you're lined with leather - in the company

of two associates known as Arty Barty and Old Dezzo. To speed our comings and goings Barty had borrowed an outboard engine from his brother. The loan, however, was hedged about with the threat of frightful reprisals if so much as 'a flick' of paint were to be scraped off the machine. Barty was concerned about this, because his brother was a vet, weighing 17 stone, and on one occasion was reported to have stunned a horse by hitting it on the head with his fist. For this reason we had taken to carrying the engine with us every time we went ashore to slake our mariners' thirst.

It was on the licensed premises of a certain Mr. Kennedy, I think, that Old Dezzo issued his ultimatum. It was positively phrased. As God was his eternal judge, Dezzo would never again put even the tip of his little finger anywhere near Barty's brother's outboard engine. He thought, in fact, that Barty and his brother's outboard engine ought to be thrown into the harbour, at the deep part where the drains emerged. Barty, he said, was only getting in his own way (a criticism difficult to analyse), and, as for the engine, it would need a rope three miles long with a horse on the end of it to get it started.

During this disagreement I'd been trying to damp down a blaze of internal fire with a pint of stout, and was surprised to find Barty suddenly snatching it out of my hand and emptying it into a bucket. He then placed the bucket under the tap of an adjacent barrel, and filled the bucket to the brim.

The landlord, taken aback by Barty's generosity, asked if it was to take away.

'It's enough,' Barty roared, 'to make a dog strike his father!'

A moment later we saw that this referred to Dezzo's accusations against the outboard engine, for Barty, by himself, hoisted the engine into the bucket and then clamped it to the back of a chair.

'Look!' cried Barty. 'A flick of me finger!'

It might, perhaps, have been because of the fury with which he pulled the cord, but the engine fired first time. Instantly the whole public-house became opaque with brown foam. The very air was made of flying stout. Great gobbets of it erupted, to splash like Niagara against the walls. By the time Barty fought his way back to the engine and switched it off the whole room had darkened down three shades, and stout was dripping from the roof. I'd never seen a bucketful of anything flung so far so fast. I'm sure that Barty would never have thought of so vivid a method of proving the engine's efficiency if he'd been drinking tea.

I recall, too, a time when I was playing golf in a West of Ireland championship, a sporting event very similar in its death-dealing qualities to Wicklow Regatta. About midnight on the second night we were playing poker in a hotel bedroom, hemmed in by crates of refreshment which had been purchased in bulk to take the strain off the legs of John Joe, the night porter.

I'd been afflicted for several hours with a hopeless succession of pairs in the lower register – mostly twos and fives – without being able to improve upon them, or, intermittently, to resist the temptation to give them an airing against what turned out every time to be at least three Jacks.

Wearying of this low-calibre ammunition, I allowed my mind to wander. It hadn't been wandering for more than a few seconds before it came up against the memory of a lady resident near a town some ninety miles away. It seemed to me I ought to be there.

I got there soon after four o'clock in the morning and padded up to the house on the grass, keeping with some difficulty – I'd brought refreshment with me – off the gravel. I located the bedroom window and tossed up a few exploratory pebbles. It was her husband who put his head out of the window, a surprise to me, since I'd believed him to be in Cork. He looked crumpled and semi-conscious, but he came to with a snap when he identified the visitor.

'What do *you* want?' he roared.

What he meant was that he knew what I wanted, but couldn't see, as things stood, how I proposed to get it. I thought it best to reply to the query in its simple form.

'Nothing, really,' I said, and walked back down the avenue, on the gravel this time, whistling and surveying, with interest, the night sky.

I only just got back to the golf club in time to bunker up with a brandy and Benedictine before stepping out on to the first tee at 9.20 a.m. to play a shot which we were unable to find later on the beach. I dare swear I should never have had the interesting experience of driving 180 miles in the middle of the night, and in the middle of a championship, to say 'Nothing, really' to a man I didn't want to see – *if* I'd been drinking sherbet.

Round another bend in memory's lane loom up the heavy figures of Matty, Mossy and Confucius Ryan – three bookmakers whom I met in a refreshment tent after the last race on the final day of Galway Races, a sporting event of four days' duration held by many to be even more destructive than Wicklow Regatta.

Matty and Mossy, holding on to one another, had just given a high, dog's note duet of the 'Rose of Tralee'. Confucius, so-called because of a chronic, yellow pallor, did not like it, and said so. He invited me to sing. 'You're the class of a fella, Mick,' he said – they'd been calling me Mick for some time – 'wit' a big neck on him.'

In this, oddly enough, he was perfectly right. My voice, on this last day,

probably owing to the heavy traffic that had been pouring down the throat, had descended into my boots – a symptom I'd often noticed before, and an indication, indeed, that all good things were about to come to an end.

I had enough spirit left, however, to oblige Confucius. Furthermore – I can't imagine how it happened – I'd just learnt all the words of 'Moonlight Becomes You'. I indicated that this would be my choice.

'Good man, Mick,' they said, respectfully, and lay back against the bar to listen.

The first note astonished me, and them. It was a full octave lower than anything I had attempted before. It was a blend of Crosby and Chaliapin, with overtones of Tallulah Bankhead. It created an immediate silence in the uproar of the tent. Men, whose lives in the horse-coping business had left them previously indifferent to the arts, now turned, as though hypnotized, to listen. A party of tinkers abandoned an altercation by the door.

> '*Moonlight becomes yoooo –*
> *Eeet shines in your hay-err – '*

The sound seemed to come out of the ground at our feet. It shook the tent like the bass notes of an organ.

> '*Aaand you certainly know the right theengs –*
> *To way-eerr –'*

Confucius took off his hat, a brown Homburg with a race-card stuck in the band. This was a signal for most of the rest of the company to uncover. They knew they were in the presence of something bigger than themselves.

> '*Aaand whaat a night to go dreee-ming –*
> *Mind if I tag along . . .'*

I threw out my arms in spontaneous appeal. A little man in a white muffler and a cloth cap was so moved that he murmured 'Come on, yourself, surr, an' welcome,' before he knew he had spoken.

> '*Eet teesent because of moonlight – although –*
> *Moonlight becomes yoooo so.'*

As a mark of gratitude, perhaps, I sang the last two lines to Confucius, my hand laid gently on his shoulder.

Silence fell. Then came a great roar of applause, followed by so many offers of refreshment – all accepted – that before I knew where I was I'd lost my bookmaking friends and had formed a new association with the proprietor of a greyhound racing track, represented to be a strong tourist attraction only fifty

miles away. It took us two days to get there. On the evening of our arrival, after the dogs had finished with the track, I took on four local athletes in a two-lap hurdle, and was beaten out of third place by a short head at the generous odds of 100/7.

But I will dally no longer with memory. The future looks even brighter than the past.

Knock the neck off that one, boy, and let's see what it holds in store.

© *from* THE COMPLEAT IMBIBER I, 1956

Claret Country

Five poems on the Médoc by
PETER DICKINSON

Table Talk: Bordeaux

An interval of this and that:—
The virtues of the plastic vat;
The lunacy of Monsieur Y,
Who's tried to make his sweet wine dry;
The wickedness of Baron G,
Who's advertising Burgundy
Right in the heart of the Médoc.
(Why, one might just as well drink Hock!
He's sold—)
        That's done it. In a flash
The conversation's back on cash:—
Will the good English go on paying

The prices caused by three dismaying
Seasons? 'Fifty-two and three—
Remember?—they got almost free;
And what about old Monsieur L
Who bought his own wine back to sell
At more than top price for his *crû*
Attained by his great rival, Q?

The talk flows on from franc to franc.
One might as well be in a bank!

Madame de S, Château C, St Emilion

Before we are even out of the car
   Clutching her shawl to her neck she's there,
      For all the world like an English aunt,
      Her brown eyes snapping, her head aslant,
As if to ask who the devil we are
   And furthermore how the devil we dare
      To cut her afternoon slumbers short
      And scatter the stones of her gravelled court.

We tender our introductions, and
   At once she's off on a high tirade
      About 'the rocket'.* She does not fail
      To shoot whenever she senses hail,
But her neighbours, who do not understand
   About science, aver that she has made
      A sudden, disastrous fall of rain.
      If she doesn't shoot they complain again.

---

*A device with a charge of silver iodide which, fired at a threatening cloud, will with luck turn hail into rain and heavy rain into light rain. In the Médoc it is in the hands of the police who discharge it to everyone's satisfaction. In St Emilion, however, it used to be fired by the army, which proved itself unable to recognize a suitable target. So now private citizens have their own rockets, if they can afford them.

Her *maître de chai*, who is tiny and bent,
  Brings us the 'sixty-two and three.
    We expectorate over the roots of a rose
    (Dorothy Perkins, of course) which grows
Up the sun-warm wall, and compliment
  Madame on its promise of quality.
    She contrives to insert a complaisant smile
    Between verb and object, for all the while

She's been in endless, effortless spate
  On the price of corks ... on her sister's sons
    Who are sots ... on the meanness of foreigners who
    To save the odd franc consume a brew
Which, despite an adequate label and date,
  Is not château-bottled. In Belgium once
    She drank (but I missed that bit) ... And, Oh,
    The crimes of the middlemen in Bordeaux.

We leave her, still in the critical vein,
  And pass her oxen ploughing among
    Her brilliant, bluey-with-sulphur vines
    Which will bear, for sure, astonishing wines
Being fed by her rocket-assisted rain
  And blessed by her fierce, beneficent tongue.
    This is a woman whom I would praise
    By drinking her wine to the end of my days.

Maître de Chai: Latour

Large, elderly, stiff, remote,
He moves like a narrow-boat
  Down the long canals between
His casks in regular line.
He does not talk about wine
  In wine-talk (you know what I mean—

The mysterious jargon in use
Among those who are fond of this juice).
   Indeed, he seems almost perverse
The way he tends to compare
One year with another year
   By calling it 'Better' or 'Worse'.

His hairy fingers stroke
The close-grained staves of oak
   Where a dribbling indigo stain
Covers the round of the cask.
'Is that fermentation?' I ask.
   He grunts and tries to explain

That the seasons tug like a tide
On the raw new wine. When, outside,
   The vines are in trivial flower
It works and moves to that pull.
And again, when the grapes are full,
   It knows, he remarks, its hour.

I feel the hair on my nape
Prickle, to think of the grape
   Being mashed, fermented, and run
Into barrels, and fined, and racked—
Being ten-times-processed, in fact—
   But moving still when the sun

Moves, here, in the wood, in the dark.
No wonder his language is stark:
   When phenomena such as these
Are part of his everyday
Problems down in the *chai*
   He needn't *make* mysteries.

On the Evidences of having Spat too Close
in the Testing-room of a First-growth Château

This purplish spot
Upon my shirt
That otherwise appears so neat—
This mark is not,
As *you* think, dirt:
No, it is '63 Lafite.

One couldn't swallow
This shrivelling brew,
Smelling of sawdust, harsh as brine.
The years that follow
Will turn it to
The fabled, violet-hinting wine.

Its price will rise
With every year
Far from my pocket as star from star;
And so I prize
The shirt I wear,
Stained with this honourable scar.

Château Ducru Beaucaillou, 1918
(In gratitude to M. Guy Schyler, who gave it to us)

This senatorial stuff was harvested
  By wives and grandfathers and children, when
  Upon the Western Front the last young men
In France were being pricked to join the dead.

Emotion is the enemy of taste:
  Dead harvesters do not affect the wine:
  'Sixteen, for instance, managed to combine
Carnage and vintage in one classic waste.

VINTAGE TALES

What right has anybody got to drink it
   Who wasn't there?
                 Well, it is at its prime—
   Polleny, firm, remarkable. What's more,
   Henceforth it will be dying all the time.
I suck and swallow. Strange indeed I think it
   That this is what the grapes were gathered for.

© *from* THE COMPLEAT IMBIBER 7, 1964

The First Man who Threw Peas at me
was a Publican

WILLIAM McGONAGALL

Poet and Tragedian

It would be a poor Imbiber who couldn't find a place
in his heart for a distinguished Abstainer, and who
more distinguished than William McGonagall (1830–
1902) Poet and Tragedian, Sweet Singer of Dundee,
who here shows himself a peerless writer of prose, as
well as the best bad poet in literary history. C.R.

My dearly beloved readers, I will begin with giving an account of my experiences amongst the publicans. Well, I must say that the first man who threw peas at me was a publican, while I was giving an entertainment to a few of my admirers in a public-house in a certain little village not far from Dundee; but, my dear friends, I wish it to be understood that the publican who threw the peas at me was not the landlord of the public-house, he was one of the party who came to hear me give my entertainment. Well, my dear readers, it was while I was singing my own song, 'The Rattling Boy from Dublin Town', that he threw the peas at me.

You must understand that the Rattling Boy was courting a lass called Biddy Brown, and the Rattling Boy chanced to meet his Biddy one night in company with another lad called Barney Magee, which, of course, he did not like to see, and he told Biddy he considered it too bad for her to be going about with another lad, and he would bid her good-bye for being untrue to him. Then Barney Magee told the Rattling Boy that Biddy Brown was his lass, and that he could easily find another – and come and have a glass, and be friends. But the Rattling Boy told Barney Magee to give his glass of strong drink to the devil! meaning, I suppose, it was only fit for devils to make use of, not for God's creatures. Because, my friends, too often has strong drink been the cause of seducing many a beautiful young woman away from her true lover, and from her parents also, by a false seducer, which, no doubt, the Rattling Boy considered Barney Magee to be. Therefore, my dear friends, the reason, I think, for the publican throwing the peas at me is because I say, to the devil with your glass, in my song, 'The Rattling Boy from Dublin', and he, no doubt, considered it had a teetotal tendency about it, and, for that reason, he had felt angry, and had thrown the peas at me.

My dear readers, my next adventure was as follows: During the Blue Ribbon Army movement in Dundee, and on the holiday week of the New Year, I was taken into a public-house by a party of my friends and admirers, and requested to give them an entertainment, for which I was to be remunerated by them. Well, my friends, after the party had got a little refreshment, and myself along with the rest, they proposed that I should give them a little entertainment, which I most willingly consented to do, knowing I would be remunerated by the company for so doing, which was the case; the money I received from them I remember amounted to four shillings and sixpence.

Of course, you all ought to know that while singing a good song, or giving a good recitation, it helps to arrest the company's attention from the drink; yes! in many cases it does, my friends. Such, at least, was the case with me – at least the publican thought so – for – what do you think? – he devised a plan to bring my entertainment to an end abruptly, and the plan was, he told the waiter to throw a wet towel at me, which, of course, the waiter did, as he was told, and I received the wet towel, full force, in the face, which staggered me no doubt, and had the desired effect of putting an end to my giving any more entertainments in his house.

My dear friends, a publican is a creature that would wish to decoy all the money out of the people's pockets that enter his house; he does not want them to give any of their money away for an intellectual entertainment. No, no! by no means; give it all to him, and crush out entertainment altogether, thereby he

would make more money if he could only do so. My dear friends, if there were more theatres in society than public-houses, it would be a much better world to live in, at least more moral; and oh! my dear friends, be advised by me. Give your money to the baker, and the butcher, also the shoemaker and the clothier, and shun the publicans; give them no money at all, for this sufficient reason, they would most willingly deprive us of all moral entertainment if we would be as silly as to allow them. They would wish us to think only about what sort of strong drink we should make use of, and to place our affections on that only, and give the most of our earnings to them; no matter whether your families starve or not, or go naked or shoeless; they care not, so as their own families are well clothed from the cold, and well fed. My dear friends, I most sincerely entreat of you to shun the publicans as you would shun the devil, because nothing good can emanate from indulging in strong drink, but only that which is evil. Turn ye, turn ye! why be a slave to the bottle? Turn to God, and He will save you.

> *I hope the day is near at hand,*
> *When strong drink will be banished from our land.*

I remember a certain publican in the city that always pretended to have a great regard for me. Well, as I chanced to be passing by his door one day he was standing in the doorway, and he called on me to come inside, and, as he had been in the habit of buying my poetry, he asked me if I was getting on well, and, of course, I told him the truth, that I was not getting on very well, that I had nothing to do, nor I had not been doing anything for three weeks past, and, worse than all, I had no poetry to sell. Then he said that was a very bad job, and that he was very sorry to hear it, and he asked me how much I would take to give an entertainment in his large back-room, and I told him the least I would take would be five shillings. Oh! very well, he replied, I will invite some of my friends and acquaintances for Friday night first, and mind, you will have to be here at seven o'clock punctual to time, so as not to keep the company waiting.

Well, when Friday came, I was there punctually at seven o'clock, and, when I arrived, he told me I was just in time, and that there was a goodly company gathered to hear me. So he bade me go ben to the big room, and that he would be ben himself – as I supposed more to look after the money than to hear me give my entertainment. Well, my readers, when I made my appearance before the company I was greeted with applause, and they told me they had met together for the evening to hear me give my entertainment. Then a round of drink was called for, and the publican answered the call. Some of the company had whisky to drink, and others had porter or ale, whichever they liked best; as for myself, I remember I had ginger-beer.

[83]

Then the chairman was elected, and I was introduced to the company by the chairman as the great poet McGonagall, who was going to give them an entertainment from his own productions; hoping they would keep good order and give me a fair hearing, and, if they would, he was sure I would please them. And when he had delivered himself so, he told me to begin, and accordingly I did so, and entertained the company for about an hour and a half. The company was highly satisfied with the entertainment I gave them, and everyone in the company gave threepence each, or sixpence each – whatever they liked, I suppose – until it amounted to five shillings. Then the chairman told the publican that five shillings had been subscribed anent the entertainment I had given, and handed it to him. Then the publican gave it to me, and I thanked him and the company for the money I received from them anent the entertainment I had given them. Then the chairman proposed that I should sing 'The Rattling Boy from Dublin' over again, and that would conclude the evening's entertainment, and that I would get another subscription, which was unanimously carried by the company, but opposed by the publican; and he told me and the company I had no right to get any more than I had bargained for.

But, my friends, his motive for objecting to me getting any more money was to get it himself anent another round of drink he guessed the party would have after I left. And such was the case, as I was told by one of the party the next day, who stayed well up to eleven o'clock, and it was after ten o'clock when I left. Now, my friends, here was a man, a publican, I may say, that pretended to be my friend, that was not satisfied with the money that he got from the company for so many rounds of drink, all through me, of course, that had brought them there to hear me give an entertainment.

My opinion is, if I had been as simple to have spent my five shillings that I got for giving my entertainment, he would not have felt satisfied either. In my opinion, he would have laughed at my simplicity for doing so. May heaven protect me from all such friends for ever, and protect everyone that reads my experiences amongst the publicans.

I remember another night while giving an entertainment in a certain public-house to my admirers, and as soon as the publican found out I was getting money for giving the entertainment, he immediately wrote a letter and addressed it to me, or caused some one else to do it for him, and one of the waiters gave it to me. I was told in that letter, by particular request, to go to Gray's Hall, where a ball was held that evening, and, at the request of the master of the ceremonies, I was requested to come along to the hall, and recite my famous poem, 'Bruce of Bannockburn' and I would be remunerated for it, and to hire a cab immediately, for the company at the ball were all very anxious to hear me.

The First Man who Threw Peas at me was a Publican

So I left the public-house directly, but I was not so foolish as to hire a cab to take me to Gray's Hall. No, my friends, I walked all the way, and called at the hall and shewed the letter to a man that was watching the hall door, and requested him to read it, and to show it to the master of the ball ceremonies, to see if I was wanted to recite my poem, 'Bruce of Bannockburn'. So the man took the letter from me and shewed it to the master of the ceremonies, and he soon returned with the letter, telling me it was a hoax, which I expected. My dear friends, this lets you see so far, as well as me, that these publicans that won't permit singing or reciting in their houses are the ones that are selfish or cunning. They know right well that while anyone is singing a song in the company, or reciting, it arrests the attention of the audience from off the drink. That is the reason, my dear friends, for the publican not allowing moral entertainments to be carried on in their houses, which I wish to impress on your minds. It is not for the sake of making a noise in their houses, as many of them say by way of an excuse. No! Believe me, they know that pleasing entertainment arrests the attention of their customers from off the drink for the time being, and that is the chief reason for them not permitting it, and, from my own experience, I know it to be the case.

My dear friends, I entreat of you all, for God's sake, to abstain from all kinds of intoxicating liquor, because seldom any good emanates from it. In the first place, if it was abolished, there would not be so much housebreaking, for this reason: When the burglar wants to break into a house, if he thinks he hasn't got enough courage to do so, he knows that if he takes a few glasses of either rum, whisky, or brandy, it will give him the courage to rob and kill honest-disposed people. Yet the Government tolerates such a demon, I may call it, to be sold in society; to help burglars and thieves to rob and kill; also to help the seducer to seduce our daughters; and to help to fill our prisons, and our lunatic asylums, and our poorhouses. Therefore, for these few sufficient reasons, I call upon you, fathers and mothers, and the friends of Christianity, and the friends of humanity,

> To join each one, with heart and hand,
> And help to banish the bane of society from our land,
> And trust in God, and worship Him,
> And denounce the publicans, because they cause sin;
> Therefore cease from strong drink,
> And you will likely do well,
> Then there's not so much danger of going to hell!

© *From* POETIC GEMS, SELECTED FROM THE WORKS OF WILLIAM McGONAGALL, WITH REMINISCENCES BY THE AUTHOR, N.D., C. 1900

[85]

Vintner's Valentine

CYRIL RAY

My glass of wine, dear Valentine,
　With what can it compare?
When ruby, with your lovely lips,
　When golden, with your hair,
The rosé with your damask cheek
　On which long lashes lie,
And in my glass of fizz I see
　The sparkle of your eye...

[86]

Mankind's Mysterious Friend

DUFF COOPER

As the week drew to its close I discovered that it was possible to get leave of absence from mid-day Saturday to ten p.m. on Sunday, and immediately applied for it. To my surprise it was granted, but it was too late to make arrangements to be with those whom I most wanted to see. To get back to London, however, and to change out of my ill-fitting private's uniform and service boots gave me the sensation of escaping from prison. I spent a dull evening with a friend who was living in a villa at Tadworth, where he was quartered. Already, after those few days, an officer in the Brigade, which he happened to be, had assumed in my eyes almost god-like proportions. On Sunday it rained all day and I left in the early afternoon, so nervous did I feel of overstaying the hour of return. I could find nobody whom I knew in London. I went to dine alone at a club. A great cloud of depression came upon me and I felt even more miserable than I had been at Bushey and without hope.

It was one of those great station-hotels of clubs where I knew nobody, but

[87]

where in those days the food was simple and good, and the wine very cheap. Also it had a library. I ordered an imperial pint of champagne, that admirable measure which like so many good things has disappeared from the world, and I took *Alice Through the Looking-Glass* to accompany me during dinner. I wrote in my diary the next day:

> As by enchantment my melancholy left me and I knew that I should not be unhappy again. Courage came back to me which I had lost and I despised myself for having done so. I went back to my flat, changed into my uniform, spoke to the Montagus, who had just returned, and motored down to Bushey feeling perfectly happy.

Whether it was the humour of Lewis Carroll or the sparkle of the widow Clicquot that had restored my spirits would be hard to say. I think it was the mating of the two. I have already made mention of the happiness I have derived throughout my life from literature, and I should here, perhaps, acknowledge the consolation I have never failed to find in the fermented juice of the grape. Writing in my sixty-fourth year, I can truthfully say that since I reached the age of discretion I have consistently drunk more than most people would say was good for me. Nor do I regret it. Wine has been to me a firm friend and a wise counsellor. Often, as on the occasion just related, wine has shown me matters in their true perspective, and has, as though by the touch of a magic wand, reduced great disasters to small inconveniences. Wine has lit up for me the pages of literature, and revealed in life romance lurking in the commonplace. Wine has made me bold but not foolish; has induced me to say silly things but not to do them. Under its influence words have often come too easily which had better not have been spoken, and letters have been written which had better not have been sent. But if such small indiscretions standing in the debit column of wine's account were added up, they would amount to nothing in comparison with the vast accumulation on the credit side.

I am proud that Belloc's great poem on wine should have been dedicated to me. I transcribe the first lines:

> To exalt, enthrone, establish and defend,
> To welcome home mankind's mysterious friend:
> Wine, true begetter of all arts that be;
> Wine, privilege of the completely free;
> Wine the recorder; Wine the sagely strong;
> Wine, bright avenger of sly-dealing wrong –
> Awake, Ausonian Muse, and sing the vineyard song!

This mysterious friend has proved a very loyal one to me, and to all those, I believe, who do not abuse friendship and who learn by experience that even

between friends excessive and coarse familiarity cannot be permitted. Nor would I be thought, while paying the homage that I owe to wine, to exclude from their share of it those who, if they cannot aspire to the high dignity of friend-ship, do at least deserve the deep gratitude that is owed to trustworthy and faithful servants. I refer to beer and spirits, which belong to a different class from that of wine but are not upon that account to be less loved and honoured.

© *From* OLD MEN FORGET, 1953

Afternoon at Chateau d'Yquem

JOSEPH WECHSBERG

*No man is born a connoisseur, but with patience
and talent you may become one.*

MONSIEUR K., SR

Monsieur K. lived in a fine old house across from an old park. There was the smell of marble and wood, and the fragrance of wine that seems to hover over the old houses of Bordeaux, whose owners have wisely invested their wealth in fine wines.

Monsieur K. was sitting in the salon as I came in. His armchair was covered with blue velvet, and his head rested on a needlepoint lace, like a gem in the jeweler's case. He was a fragile, white-haired man with a finely shaped head, delicate features, and the hands of an artist. His art was the wine of Bordeaux. In this city, where fake experts don't last long, Monsieur K. has been respected

for decades as one of the great artists of wine. I'd known him for years. He told me how pleased he was to see me again.

'Sit down, sit down,' he said, pointing vaguely into space with no chair in it to sit on. 'I've been trying to decide about the wines that we are going to have with our lunch.'

In the adjoining dining-room the table was set up in bourgeois style. Long sticks of white bread, hors-d'oeuvres, and olives were already prepared. Several decanters and wine bottles were standing on the buffet.

'Sometimes my wife can't make up her mind what to cook, and naturally I can't make up my mind before she's made up hers. People make much fuss about great vintages and fine *crus* but they pay too little attention to the relationship of food and wines. They commit the heresy of serving older, full-bodied wines before younger, elegant ones. They serve the liqueurish wines of Sauternes, Barsac, Monbazillac, Anjou, and Vouvray at the beginning of the meal. Afterward, of course, all other wines appear dull and as mild as milk. People waste fine wines by serving them with salad, the enemy of wine. The only liquid that goes with salad is a glass of mineral water.'

Monsieur K. shook his head in resignation. *Rien à faire*, he said, the world was going to the dogs. People would enjoy wines much more if they would follow the simple rules – rules that have been set by the palate, not by wine growers or professional gourmets. With fish, oysters, other sea food, and hors-d'œuvres, serve Chablis, Pouilly-Fuissé, Puligny-Montrachet, Chassagne-Montrachet, Sancerre-Sauvignon, Vouvray *sec*, Graves *sec*, Tavel, Hermitage *blanc*, Montrachet, Alsace. With white meat and fowl, serve red Bordeaux from the Médoc or Graves region; Beaujolais and light red Burgundies; Chinon, Arbois, Bourgeuil. With red meat, game, *foie gras* and cheese, serve Pomerol, Saint-Émilion, Néac; Beaune, Pommard, Volnay, Corton, Nuits-Saint-Georges, Clos Vougeot, Musigny, Romanée, Chambertin; Moulin-à-Vent, Morgon, Juliénas; Hermitage *rouge*, Côte Rôtie, Châteauneuf-du-Pape.

'People serve white wines ice-cold when they ought to be moderately chilled,' said Monsieur K. 'Cold wine never offers its full taste. Even here in Bordeaux people don't know that red wines need time and warmth to release their flavors. They bring their bottles up from the cellars ten minutes before the meal. Sometimes they place them near the stove. *Ah, mais ça se casse!* The sediments fall down, the wine breaks. A few weeks ago a dinner was given here for some ship's captains. I was asked to select the wines. The following day no one called to commend me on my choice – which was unusual. So I investigated. The stewards had put the bottles into a bathtub filled with warm water to bring them up to room temperature. *Right here in Bordeaux!*'

Monsieur K. put the tips of his fingers together and gave the ceiling a contemplative stare. 'People treat wine as if it were a soulless liquid. But wine is a living organism. Its cells act like the cells of a human being. Wine lives even when it seems to be dead in the bottle. Believe me, I've stopped going out to restaurants. I just can't stand the sight of a *type* called *sommelier* who wears around his neck a chain that ought to be tied to his leg. He's a criminal, a murderer! He swings a fine old bottle as though it were a soft-ball. He's never heard of the sediments, a sign of maturity and age, which develop over years of careful storing and must not be disturbed. He doesn't know that the cork must be drawn slowly and steadily, without haste or jerking. He forgets to clean the inside lip of the bottle with a white cloth and to sniff at the cork. Perhaps he knows that wine bottles are stored horizontally, and Cognacs and Armagnacs are not, because they would burn the cork. But does he know what a wine cellar should be like – clean, dark, well aired, but without draughts, and in a place that has no street trepidations. Ah, it is all very, very sad.'

He got up, and returned with a file containing charts and statistics.

'My little treasure chest. Charts for every year since 1847, giving the exact number of rainy days, the summary of medium temperatures for each month of the year, and the hours of sunshine. There seems to be a sort of recurrent parallelism between certain vintages, every thirty or fifty years. Either they cross one another or they meet in pairs. The cycles would be almost perfect if the war years hadn't created disturbances that were not to be expected. Take, for instance, 1895 and 1945. Both vintages have the same characteristics. The red wines were full-bodied and "roasted", as we call it, having been produced from overripe grapes. The wines were sweet, oily, round, and full of sap. The white wines were sweet, flavory, *savoureux*. Similar analogies exist between 1896 and 1946. Both years produced wines that were harmonious, elegant, deep-colored.'

Mme K. came in, a white-haired woman of great dignity, dressed in black. She said lunch was ready. Her husband didn't look up from his charts.

'The wines of 1868 and 1869 are similar to those of 1898 and 1899, exactly thirty years later, and again to those of 1928 and 1929. Always an outstanding year followed by a great one. The years of 1869, 1899, and 1929 have produced wines that are almost strikingly similar: round and oily, soft, yet with lots of life, near-perfect wines. Note too that the 1898 and 1928 are still growing in quality, while the 1899 and 1929 are either at their height or declining. *Ça c'est vraiment curieux!* The charts don't lie, my friend. With the help of those charts my father would be able to forecast the quality of the future harvest as early as June. He made a fortune that way. He made only one

mistake, in 1858, when he didn't know that mildew can ruin a harvest. Almost broke him.'

Monsieur K. gazed fondly at a framed portrait on the wall. It showed a sumptuously bearded gentleman radiating the confidence that comes from having remade one's fortune after being broke. Mme K. took advantage of the momentary lull in her husband's monologue to point at the table, with the desperate urgency of the hostess who knows that the roast in the oven is getting drier every moment. As we walked into the dining-room, Monsieur K. was reminiscing about his father.

'He used to say: "No man is born a connoisseur, but with patience and talent you may become one." But it takes years, many years. When I was four years old, my father let me taste some wine and asked me how I liked it. There never was a meal in our house when wine wasn't discussed at great length. You can't help learning that way.'

Lunch was good and the wines were superb. There was a Margaux 1900 which Monsieur K. had decanted a few hours earlier, holding the neck of the bottle against a candle to see when the sediments started to come and it was time to stop pouring. The Margaux was served with a Roquefort that was not too strong in flavor.

Monsieur K. gazed thoughtfully at the robe of the wine, holding his glass against the light. 'This Margaux gives me great satisfaction. Back in 1901, when I was a young man, my father and a friend of his went out to the vineyards of Margaux to buy some of the young wines. I was permitted to go along. They tasted this wine, which was then only a few months old. Must have been quite hard on the tongue. My father's friend said: "*Il est bon mais trop gentil.*" My father shook his head. "This wine will be great in fifty years," he said. How right he was! Papa was a genius.'

The wines of Margaux have always been my favourites for their delicacy, aroma, and beautiful colour, and this Margaux seemed to combine all their virtues. It was round and flavoury, soft and elegant, truly a great wine.

'I gave a little dinner a few months ago for twelve friends,' Monsieur K. said. 'All of them are lovers of fine wine. I served them a Château Gruaud 1875, without showing them the label. They were to guess the origin and the year. All came pretty close. Some voted for the Pontet-Canet 1875, and some thought it was a Léoville-Las-Cases 1871. Everybody agreed that the 1875 was *une exquise jeune fille*. Still, these day some people make much too much fuss about vintages. After all, there have been only four unforgettable vintages in the past hundred years: 1847, 1875, 1900, and 1929.'

Mme K., who, in the tradition of long-suffering French wives, had not spoken up while her husband was holding forth, asked me to take another piece of the *tarte aux fraises*. Her husband poured the wine, a liqueurish Château d'Yquem 1899.

'No matter what some people may say about Bordeaux wines, they can't say anything about Yquem,' he said, with some asperity. 'Yquem is perfection. I chose this wine forty-five years ago. It was the month before we got married.'

'That was the Armagnac,' said Mme K.

'Oh, yes. I'm sorry, *ma chère*. It was the Armagnac. We will have it later. It is pure perfume – all the sharpness and fire have gone.' He gently placed his hand on the arm of his wife. 'Forty-five years isn't so long in Bordeaux. At a banquet at Château d'Yquem, a few months ago, they had twenty couples, each of them older than eighty years....' He looked at me and said: 'Why don't we drive out to Yquem? The afternoon is pleasant.'

An hour later we arrived at the gravel-covered courtyard of Château d'Yquem, a large, medieval stone structure with walls a yard thick and a round watchtower overlooking the gentle slopes of the Sauternes district. A heavy-set, elderly man with a blue beret and heavy bedroom slippers welcomed us. He seemed to be a friend of Monsieur K., who introduced M. Henriot, the *régisseur*. It must be true, as they say in Bordeaux, that people take on the color of the wine that they 'work' and drink. M. Landèche's face had had the reddish color of the grapes of Château Lafite-Rothschild. And M. Henriot's hue reflected the golden glow of the wines of Château d'Yquem.

We walked past the administration buildings inside the courtyard. A white-haired patriarch in bedroom slippers came out and vigorously shook hands with

Monsieur K. He was the château's bookkeeper and had been employed here fifty-nine years.

'I came in 1893,' he said, and rubbed his hands. He seemed none the worse for wear. 'It was a golden age. A bottle of Château Yquem cost fifty sous.'

'Fifty *gold* sous,' Monsieur K. explained.

'Yes,' said the bookkeeper. 'How easy it was to keep books! Today one needs so much space to write down all the large figures. Did the gentlemen taste our new wine, Léopold?'

'I was just going to take them there,' said M. Henriot. 'Why don't you come along?'

We walked over a gravelled path. In front of a small house a parchment-faced, toothless woman was knitting.

'She was ninety-three last Easter,' said the bookkeeper. 'Last year, at the dance that Monsieur le Marquis gives at the end of the harvest, she was dancing with me and the other young men. She has her glass of Yquem every night after dinner.'

'Maybe a couple of glasses,' said M. Henriot. The young men smiled and Monsieur K. clucked his tongue appreciatively.

Presently we were in the cellar. I saw rows of barrels of wine forming straight lines, like soldiers at a parade. M. Henriot, moving about silently in his heavy slippers, brought us samples. The one-year-old wine was still somewhat dry and rough-cornered, but the two-year-old was sweet and luscious, and already had the peculiar flavour of Yquem. I took a swallow, and then I drank up my glass.

M. Henriot chuckled. '*Doucement, doucement,*' he said. 'This wine is made of overripe grapes. *La pourriture noble*, we call it. It contains more alcohol than any of the red wines in the Médoc. Ah, our wonderful, wonderful Sauternes!'

His face was brightened by the supreme bliss that I had noticed earlier on on M. Landèche's and Monsieur K.'s faces when they tasted *their* wines. 'Isn't it a ray of sunshine, caught in the glass – a bowl of liquid gold?'

We moved to another barrel, and then to the one behind, sampling more wines. A mood of contentment seemed to settle down over the cellar, and us. The old bookkeeper talked of the Cardinal de Sourdis, an archbishop of Bordeaux in the seventeenth century, who had greeted a bottle of Sauternes with the words: '*Je te salue, oh, roi des vins,*' and Monsieur K. sat on a barrel, dangling his thin legs, quoting Baudelaire,

J'allumerai les yeux de ta femme ravie,
A ton fils je rendrai sa force et ses couleurs....

From the château's chapel came the sound of the Angelus bell. Through the open door of the cellar I saw the sun go down behind the softly rounded slopes of Sauternes with their rows of Semillon and Sauvignon vines. The sky took on the golden glow of the liquid in my glass, and the air had a mellow fragrance. M. Henriot shuffled around in his slippers, refilling our glasses with the liquid gold of Yquem.

© *From* BLUE TROUT AND BLACK TRUFFLES, 1953

The Case of Yquem

GODFREY SMITH

The Grapevine (Aristide Maillol)

For thirty years the secret has lain on my heart; at last it can be told. At last I can reveal why the lovely word 'Yquem', the name of one of the greatest wines the world has ever known, has made me start with guilt these last three decades like a mass murderer not yet brought to book.

Come back with me, if you will, to the year 1950. The King was still on the throne, Clem Attlee still led the first post-war Labour Government, and we still had rationing. At Oxford, where I was then an undergraduate, a famous college notice proclaimed: 'Will Gentlemen Under Eighteen Kindly Collect Their Bananas From The Buttery'.

The influence of *Brideshead Revisited* still hung heavily over us all. Undergraduates actually carried teddy bears in the streets, and plovers' eggs were at a distinct premium. In the Oxford Union, the nursery of Gladstone and Asquith, Curzon and FE Smith, the smartest speeches were made late at night under the influence of the beneficent Bollinger. The house was packed for the pyrotechnic performances of the young Ken Tynan. Anthony Wedgwood Benn had just been President, and so had a promising lad called Robin Day. In Michaelmas term 1950 it was my turn to occupy that illustrious chair. My treasurer was an amusing young rascal and gifted mimic called Jeremy Thorpe. My librarian (and thus in Union tradition deputy) was an already grave elder statesman of twenty-two called William Rees-Mogg.

Among the many pleasures and privileges of his office, the President of the Oxford Union receives an allowance to entertain his distinguished guests. It was – and no doubt still is – a modest sum, but, carefully husbanded, it will just do the trick. Obviously, if you could raise a bit more privately you could push the boat out appropriately.

My future father-in-law, a thoughtful and generous man, had most kindly offered to advance me a further sum, to be repaid against my future putative earnings, with which to push the boat out. I did my best to see that his generosity was in no whit wasted.

One of the happy duties that fell on me during my term of office was to arrange the unveiling of the portrait – newly painted by the distinguished academician James Gunn – of our eminent ex-President Hilaire Belloc. He was now a very frail old man, too ill to be with us, but he would listen to the occasion on the radio, for it was to be broadcast. The unveiling would be done by Duff Cooper, first Lord Norwich, soldier, statesman, poet, husband of the legendary Diana Cooper, and celebrated authority on wine.

My young mind was greatly exercised over what wine I could possibly give the great man on that historic evening. My own knowledge of the subject at the time was sketchy to say the least. Like most of my contemporaries, I drank whatever came to hand. There was Morrell's bitter in the buttery, and I drank Harvey's Bristol Cream in the Union Bar. I drank plonk at parties and bubbly at Commem Balls. I drank with a will and was frankly not too fussy about what went down the hatch. For Duff Cooper, clearly though, I would have to stop and take thought. I called for the Steward of the Oxford Union, the great and good Mr Dubber, the Jeeves of our day.

'Yes sir?' enquired Mr Dubber, materialising as ever from nowhere.

'Mr Dubber,' I said, 'I have a problem. Lord Norwich, a formidable authority on wine, is dining with us when we unveil the Belloc portrait. We must give him some good wine.'

'Indeed we must sir.' There was a discreet pause. Mr Dubber would never be so ill-bred as to obtrude his own opinions.

'Mr Dubber, could you find me a case of Yquem?'

'I'm sure I could sir.'

'Then let us serve that with the Duff Cooper dinner.'

'Very good sir.'

Now up to that moment, I had never tasted Yquem. I had read somewhere that it was a king among wines, so delicious indeed, as to be *hors concours*. It seemed to me that Duff Cooper would enjoy a glass or two.

The great day dawned. The great man duly presented himself, full of years of wisdom and wine, and our glittering party moved into dinner. Duff sat on my right. The waiters circled busily. We were to have – how could I forget? – roast beef and Yorkshire pudding, with roast spuds and all the usual trimmings. The wine waiter hovered with the first Yquem for me to sip. I noted with a slight start that it was white, and took my first taste of the magnificent stuff. Thus, rather later in the day, did I realise that Yquem is a sweet wine; monstrously, intoxicatingly, gloriously, sweet; as sweet as angels' tears. Rather rum stuff though to be serving with the beef and pud. However, it was too late to go back now. I nodded approval, and the waiter poured the golden nectar into Duff Cooper's glass. I watched horrified. He picked it up, and took a good swill. The roof did not fall in. After all, he had been in some pretty tough corners, both on the battlefield and at the hustings in his long career, and I supposed it must have seemed a minor hazard to him, a fairly typical bit of undergraduate eccentricity. He drank some more.

The night passed away. Duff Cooper unveiled the portrait with a typically graceful speech. He passed no comment on the wine, and the guilty secret lay heavily on my soul all those thirty years. Then one happy day recently I met Michael Broadbent of Christie's, that great and good Master of Wine, and told him the whole sorry story. To my relief, he just laughed.

'The truth is,' he explained to me, 'that you *can't* eat the wrong thing with Yquem. It's a bit like saying the Derby winner ran too fast. The owner of Yquem, you know, drinks his with things like pâté de fois gras.'

I felt a great invisible weight lift from my shoulders. I felt as a man must do who has just risen from his first confessional after committing a *crime passionel*. I felt, not to put too fine a point on it, like a free man again. And what, I asked Michael, is the ideal way to drink Yquem? He said that everybody would have his own ideas about that; 'for myself, though, I like to drink it with a nectarine, on a perfect summer's evening, with one or two good friends'.

It is too late now to offer it to Duff Cooper in those surroundings. However, I could offer it in lieu to his son John Julius Norwich, writer and broadcaster, who I am sure would not say no to it. The only snag is, what will a case set me back? At a recent auction, a bottle of 1949 Yquem – and manifestly we could not have drunk anything later that day in 1950 – was sold for £82. One

bottle! The case I bought from Mr Dubber so lightheartedly that day would now set me back just under £1,000. Well, they do say we have to pay for our mistakes.

from [PROVENANCE TO BE RESEARCHED]

Arketall

Harold Nicolson

The following is from a collection introduced by an author's note that it would be improper on my part to omit:

> Many of the following sketches are purely imaginary. Such truths as they may contain are only half-truths.
> *Tehran,*   H.N.
> *December* 30, 1926

... but the names are the real names of real people: even Lord Curzon once moved among mere mortals ...

C.R.

I

The train was waiting at Victoria Station and there remained but three minutes to the time when it was scheduled to leave. In front of the Pullman reserved for Lord Curzon clustered the photographers, holding their hooded cameras ungainlily. The station-master gazed towards the barrier. Already the two typists were ensconced in the saloon: Sir William Tyrrell in the next compartment had disappeared behind a newspaper: the red despatch boxes were piled upon the rack, and on the linoleum of the gangway Lord Curzon's armorial dressing-case lay cheek by jowl with the fibre of Miss Petticue's portmanteau. I waited with Allen Leeper on the platform. We were joined by Mr. Emmott of Reuter's. 'Is the Marquis often as late as this?' he inquired. 'Lord Curzon,' I answered, 'is never late', and as I said the words a slight stir was observable at the barrier. Majestically, and as if he were carrying his own howdah, Lord Curzon proceeded up the platform accompanied by the police, paused for a moment while the cameras clicked, smiled graciously upon the station-master, and entered the Pullman. A whistle shrieked, a flag fluttered, the crowd stood back from the train and began to wave expectantly. It was then that I first saw Arketall. He was running with haste but dignity along the platform: in his left hand he held his bowler, and in his right a green baize foot-rest. He jumped on to the step as the train was already moving. 'Crakey,' said Arketall, as he entered the saloon.

Arketall

2

Leeper and I sat opposite each other, going through the telegrams which had been sent down to the station from the Foreign Office. We sat there in the green morocco chairs of the Southern Railway: the marquetry on the panels behind us squeaked softly: the metal reading lamp chinked ever so slightly against the glass top of the table: to our right the houses of Purley, to our left the houses of Lewisham, passed rapidly below us in the autumn sunshine: someone came and told Leeper that he was wanted by Lord Curzon. I pushed the telegrams aside and leant back in my chair. Miss Petticue was reading the *Royal* magazine: Miss Bridges was reading her own passport: I had ample time to study Arketall.

He sat opposite to me at the end of the saloon. A man, I should have said, of about fifty-five; a tall man, at first impression, with a large naked face and large white bony hands. The fine Victorian modelling of his brow and chin was marred by a puffy weakness around the eyes and mouth: at certain angles the thoughtful refinement of his features suggested a drawing of Mr. Galsworthy by George Richmond: he would then shift his position, the illusion would pass, there would be a touch of red ink around the eyelids, a touch of violet ink about the lips: the pallor of his cheeks, the little bleached ridges around his mouth, would lose all suggestion of asceticism: when he leant forward in the full light of the window he had the appearance of an aged and dissolute pro-consul. His face, if he will forgive my saying so, seemed at such moments, self-indulgent. 'That man,' I reflected, 'drinks.'

I was well aware of the circumstances in which at the last moment Lord Curzon had engaged Arketall as his valet. Three days before we were due to leave for Lausanne, I had walked across to Carlton House Terrace with some papers that were urgently required. The Secretary of State was undergoing one of his recurrent attacks of phlebitis and I was taken up to his bedroom. I gave him the papers and he began to look at them, his lips, as was his wont, moving

rapidly in a faint, but not unpleasant, whisper as he read the documents. My
eyes wandered around the room. It was a small room with but one window
which looked over the park: there was a white washing-stand, a servant's chest
of drawers, and a cheap brass bedstead: the walls were papered with a simple
pattern of sweet-pea, and there were some photographs and a brown wooden
hair-brush upon the dressing-table: on the small mantelpiece beside me I noticed a washing-list, a bone collar-stud, and two pieces of string. It was like a
single bedroom in one of the Gordon Hotels: the only luxuries were an elaborate
telephone affixed to the wall beside the bed, and a large box of crystallised
fruits upon a side-table. The problem of Lord Curzon's personality, which had
become almost an obsession to me, was enhanced by the sight of these acces-
sories. My eyes wandered round the room in mute surprise. They returned
finally to the figure in the bed. He was no longer looking at the documents, he
was looking at me. 'You are observing,' he said, 'the simple squalor of my
bedroom. I can assure you, however, that my wife's apartments are of the most
unexămpled magnificence.' And at this his shoulders shook with that infectious
laughter of his, that rich eighteenth-century amusement. 'You have also,' he
continued, 'observed the telephone. A disăstrous invention, my dear Nicolson,
but it has its uses. Thus if I make upon this ivory lever a slight pressure to
deflect it to the right, a mere *exiguum clinamen*, the whole secrets of my household are revealed to me. I overhear. This morning, for instance, when thus
switched on (I think that is the correct term) to the universe, the bell rung. A
voice said, "Is that you, Alf, and 'ow's it feeling this morning? I 'ad a devil of
a time coming in with the milk like that." "My dear young lady," I answered,
"you are singularly mistaken. You are not speaking to Mr. Alfred Horlick, you
are speaking to Lord Curzon himself." The noises, I may say, which greeted
me from the other end indicated that my words had produced an effect which
was positively blăsting. And Horlick, an excellent valet, leaves me to-morrow.'

Victim of such coincidences did Arketall sit there that morning in the Pullman with a small and incongruous bowler perched upon his head. He became
slightly uneasy at my scrutiny: he reached for his suit-case and extracted *John
o' London's Weekly:* I returned to my telegrams. The train skimmed tinkling
and direct above the Weald of Kent.

Arketall

3

Our arrival at Dover somewhat disconcerted Arketall. It was evident that he was proud of his competence as a travelling valet and anxious to win confidence by a brisk display of merit. Before the train had come to a standstill he was out on the platform, his face assuming the expression of 'Leave everything to me.' He was at once brushed aside by an inspector of police and two Foreign Office messengers. A phalanx of porters stood behind the inspector and leapt upon our baggage. The Foreign Office messengers seized the despatch boxes. Before Arketall had realised what had happened, Lord Curzon was walking slowly towards the boat chatting to the inspector with not unconscious affability. We strolled behind. Arketall came up to me and murmured something about passports. I waved him aside. There was a man beside the gangway with a cinematograph, the handle of which he began to turn gently as we approached. I glance behind me at Arketall. His attitude had stiffened suddenly into the processional. 'Arketall,' I said to him, 'you have forgotten the foot-rest.' 'Crakey!' he exclaimed as he turned to run towards the train. The other passengers were by then beginning to dribble through the pens in which they had been herded: I leant over the taffrail, watching the single agitation meeting the multiple agitation: widows hurrying along searching frantically in their reticules for those yellow tickets which would take them to Bordighera: Arketall, in acute anxiety, breasting this fumbling torrent with his bowler in his hand. A policeman touched me on the shoulder: he was holding the foot-rest. 'His lordship generally requires this with him on the voyage.' But by then Arketall was but a distant dome-shaped head bobbing against a panic stream. The little cords that tied the awning above me were pattering against the stays in an off-shore wind: in the gap between the pier-heads a swell tumbled into foam, the inner harbour was wrinkled with scudding frowns: clearly we were in for a rough crossing. I took the foot-rest to Lord Curzon. He was sitting at his cabin table writing on loose sheets of foolscap in a huge flowing hand: his pencil dashed over the paper with incredible velocity: his lips moved: from time to time he would impatiently throw a finished sheet upon the chintz settee beside him. I adjusted the foot-rest. He groaned slightly as he moved his leg. He was much too occupied to notice my ministrations. I returned to the deck outside. A voice wailed to me from the shore: 'It's gone; it's gone.' Arketall flung into the words that forlorn intensity which throbs in the earlier poems of Lord Tennyson. I replied by reassuring gestures indicative that he should come on board. He was mopping his forehead with a large linen handkerchief: little white drops were still forming on it as he stood panting beside me. 'Crakey,' he gasped. 'You had better go downstairs,' I answered, 'it is going to be rough.' He closed one eye at me. 'A little peg ay don't think.' His words, at the moment, had little apparent meaning.

4

I did not see Arketall again until we were approaching Calais. I found him talking to Sir William Tyrrell outside the cabin. 'Now Ostend,' he was saying, 'that's another question. Nane francs a day and no questions asked.' 'And no questions asked,' he repeated looking wistfully at the sand dunes. The inspector came up to me with a packet of passports: he said he would hand them over to the *commissaire de police* on arrival. I took them from him, desiring to solve a problem which had often assailed me, namely, whether Lord Curzon made out a passport for himself. It was there all right – 'We George Nathaniel', and then his name written again in the blank spaces. That amused me, and I was still considering the curious associations evoked by such official Narcissism when we sidled up to the Calais landing-stage. The gangway was immediately opposite Lord Curzon's cabin: on the pier below stood the Consul in a top-hat, and some French officials: I went in to Lord Curzon and told him we were arriving: he was still writing hard, and paid no attention: on the settee beside him was a pile of foolscap and at least twenty envelopes stamped and addressed. A muffled jerk showed that we were already alongside. Sighing deeply Lord Curzon addressed and stamped the last envelope. 'Send me that valet man,' he said. I fetched Arketall, telling him to hurry as the other passengers were being kept waiting: there they were on my left secured by a cord across the deck, a serried wedge of passengers looking their part. Lord Curzon emerged genially from his cabin at the exact moment the gangway was fixed: Arketall followed with the foot-rest: he stumbled as he stepped on to the gangway and clasped the rail. 'Yes, I thought he was drunk,' said Sir W. Tyrrell as we followed in our correct order. Lord Curzon was being greeted by the Representative of the French Republic. He moved slowly towards the train, leaning on his ebony cane; behind him zigzagged Arketall, clasping the green baize foot-rest. 'Hadn't we better warn the Marquis ...?' I asked. 'Oh, he'll notice it soon enough.' Lord Curzon had paused by the train to say a few chosen words to the Consul. Behind him stood Arketall, very rigid as to the feet, but swaying slightly with the upper part of the body, bending slowly forwards and then straightening himself with a jerk. We left for Paris.

5

The next thirty-six hours are somewhat of a blur in my memory. I can recall M. William Martin at the Gare du Nord and other top-hats raised simultaneously, and the flash and subsequent smell of magnesium wire lighting rows of white featureless faces beyond the barrier: a group of Americans pausing to stare at us, cocktail in hand, as we entered the Ritz – 'Why, look, Mrs. Cameron ...' and then the figure of Mr. Ellis, pale and courtly, standing erect beside Lord Curzon in the lift: the corridor stretching white, airless, unwindowed, the little lighted globes in the ceiling, the four detectives grouped together, a bottle of Evian and two glasses on a Saratoga trunk. I remember also a late dinner and Olivier ministering to Lord Curzon and yet not ignoring us – Olivier blending with a masterly precision the servile and the protective, the deferential and the condescending. And then the following day the familiar conference atmosphere: the crackle of Rolls-Royces upon the raked and watered gravel in front of the Affaires Étrangères: the slow ascent, maps, despatch boxes, politeness, up the wide stone staircase: the two huissiers in evening dress and silver chains, that huissier with a white nose, that other huissier whose nose is red: the first ante-room, gold and damask, the second soft-carpeted ante-room, damask and gold: the Salle de l'Horloge – green rectangles of tables, a perspective of pink rectangles of blotting-paper: M. Poincaré advancing from a group by the furthest window: the symmetry of alignment broken suddenly by papers on the green cloth, protruding edges of maps, despatch boxes with open lids, secretaries bending from behind over their employers, the interpreter sitting with his pencils and note-book by himself: the soft hum of traffic along the Quai d'Orsay.

We lunched that day with Madame Poincaré and afterwards the discussions continued: at 4 p.m. the chandeliers leapt in successive tiers to brilliance; the white and scarlet benches in the window recesses were hidden one by one as the silk curtains were drawn across them, and at five we had tea and macaroons in the large white room beyond. At nine we returned exhausted to our dinner; we were all to start for Lausanne next morning at 7.30.

We gathered sleepily at 7.5 a.m. in the hall of the Ritz: the revolving glass door was clamped open and a man in a striped apron was shaking an india-rubber mat out on to the Place Vendôme: the luggage had already preceded us, the typists were sitting in the third motor rather pinched and blue: we waited for Lord Curzon. At 7.16 a.m. he appeared from the lift escorted by Mr. Ellis. He climbed slowly into the motor, falling back on to the cushions with a sigh of pain: he beckoned to me: 'I shall want my foot-rest.' I dashed back into the hotel to search for Arketall. Mr. Ellis was standing by the staircase, and as I approached him I could hear someone pattering above me down the stairs: at the last turning there was a bump and a sudden exclamation, and Arketall shot round and down the staircase like a bob-sleigh, landing beside me with his feet in the air and the foot-rest raised above him. 'Crakey,' he remarked. We had by then only eleven minutes in which to reach the Gare de Lyon. The three motors swayed and dashed along the boulevards like fire-escapes to an incessant noise of Claxons. Then very slowly, processionally, sleepily we walked up through the station towards the platform. M. Poincaré in a black silk cap with a peak was waiting, a little irritably I thought, beside the train. There was a saloon for the French Delegation, a saloon for the British Delegation, and separating them a satin-wood drawing-room carriage and a dining-car. The large white clocks marked 7.29 as we entered the train. At 7.30 we slid out into the grey morning past a stiff line of saluting police and railway officials. Arketall was standing beside me: 'Ay left me 'at behind,' he remarked in sudden dismay. I had a picture of that disgraceful bowler lying upwards on the stair carpet of the Ritz: 'Tiens,' they would exclaim, 'le chapeau de Lord Curzon.' 'You can get another,' I answered, 'at Lausanne.' Miss Petticue came up to me holding a bowler. 'They threw this into our motor as we were leaving the Ritz.' I handed it in silence to Arketall.

6

For the greater part of that twelve-hour journey we sat in the drawing-room carriage discussing with our French colleagues the procedure of the impending conference: from time to time a Frenchman would rise and retire to the back of the train to consult M. Poincaré: from time to time Allen Leeper or I would make our way to the front of the train to consult Lord Curzon: outside his door Arketall sat on a spring bracket-seat which let down on to the corridor: he would stand up when we came, and the seat would fly up smack against the wood-work: Arketall looked shaken and unwell. Lord Curzon in his *coupé* carriage reclined in a dove-coloured armchair with his leg stretched out on the foot-rest. On the table beside him were at least thirty envelopes stamped and addressed: he did not appear to relish our interruptions.

Towards evening the lights were lit in that satin-wood saloon. We sat there, M. Barrère, General Weygand, Admiral Lacaze, Sir William Tyrrell, Laroche, Massigli, Allen Leeper and myself. The discussion had by then become desultory: from time to time a station would leap up at us from the gathering dusk, flick past the train in a sudden rectangle of illuminated but unfocussed shapes, be lost again in the brooding glimmer of the Côte d'Or. We stopped at Pontarlier and telephoned to M. Mussolini. He answered from Locarno. He wanted us to dine with him that night at Vevey. We pattered up and down the platform conveying messages from M. Poincaré to Lord Curzon, from Lord Curzon to M. Poincaré. It was agreed that they would both proceed to Vevey, and then the train slid onwards down upon Lausanne. Lord Curzon in his dove-coloured arm-chair was slightly petulant. He was all for dining with M. Mussolini but would have preferred another night. 'And why Vevey?' he said 'Why indeed?' I echoed. Lord Curzon sighed deeply and went on writing, writing. I left him and stood in the corridor. Arketall had pulled up the blind, and as the train jigged off to the left over some points a row of distant lights swung round to us, low lying, coruscating, white and hard. 'Evian,' I said to Arketall. 'Ho indeed,' he answered. Ten minutes later, the train came to rest in the station of Lausanne: there was a pause and silence: the arc-lamps on the platform threw white shapes across the corridor, dimming our own lights, which but a few minutes before had seemed so garish against the darkness. I returned to Lord Curzon's compartment. 'I think,' he said, 'that you and Leeper had better get out here. It is quite unnecessary for you to come on to Vevey.' 'Oh, but, sir ...' I protested. 'Quite unnecessary,' he repeated. I usually enjoyed an argument with Lord Curzon, but there was something in his voice which indicated that any argument at that moment would be misplaced. I went and told Leeper: we both seized our despatch boxes and climbed down on to the platform. Bill Bentinck, who had been sent on two days before to complete arrangements, came up to us, immaculate, adolescent and so reliable. 'There are four motors,' he said, 'and a lorry for the luggage.' 'The Marquis isn't coming,' I informed him, 'he and M. Poincaré are going on to Vevey to dine with Mussolini. They won't get back here till midnight.' 'Oh Lud,' he exclaimed, 'and there's a vast crowd outside and the Mayor of Lausanne.' 'Lud,' I echoed, and at that the slim presidential train began to slide past us towards the night and Mussolini. It was only then that I noticed that the platform was empty from excess rather than from lack of public interest: behind the barrier, behind a double row of police, stretched the expectant citizens of the Swiss Confederation. On the wide bare desert of the platform stood Leeper in a little brown hat, myself in a little black hat, and Arketall in his recovered bowler: Miss Petticue: Miss Bridges: pitilessly the glare of forty arc-lamps beat down upon our isolation and inadequacy. We walked (with dignity I feel) towards the barrier: at our approach the magnesium wire flashed up into its own smoke and there was a stir of excitement in the crowd: somebody cheered: Arketall raised his bowler in acknowledgement: the cheers were repeated: he held his bowler raised at exactly the correct angle above his head: the Mayor advanced towards him. I intervened at that moment and explained the situation. The Mayor turned from me, a little curtly perhaps, and said something to the police inspector. The wide lane which had been kept open for us ceased suddenly to be a lane and became a crowd leaving a station: we left with it. In a few minutes we were hooting our way under the railway bridge and down to Ouchy.

Arketall

7

The hall of the Beau Rivage was crowded with hotel managers and journalists. The former bowed ingratiatingly at our entry: the latter, who had been sitting together at little tables drinking sherry, rose as a man to greet us. There was Mr. Walter, and Mr. Pirrie Gordon, and Mr. Ward Price, and Mr. Ryall. There were a great many others whom I did not know: they looked diverse and yet convivial: I like journalists in principle and was extremely sorry to disappoint them: at no moment of my life have I desired so acutely to be important. Through all this gratuitous humiliation I was conscious, however, of a thin thread somewhere within me of self-esteem. I lay idly in my bath trying to work this vaguely apprehended fibre of pleasure into the central focus of my consciousness, which seemed in its turn wholly occupied by pain: I tested myself in successive phases: the platform, solid pain: the exit from the platform, pain unrelieved: it was only when I went back to the phase in the motor that I ceased inwardly to wince. Leeper, rather tired and thinking silently about Rumania, had sat beside me; but Arketall, on the strapontin opposite, was full of talk. 'Very civil,' he had said, 'these Swiss people. Now ay remember when ay was with a Columbian gentleman, we went to Zurich. You know Zurich, sir? Well, it was lake this . . .' Yes, Arketall at that moment had called me 'sir': up to that moment he had treated me solely as a colleague. Something in the force of my personality or in Lord Curzon's absence had elevated me to a higher level of regard. I was gratified on discovering this, and lay back in my bath thinking affectionately of Lord Curzon, who at that moment must have been descending on to the platform at Vevey. Sir William Tyrrell would have to carry the foot-rest: I did so hope that, if Lord Curzon got tired, Sir William would be able to soothe him down.

We dined downstairs in the restaurant. The remainder of the Delegation had assembled by earlier trains. There was General Burnett-Stuart with a military staff, and Sir Roger Keyes with naval assistants: there was Mr. S.D. Waley of the Treasury, and Mr. Payne of the Board of Trade: our own Secretariat was under the charge of Tom Spring Rice: there was a young man of extreme elegance who looked after the maps: there was an accountant and two further lady typists, and there was Mr. McClure for the Press. Undoubtedly we were an imposing collection. M. Duca and M. Diamandy, the Rumanian representatives, were seated at a further table; they came across to us and gave us caviare out of a flat tin box. I was pleased at this, mainly for Allen Leeper's sake, since, although in general the most stimulating of companions, he is apt at moments to brood about Rumania in silent suffering: with their arrival his pang had found a voice. It was a pleasant dinner if I remember rightly, and when it was over, Leeper and I ascended to put the final touches to Lord Curzon's suite. A large drawing-room on the first floor gazing from its three high windows upon the lake: on the left a dining-room, on the right a bedroom with baths beyond. The drawing-room was sprinkled with little white armchairs and tables looking very occasional: there were palms and chrysanthemums in a large brass jardinière: there was a little bean-shaped bureau, and on the walls some coloured prints of ladies in green riding-habits descending the steps of Chambord, Chenonceaux and Blois. We removed these pictures and secured a larger writing-table. We sent for more flowers, and arranged some newspapers and brandy and soda upon a side table. In the bedroom next door Arketall was unpacking several trunks: I looked in on him: he was not inclined for conversation, but hiccoughed gently to himself as he swayed, now over the Marquis's black suits and now over his grey. It was by then 11.30: a telephone message came in from Vevey to say that Lord Curzon should reach Lausanne about midnight: we descended to the hall to await his arrival.

8

At 12.10 there was a stir at the front door and the managers dashed to the entrance. They returned in triumph, escorting a small brown gentleman in a

brown suit and very white shirt-cuffs. He carried a brown bowler in his left hand and his right was thrust into his waistcoat. The iris of his eyes was entirely surrounded by white, a phenomenon which I had hitherto observed only in the photographs of distinguished mesmerists. He was followed by three or four other gentlemen and two boy-scouts in black shirts. An electric tremor ran through the assembled journalists. 'Mussolini,' they whispered in amazement. I turned to Allen Leeper. 'Really,' I remarked, 'that was very odd indeed.' 'It was,' he answered.

Ten minutes later the glass doors again gyrated and Lord Curzon, magnificent and smiling, stood upon the threshold. Slowly and benignly he bowed to the managers: to the journalists he made a friendly gesture at once welcoming and dismissive: he proceeded to the lift. Seizing the green foot-rest from Sir William Tyrrell, I hurried through the crowd towards the staircase: 'Tiens,' exclaimed a French journalist, indicating the foot-rest, 'le trône de Bagdad.' I pushed past him and arrived on the first floor just as Lord Curzon was leaving the lift. He paused at the doorway of his apartment and surveyed it. 'How ghăstly!' he sighed. He walked towards the window, pulled aside the yellow cretonne curtain, and gazed across to the lights of Evian. 'How positively ghăstly,' he repeated. We helped him out of his large Lovat mixture greatcoat; we propped the ebony cane against the white wall: we pulled up the least diminutive of the sixteen armchairs, and we placed the foot-rest in position. He sank back, sipped at a brandy-and-soda, sighed deeply, and then embarked on a narrative of the Vevey conference.

Ah, those Curzonian dissertations! No small thing has passed from my life now they are silenced. As if some stately procession proceeding orderly through Arcs de Triomphe along a straight wide avenue: outriders, escorts, bands; the perfection of accoutrements, the precise marshalling of detail, the sense of conscious continuity, the sense of absolute control. The voice rising at moments in almost histrionic scorn or dropping at moments into a hush of sudden emotion; and then a flash of March sunshine, a sudden dart of eighteenth-century humour, a pause while his wide shoulders rose and fell in rich amusement. And all this under a cloud of exhaustion, under a cloud of persistent pain.

The glamour of this particular discourse was somewhat dimmed for me by anxiety on behalf of Arketall. The door into the bedroom was open, and there came from it the sound of cupboards opening and shutting, the sound at intervals of a hiccough inadequately suppressed. 'We had by then,' Lord Curzon was saying, 'reached the last point of the six which I have grouped under category A. Mussolini had as yet not fully grasped my intention; with the assistance of that dilapidated marmoset who acts as his mentor I regained my point of departure: the status of pertinenza, I explained ...'

''Ic' came loudly from the adjoining room. Lord Curzon paused. My eyes met those of Allen Leeper and I motioned to him to close the door.

'... the status of pertinenza, I explained, was in no way identical with what we regard as domicile. Poincaré, who on all such points, is exásperatingly punctilious, insisted on interrupting. He maintained ...'

''Ic,' said Arketall from the next room. Leeper had by then reached the doorway and closed it abruptly. 'What was that?' said Lord Curzon, turning a petulant eye in my direction. 'It is your servant, sir, unpacking some clothes.'

'He maintained that the *droit d'établissement* ...'

The procession had re-formed and continued its stately progress: it continued until 2 a.m.: the Marquis then dismissed us: he said he had letters to write as well as a report for the Cabinet; he had by then to our certain knowledge been working without interruption for nineteen hours; and yet in the morning there was a report of eight pages for the Cabinet, and on the table in the passage twenty-two letters addressed and stamped – or, as he himself would have said, 'stamped and directed.'

9

Next morning there was to be a meeting to continue the conversations begun at Vevey. We arranged a large table in Lord Curzon's room and placed paper and pencils at intervals. The Marquis sat at his desk writing rapidly. Punctually at eleven both doors were flung open by Arketall. 'Excellence Poyncarry,' he bawled, 'and General Wiggand.' Lord Curzon rose genially to meet them, and conducted them to the table. They sat down and waited for M. Mussolini. General Weygand began drawing little squares and triangles on the sheet before him. M. Poincaré rose and walked up and down the room in obvious impatience, flicking his pince-nez against his thumb-nail. From time to time he would pause at one of the windows, looking at the grey fog which crept among the conifers. Lord Curzon kept on sending me with messages to the Duce urging him to come. I did not execute these missions, knowing them to be of no avail, but I had several pleasant chats in the passage with Mario Pansa, who was acting as M. Mussolini's personal secretary. From time to time I would return to Lord Curzon's room and assure them all that M. Mussolini was on his way. I would then resume my talks with Mario, whose gay Harrovian chatter relieved a situation which but for him I might have found a trifle tense. When, at 11.35, M. Mussolini actually did come, he came very quickly. Pushing Arketall aside, His Excellency shot into the room like a brown thunderbolt, stopped short, clicked his heels, bowed and exclaimed, 'Je vous salue, Messieurs.' They then sat down at the table, and we sat behind. The maps were spread in convenient places; the interpreter sharpened his pencil. The Vevey conversations were resumed.

That evening M. Poincaré returned to Paris, and M. Mussolini to Rome: Lord Curzon was left pre-eminent over a Conference consisting mostly of Ambassadors. There was M. Barrère and M. Bompard for France: and for Italy the aged Marchese Garroni: Ismet Pasha, deaf and boyish, coped with a large and resentful Turkish delegation: M. Venizelos, troubled but conciliatory, spoke for Greece: at moments, even, the mezzo-soprano of M. Tchicherine would quaver into our discussion. And as the days passed, Arketall, to my despair, entered visibly on a decline.

10

We found it difficult to induce Lord Curzon to treat the problem seriously. On the second morning Arketall, in helping his master on with his socks, had slipped and fallen. 'Arketall,' Lord Curzon had remonstrated, 'you are either very ill or very drunk.' 'Both, m' Lord,' Arketall had answered. Lord Curzon was so pleased with this response that his affection for Arketall became unas-

sailable. We grew seriously uneasy. I found him one morning standing by the side-table in the dining-room pouring liqueur-brandy into a claret glass. He winked slowly at me and placed a shaky forefinger beside his nose. I was incensed at this gesture of confederacy: I told Bill Bentinck that the Marquis must again be warned. But unfortunately that morning Marchese Garroni had, in Lord Curzon's presence, mistaken Arketall for Sir Roger Keyes, had seized both his hands and had assured him in a torrent of Genoese French how great a debt, how unforgettable a debt, Italy owed to the noble and generous British Navy. Lord Curzon was so delighted by this incident that our warnings fell on even deafer ears. A catastrophe was imminent, and it came.

The Hôtel Beau Rivage at Ouchy consists of two wings joined together by a large suite of ball-rooms and dining-rooms. In the evening the natives of Lausanne and the visitors undergoing either education or treatment would gather in the foyer to listen to the band, to watch the dancing, and to observe the diplomatists and journalists passing backwards and forwards on hurried and mysterious errands. Saturday was the gala night, and on Saturdays I would generally slip down after eleven and sit there admiring the couples jerking together in the ball-room. There was an American woman of great distinction, who wore a stomacher of diamonds: there was a greedy-looking Cuban woman in a wheeled basket chair: there was Prince Nicholas of Russia, who was staying at a neighbouring pension and who danced with all the young ladies. It was a pleasant sight, and on the second Saturday I induced Lord Curzon to come and watch it. He stood there by the entrance to the ball-room leaning on his ebony cane, and smiling genially at the diverse couples who jigged and twirled before him. I observed the American lady syncopating towards us in the arms of a distinguished-looking gentleman in evening dress. I called Lord Curzon's attention to her, warning him to observe her stomacher as she passed. He glanced towards her and grasped my arm. 'Surely,' he said, 'surely that can't be Arketall?' It was Arketall, and he recognised us at the same moment. In trying to wince away from the cold inquiry in Lord Curzon's eye, he slipped between the legs of the American lady and brought her down upon him. Lord Curzon had turned abruptly and was walking back across the foyer. I ran after him. 'I think,' he said, 'that Arketall had better leave. He had better leave early to-morrow.'

I returned to the ball-room and accompanied Arketall to his room. He was somewhat dazed by his experience and he followed me meekly. I told him that there was a train at 7.30 next morning and he had better leave by it. He plunged under the bed and began pulling out his portmanteau: it refused to move and he tugged at it viciously: three empty bottles of Benedictine and a bottle of

Grand Marnier shot out into the room, followed by the trunk. Arketall sat on the floor, nodding at the empty bottles. 'You must pull yourself together,' I said. 'You should at least assist us to minimise the scandal which your conduct has caused.' 'Never,' he hiccoughed vaguely, 'not no more.'

II

I did not witness his departure. I merely heard next morning that he had gone. While having breakfast I received a message that Lord Curzon wished to see me urgently. I found him in his dressing-gown. He was half angry and half amused. 'That indefinite Arketall,' he said, 'has stolen my trousers.' 'Not *all* your trousers?' I asked in some confusion. 'Yes, *all* of them, except these.' Lord Curzon was wearing his evening trousers of the night before. I glanced at my watch. There was still an hour before the meeting of the Conference, but by this time Arketall must have reached Pontarlier. I ran for Bill Bentinck and told him to telephone to the frontier police: 'Don't say trousers,' I shouted after him, 'say "quelques effets".' I then secured the manager and proceeded to Arketall's room. We looked in, over and under the cupboard and into the chest of drawers: I peered under the bed; there were three more bottles of Benedictine against the wall, but otherwise the space was empty. The manager and I looked at each other in despair. 'C'est inénarrable,' he muttered, 'complètement inérarrable.' I sat down wearily on the bed to consider our position. I jumped up again immediately and pulled back the bed-spread. Upon the crumpled bed-clothes lay a trouser-press bursting with Lord Curzon's trousers. I sent the manager to stop Bill Bentinck telephoning; myself I clasped the trouser-press and returned in triumph to Lord Curzon. He was seated at his writing-table, his pencil dashing across sheets of foolscap, his lips moving. I stood there waiting. When he had finished four or five sheets and cast them from him he turned to me indignantly. His face relaxed into a smile and then extended into that irresistible laugh of his, that endearing boyish sense of farce. 'Thank you,'

he said, 'I shall now complete my toilet. There will only be Leeper to dinner to-night, and as a reward I shall give you my celebrated imitation of Tennyson reciting "Tears, idle tears".'

He kept his promise. It was an amazing performance. We expressed our admiration and our gratitude. A sudden wave of depression descended upon Lord Curzon. 'Ah, yes,' he sighed, 'ah yes. I know. All that was years ago, when I was young and could still laŭgh at my elders. But all young men are remorseless. You will go upstairs this evening and chǎff me behind my back. You will give imitations in after life of the old buffer imitating Tennyson. And so it continues.' He sighed deeply. And then he grinned. 'I am sorry,' he said, 'for Arketall. I liked that man.'

© *from* SOME PEOPLE, 1927

For a Wine Festival

VERNON WATKINS

Now the late fruits are in.
Now moves the leaf-starred year
Down, in the sun's decline.
Stoop. Have no fear.
Glance at the burdened tree:
Dark is the grape's wild skin.
Dance, limbs, be free.
Bring the bright clusters here
And crush them into wine.

Acorns from yellow boughs
Drop to the listening ground.
Spirits who never tire,
Dance, dance your round.

Vintage Tales

Old roots, old thoughts and dry,
Catch, as your footprints rouse
Flames where they fly,
Knowing the year has found
Its own more secret fire.

Nothing supreme shall pass.
Earth to an ember gone
Wears but the death it feigns
And still burns on.
One note more true than time
And shattered falls his glass.
Steal, steal from rhyme:
Take from the glass that shone
The vintage that remains.

© *from* THE COMPLEAT IMBIBER 11, 1970

Islands and Spirits

RONALD BRYDEN

The national spirit of my native country first blazed over my horizon when I was six. I had wakened in those appalling hours children love, when in the half-dark before dawn they find themselves alone and free in a silent world depopulated of adults. I wandered out on the verandah which circled our bungalow in the hills behind Port-of-Spain, barefoot, shivering pleasurably in my pyjamas, looking for one of the dogs to talk to. It could not be as early as it felt, already there was a pinkish glow in the sky over the town – I could just make out, as I passed their open doors, the humps of my brothers, of my parents, under their mosquito nets, and savour the power of the waking over the sleeping. On the steps down to the garden, still a dark, bushy blur smelling of wetness and snails, I found one of the dogs sleeping, and squatted on the step above, warming my feet under him, while I thought. Something was unusual. Port-of-Spain lay directly south of us, over a low spur of hills. Even at Christmas, when the sun (my father had explained to us) travelled south of

the Guianas, the farthest south anyone had heard of, it had no business rising there; and we had had Christmas. I went through on my fingers the rhyme my father had used to teach us the points of the compass – I discovered years later it was a parody of Lord Tennyson's agonised religious questings in 'In Memoriam':

The golden sun sinks in the West
And rises in the East each day,
And westward once more takes its way.
I cannot think but this is best.

I scanned again the glow in the sky. The golden sun had elected this morning, apparently, to rise in the south, out of the huge, calm harbour which lay between Trinidad and the mountains of Venezuela. Prodding the dog with my foot, I padded back into the sleeping house to shake my father's shoulder and inform him that something had gone wrong with the Victorian universe.

That was the extent of my participation in the most momentous event of my West Indian childhood, the burning of the Trinidad Government rum bond. Later, however, I was to hear its details over and over – it became a classic theme of calypso, holding its own with such subsequent epic matter as Mrs Simpson or the visit of the Graf Zeppelin. No one ever discovered how the fire started: a night-watchman, as I remember, was trapped in the flames, and it was presumed he had lit an incautious cigarette. The first anyone knew was when, with a roar of exploding casks, the flames leapt through the roof of the great old nineteenth-century warehouse on Marine Square, scorching the royal palms which stood with white-washed feet outside all official buildings, and lighting up the entire waterfront. Thousands of barrels, millions of dollars' worth of rum lying bonded there waiting maturity, blazed skyward in a glare of orange which flickered over the wooden façade of the old Roman Catholic cathedral, the iron-balconied stores and sailors' bars, the painted shutters of the Ice House and Union Club, the peeling ones of the Hotel Miranda. Thousands of gallons ran flaming down the gutters, hissing past the feet of the beggars who slept wrapped in sacking under the trees of the square.

The city woke to a lurid reek and crashing as of bombardment. Through dark dawn streets the slum-dwellers of the waterfront pelted. As the word spread, they began to arrive with vessels. Women ran jiggling enamelled sauce-pans. Children sprinted with small chamber-pots. They scooped up flaming liquor in china washbasins. They bore it away smoking in flowered bedroom jugs. The less provident drank on the spot from mugs and porridge-tins. The beggars baled it up in the calabashes they begged with. The square began to fill with people on foot, on bicycles, in singlets and slippers; with the donkey carts of market-women rumbling in from the countryside before sunrise. They began to offer bakes, curry and salt fish for sale. Indian coconut-vendors struck up a sweating trade, hacking nuts open with cutlasses and selling the water as a mixer. Cars began to pour in from the wealthier suburbs along the hills and seashore, back seats crammed with half-dressed, shouting children. The fire-brigades also arrived – too late, as usual, to do much about the fire, but in time to enhance the spectacle by displays of ladder-drill and by turning their hoses on the surrounding roofs where small boys perched in rows like nesting rice-birds.

The mayor came, buttoning himself, and the square began to look like a Hieronymus Bosch *kermesse*. Everyone stood drinking and laughing under the trees, as if at a municipal cocktail party. The Ice House threw open its shutters and started selling ice. White businessmen, pyjama jackets tucked into their trousers, appeared with glasses in hand on the Union Club verandah. At the Miranda, a few doors down, the girls crowded the balustrades in dirty kimonos, waving to people they knew in the crowd. Now and then there would be a wave of cheering as a popular city-councillor appeared, or the top of a palm blazed up like a Roman candle. At any moment, one felt, the Governor would arrive on horseback, dressed as for the annual police review, in full tropical white, pith helmet and cock feathers. A few bold young men pretended to eat fire, scooping burning rum to their lips and blowing out the flames; a giggling circle gathered to watch the sideshow. Here and there, drunken dancing began to break out. And still the crack of staves splitting red-hot hoops rang out like pistol-shots in the holocaust, and rivers of blazing rum deluged the gutters, coursing across the square and down storm-drains to the harbour, where it burned on the water beside the customs house, lividly silhouetting the schooners at their moorings against the thinning grey dawn.

That, more or less, is how it was told to me. The fire did not burn itself out for nearly thirty-six hours. The dogs were drunk for days.

Ever since, rum has been for me the drink of communal merrymaking, of national occasions and public joy. Wine always seems to me essentially intimate, gin positively conspiratorial and brandy Byronic and solitary. Whisky is convivial, but cosily, in small groups, and beer too watery to lead to more than singing and sickness. But something in the nature of rum, I find, goes beyond gregariousness, fitting it for drinks all round, toasting admirals, carousing in the streets, precipitating mutinies, throwing up barricades and celebrating victories afterwards. I can't imagine a holiday, fiesta or fête without rum. Well, not what we called a fête in the West Indies.

I can't remember when I first tasted it, nor a time when I didn't know what it tasted like. It stood about us in our infancy like cooking oil, Lysol or any household liquid. My father's decanters of sherry, whisky and port lived locked in the mahogany sideboard which came from his mother's house in Barbados, but the rum lived in the kitchen, on the same open shelf as the rice, tea and washing soda, to be used as needed. It was there as a disinfectant if a maid cut her finger; as a restorative if a tarantula bit the yard-boy; as a sunburn lotion, mixed with milk, to bathe our crimson shoulders after a long Sunday on the beach. It was there to inspire the cook, who grumbled much of the day, but at nightfall became mellow and raucous, singing shrill Congregational hymns among her coal-pots. It was there for postmen and garbage-collectors at Christmas; for carpenters who came to build rabbit-hutches or screens against vampire bats; for the small Indian cowman when he delivered a calf, or the little Chinese who brought oysters from the Caroni swamp, where they grew on the mangroves ('Ever see an oyster which grew on a tree?' my father would say, grinning at the grain and dry-goods salesman who came out from Manchester and Montreal). All through my childhood, I was used to the sight of delivery-boys, odd-job men and veterinary surgeons standing at the back steps, saying 'Thank you, suh', and draining a tumbler of warm, neat rum without blinking.

We knew it from sipping furtively at glasses left half-full by guests – rum-punches after Sunday morning oyster parties, rum-and-sodas after games of tennis, rum cocktails which my mother's women friends favoured: pure rum, shaken with sugar, ice and Angostura, and gulped down while the maid stood waiting with a tray to take the glasses for refilling. When my eldest brother was old enough for dances, his friends revealed a new range of rum-mixtures – rum and ginger-ale, rum and Coca-cola, even rum and ginger-beer. We knew it as a flavouring in ice-cream and puddings: doused on to cake left over from tea to make a trifle if guests stayed unexpectedly to dinner, or flickering in blue flames over the annual plum-pudding which rounded off Christmas dinner with huge dollops of rum-butter, usually in temperatures between eighty and ninety in the shade.

We knew it from sucking experimentally the red streaks of fermentation in the sugar-cane our mother made us chew for the sake of our teeth – the negroes, she explained, had strong white teeth although they never owned tooth-brushes because, from slavery times, they had exercised their gums chewing the coarse cane pith. We knew its taste on the air, borne into the car as we drove across the centre of the island between the big sugar-estates – Brechin Castle, Caroni, Golden Grove – the refinery chimneys visible for miles across the flat cane-fields: acres of pale, giant grass taller than a man, watered by slow, molasses-coloured rivers; silvery in the sun, blue in its under-shadows, tufted toward crop-time with feathery, steel-blue spears. From the mountains which ran along the north of the island, you could look for fifty miles over unbroken fields as level as Lincolnshire, and image you smelled rising from them the heady, vegetable fermentation of rum.

We found out early that we inhabited, more or less, a one-crop economy. Nearly everyone we knew lived, directly or indirectly, by the sugar industry. For a time, we believed everyone had his own family rum – distilled on family estates or bottled by family firms. We vied at school in precocious expertise: 'You-all make rum too thick for me, man. Give me a nice, dry rum like ours, every time.' 'You mean you don't like rum that is *rum*, is what you mean!' I was in a strong position, for my father imported a fine, light rum bottled by *his* father's firm in Barbados, and most Trinidadians had to admit that Barbadian rum was better than their own. They did so reluctantly, for Trinidadians hated Barbados. They hated its airs about its coral beaches and its Englishness and its respectability. Barbados had belonged to Britain since 1625, and was small, clean, domesticated and Protestant. Every square inch of its soil was cultivated with sugar-cane, and from the air, Barbadians boasted, you could mistake its calm greenness for a corner of Dorset. Its doorsteps were whitewashed, its sands were brilliant as diamonds, and its races maintained a parallel purity – to people of my grandparents' generation, the undiluted whiteness and blackness of Barbadian faces was the outward, visible sign of triumphant morality. Barbadians prided themselves on wearing starched collars and alpaca jackets, dressing for work exactly like London clerks in July, on reading their Bibles, knowing their places and fielding the whitest-flannelled cricket teams in the Caribbean.

Trinidad, on the other hand, sprawling off the mouth of the Orinoco, had been Spanish until 1798, French-speaking for some decades after (the Revolution flooded it with French planters fleeing Martinique), and was large, jungly, easy-going and Roman Catholic. Its beaches were brown, its waters brackish with Orinoco silt, its mountains tangled with rain-forest and loud with monkeys; its old French houses were elegant but ramshackle and its races miscegenated like Brazilians. Descendants of slaves interbred with descendants of their owners, Lebanese traders married Portuguese Jews, Chinese emigrants from Canton bought the daughters of Indian indentured labourers, brought from Madras to replace the freed slaves on the estates they deserted. Few families claimed confidently to be pure white Caucasian, and fewer still believed them. Trinidad went in for carnivals, Creole cooking and *crimes passionels*. Geologically, it was a severed finger of Latin America, and it behaved like one.

Both my parents, therefore, had dismayed their own by deciding to settle in

Trinidad when they married. To my father's Barbadian family and my mother's Jamaican one, they might as well have announced their intention to migrate to New Guinea. Whenever we were taken on visits to Barbados (overnight on a neat little Dutch steamer plying from Curacao to Rotterdam), my father's mother would hand our clothes to her laundress, lead us to her dining-room, with its big windows overlooking the roofs, masts and funnels of Bridgetown harbour, and urge us mournfully to eat some wholesome English food while we had the opportunity. My mother had once revealed to her that Trinidadians cooked with oil and regarded iguanas as a delicacy; she had never forgotten it. By plain English food she meant, as likely as not, sea eggs, flying fish, rice, pigeon-peas, yams and plantains; but everything was boiled and grilled as in her English girlhood, and served at the Victorian meal-hours. My grandfather left for his office at seven-thirty, and returned at ten for a breakfast of kidneys, kedgeree, ham, kippers and corn fritters. Luncheon – they had modernised only the name – came when he finished work, between two and three, and was followed by an elaborate tea at five and dinner at nine. At each meal, we would be stuffed till our stomachs were tight as cushions, against our return to Trinidad's oily and heathen cuisine.

The old meal-hours survived in Barbados partly out of unshakeable conviction that all things British were best, partly for their conveniences for estate-owners, whom they enabled to ride round their acres before the sun was high, complete their indoor work before the first rum-punch and luncheon, and sleep in the baking hours from three to five. My grandfather liked them because they enabled him to finish his work in the cool of the morning, join his cronies at his club for a long drink at midday, and go swimming at the Royal Barbados Yacht Club every afternoon. He had won medals as a young clerk in London for the breast-stroke, and I suspect it was the prospect of a daily dip in the Caribbean that had persuaded him to emigrate in the 1880s. He would lead us out into the opal water, butting through it with his big guardsman's torso, then sink suddenly and emerge with the ends of his white Kaiser Wilhelm moustache dripping. We paddled behind like puppies as he forged out toward the ships with old-fashioned, dignified strokes, pointing out how clearly we could still see the bottom fifty yards from the shore. 'You can't do that in Trinidad, can you now?' he would ask reprovingly, and then lead us ashore to be filled with dazingly rich egg-nogs from the Yacht Club bar. We were not allowed rum in ours, as his had, but the barman would monogram the foam on top with our initials in Angostura. When we complained to my grandfather that the neighbouring Aquatic Club had a longer beach than the yacht club, and a thrilling old pier with a dance-floor and diving-boards at the end, he would

point out gently that persons of colour, no doubt respectable enough folk in themselves but not the kind of company in which a gentleman would wish to bathe, were admitted to membership there, and besides that the barman would not know our initials.

Rum-punch is the drink I associate with him, however – he could no more have called it planter's punch than bring himself to address one of the American tourists who did, still rare and laughable phenomena, in their dark spectacles and ill-fitting shorts, at our end of the islands in those days. It was he who taught me the Barbados recipe for it: 'One of bitter, two of sweet, three of strong and four of weak.' 'Bitter' was the juice of fresh limes (Barbadians, unable to conceive any other purpose for them, called them punchberries); sweet was sugar-water or grenadine; weak – this was why it quenched thirst so effectively – was simply ice and water, and strong, my grandfather finished roundly, should always be 'a decent Bubbaijan rum'. Piously lightening our Trinidadian darkness, he would explain why: 'Those people down in Trinidad, boy, they tap the rum from the *bottom*. They draw off the lees and that mess so the rum tastes of molasses. Here in Bubbadus, we tap the vat ten inches from the bottom, so we draw just the good, pure spirit. I wouldn't feed that trash at the bottom of the cask to hawgs. But down in Trinidad, o' course, they don't know better.'

My father, grinning, would agree with him. He had inherited the English-Barbadian taste for rum as a sort of whisky substitute, a dry, light spirit to be taken with soda. He had inherited, too, the Barbadian accent: within a day or two of arrival, he and the old man would be arguing away in its broad, infectious drawl, all rolling r's and West Country 'oi' sounds, overlaying five years of English public school, fifteen of Trinidad sing-song. Presumably it was the same accent brought out to the plantations by the transported Cromwellian prisoners who had given sugar-spirit its name, the Cornish word 'rumbullion' – an uproar – and later shortened it to rumbo, and then to rum. Certainly there were still villages, up the leeward coast, of ragged, tow-haired whites with pale blue eyes and bare feet, who answered to old Devon and Somerset names and were called 'Red-Legs'. And years later, in Cambridge, I saw a production of *Julius Caesar* acted in as close approximation to Jacobean speech and costume as a scholarly committee of phoneticists and Shakespearians could reconstruct. To me, the stage seemed crowded with pantalooned Barbadians, sounding marvellously, as they tossed their sweaty nightcaps in the air and howled for the blood of Cinna the Poet, like my grandfather at ease under the Yacht Club casuarinas, scornfully denouncing the molasses-content of Trinidad rum.

My mother, who cared little for spirits, stayed out of most discussions of this kind, but occasionally, sorely tried, she would let fall with mild snobbery the fact that her people in Jamaica were close friends with the family whose name was the greatest in the West Indies and outside it – the Myerses. 'Well, of course, I don't care for any of it much, but I do know Horace Myers used to say no rum was worth drinking before seven years.' Her father had been an undistinguished officer in the Jamaican excise and poor as a church mouse, but in the tiny, ancient community of the Jamaica Jews – their synagogue was older than the oldest in London: Cromwell's permission for the founding of Bevis Marks was a reward for one of its members who guided the Commonwealth fleet which took the island from the Spaniards – in their tiny, closed community his children and the young Myerses had attended each others' parties, pulled each others' hair and scampered all over the Myerses' magnificent country place in the Blue Mountains above Kingston. It figured again and again in my mother's Jamaican stories – its gardens, its Italian floors, its horses, and its river plunging down through tree-ferns to a private pool – and throughout our childhood the Myerses were held up to us as glittering examples both of the fact that Money did not necessarily bring Happiness (though we never learned precisely wherein their griefs lay) and of the ultimate in luxury and cultivation. They became part of a fabulous picture in our minds of my mother's birthplace as an island where people habitually indulged in things – watching polo, waltz- ing with English officers from the Garrison, staying in mountain hotels, coping with earthquakes and hurricanes – more exciting and complex than were dreamed of at our end of the Caribbean. Had we been capable of the dis- tinction, we should have judged that, while Barbados in its small way was a culture and Trinidad something vaguer and more straggly, Jamaica must be a civilisation.

My chance to verify this came when I was seven and my mother's father eighty. His children called a great family reunion for his birthday, and my mother, packing innumerable trunks with clothes, medicines, presents and our own sheets and pillowcases, set off in a banana-boat with the two youngest of us and our fat coloured nurse, Gladys, on the nine-day voyage up the coast of Central America. Certainly the trip was the biggest experience of my first ten years. We stopped at the port for Caracas, drove over the mountains and saw the house where Bolivar died, a dank old Spanish mansion with a mildewed patio. We stopped at Santa Marta in Colombia, where a single snow-crowned peak towered 17,000 feet above the vast, stifling bay Conrad used as the setting for *Nostromo*. We stopped at Panama, and saw an American battleship rising like a steel alligator through the Gatun Locks. We stopped at every banana- port around the Caribbean, and in each watched the bananas loaded into the night: lines of stevedores with green bunches on their shoulders filing, in the flickering light of kerosene flares in decapitated rum-bottles, up the gangway past the khaki-clad tallyman. As they passed, he swung up his cutlass as if to behead them, and then swiped it sharply down behind them, neatly severing the stalk from each bunch – that was his tally. We were in United Fruit Company territory now, and in each port my mother would recognise some of the officials who came aboard as young men who had passed through the empire's Kingston offices when she had worked there as a secretary before her marriage. And finally one morning, a blue mountain rose from the sea, and we sailed past the weather-beaten vestige of Port-Royal on its forlorn sandspit, over the drowned buildings which had sunk in its great seventeenth-century earth-quake, and across Kingston's landlocked harbour to the United Fruit dock where my aunts and uncles and grandfather were waiting.

The first thing I noticed was that they were dressed as I had never seen people dressed before. The men wore creamy, silky-looking suits and shoes of two colours. The women were hatted, and clad in lace, flowered chiffon, *crêpe-de-chine*. Some carried fans; some may even have worn gloves. In their midst stood my grandfather, noble in white linen, a broad white Panama hat in one hand, a cane in the other. They wept; they kissed us; they took us to their bosoms in a daze of scent and emotion and large open cars. When we regained consciousness, we were in a garden of giant dahlias and blazing canna lilies even larger than the flowers on my aunts' dresses, which seemed more gardened, more garden-like, than any in Barbados or Trinidad. Under older, leafier trees than those we knew, people even more dressily dressed chatted noisily but negligently in ornate wicker chairs, waving cigars and drinking gin-and-lime. Then we were at an immensely long table (all my grandfather's nine children and their families gathered for Sabbath-eve supper every Friday night) eating a huge meal of innumerable strange courses ('You mean you don't eat ackies in Trinidad? How else can you serve salt fish?') and drinking – even in my daze I was impressed – wine. Everyone was talking at once, but always stopped when my grandfather looked up, raising his pince-nez to his nose, freeing the black ribbon from the white rose in his lapel. When he had spoken, he would complete the gesture with a faint inclination of his freckled old hand towards the person he had interrupted. His movements were slow, formal and authoritative; he had been known to dismiss a middle-aged son to his room for coming to breakfast with his collar unbuttoned. Now he beamed on his sons and daughters patriar-chally. Cigars were brought, and a decanter of something dark brown, almost as black as the mahogany table. 'This is a gift of our good friend Horace,' he said, filling his glass and raising it. 'We will use it to welcome Flo and her sons at the end of their voyage.' It was my first encounter with Jamaican rum, and the first time I had seen rum drunk as a liqueur.

The difference of their rum, as I came to know it later, seemed to sum up the difference of Jamaicans from the other West Indians I knew. It was older, richer, more aromatic than our rums; too strong and sweet to take in at a mouthful; and it was a legacy of the English eighteenth century which had evolved in the tropics into something indigenous and exotic. Long ago, during the Georgian wars against France and Spain, Jamaicans had developed a way of shipping economically the rum with which they supplied the British navy. They simply distilled a double-strength, heavy concentrate which on arrival could be diluted back to normal strength by mixing it half-and-half with water. But generations of sailors had grown attached to the undiluted brown swig, and later generations of Jamaican planters had adopted it too. They converted it to a drink which combined for them the functions of port and brandy – a sugared, full-bodied, fierily fortifying after-dinner tipple. All the best Jamaican rums aspired to the condition of liqueurs, and this was why they were matured longer than our lighter spirits. Even in fruit-punches, they were more clinging, more scented and languorous than other rums, requiring longer sitting over before lunch and longer siestas after. They had become an expression of the odd, overblown transplanting of Georgian and Anglo-Indian manners which had grown into Jamaica's leisurely, floridly formal and unique way of life.

They had more history, that was what it amounted to. Jamaica had always been the richest of the islands, which was another way of saying it was the colony where slavery had taken deepest root. I became aware in Jamaica for the first time of the ubiquitous, inescapable legacies of the Trade. Barbados was too small, Trinidad too parvenu, for the system to have become institutionalised there, but wherever you went in Jamaica you saw its monuments – the huge, improvident cattle-pens in the hills, the old estate-mansions tumbled into desolation, the ruined, overgrown slave-barracks still inhabited here and there. The names of the old slave-owning families – the de Lissers, the Moulton-Barretts, the Marquesses of Sligo – were still to be heard in the island, servants still referred to their employers as 'master' and 'mistress'. You would meet children walking along country roads with both hands on their heads – only years later did I recognise it as a posture to be found in old prints, and nowhere else, of slave-auctions. Up in the crumpled pink valleys of the Cockpit Country, beyond Spanish Town and Mandeville, you could still find villages of Maroons, the escaped slaves who had hidden out there, set up their own polity and eventually won a kind of autonomy in the great slave revolt of 1795.

And there was still hatred. Trinidad was too French and Spanish ever to have known a rigid colour bar, Barbados had never known anything else; but in Jamaica the custom of providing young English overseers with concubines from among the slave-girls on the estates had created a large population of mixed blood, a many-shaded middle-class agonisingly suspended between an English inheritance and bitter loathing of it. It was they who gave Jamaica its distinctive English un-Englishness, its peculiar flavour of the familiar grown alien and strangely-coloured. It was they who locked Jamaica's races in uniquely understanding antagonism: a combination and a hostility which required uniquely powerful fuel to explode.

Don't misunderstand me. I'm not trying to be frivolous about the part played by the different islands' rums in the rioting which blazed through the West Indies in 1938. That amounted to a national rebellion, one of the first in the British Empire, and laid the foundations of the independence the islands have finally won in the last few years. But reverence for the origins of my nation's freedom shouldn't obscure the fact that those chain explosions were ignited by hunger, racial resentment and rum; and I think one can trace a connection between the different courses violence took in the islands and the differences between their rums. In Trinidad, the distressed sugar-workers had been parading their grievances fairly peacefully for months before the outbreak (a Royal Commission, after the event, reduced these to Micawberishly stark simplicity: it estimated that the minimum sum necessary to nourish and shelter one person adequately at prevailing prices was about one West Indian dollar a day, and the average actual sugar-worker's wage about sixty cents). A few cane-fields had been burned, but that happened every year. One hot night, some women were gathered outside a rum-shop in southern Trinidad when an unpopular police-sergeant came up and asked if they had seen a man wanted as an agitator. Insults were exchanged, then blows; suddenly they were on him, scratching, dragging him behind the shop, pouring kerosene on him. A match was lit, and for five days panic swept the island. It was bloody, passionate, terrifying and suddenly over. A grey Navy cruiser stood in Port-of-Spain harbour, the stores repaired their windows and everyone went sullenly back to work. It was like a grim version of the annual carnival, with two days of frenetic dancing in the streets ending in hang-over and penitence on Ash Wednesday, or like one of the many *crimes passionels* in the Trinidad papers, by rum-crazed Indians chopping their wives with cutlasses.

In Barbados the riots were even briefer and more light-headed. Some shops were looted and some old scores settled, but no one really expected to alter the order of things. It was the rioting in Jamaica which was serious, an eruption of slow, dark, historic forces. It was not only the sugar-workers who rose, but townspeople, labourers, peasant-farmers from the mountains; there were demonstrations all over the island. It was a national rising on the same scale as the great Port Morant rebellion of 1865, which became an imperial issue at Westminster, with Carlyle, Tennyson and Kingsley defending the repressive measures of Governor Eyre against a committee led by John Stuart Mill. It produced two national leaders – Alexander Bustamente, who led the Kingston demonstrators, and his cousin Norman Manley, a barrister who defended him at his trial for inciting violence. The Jamaican outbreak of 1938 was the bitterest in the islands, and the longest. It never really ended, but went on smouldering sluggishly until internal self-government was granted after the war, as the basis of Jamaica's curious, ingrown, intense political life.

I left the West Indies in 1941 to go to school and university in Canada, and it was there, I suppose, that I formed my drinking habits. I developed a taste for long, fruity American gin-drinks, and for Canadian rye whisky – the first drunken parties I went on were after football games in Toronto, starting with a bottle of rye and a blanket on the chilly bleachers of the university stadium and ending with a case of it and several hundred people in a small hotel room. But my attitudes to drinking had formed earlier: I could never understand the Canadian and American fuss about liquor, the elaborate Ontario laws which prevented you from buying spirits in bars or restaurants, but compelled you to queue in bleak government liquor stores and bear off your wrapped bottle furtively to your home or hotel. Even when my Canadian friends denounced the system, and the whole Prohibition legacy of ideas behind it, they seemed to assume that the alternative lay between what the authorities feared, a North American proclivity for 'drinking to get drunk', and a civilised, European notion of 'drinking for pleasure'. I could not make them understand that there might be a third alternative, drinking as West Indians drank rum: simply as part of your geography, your nationality, your culture, without question or discussion or even noticing it much, simply because it was part of your life, of certain occasions, because everyone drank it, because it was there.

Certainly I should never have thought about rum if I had never left the West Indies. It took a drink in a Martiniquan bar in Paris to wake me up to how much of my life was bound up with it. At the first sniff, I was overwhelmed by a flood of images and associations. It was my equivalent of Proust's *madeleine*: back rushed everything and everyone I had known, the smells and heat and sounds of the Caribbean. I suppose there are three things which make cultures truly indigenous – a particular stone or brick-clay which distinguishes their architecture, a particular mode of weaving and a particular fermented juice.

Cement is eliminating the first, nylon the second, and eventually, I suppose, world trade will make the third meaningless, too. It seems a pity. Everything else we had in the West Indies came from elsewhere – our architecture, our laws, our cooking, our meal-times, ourselves. Our individuality was a pathetic colonial matter of limitation, of the odd private values families would build up around a few random cultural totems – an old Caruso record, a shelf of damp-stained Waverley novels, an inherited recipe, a sheaf of Edwardian sheet-music brought back from some visit to Europe years ago. But rum was our own, and the occasions and habits it made. It was our link with our geography, our one strand of nativeness. All the rest of our education and culture pointed us elsewhere. Only rum pointed us home.

I'm not sure to what extent it still does so. When I returned to the West Indies in the late 'forties, prosperity had transformed the islands. American bases and tourism had brought dollars to most of them – their effect on Trinidad was the subject of the calypso, 'Rum and Coca-Cola'. The dislocation of European agriculture and industry had created a boom in sugar and rum. More rum than ever was being exported – big names, Fernandes, Lemon Hart, Mount Gay, had pushed out small ones like my grandfather's – but less was being drunk. With their new money, people were drinking whisky – its import had become a staple of my father's business. It was the drink you were offered after tennis parties, the drink my mother's friends sipped on their verandahs after bridge. Even in the sailors' bars, it threatened to outstrip rum. Only the poor still drank rum, and the young – the bank-clerks and debutantes I mixed with during the year I worked on the Trinidad newspaper refreshed themselves between dances with rum-and-ginger, rum-and-coke, and sometimes took half a dozen water melons and a thermos of rum-punch as a day's sustenance on the beach. But they did so shamefacedly, meaning to change as soon as they could afford to. It was brands of whisky they talked about and compared now. It was not like being back home, it was like being anywhere.

Only once did I feel I'd stumbled on the West Indies of my youth. At the end of my year with the paper, they held a staff dinner at an old, rather doubtful hotel off Marine Square with elaborate wooden fan-lights and Chinese calendars on the walls. On arrival, I was handed a half-tumbler of neat rum. I looked around desperately for a waitress. Beside me, one of the leader-writers, an ebony-skinned Trotskyite, was arguing with a young Indian court-reporter about Federation. 'How you going to make one nation with all them small-islanders and Jamaicans, tell me that?' he was saying. 'Jamaica – you can't even drink their rum!' He tipped up his iceless, undiluted glass and swallowed scornfully. A waitress leaned over me affectionately. 'You wanted something?'

she asked. 'No, it doesn't matter,' I said and gulped my rum agonisingly, feeling for the first time that I had achieved the maturity all my childhood had defined for me.

© *from* THE COMPLEAT IMBIBER 6, 1963

The Expense of Spirits Is a Crying Shame

WENDY COPE

The Expense of Spirit in a Waste of Shame is Lust in Action . . .
SHAKESPEARE, SONNETS, 129

The expense of spirits is a crying shame;
So is the cost of wine. What bard today
Can live like old Khayyam? It's not the same –
A loaf and Thou and Tesco's beaujolais.
I had this bird called Sharon, fond of gin –
Could knock back six or seven. At the price,
I paid a high wage for each hour of sin
And that was why I only had her twice.
Then there was Tracy, who drank rum and coke –
So beautiful I didn't mind at first
But love grows colder. Now some other bloke
Is subsidising Tracy and her thirst.
I need a woman, honest and sincere,
Who'll come across on half a pint of beer.

© *from* STRUGNELL'S SONNETS

Down Where the Würzburger Flows

LUDWIG BEMELMANS

I know about beer, because it flows in my veins; my great-grandfather was a brewer in the best hops country of southern Germany, and over the vast stone portal of the brewery was written:

Hopfen und Maltz
Gott erhalt's.

The peculiarly built, long, heavy wagons which cradle the oaken barrels were pulled by stout Lippizaners, weighing tons apiece, and the colour of beer, with manes like foam. They moved with slow dignity – and when they came out of the brewery, pounding their heavy, shaggy hoofs on the creosote blocks of the pavement, sounded like thunder. This majestic tempo was kept up until the beer arrived in vast limestone caves, where it was rested or *gelagered* (hence the word 'lager' beer) for six months. After that the barrels were carefully loaded again, and the beer was delivered to the various places which are called *Wirt-*

schaften, where it was poured and tasted with the ceremony and nervosity that is given in other regions of Europe to great wine.

As wine has a bouquet, so has beer. It is said of good, dark beer that it tastes like licking a dusty windowpane. That may not be everyone's idea of pleasure, but an experienced beer drinker knows what I mean; it is a dusty, a fine antique, dusty, musty – a taste that is perfection.

As does wine, so does beer reflect its native landscape. If you have been out in the vineyards of France, the wine will bring them back to you. You can see the flowered fields of Alsace with the aid of a glass of *Gewürztraminer*, you can conjure up the faces of the *Bordelais* when you drink their wine; and the *Boxbeutel* of Würzburg clearly reproduces for you the stony fields on which this superb wine grows.

Of beer, the same is true. The scene is more solid; it is a heavier canvas, determined in line and colour. Not only does beer reflect; it is stronger, it is also determined. It has created a certain kind of furniture, interiors, vehicles; influenced mores, dress, and the shape of people. It has even changed language, medicine, and the law.

In the south of Germany, whence the best brews come and where the cathedral of brewing, the Academy of Weihenstephan, is located, the number of breweries is easily determined in any given community simply by counting the church steeples. For every one there is, there is also a brewery.

Drinking here is a devotional rite, by people who have for generations given themselves to it. The South Germans are a kind of surviving Neanderthaler, with skulls of stone. In character, they are comparable to the Irish, of the same manic–depressive character. Their soul is a ponderous mechanism, and when set in motion by sentimental impulse or agitated anger it moves the man slowly at first but with mountain-moving might.

The heavy beer is blamed for that.

The beerpeople of the south of Germany should be of the greatest interest to the student of abnormal anthropology.

The children of beerpeople grow up normally, with here and there one that has an abnormally large head – which is called a *Wasserkopf*, or waterhead. The local joke on this subject goes like this:

Two men stand on a street corner and one says, 'Oh, look at the boy with the *Wasserkopf*.'

The other says, 'That's my son.'

'Looks good on him,' answers the other.

As time passes, all but the *Wasserköpfe* look for girls to marry. The requirements are easily met, the conditions easy. They have to be sound in front

[137]

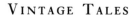

and back, stand on solid legs, and have able hands. Beauty is not *ausschlaggebend* and the dowry is not as important as it is in France. The mating season is brief. The rites of love are an awkward kind of stumbling about, a dance of love as it is performed by the *Auerhahn*, a local bird that, with half-closed eyes, becomes ill with passion and almost topples off the trees. He is often shot during these exercises. The tail feathers of the *Auerhahn*, forming the outline of a *Lyra*, are a favourite decoration of the headgear of the man of the beerworld. He is married now, and produces children – statistics show an average of four – and, towards the last, he withdraws from woman as such. She goes to the *Kirch*, the *Kinder*, and the *Küche*, and he to the *Wirtschaft*.

The beer here has influenced the décor of the *Wirtschaft*, with heads of game on the wall and frescoes interwoven with poetry:

> *Leberwurscht für den Durscht*
> *Blunzeduft mit Kraut –*
> *Wenn der Bauer Hunger hat*
> *frisst ers z'amt der Haut.*

The author of this verse was my maternal grandfather, Ludwig Fischer. Translate it I cannot, but it wants to say:

> Liver sausage for the thirst
> the aroma of blood sausage and cabbage
> when the peasant is hungry
> he devours it ['fressen' is not translatable]
> 'z'amt der Haut' – means with the skin.

The tables are solid and the influence of beer on the chairs is remarkable. They are heavy, made mostly of oak. The good ones have a face carved into the part against which you put your back. The seat is wooden also and so planed that it conforms to the anatomy of the local males; that is, you can place a large trunk on it and it will be safe and not wobble. Into the seat the four solid legs are placed, and here the Irish resemblance is again apparent. These legs are not glued or screwed into the seat, but merely inserted, so that with a good strong twist of the wrist you can remove them and work with them as with a shillelagh.

Now as to the man who sits on the chair – he is self-contained and quiet (unless enraged); he is honest, loves his country, goes to church. Beer has also influenced him. First of all, he is there on its account and on no other. He enters the *Wirtschaft*, goes to his chair, and a grunt and a nod serve him for the first half-hour. The waitress knows his wants and puts the first heavy stein in front of him.

[138]

During the first half-hour the true 'Spezi' as he is called – and which perhaps means 'specialist' – folds his hands and contemplates his beer. He might lift his head and look beyond his part of the *Stammtisch* to see if any hostile element is present. (Anyone from another city is a foreigner.) If he sees a friend there is another grunt. He does not call the waitress for another beer because when he wants one he merely leaves the cover on his mug open in upstanding position; that is the signal to the waitress to hit him again.

He usually eats at home. If he eats at the *Wirtschaft* he eats the same diet as his *Frau* prepares – radishes, pumpernickel, potato dumplings (which must be torn apart, not cut, or the cook's heart is broken), *Schweinebraten, Gänsbraten mit Rotkraut, Leberwurscht und Blutwurscht.*

All this gives him a liver like the geese of *pâté de fois gras* fame. He drinks himself to death at about the same age the American executive works himself to death.

He sits there like a frog that has swallowed a stone and is unable to move, his laughter is bitter, his words are few. The beerworld has formulated the language into a kind of ponderous audible shorthand. To illustrate this I will give here a quick sampler of this curious means of communication, of its meaning in High German and also in English.

> *How do you do?*
> High German: Wie geht es Ihnen?
> Beer: Grüassdi
>
> *What are you doing?*
> High German: Wie geht hier vor?
> Beer: Wastuastdenn
>
> *We're cleaning*
> High German: Wir machen rein
> Beer: Ramma tamma
>
> *At home*
> High German: Zu Hause
> Beer: Dahoam

My grandfather was an exceptionally well-preserved Neanderthaler. He was in the war of 1870, and was hit by a projectile at close range. It merely left a small dent in his skull. The brewmaster was with him at the time and lost a leg. It worked a certain benefit for them, for they split their shoes, Grandfather wearing the right one and the brewmaster the left. O'Papa, as the grandfather is called in southern Germany, lost the use of his left leg – a martyr to his brewery.

He drank a minimum of thirty liters of beer a day, consuming this in one after the other of all the *Wirtschaften* in and around Regensburg, where our beer was sold. This is called *Kundschafttrinken* and is related to the present-day practice of taking out the client. As a consequence he traveled in a wheel chair from tavern to inn to Rathskeller, one leg raised in a vast packing of cotton-wool, the other down, with the foot stuck into an old-fashioned boot with elastic sides.

As he moved through the streets of the old city he waved his cane over the gouty leg to keep anyone from approaching it. He had a theory that every human being was filled with electricity and if too close to his leg started the pain. This pain was very curious, for he made sounds as if he heard jokes – he laughed from pain – hi-hi, ha-ha – and made faces.

The advanced age of O'Papa and the great volume of liquids he took posed a great problem, and it was again beer that conditioned the construction of the wheel chair. It had a tank at the bottom down to which a rubber tube led, a device that allowed O'Papa to ease himself without getting out of his chair.

The first time that my peculiar talents asserted themselves was in our beer garden in Regensburg. O'Papa was sleeping in his easy chair, the waters of the Danube lapped against the stone walls of the beer garden, the green candelabra of the chestnut trees were alight with white and pink blossoms. I crawled under the chair and I took the end of the rubber tube from the tank and stuck it into O'Papa's shoe. The only one who knew it was Fafner, an alcoholic dachshund – and also a Spezi on beer – he knew all the good ones.

All this, so long ago and far away, comes back to me with sharpest clarity when I sit with one of the good beers, with *Loewenbräu, Würzburger, Kulmbacher, Paulaner* – there isn't a bad one in that region, even in the places that have only one church steeple.

© *from* THE WORLD OF BEMELMANS, 1955

Another Temple Gone

C. E. MONTAGUE

They say that there may be a speck of quiet lodged at the central point of a cyclone. Round it everything goes whirling. It alone sits at its ease, as still as the end of an axle that lets the wheel, all about it, whirl any wild way it likes.

That was the way at Gartumna in those distant years when the 'land war' was blowing great guns all over the rest of the County Clare. Gartumna lay just at the midst of that tempest. But not a leaf stirred in the place. You paid your rent if you could; for the coat that the old colonel had on his back – and he never out of the township – was that worn you'd be sorry. Suppose you hadn't the cash, still you were not 'put out of it'. All that you'd have to suffer was that good man buzzing about your holding, wanting to help; he would be all in a fidget trying to call to mind the way that some heathen Dane, that he had known when a boy, used to bedevil salt butter back into fresh – that, or how Montenegrins would fatten a pig on any wisp of old trash that would come blowing down the high road. A kind man, though he never got quit of the queer dream he had that he knew how to farm.

Another practising Christian we had was Father O'Reilly. None of the sort that would charge you half the girl's fortune before they'd let the young people set foot in the church. And, when it was done, he'd come to the party and sing the best song of anyone there. However, at practical goodness Tom Farrell left the entire field at the post. Tom had good means; a farm in fee-simple – the land, he would often tell us, the finest in Ireland, 'every pitaty the weight of the world if you'd take it up in your hand'; turf coming all but in at the door to be cut; besides the full of a creel of fish in no more than the time you'd take dropping a fly on the stream: the keeper had married Tom's sister. People would say 'Ach, the match Tom would be for a girl!' and gossips liked counting the 'terrible sum' that he might leave when he'd die if only he knew how to set any sort of value on money. But this he did not. The widow Burke, who knew more about life than a body might think, said Tom would never be high in the world because no one could come and ask for a thing but he'd give it to them. Then, as she warmed to the grateful labour of letting you know what was what, the widow might add: 'I question will Tom ever make a threepenny piece, or a penny itself, out of that old construction he has away there in the bog.'

At these words a hearer would give a slight start and glance cannily round, knowing that it would be no sort of manners to give a decent body like Sergeant Maguire the botheration and torment of hearing the like of that said out aloud. But the sergeant would never be there. For he too had his fine social instincts. He would be half a mile off, intent on his duty, commanding the two decent lads that were smoking their pipes, one on each of his flanks, in the tin police hut away down the road. Gartumna did not doubt that this tactful officer knew more than he ever let on. A man of his parts must surely have seen, if not smelt, that no unclean or common whiskey, out of a shop, had emitted the mellow sunshine transfiguring recent christenings and wakes. But who so coarse as to bring a functionary so right-minded up against the brute choice between falling openly short in professional zeal and wounding the gentle bosom of Gartumna's peace?

And yet the widow's sonorous soprano, or somebody else's, may have been raised once too often on this precarious theme. For, on one of the warmest June mornings that ever came out of the sky, Sergeant Maguire paraded his whole army of two, in line, on a front of one mile, with himself as centre file and file of direction, and marched out in this extremely open order into the fawn-coloured wilderness of the bog. 'You'll understand, the two yous,' he had said to his right flank, Constable Boam, and to Constable Duffy, his left, 'that this is a sweeping or dragging movement that we're making.'

The sun was high already – your feverish early starts were no craze of the sergeant's. The air over the bog had tuned up for the day to its loudest and most multitudinous hum and hot click of grasshoppers and bees; all the fawn surface swam in a water-coloured quiver of glare; the coarse, juiceless grass and old roots, leathery and slippery, tripped up the three beaters' feet. Hour by hour the long morning greased and begrimed the three clean-shaven, good-soldier faces that he set out on the quest; noon came blazingly on – its savage vertical pressure seemed to quell and mute with an excess of heat the tropical buzz of all the basking bog life that the morning's sunshine had inspirited; another hour and the bog was swooning, as old poets say, under the embraces of the sun her friend, when a thin column of more intensely quivering air, a hundred yards off to the sergeant's half-left, betrayed some source of an ardour still more fiery than the sun's. Then it was all over. The hunting was done: nothing left but to whistle in his flank men and go over the haul.

The tub and worm of the illicit still had not been really hidden; they were just formally screened with a few blocks of turf as though in silent appeal to the delicacy of mankind to accept as adequate this symbolic tribute to the convention of a seemly reticence. Farrell, a little, neatly-made, fine-featured man with a set, contained face, but with all the nervousness of him quivering out into the restless tips of his small, pointed fingers, gazed at the three stolid uniformed bulks, so much grosser than he, while they disrobed his beloved machinery of that decent light vesture of turf and rummaged with large, coarse hands among the mysteries of his craft. He wore the Quakerish black suit and the broad and low-crowned soft black hat in which a respectable farmer makes his soul on a Sunday morning. Silent, and seemingly not shamed, nor yet enraged, neither the misdemeanant caught in the act nor the parent incensed by a menace to its one child, he looked on, grave and almost compassionate.

Sergeant Maguire, too, may have had his own sense of our kind's tragic blindness quickened just then – that a man, a poor passionate man, should so rush upon his own undoing! 'Ach, it's a pity of you, Farrell,' he presently said, 'A pity! You with the grand means that you have of your own! An' you distilling pocheen!'

'Pocheen!' The little, precise, nervous voice of Farrell ran up into a treble of melancholy scorn. With an austere quality in his movements he drew a brown stone-ware jug from among some heaped cubes of turf that the barbarians had not yet disarranged. From another recess he took a squat tumbler. Into this he poured from the jar enough to fill a liqueur-glass rather smaller than most. 'Tell me,' he bade almost sternly, holding the tumbler out to Maguire, 'd'ye call that pocheen?'

'Ye can take a sup first,' was the canny reply. Maguire had heard how Eastern kings always made cooks and premiers taste first.

Farrell absorbed the tot, drop by drop. He did not cross himself first, but there was something about his way of addressing himself to the draught that would make you think of a man crossing himself before some devout exercise, or taking the shoes from off his feet before stepping on holy ground. As the potion irrigated his soul he seemed to draw off from the touch of this clamorous world into some cloistral retreat. From these contemplative shades he emerged, controlling a sigh, a little time after the last drop had done its good office. He poured out for Maguire.

'Well, here's luck,' said the sergeant, raising the glass, 'and a light sentence beyond.' The good fellow's tone conveyed what the etiquette of the service would not allow him to say – that in the day of judgment every mitigating circumstance would be freshly remembered.

Up to his fortieth year Maguire, conversing with the baser liquors of this world and not with philtres of transfiguration, had counted it sin to drink his whiskey as if it would burn him. So the whole of the tot was now about to descend his large-bore throat in close order, as charges of shot proceed through the barrel of a gun. But the needful peristaltic action of the gullet had scarcely commenced when certain tidings of great joy were taken in at the palate and forwarded express to an astonished brain. 'Mother of God!' the sergeant exclaimed. 'What sort of hivven's delight is this you've invented for all souls in glory?'

A sombre satisfaction gleamed out of Farrell's monkish face. Truth was coming into its own, if only too late. The heathen were seeing the light. 'It's the stuff,' he said, gravely, 'that made the old gods of the Greeks and Romans feel sure they were gods.'

'Be cripes, they were right,' asseverated Maguire. He was imbibing drop by drop now, as the wise poets of all times have done, and not as the topers, the swillers of cocktails, punch and cup, and the like, things only fit to fill up the beasts that perish. Not hoggishness only, but infinite loss would it have seemed to let any one drop go about its good work as a mere jostled atom, lost in a mob of others.

Farrell, after a short pause to collect his thoughts, was stating another instalment of the facts. 'There's a soul and a body,' he said, 'to everything else, the same as ourselves. Any malt you'll have drunk, to this day, was the body of whiskey only – the match of these old lumps of flesh that we're all of us draggin' about till we die. The soul of the stuff's what you've got in your hand.'

'It is that,' said the sergeant, and chewed the last drop like a lozenge. He now perceived that the use of large, bold, noble figures of speech, like this of Farrell's, was really the only way to express the wonderful thoughts filling up a man's mind when he is at his best. That was the characteristic virtue of Farrell's handiwork. Its merely material parts were, it is true, pleasant enough. They seemed, while you sipped, to be honey, warm sunshine embedded in amber and topaz, the animating essence of lustrous brown velvet, and some solution of all the mellowest varnish that ever ripened for eye or ear the glow of Dutch landscape or Cremona fiddle. No sooner, however, did this potable sum of all the higher physical embodiments of geniality and ardour enter your frame than a major miracle happened in the domain of the spirit: you suddenly saw that the most freely soaring poetry, all wild graces and quick turns and abrupt calls on your wits, was just the most exact, business-like way of treating the urgent practical concerns of mankind.

So the sergeant's receivers were well tuned to take in great truths when Farrell, first measuring out the due dram for Constable Duffy, resumed, 'You'll remember the priest that died on us last year?'

'I do that, rest his soul,' said each of the other two Catholics. Constable Boam was only a lad out of London, jumped by some favour into the force. But a good lad.

'Ye'll remember,' Farrell continued, 'the state he was in, at the end? Perished with thinness, and he filled with the spirit of God the way you'd see the soul of him shining out through the little worn webbin' of flesh he had on, the match for a flame that's in one of the Chinese lanterns you'd see made of paper. Using up the whole of his body, that's what the soul of him was – convertin' the flesh of it bit by bit into soul till hardly a tittle of body was left to put in the ground. You could lift the whole with a finger.'

'Now, aren't ye the gifted man?' The words seemed to break, of themselves, out of Constable Duffy. Rapt with the view of entire new worlds of thought, and the feel of new powers for tackling them, Duffy gazed open-lipped and wide-eyed at Farrell the giver.

Farrell's face acknowledged, with no touch of wicked pride, this homage to truth. *Non nobis, Domine.* Austere, sacerdotal, Farrell inspected the second enraptured proselyte. Then he went on, his eyes well fixed on some object or other far out on the great bog's murmurous waste – the wilfully self-mesmerising stare of the mystic far gone. 'The body's the real old curse. Not a thing in the world but it's kept out of being the grand thing it's got the means to be

[145]

if it hadn't a hunk of a body always holding it back. You can't even have all the good there is in a song without some old blether of words would go wrong on your tongue as likely as not. And in Ireland the glory an' wonder that's sent by the will of God to gladden the heart of a man has never got shut till this day of sour old mashes of barley and malt and God alone knows what sort of dish-washin's fit to make a cow vomit, or poisons would blister half the lining off the inside of an ass.'

Constable Duffy was no man of words. But just at this moment he gained his first distinct view of philosophy's fundamental distinction between matter and form; the prospect so ravished his whole being that as he handed in the drained tumbler to Farrell he murmured in a kind of pensive ecstasy, 'Hurroosh to your soul!' and for a long time afterwards was utterly lost in the joys of contemplation.

Constable Boam's revisionary interest in paradise had now matured. While Farrell ministered to Boam, the grapes of the new wine of thought began abruptly to stammer through the lips of the sergeant. 'Aye! Every man has a pack of old trash discommodin' his soul. Pitaties and meal and the like – worked up into flesh on the man. An' the whole of it made of the dirt in the fields, a month or two back! The way it's a full barrow-load of the land will be walking on every two legs that you'd see shankin' past! It's what he's come out of. And what he goes back into being. Aye, and what he can't do without having, as long as he lasts. An' yet it's not he. An' yet he must keep a fast hold on it always, or else he'll be dead. An' yet I'll engage he'll have to be fighting it always – it and the sloth it would put on the grand venomous life he has in him. God help us, it's difficult.' Along the mazy path that has ever followed in the wake of Socrates the sergeant's mind slowly tottered, clinging at each turn to some reminiscence of Farrell's golden words, as a child makes its first adventurous journey on foot across the wide nursery floor, working from chair to chair for occasional support.

'Sorra a scrap of difficulty about it,' Farrell assured him, 'once you've got it firm set in your mind that it's all an everlastin' turnin' of body into soul that's required. All of a man's body that's nothing at all but body is nothing but divvil. The job is to cut a good share of it right out of you, clever and clean, an' then to inspirit the whole of the bit you have left with all the will and force of your soul till it's soul itself that the whole has become, or the next thing to the whole, the way the persons that lay you out after you die and the soul has quitted would wonder to see the weeny scrap that was left for anybody to wake. You could take anything that there is in the world and go on scourin' and scourin' away at the dross it has about it and so releasin' the workin's of good

till you'd have the thing that was nine parts body and one part soul at the start changed to the other way round, aye and more. By the grace of God that's the work I've been at in this place. Half-way am I now, as you can see for yourselves, to transformin' the body of any slushy old drink you'd get in a town into the soul of all kindness an' joy that our blessed Lord put into the water the good people had at the wedding. Nothin' at all to do but walk straight on, the way I was going, to work the stuff up to the pitch that you'd not feel it wettin' your throat, but only the love of God and of man an' the true wisdom of life, and comprehension of this and of that, flowin' softly into your mind. Divvil a thing stood in me way, save only' – here the mild-hearted fanatic stooped for a moment from the heights where his spirit abode to note with a wan smile of indulgence a little infirmity of mankind's – 'a few of the boys do be lying around in the bog, the way they have me worn with the fear they'd lap the stuff hot out of the tub and be killed if I'd turn me back for one instant.'

'They'll quit, from this out,' the sergeant said, with immense decision. 'I'll not have any mischievous trash of the sort molestin' a man at his work.'

'Ow, it's a wonderful country!' Constable Boam breathed to himself. The words had been rising to Boam's Cockney lips at almost every turn of affairs since his landfall at Kingstown. Now they came soft and low, soft and low. A peace passing all understanding had just invaded the wondering Englishman's mind.

Let not the English be tempted to think that by no other race can a law be dodged for a long time without scandal. Neither the sergeant nor either man of his force was ever a shade the worse for liquor that summer. To Tom's priestly passion for purging more and yet more of the baser alloys out of the true cult there responded a lofty impulse, among the faithful, to keep undeflowered by any beastlike excess the magical garden of which he had given them the key.

For it was none of your common tavern practice to look in at Tom's when the loud afternoon hum of the bees was declining reposefully towards the cool velvety playtime of bats and fat moths. All that plays and the opera, lift of romance and the high, vibrant pitch of great verse are to you lucky persons of culture; travel, adventure, the throwing wide open of sudden new windows for pent minds to stare out, the brave stir of mystical gifts in the heart, gleams of enchanting light cast on places unthought of, annunciatory visits of that exalting sense of approach to some fiery core of all life, watch-tower and power-house both, whence he who attains might see all manner of things run radiantly clear in their courses and passionately right. The police did not offer this account of their spiritual sensations at Tom's, any more than the rest of Gartumna did. But all this, or a vision of this, was for mankind to enjoy as it took its ease on the crumbling heaps of dry turf by the still, what time the inquisitive owls were just beginning to float in soundless circles overhead. From some dull and chilly outer rim of existence each little group of Tom's friends would draw together towards a glowing focus at which the nagging 'No,' 'No,' 'No' of life's common hardness was sure to give place to the benedictive 'Yes,' 'Yes,' 'O yes' of a benignly penetrative understanding of earth, heaven, and everything else. Who such a beast as to attempt to debauch the delicate fairy conducting these mysteries? Too good to imperil, they seemed, besides, too wonderful to end. Dust, all the same, hath dimmed Helen's eyes, which seemed to so many people as if their light could not go out.

All revolutions, some pundits say, are, at bottom, affairs of finance. And Mrs Burke had diagnosed truly. Tom bore within him the germ of that mortal illness of giving away all before him. His reign in all hearts at Gartumna resembled that of the Roi Soleil over France, both in the measureless glory of its meridian and in the fundamental insolvency of its afternoon. He had always given the work of his hands, to the worthy, free and without price. The fitness to receive was all; something sacramental about the consumption of his latest masterpiece by small, close-drawn parties of beautiful souls made the passing of coin at such seasons abhorrent to Tom. 'Would you have me keep a shebeen?' he had indignantly asked, when the sergeant made a stout, shamefaced effort to pay. So from day to day they kept up an urbane routine, month after month. Tom would always proffer the squat glass with a shy, tentative gesture; this made it clear that in the sight of God, so to speak, no such freedom had ever been taken, or thought of, before. The sergeant would always accept in the jocose, casual tone of a martinet making one playful and really quite absurd exception to his rules, the case being one which, anyhow, cannot recur, so that there need be no uneasiness about setting up a precedent now. But all summers end, and urbanity butters no parsnips.

[148]

The brownness of later August was deepening round Tom's place of research before he saw that the thing couldn't go on as it was. That evening, when the day's tide of civilian beneficiaries had tactfully receded from the still, and the police, their normal successors, had laid rifle and helmet aside, Tom held up his dreadful secret from minute to minute while the grey moth of twilight darkened on into brown moth-coloured night. He tried to begin telling, but found he couldn't trust both his voice and his face at the same time. As soon as his face could no longer be clearly seen he worked up a prodigious assumption of calm and said to the three monumental silhouettes planted black on their three plinths of turf, 'I'm ruined! Apt you'll be to find me quit out of the place if you come back in two days or three.'

The sergeant leapt off his plinth, levered up by the shock; 'God help us!' he said. 'What wild trash are you just after gabbing?'

'Me fortune's destroyed,' Tom pursued. His face had crumpled up with distress as soon as he began; but the kind darkness hid that: his voice was in fairly good preservation. 'I borrowed the full of the worth of me holding to get – ' and no doubt he was going on, 'get along with the work I'm at here,' but felt, perhaps, that this would not be quite the thing, considering. So he broke off and said only, 'The back of me hand to the Jew mortgagee that's foreclosin'.'

'God help us!' again said the sergeant. 'And we drinking the creature out of house and home a good while back! Men! –' He abruptly stiffened all the muscles of Duffy and Boam with the cogent parade voice that braces standing-easy into standing-at-ease. Then he thought for a moment. O, there was plenty to think of. Tom, the decent body, put out of his farm by the sheriff. Police aid, no doubt, requisitioned. The whole district, perhaps, in a hullabaloo, like all those around it. The Garden of Eden going straight back to prairie. He must be firm. 'Men,' he resumed, 'are we standin' by to see a man ruined that's done the right thing by ourselves? I'll engage it's a mod'rate share only of cash he'll require to get on in peace with his work. An' the three of us unmarried men, with full pay and allowances!'

The heart of the ancient and good-natured people of England aligned itself instantly with the chivalrous spirit of the Gael. 'Thet's right, sawgeant,' said the Constable Boam.

Constable Duffy's range of expression had not the width to cover fully the whole diversity of life. He ejaculated, 'Hurroosh to your souls! Five shillin's a week.'

'Sime 'ere,' subjoined Boam.

'Mine's ten,' said Maguire, 'I've got me rank to remember.'

So swiftly and smoothly may any man's business pass, with seeming success,

[149]

into a small limited company. Farrell, the innocent Farrell, took heart afresh and toiled on at the disengagement of Bacchus, the actual godhead, from out his too, too solid coatings of flesh. The force stilled the first wild fears of its heart and felt it was getting good value for its money – a quiet beat for the body, and for the soul an ever open line of communication with the Infinite. Through all Gartumna a warning shudder had run at the first crisis. Now the world seemed safe again; the civilian lamb lay down once more beside the three large lions of the law, dreaming it to be enough that these were no man-eaters. Children all, chasing a butterfly farther and farther into the wilds, under a blackening sky. While they chased, the good old Resident Magistrate, Ponting, was dying of some sudden internal queerness he had, he that had never done harm to a soul if looking the other way could prevent it. And into Old Ponto's seat was climbing a raging dragon of what a blind world calls efficiency.

Major Coburn, came, in fact, of that redoubtable breed of superdragons, the virtuous, masterful, hundred-eyed cavalry sergeants who carve their way to commissions somewhat late in their careers. Precise as some old maids of exemplary life, as fully posted up in the tricks of the crowd that they have left as a schoolboy turned by magic into a master, they burn with a fierce clear flame of desire to make up the enjoyable arrears of discipline that they might, under luckier stars, have exercised in their youth.

He sent for Sergeant Maguire. Quin, the district inspector – quite enough of an Argus himself without extra prompting – was there when the sergeant marched into the major's room. To outward view at this moment Maguire was fashioned out of first-rate wood. Within, he was but a tingling system of apprehensions. First, with gimlet eyes the two superiors perforated his outer timbers in numerous places, gravely demoralising the nerve centres within. When these exploratory borings had gone pretty far the crimelessness of Gartumna was touched upon – in a spirit of coarse curiosity far, far from felicitation.

Maguire faintly propounded the notion that keeping the law was just a hobby rife among the wayward natives.

'They're queer bodies,' he said in conclusion.

No fantasy like that could be expected to weigh up with a new broom possessed with its first fine passion for sweeping. 'Don't tell *me*,' the major snapped. His voice vibrated abominably with menace. 'You know as well as I do, sergeant, the sort of a squadron it is where a man's never crimed.' He paused, to let this baleful thrust tell its tale in the agonised sergeant's vitals. Then he went on, 'And you know what it means,' and again he paused and the four gimlet eyes resumed their kindly task of puncturing him at assorted points.

To Maguire's previous distresses was now added the choice mortification which always attends the discovery that you have been firing off an abstract and friarly morality at heavily armour-plated men of the world. With no loss of penetrative power, the major continued, 'Screening – that's what it means. Sergeants who need the stripes taking off them – that's what it means. Go back to your duty and see to it.'

Sergeant Maguire withdrew.

'He'd not comperhend. He'd not comperhend,' the sergeant despairfully told himself, over and over again, as he legged back the four miles to Gartumna under the early-falling September dew. If only the darkened mind of Major Coburn *could* gain understanding! Anybody on earth, you might think, if he had any wit at all to know good from bad, must see that this was a case in a thousand – that here, if ever in man's history, the spirit which giveth life was being borne down by the letter that killeth. But that body Coburn – ! Maguire had been a soldier: he knew those middle-aged rankers. 'Shut-headed cattle!' he groaned to himself. 'No doin' anything with them.' The dew was quite heavy. Sundown, autumn, and all that was best in the world going the way of honeysuckle and rose.

It seemed next morning as if that summer's glowing pomp of lustrous months were taking its leave with a grand gesture of self-revival on the eve of extinction, as famous actors will bend up every nerve in order to be most greatly their old selves on the night of farewell. Midsummer heat was burning again, and the quicksilvery haze shimmered over the bog when Maguire went out alone to see Farrell, just as the sergeant remembered it on the day when the scorched air from the furnace first showed him the still. Farrell, a little leaner now, a little less natty in his clothes, a little more absent-eyed with the intensity of a single absorption, raised from his work the patiently welcoming face of genius called away by affairs of this world from its heavenly traffic with miracles.

'All destroyed, Tom,' the sergeant said quickly. The longer he waited to bash in the unsuspecting up-turned face of Farrell's child-like happiness the more impracticable would it have grown. 'The glory,' he added by way of detail, 'is departed entirely.'

Farrell stared. He did not yet take it in well enough to be broken.

'It's this devastatin' divvil,' the sergeant went on, 'that they've sent us in lieu of Old Ponto – God rest his kind soul!'

Farrell did not seem to have even heard of that sinister accession. They say there were Paris fiddlers who fiddled right through the French Revolution and did not hear about the Bastille or the Terror. Live with the gods and deal with the Absolute Good, and Amurath's succession to Amurath may not excite you.

'God help the man – can't he see he's destroyed?' Fretful and raw from a

night of wakeful distress, the sergeant spoke almost crossly, although it was for Tom that he felt most sorely in all that over-shadowed world.

The worker in the deep mine whence perfection is hewn peered, as it were, half-abstractedly up the shaft.

The disorganised sergeant veered abruptly all the way round from pettishness to compunction. 'Dear knows,' he said, 'that it's sorry I am for ye, Tom.' He collected himself to give particulars of the catastrophe. 'A hustlin' kind of a body,' he ended, 'et up with zeal till he'd turn the grand world that we have into a parcel of old rags and bones and scrap iron before you could hold him at all. An' what divvil's work would he have me be at, for a start, but clap somebody into the jug, good, bad, or indifferent? *Now* do ye see? There isn't a soul in the place but yourself that does the least taste of a thing that any court in the wide world could convict for. What with you and the old priest and the new, and the old colonel below, you've made the whole of the people a very fair match for the innocent saints of God. An' this flea of a creature you couldn't even trust to be quiet an' not stravadin' out over the bog by himself like a spy, the way he'd soon have the whole set of us supping' tribulation with a spoon of sorrow.'

Farrell subsided on one of the seat-like piles of sunned peat. The fearful truth had begun to sink in. He sat for a while silent, tasting the bitter cup.

The heat that day was a wonder. Has anyone reading this ever been in the Crown Court of Assizes when three o'clock on a torrid dog-day comes in the dead vast and middle of some commonplace murder case, of poignant interest to no one except the accused? Like breeze and bird and flower in the song, judge and usher, counsel and witnesses, all the unimperilled parties alike 'confess the hour'. Questions are slowly thought of by the Bar and languidly put; the lifeless answers are listlessly heard; motes of dust lazily stirring in shafts of glare thrown from side windows to help to drowse you as though they were poppy seeds to inhale; all eyes, except one pair, are beginning to glaze; the whole majestic machine of justice seems to flag and slow down as if it might soon subside into utter siesta, just where it is, like a sun-drugged Neapolitan pavior asleep on his unfinished pavement. Only the shabby party penned in the dock is proof against all the pharmacopœia of opiates. Ceaselessly shifting his feet, resettling his neckcloth, hunting from each sleepy face to the next for some gleam of hope for himself, he would show, were anyone there not too deeply lulled to observe, how far the proper quality and quantity of torment is capable of resisting the action of nature's own anodynes.

Out in the bog a rude likeness of that vigil of pain, set amidst the creeping peace of the lotus, was now being staged. Under the rising heat of that tropical day the whole murmurous pulse of the bog, its flies and old bees, all its audible infestation with life seemed to be sinking right down into torpor while Sergeant Maguire's woebegone narrative dribbled off into silence and Tom came to the last of his hopeless questions. Questions? No; mere ineffectual sniffings among the bars of the closed cage of their fate. They both lay back on the warm turf, some ten feet apart, Tom staring up blankly straight into the unpitying blue while the sergeant stuck it out numbly within the darkened dome of his helmet, held over his face, striving within the rosy gloom of that tabernacle to gather up all his strength for the terrible plunge.

The plunge had to come. The sergeant rose on one elbow. He marshalled his voice. 'There's the one way of it, Tom,' he got out at last. 'Will you quite out of this and away to the States before I lose all me power to keep a hand off you?'

Farrell partly rose, too. His mind had not yet journeyed so far as the sergeant's along the hard road.

'I'll make up the fare from me savings,' the sergeant said humbly.

Farrell turned upon him a void, desolate face. The sergeant hurried on: 'The three of us down below will clear up when you're gone. An' we'll sling the still for you into the bog-hole. Aye, be sections, will we. An' everything.'

Farrell seemed to be eyeing at every part of its bald surface the dead wall of necessity. That scrutiny ended, he quietly said, 'Me heart's broke,' and lay back again flat on the peat. So did the sergeant. Nothing stirred for a while except for the agonized quiver and quake of the burnt air over the homely drain-pipe chimney of Tom's moribund furnace.

The sergeant wangled a day's leave of absence to go down to Queenstown the day Farrell sailed for New York. Farrell, absently waving a hand from some crowded lower deck of the departing ship, was a figure of high tragic value. The sergeant came away from the quay with his whole spirit laid waste –

altruistic provinces and egoistic alike; his very soul sown with salt. He had been near the centre of life all the summer and felt the beat of its heart; now he was somewhere far out on its chill, charmless periphery – 'As the earth when leaves are dead.' He had not read Shelley. Still, just the same thing.

'I've done my duty,' he said in an almost God-cursing tone as the three of them sat in the tin hut that night, among ashes, and heard the hard perpetual knock of the rain on the roof, 'an' I've done down meself.'

'Aye, and the whole of us,' Constable Duffy lamented, not meaning reproach, but sympathy only; just his part in the common threnody, antiphone answering unto phone.

Constable Boam had a part in it, too: ''Eaven an' 'Ell, 'Eaven an' 'Ell' – he almost chanted his dreary conspectus of their vicissitudes. 'Ow! a proper mix-up! Gord! it's a wonderful country!'

Nothing more was heard of Farrell. He may have died before he could bring back into use, beside the waters of Babylon, that one talent which 'twas death to hide. Or the talent itself may have died out in his bosom. Abrupt terminations have ere now been put to the infinite; did not Shakespeare dry up, for no visible cause, when he moved back to Stratford? All that we know is that Tom's genius can never have got into its full swing in the States. For, if it had, the States could never have gone to the desperate lengths that they afterwards did against the god of his worship.

© *from* FIERY PARTICLES, 1925

Civilization's Emblem

SANCHE DE GRAMONT

The bottle of wine is an emblem of French civilization. Because wine lives, ages, and changes in the bottle, it lends itself to personalization. It is attributed a soul, a temperament, qualities of wit and wisdom which are the fluid concentrate of a superior way of life. It is a way of life that can be sampled by uncorking a bottle. Something so prestigious must be beneficial, and the conviction is held that wine, like an old and loyal friend, can do no harm. It is the antidote for alcholism, the ray of sunshine in the trenches, the glass of morning cheer, the national and patriotic beverage, nourishing, antiseptic, and tonic.

More than that, the ability to appreciate wine is seen as a sign of general perspicacity, while, as Baudelaire said, someone who drinks only water must have a secret to conceal from his fellowman. Against the French tendency toward suspicion, wine provides a bond of fellowship, and against tightfistedness, something which it is natural to share. The measure of Voltaire's stinginess is that he gave his guests *vin ordinaire* and kept Corton for himself. On the one

hand the qualities of the wine – delicacy, finesse, and continuous excellence – are transferred to the people who made it. On the other, the qualities of the country are attributed to the wine, so that each bottle is said to be the expression of a thousand years of history and a fertile and harmonious landscape. Frenchmen have always found in wine qualities which defy analysis of its ingredients – Pasteur found philosophy, Montaigne wit, Baudelaire inspiration that turned a mole into an eagle, and Montesquieu a way to spur love. The role of wine has not changed since the Gothic cathedrals were built; it is still sacramental.

© *from* THE FRENCH, 1969

The Plaint of a Frenchwoman in an English Hospital
(WORLD WAR ONE)

STEPHEN GWYNN

They bid me eat; – I am too tired for food;
Yet if I were at home, we have a wine,
Valiant and generous, that quickly could
Scatter this wretched listlessness of mine.

Grandfather bottled it; yet, strong and bright
As fresh blood flowing after all these years,
It drowns in rich effusion of delight
All that might otherwise be steeped in tears.

The vineyard plot is walled, and all about
Peach-trees are trained, wherever the sun reaches,
For vineyard wisdom holds beyond a doubt
That wine draws influence from neighbouring peaches.

VINTAGE TALES

When the green clusters have begun to form,
Peach-blossom's scent already fills the air,
And when the purpling skins feel autumn warm,
The breath of ripened peach is everywhere.

Close packed like honeycomb, along each range,
Each bunch seeks help to plump its lovely shape
And, neighboured as they are, it would be strange
If their juice tasted only of the grape.

This consecrated spot, the wine it yields,
Part of our blood almost, our very life,
What of them now? since in our cherished fields
The stranger lords it, victor in the strife.

My father keeps (alas! should I say, kept?)
The precious store in some close hidden place,
Yet who can tell but treachery has crept
In, to work profanation and disgrace.

If so, what alien lout swills that rich spoil?
Are vines supplanted by some vulgar crop
Wrecking the balanced finish of a soil
Tended through generations without stop?

I know not; only this I know – our wine
Had such a sovereign excellence and power
That no fatigue, no care with which men pine,
Could last against it for a single hour.

May God preserve that vineyard to its use –
Or may He smite with an unsparing hand
Whatever baseness intervenes to loose
The sacred tie between us and our land.

© *from the magazine of* THE INTERNATIONAL WINE AND FOOD SOCIETY,

Vivandière

JAMES LAVER

THE men of the French Revolutionary armies began by wearing whatever garments they could lay their hands on, but their woman auxiliaries and camp-followers soon began to fancy themselves in uniform – if 'uniform' is the word. An engraving exists showing a *cantinière** in the early 1790s. Her outfit consisted of a tight-fitting but *décolleté* tunic adorned with many small buttons and piped in red, with small, turned-up red cuffs. With this she wore an ankle-length blue skirt and the *bouffant* fichu familiar to us in pictures of such heroines of the Revolution as Charlotte Corday.

Successful looting soon enabled the Revolutionary soldiers to improve their attire. The women camp-followers shared in this increasing prosperity; and a contemporary writer feels able to remark that, 'being a *cantinière* is a *beau métier*.

*Military historians distinguish between the *vivandière* who followed the troops in their campaigns and the *cantinière* who stayed in barracks; but in practice the two terms are often treated as interchangeable.

[159]

These ladies usually start by following some soldier who has inspired tender sentiments in their hearts, and they begin by marching along on foot with a small barrel of brandy at their girdle. A week later, someone has found them a horse which carries not only the rider but casks, cheeses and sausages on each side, before and behind, and cleverly arranged to balance the load.

'Before a month is out, the horse has been exchanged for a waggon with two horses, full of provisions of every kind, proof of the growing prosperity of their enterprise....

'It is comical to see these ladies dressed in robes of velvet and satin found by the soldiers and exchanged for a few glasses of brandy. The rest of their toilet is not in harmony, for hussar boots or a police cap complete it in a fashion grotesque enough. Imagine a woman thus clad, astride a horse flanked by two enormous panniers, and you will have an idea of the bizarre appearance thus presented.'

Under Napoleon, armies became more professional and the idea was born of allocating a certain number of *vivandières* to each regiment and of clothing them in a version of the regimental uniform. What a field was thus opened to the military tailors, and with what enthusiasm they responded, reaching the limit of exuberance under the Second Empire! Here was no question of the drab monotony of modern military costume. There were grenadiers and *voltigeurs*, guards and troops of the Line, *sapeurs* and *chasseurs* and *zouaves*: and all that was only the infantry. It was in the cavalry that the designers really let themselves go, with cuirassiers, guides and *chasseurs à cheval*, hussars and lancers and heavy dragoons, not to mention the artillery and the engineers, in a whole range of fantastic habiliments.

The most splendid were, naturally, the *vivandières* of the Guards. In the first place, there were more of them, for the regulations allowed twenty for each regiment of grenadiers and *voltigeurs*, the Line regiments having to make do with a smaller number. Also, the Guards had higher pay and were therefore more able to indulge in what a contemporary calls, '*les douceurs de la cantine*'. It was a fine sight, he says, to see the *vivandières* of the Guards, in brilliant uniforms, marching proudly in step and, if they were not all pretty, they all had a certain *chic*.

One of the most picturesque of the uniforms was that of the *vivandières* attached to the Zouaves de la Garde. The costume is described as dazzling, '*tout soutaché de jaune*'... 'On the head is a red cap round which is rolled a white turban striped with yellow silk, the jonquil-coloured tassel falling gracefully on the shoulder. A blue Zouave jacket with yellow trimmings covers the oriental waistcoat adorned with little round gilded buttons. A girdle of azure silk encircles the waist and the costume is completed by a royal blue skirt with three rows of yellow silk at the bottom and partly covered by a little black apron, baggy red Zouave trousers and white gaiters. At the left side she wears a miniature oriental sabre.'

In similar fashion the uniform of all the *vivandières* echoed that of the regiments to which they were attached. The artillery women wore busbies with a white and red cockade, those of the *sapeurs* a cocked hat with a red and yellow plume. And it was in such accoutrements that they actually served in the field.

The height of absurdity was reached by the projected uniform of the *vivandières* of the Cent-Gardes, or more properly the '*Escadron des Cent-Gardes à cheval*, forming part of the Garde Impériale. It was decided that this *élite* body should be *doté d'une cantinière* and much thought was given to devising a suitable costume. It was to consist of a blue tunic with knee-length panniers with scarlet revers. Under the tunic was a white skirt bordered with gold, and white cloth breeches fitting into knee-high boots. The bodice of cloth of silver, and adorned with gold buttons, was made to resemble a cuirass, but with a very narrow waist. The helmet was silver and gold with a white mane and a red cockade. White gloves and the obligatory little barrel of cognac completed the outfit.

This gorgeous uniform was worn by *la baronne* Verly at a ball at the Tuileries in order that the Emperor and Empress might judge the effect. They were presumably delighted but unfortunately '*par suite de raisons budgétaires*' it was decided that the Cent-Gardes should not have a *cantinière* after all. So this '*magnifique tenue fut l'unique confectionnée*'. The *baronne* Verly was the only woman who ever wore it.

The British Army never had any uniformed *vivandières* but the Piedmontese Army copied the French alongside whom it fought at Magenta and Solferino. Indeed it was in the Italian Army, modelled on that of Piedmont, that the *vivandières* lasted longest, not being finally abolished until 1920. The services they rendered – or some of them, at any rate – have now been taken over by official organizations. The N.A.A.F.I. is no doubt more efficient, but its women are hardly so dashingly dressed as the *vivandières* of the Second Empire.

© *from* THE COMPLEAT IMBIBER 9, 1967

Bedside Manners

JOHN TIMBS

Dr. George Fordyce, the anatomist and chemical lecturer, was accustomed to dine every day, for more than twenty years, at Dolly's chop-house, in Queen's Head Passage, Paternoster Row. His researches in comparative anatomy had led him to conclude that man, through custom, eats oftener than nature requires, one meal a day being sufficient for that noble animal, the lion. He made the experiment on himself at his favourite dining-house, and, finding it successful, he continued the following regimen for the above term of years.

At four o'clock, his accustomed dinner hour, he entered Dolly's chop-house, and took his seat at a table always reserved for him, on which were instantly placed a silver tankard full of strong ale, a bottle of port-wine, and a measure containing a quarter of a pint of brandy. The moment the waiter announced him, the cook put a pound-and-a-half of rump-steak on the grid-iron; and on the table some delicate trifle, as a *bonne bouche*, to serve until the steak was ready. This delicacy was sometimes half a broiled chicken, sometimes a plate of fish; when he had eaten this, he took a glass of his brandy, and then proceeded to devour his steak. We say devour, because he always ate as rapidly as if eating for a wager. When he had finished his meat, he took the remainder of his brandy, having, during his dinner, drunk the tankard of ale, and afterwards the bottle of port.

The Doctor then adjourned to the Chapter Coffee-house, in Paternoster Row, and stayed while he sipped a glass of brandy and water. It was then his habit to take another at the London Coffee-house, and a third at the Oxford, after which he returned to his house in Essex Street, to give his lecture on chemistry. He made no other meal till his return the next day, at four o'clock, to Dolly's.

Dr. Fordyce's intemperate habits sometimes placed his reputation, as well as the lives of his patients, in jeopardy. One evening he was called away from a drinking-bout, to see a lady of title, who was supposed to have been taken suddenly ill. Arrived at the apartment of his patient, the Doctor seated himself by her side, and having listened to the recital of a train of symptoms, which appeared rather anomalous, he next proceeded to examine the state of her pulse. He tried to reckon the number of its beats; the more he endeavoured to do this, the more his brain whirled, and the less was his self-control. Conscious of the cause of his difficulty and in a moment of irritation, he inadvertently blurted out, 'Drunk, by Jove!' The lady heard the remark, but remained silent; and the Doctor having prescribed a mild remedy, one which he invariably took on such occasions, he shortly afterwards departed.

At an early hour next morning he was roused by a somewhat imperative message from his patient of the previous evening, to attend her immediately; and he at once concluded that the object of this summons was either to inveigh against him for the state in which he had visited her on the former occasion, or perhaps for having administered too potent a medicine. Ill at ease from these reflections, he entered the lady's room, fully prepared for a severe reprimand. The patient, however, began by thanking him for his immediate attention, and then proceeded to say how much she had been struck by his discernment on the previous evening; confessed that she was occasionally addicted to the error which he had detected; and concluded by saying that her object in sending for him so early was to obtain a promise that he would hold inviolably secret the condition in which he found her. 'You may depend upon me, madam,' replied Dr. Fordyce, with a countenance which had not altered since the commencement of the patient's story; 'I shall be silent as the grave.'

© *from* ENGLISH ECCENTRICS AND ECCENTRICITIES 1866

Confessions of a Bootlegger

JOSEPH WECHSBERG

My career as a bootlegger was criminally unspectacular but educationally rewarding. I never made the inner circle of Mr. Capone's henchmen, but I learned a few things about drinking.

The year was 1928, and I was the second violinist with the ship's orchestra on *La Bourdonnaise*, a rather decrepit Compagnie Générale Transatlantique vessel that was said not to be listed as an asset on the balance sheets of the company; maybe it was carried as a liability. *La Bourdonnaise* had neither a working schedule nor working lifeboats, her machines often broke down in moments of emotional stress, and once we lost part of the only funnel we had. At night, when you came down to the state-rooms, something might cross your path that was too small to be a cat and too big to be a mouse. It wasn't a ladies ship. But when you are twenty-one and eager to see the world, minor inconveniences don't bother you. Not only did I see the world but I was getting paid for it; a thousand francs a month, and I got fine French food free of charge and lots of wines.

Unlike her celebrated sisters, the *France*, *Paris* and *Ile-de-France*, which sailed in a blaze of glory, gala and champagne from Le Havre, *La Bourdonnaise* made an unpublicised, shamefaced and totally unnoticed getaway from an open pier on the Quai des Chartrons in Bordeaux. She used to sail in the morning hours when decent people are asleep in Bordeaux. We members of the four-man ship's orchestra would take the night train from the Gare d'Orleans in Paris which got us into Bordeaux in the pale, dry-sherry light of dawn. We piled into an old, enormous and ramshackle taxicab with our instruments, Maurice's two 'celli, one with a detachable back, the large and small drums, our luggage, piles of sheet music including the latest Broadway hits, 'Ain't She Sweet' and 'Singing in the Rain', and odds-and-ends. The driver would curse, and Maurice, our 'cello player and *chef d'orchestre*, would appease him by telling him to stop in front of a *bistro* where they started off the young day with a couple of glasses of Pernod.

The shabby waterfront buildings on the Quai des Chartrons were a depressing sight. Little did I know then that they housed the offices of *l'aristocratie du bouchon*, the rich Bordeaux brokers and shippers, and that under the cobblestone street large cellars extended, piled up high with a magnificent roll-call of claret vintages. I didn't even know what a vintage was. I'd been brought up in Czechoslovakia, a beer democracy, and when I'd come to Paris in 1927, I was able to afford only *pinard*, the Frenchman's *vin ordinaire*. We were always swimming in *pinard*, when Maurice was around. He liked wine that had plenty of things in it – tannin, acid alcohol and pieces of cork – which looked like the *chabrot*, the wine soup that the cellar-workers in Bordeaux eat from barrel tops. Wine, Maurice used to say, was to be chewed and swallowed, not to be tasted and sipped. After the third bottle, he said, it didn't matter any more. The trouble was that after the second bottle his hands began to tremble, which didn't bother us in the *presto* passages of Rossini's 'William Tell' overture but created embarrassment during the slow *legato* phrases in the 'Manon' (Massenet) fantasy. If you happened to travel on *La Bourdonnaise* in the summer of 1928, you may have been bothered by the orchestra playing 'William Tell' three times in a row. The next day Maurice would get on the wagon; that is, he would add one-quarter of water to three-quarters of *pinard*, but that was as far as he would go. He was the most pleasant alcoholic anonymous I've ever known; he had a heart of gold and his happiness was infectious. Ever since, I've been fond of wine-drinkers. I was less fond of Lucien, our first violinist, a smooth Frenchman subsisting almost entirely on Armagnac, and of our pianist, a White Russian from Vladivostok, who drank milk in his rare moments of exuberance and vodka during his prolonged attacks of depression. None of us would lower

[165]

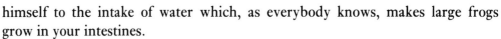

himself to the intake of water which, as everybody knows, makes large frogs grow in your intestines.

In those happy days we ship's musicians had no union cards, little discipline and no steady working hours to speak of. We mingled with the passengers, had two first-class state-rooms for ourselves and an empty one for our instruments, and ate our meals in the first-class dining-room prior to the service, in the company of precocious gnomes and dour Canadian ladies who were said to resent the sight of wine bottles on the tables. We had two bottles of wine apiece with each meal, called simply 'red' and 'white'. This was before the French legislature came up with the intricate *Appellation d'Origine* laws, so I couldn't tell you what was in the bottles; probably something that had arrived in Burgundy or Bordeaux after a long trip from the south of France in long trucks looking exactly like gasolene trucks. In fact, Maurice claimed that sometimes they mixed up the trucks and sent the wines in gasolene trucks, and he was able to discern the fine nuances in bouquet between, say, an oily round Shell and a not yet fully matured Mobiloil. That wouldn't bother him, as long as there was plenty of it. We never touched the white wines. Maurice said they were almost as dangerous as water. Made small frogs grow in your stomach. He would tell us to take the bottles down and store them under the beds.

I noticed other things on this trip. The first violinist, an expert chemist, skilfully diluted the contents of gin, rum, Scotch whisky, benedictine and cognac bottles which he bought at the crew's fifty per cent reduction from the second-class barman. (In those days of Honesty, it was 'second', not 'cabin' class.) The Vladivostok pianist raided the passengers' tables after each meal and brought the bottles down. It was a long trip, eleven days, by way of Vigo and Santander, where we embarked Spanish nuns and refugees from a late Inquisition, and Halifax, where we disembarked the wine-hating Canadian ladies. There were no Americans aboard; I suppose they never knew that our ship existed. We were never mentioned at the Transat headquarters in Rue Auber, Paris. Maurice had a theory that they wanted to pass us off as a disreputable Cunarder.

In the circumstances I was surprised that all people working aboard – stewards, cooks, *marins*, *femmes de chambre*, barmen – seemed to be in a happy frame of mind, and were fond of our ship. When I asked the second-class barman, a virtuoso with a heart of gold who diluted his cognacs and often offered me a glass of *brut* champagne which he charged to a tipsy passenger, why on earth he didn't work on the luxurious *Ile-de-France*, always crowded with millionaires, and what the French call *poules de luxe*, he winked at me and said, 'Are you kidding, *mon petit?*' I began to feel like the girl whose mother hadn't told her, but I kept my mouth shut, like President Coolidge.

A few hours before we arrived in New York, Lucien began to stack up the bottles in the empty cabin, which was used to park our instruments, while Maurice knocked down closets and arranged for a sort of makeshift bar. It was easy to take apart the cabin, since *La Bourdonnaise* was held together only by a few rusty nails and the happy spirit of its crew. The Vladivostok pianist swiped mouthwash glasses from nearby state-rooms. Maurice stored six bottles of horribly sweet *'gout Américain'* champagne in his second 'cello, the one with the detachable back that also contained his collection of interesting photographs.

We passed the French Line Pier 57, located at the foot of West Fourteenth Street, where the *Ile-de-France* was lying. Our foghorn greeted her but they didn't answer, ashamed of their shabby relations. The second-class barman spat over the railing and said something terrible. Our boat went up all the way to the last pier, at the foot of West Fifty-ninth Street, across from an ugly row of tall chimneys belonging to the municipal garbage disposal plant. There was an awful smell and the neighbourhood was depressing, with dirty streets and dirty mongrel dogs, but, on the other hand, said the barman, there was only one customs man at the gangway. At the *Ile-de-France* there were sometimes as many as ten, and armed police. Maurice said he didn't care about the neighbourhood; he had never set foot in America since Prohibition began. He was a man of unusual strength of character.

The customs man at the gangway seemed to be a friend of Maurice's, for he came to our state-room and was given a water-glass filled with Scotch whisky – from an undiluted bottle, I noticed with amazement. In the afternoon Maurice sent me to a drugstore in Columbus Circle with a list of telephone numbers. I was to dial and say, '*La Bourdonnaise* is here', or something to that effect. I couldn't say more anyway, since I knew only twenty-four English words, most of them not to be used over the telephone. I had no trouble though; the parties at the other end of the wire exclaimed hosannahs when I made my terse announcement. They had no difficulty in understanding my pitiful English. I went back to the ship. Our White Russian was just welcoming two straw-hatted, prosperous citizens who looked like, and were, millionaires. He winked at the customs man and said the gentlemen were friends of the musicians. The customs man nodded understandingly.

'Music makes friends all over the world,' he said sententiously. One of the millionaires laughed so hard he dropped his straw hat.

There were already about a dozen friends of music in our state-rooms. All looked prosperous and happy, and all had glasses in their hands. They sat on 'cello cases, beds, on the floor, and, if memory serves me right, two squatted, fully clothed, in the empty bathtub. Lucien washed out glasses in the wash-basin, and Maurice filled them and took in the money. Some friends of music seemed in an awful hurry to get drunk; they said they had to make the 5.16 for Westport. One who was said to be a president of something really big got red in his face and fell flat down on his stomach. I had to summon the ship's doctor, who shrugged and said, '*Ces pauvres types- ils ne savent pas boire.*' We brought the president back to life in no time by throwing a glass of water into his face and a cup of black coffee into his stomach. He opened his eyes and asked for something to make him fully awake, preferably gin. I indicated in delicate sign language that maybe he shouldn't drink any more, and he pointed at his stomach and said, 'Son, what you've got in here, no one can take away from you,' and then he began to cry. It was very pathetic. Maurice said 'Pro-hibition!' and spat out in contempt.

Some friends of music shook hands all round, paid and said goodbye, but before they were allowed to leave the cabins, Maurice made them rinse their mouths with a special mixture he had prepared, and each was given a coffee bean and asked to bite and chew it. Maurice would sniff at each man's breath and, if there was a trace of liquor, the man had to take a drink of milk. The presidents slapped our backs and told us we were their friends for ever and to come and see them any time. That made me feel good. I had hardly arrived in the United States and had already made so many friends among the country's presidents.

The customs man of the afternoon had been relieved by a tough-looking specimen who wasn't so tough, though, when he ate dinner with us later that night. Our *chef de cuisine* was a Provençal who would have put garlic even into his grandmother's berry wine. That night he'd made a *daube chaude à la Prov-ençale*, the memory of which still gives me slight indigestion. The tough customs man and a late friend of music, a double-chinned corporation president, drank Scotch whisky out of water-glasses during the whole meal. It seems they took a dim view of wine, a sissified beverage, and the president said, 'Whisky's the only thing that will go with everything, from apéritif to digestif'. Everybody exploded into laughter at this bit of alcoholic *savoir faire*. The president wasn't able to get down to the nearest taxi. We took him to an empty state-room where he slept it off. It was a busy night. We were washing glasses and re-plenishing our stocks for the morning when early friends of music would drop in for a quick one on the way back to their downtown offices, and they would probably come back in the afternoon.

'That's the beauty of being anchored up here where no one gets suspicious

like down there on the West Fourteenth Street pier,' Maurice said. I began to understand why the barman didn't want to work on the *Ile-de-France*.

Later, Maurice conducted an interesting physical experiment, letting a bottle of champagne dangle down on a line from the promenade deck. The way Maurice explained it you lowered the line, and the line came back again with a ten-dollar note tied to its end, or maybe I have it wrong and the ten-dollar bill came up *before* the champagne was let down to the two men in the small boat there. I asked Maurice whether it wouldn't hurt the champagne when it touched sea-water, and he said, *au contraire*, it would improve the sweet champagne when it got 'neutralised' by the dirty salt-water. As you can see, Maurice was also something of a basic chemist. He always told me never to touch sweet champagne or that absurd concoction called 'dry sauternes', and never to mix caviare with onions or *anything* with margarine. That was sound advice which I've never forgotten.

When *La Bourdonnaise* left New York, we put back the closets and beds, threw the empty bottles out of the port-hole and divided the proceeds. My part was over five times my monthly salary as musician. At lunch the next day, Maurice slapped a fifty-dollar bill on the table and said everybody could order his favourite bottle, he was going to pay for it. The Vladivostok pianist ordered milk and vodka, this being his mixed-up day; Lucien got the most expensive bottle of Armagnac, and I chose a bottle of something called Château Lafite because I liked the bucolic picture on the label, showing an elegant château and people harvesting in front of it. My method of choosing wine according to the design of the label turned out to be right: Lafite-Rothschild is still one of my favourites, which I'll gladly take even in an off-year, thank you. My career as a bootlegger came to an end shortly thereafter when I was unfortunately transferred to the orchestra of the *Ile-de-France*, but I'll always remember my days on *La Bourdonnaise* which gave me a sound and basic alcoholic education. I still dislike sweet champagnes and wines misnamed 'dry sauternes', and I've become very fond of the châteaux of the Médoc, even including the ones that have no beautiful labels.

© *from* THE COMPLEAT IMBIBER 2, 1958

Love Potion

E. J. Kahn Jr

In South Africa and in Mexico, a young man may drink anything that comes to hand during the week, but when he takes his best girl out on a Saturday night, he treats her to a Coca-Cola. Or so say Coca-Cola people, whose observations, of course, are derived less from double-dating than from case-sale statistics. There is plenty of evidence that to Coca-Cola men the course of true love runs smoothest when it runs delicious and refreshing. In the company's advertisements, which try manfully to equate the beverage with 'the heart-thumping happiness of boy getting acquainted with girl', it is made explicit that boy who first gets Coke to girl gets girl, too. In private, Coca-Cola men tend to speak more bluntly. 'You want to know what makes Coke so romantic to so many people?' one of them once said to an acquaintance. 'Well, maybe that starry-eyed kid who lives next door to you was sitting in a drugstore booth with his girl one night, and maybe they were drinking Coke, and maybe while they were drinking that Coke was the first time that girl let that boy put his hand on her leg.'

© *from* THE BIG DRINK, 1960

Not the Real Thing...

DEREK COOPER

One of my favourite axioms about drink, filed in the daybook under the heading 'Messages, Inspirational', comes from the Vice-President for New Products and New Packaging of the Coca-Cola Corporation. 'It's the mystique,' he pronounced, 'that counts most in sales – what a drink gives to the soul rather than the body'.

What state a soul, bathed in a lifetime of carbonated pop, would manifest to St Peter is better left unimagined. Presumably, being incorporeal, it would not be pitted nor eroded as might the teeth. Perhaps Coca-Cola does give more to the soul than the body. Physically, it's a non-nutritious drink which makes you thirsty for more and its taste, although complex, could hardly be described as adult. And yet it has been as much a part of the American way of life in peace and war as Lil' Orphan Annie or the Ku Klux Klan. The Coca-Cola Corporation, which keeps a vault full of vice-presidents specialising in home-spun quotes, was even able to produce an executive who declaimed at the height of the south-east Asian involvement: 'When a soldier in Vietnam has a Coke it satisfies his need to identify with the American tradition and way of life. It reminds him of what he's fighting for.'

I've often wondered what it is about Coke that has made it the most widely drunk non-alcoholic drink in the world. Others wonder too. Izrail Iskovich Brekhman, professor at the Institute of Marine Biology in Vladivostok, in a recent dissertation on the effect of drugs, diet and pollution on health, claimed that in America one-fifth of a bottle of Coke per head per day (5,000 million dollars a year) was being downed and up to 85 per cent of hospital patients were constantly imbibing Coke and its rivals.

The Coca-Cola Corporation exports the flavouring syrups to 160 countries, where they are watered down and carbonated by local franchisees. The formula has certainly changed since the drink was invented by John S. Pemberton of Atlanta in 1886, in the days when the coca leaf and its stimulating properties were first being exploited. The current formula is known only to two executives (so folk myth relates), who never board the same plane.

Phosphoric acid, cola nut extract, vanillin, nutmeg, neroli, coriander, tartaric acid, caramel, caffeine, cinnamon, vegetable glycerin, lavender, extract of guarana, lime juice and citrus oil are believed to be variously present in the cola drinks, but one thing no cola contains today is even the slightest suggestion of cocaine. The Harrison Narcotics Act, which made cocaine illegal in 1914, also outlawed the most famous coca-wine tonic ever marketed, Vin Mariani à la Coca du Perou, the invention of a Corsican-born pharmacist, Angelo Mariani. He mixed extract of coca leaves with claret and dispensed it to a growing circle of *fin-de-siècle* enthusiasts in Paris. Toward the end of his life Mariani was to claim that 'Vin Mariani has never produced *cocainisme*, nor any other unpleasant effects', but it certainly had a high to which even the finest Médoc had never aspired.

Its popularity began in operatic circles, where it was soon discovered that a glass or two of Mariani's 'wine' relaxed the throat muscles like nothing ever known before. Even Pope Leo XIII endorsed the product and presented Mariani with a gold medal. Sarah Bernhardt drank it before every performance and was thrilled to find it on sale widely in New York and Chicago: 'It has, as always, largely helped to give me that strength so necessary in the performance of the arduous duties which I have imposed upon myself.'

Emile Bergerat, the littérateur, wrote: 'One glass of coca wine for an article and two glasses for an aquarelle – that's my dosage. But the real genius is at the bottom of the bottle.'

It was not only poets, painters and politicians who extended their range with

coca. When Louis Blériot flew from Calais to Dover in 1909 he took the precaution of loading a small flask of Vin Mariani for the historic 25-minute flight. 'And it was a great help. Its energetic action sustained me during the crossing of the Channel.' Mariani grew coca plants in his greenhouse at Neuilly more for the pleasure it gave him than for commercial purposes and, as he contemplated his growing fame and wealth, letters of gratitude flowed in by every post, 'Mariani, your wine is digestive, comforting and tonic,' wrote Edmond Rostand, author of *Cyrano de Bergerac*. 'I always have a bottle handy to my work-table.' Anatole France claimed that, in his experience, Mariani's wine 'spreads a subtle fire through the organism'.

In 1895, in a masterstroke of advertising, Mariani published the first volume of *Les Figures Contemporaines*, in which world leaders gratuitously provided him with a poem, a drawing, a phrase of music, depending on their artistic talents, in gratitude for the uplifting effect of the wine. Edison sent a photograph (not a phonograph), President McKinley a letter and H.G. Wells drew two Before and After cartoons: the first showing him looking rundown and miserable, the second, after a swig of the wine, remarkably bucked up.

Mariani became a universal hero. 'We no longer say Hail Mary,' blasphemed the dramatist Emile Fabre, 'but Hail Mariani'. The recipe for Mariani's particular *vinum cocae* died with him in 1914 and it suddenly stopped snowing in many an atelier and green room. The miracle drink purveyed for so long from 41, Bd Haussmann was no more. Secret Coca-Cola may be; narcotic never.

© *From* THE OBSERVER COLOUR MAGAZINE, 27 JULY 1980.

North of San Francisco

PETER DICKINSON

I was on that coast for seven shuttlecock days
   And even now I'm afraid to unpack my mind,
   Knowing that under the straining lid I will find
My thoughts in a random, undisentanglable maze,
   Crammed to a pellet – a Japanese paper flower
   Which you drop in water and watch expand by the hour.

Ah well. Click, click. This bottle has nosed to the top.
   Some oddments cling to it while I wriggle it clear:
   Friesians grazing a hillside as brown as beer;
A blue-gum grove that reeks like a chemist's shop;
   Three buzzards quartering the enormous calm;
   An orange butterfly, big as a child's spread palm.

North of San Francisco

Lunch on my one free day, my single chance
   To see beyond that clanging, self-conscious town.
   We found a dirt-road over a loping down
And sat in the sun, and munched, as if it were France –
   Paté and bread, and peaches, all of them fine,
   Washed down with this self-same bottle of local wine.

A Pinot Noir, black-purple, muscular. Pressed
   By monks, the label averred. A real surprise.
   Too good for a picnic, bullying exercise
On our city-fagged limbs. So we drove a few miles west
   And paddled solemnly (me in my early forties)
   In the booming ocean that so astonished stout Cortes.

© *from* THE COMPLEAT IMBIBER 10, 1969

Grandmother Clatterwick and Mr McGuffog:
a Story

MICHAEL GILBERT

When I qualified as a solicitor, one of the first clients I took on was Grandmother Clatterwick. I did so with some trepidation. I was a young lawyer and she was a formidable old lady, as tough and as straight as one of the whale-bone inserts in her own corsets. Surprisingly, we got on well together. My mother, who died in the same year as my father, had been her youngest and favourite daughter, and I think some of the affection washed off on to me. As the years went by it became a source of sadness to me to see her estate diminish. Not that there was any question of her sinking into poverty. Her husband, Herbert Clatterwick, had been a strange, silent man who had known nothing about anything except South American mining shares; but he had understood them well enough to make a comfortable fortune on the Stock Exchange, all of which was left to his widow, along with Hambone Manor and its park. Unfortunately the money was all unearned income, and as taxation bit into it more and more deeply, pieces of the park had to be sold, wings of the Manor shut off, and servants dismissed or not replaced.

In the end, Grandmother Clatterwick lived in the south wing, attended only by the faithful McGuffog, assisted by a couple of villagers who came up by day and did the cleaning and cooking.

McGuffog had started life at the Manor as gardener's boy, had graduated through the pantry to assistant butler, and was now butler, gardener, and handyman combined. When I went down, as I did from time to time, to talk business, and stayed the night, McGuffog would wait upon the two of us, through a ritual meal. After dinner he would bring the coffee into the drawing room, place a log or two on the fire, enquire whether anything else was wanted, and retire to the flat which had been fitted out for him in the stable block. There were, in fact, a dozen bedrooms he could have used in the house itself, but when the last of the resident servants left, my grandmother's sense of propriety would not allow her to sleep alone in the house with a man. She was seventy-five at the time.

All these thoughts and these memories of my grandmother were in my mind as we sat round the desk in my office that spring morning a week after her funeral.

The aunts were all there. Aunt Gertrude, a dry and intellectual spinster; Aunt Valerie, who had married Dr Moffat and produced two ghastly children called George and Mary, and Aunt Alexandra, who had married a Major Lumsden, and persuaded him to resign from his cavalry regiment to listen to her talk.

'*Why* did she leave no will?' asked Aunt Alexandra. 'You were her solicitor. It was surely your duty to see that she made one. Isn't that what lawyers are for?'

'Don't be absurd,' said Aunt Gertrude. 'As if anyone, let alone her own grandson, could have persuaded Mother to do anything she didn't wish to.'

'Does it make any difference?' asked Aunt Valerie. 'As I understand the law – you must correct me if I'm wrong, dear – her money is divided into four equal shares. Not that I mind for myself. I was thinking only of George and Mary.'

Aunt Gertrude cackled sardonically. It was well known in the family that Valerie excused any selfishness by passing it on, second-hand, to her revolting children.

I took over to prevent a fight. 'That's quite correct. The property passes to the children equally, *per stirpes*. That is to say . . .'

'No need to explain,' said Aunt Gertrude. 'I haven't forgotten the Latin I learnt at school,' and she shot a glance at her sisters which implied quite clearly that she suspected they had.

'How much will the estate amount to?' enquired Dr Moffat.

'It's difficult to say. Estate duty will account for a slice of it. And the Manor will have to be sold.'

'No one will give a penny for it,' said Aunt Gertrude. 'A rambling great place, in a shocking state of repair.'

'What about stocks and shares and things like that?' asked Aunt Valerie.

I said: 'I understand that Granny had been using capital quite a bit during recent years. She wouldn't have needed much since we bought her that annuity – that cost capital too, of course. But there must be quite a lot left. And although we may not get much for the Manor, there were one or two nice things in it. It's a couple of years since I've been down there, but I remember an attributed Morland in the drawing room. That was insured for £5,000. And I think there was an Etty, in the dining room.'

'I was rather more regular in my visits,' said Dr Moffat reprovingly.

'For George and Mary's sake,' said Aunt Gertrude under her breath.

'. . . And I was actually there a fortnight before her decease. It struck me that she had become somewhat eccentric. We had a good dinner, as usual, but what do you suppose we were offered to drink with it?'

We could none of us guess.

'A very large bottle of raspberry wine.'

I could hardly conceal my delight. My uncle is the complete wine snob. By this I mean that he reads books about wine, belongs to all the wine societies, has a cupboard full of wine lists and the catalogues of wine auctions, talks endlessly about vintages and *crus* – and has less taste and discernment than a camel. On one occasion when we had him to dinner I emptied a bottle of red wine, which I had bought for two francs fifty at a grocer's shop in France, into an old Château Margaux bottle which I happened to have, and received the warmest commendation of my choice. 'Superb bouquet, my boy. One can almost taste the violets in it.' I could visualise exactly his expression when offered a bottle of raspberry wine.

'Apparently,' said Aunt Valerie, 'she had been making quite a thing of it. McGuffog, who had been helping her to brew it, told us that she had more than two thousand bottles of it in the cellar.'

'Of raspberry wine?'

'Not all raspberry. There was raspberry, plum and turnip wine, blackcurrant and redcurrant cordial, and elder-flower champagne. And half a dozen other nauseating brews too, I don't doubt.'

Major Lumsden was a silent man, as anyone would be who was married to my Aunt Alexandra, but he had a kind heart. He said: 'Talking about that fellow McGuffog, are we going to do anything for him?'

'I was thinking about that,' I said. 'He looked after Granny for more than forty years. If I could have persuaded her to make a will, I'm sure she'd have left him something.'

'But she didn't make a will,' said Aunt Valerie sharply.

'All the same . . .' said the Major.

'As a matter of fact,' I said, 'I had a letter from McGuffog only this morning. I won't bother to read it all to you, although it's surprisingly well composed. . . .'

'He must be reasonably competent,' said Aunt Valerie. 'After all, he used to manage a very large household. Larger than any of *us* has had to deal with.'

'Quite so,' I said. 'Well, this is the passage that I wanted to read you: "I realise that Mrs Clatterwick didn't approve of will-making. She has often told me so. There couldn't therefore be any question of a legacy. However . . ."'

As I turned the page, I was aware of five pairs of eyes on me. One pair sardonic, one kindly, the other three frankly greedy.

'"It did occur to me to wonder whether the family would agree to me taking over the unused stock of home-made wine. I co-operated with Mrs Clatterwick in getting together what must, I venture to think, be a unique collection of vintages."'

'If *that's* all he wants,' said Aunt Valerie, striving to keep the relief out of her voice, 'I should be the first to agree.'

The others nodded. Major Lumsden said, 'Don't you think some sort of pension . . .' but was decisively overruled.

'All right,' I said, 'I'll tell him. He can store it in the old stable block. And I assume you'll let him keep on his flat until the house is sold?'

'If the people who buy the house have got an atom of sense,' said Aunt Gertrude, 'they'll take McGuffog on with the house. Servants like that don't grow on trees.'

The winding up of an intestate estate, particularly the estate of an old and secretive lady, is not a quick matter. But as the months slipped by, and the answers came in from banks and stockbrokers and insurance companies, I began to feel the first stirrings of unease. There was so much less in the estate than I had expected.

It was true, as I had told her daughters, that Grandmother Clatterwick had been nibbling into capital for years. But when I finally persuaded her to put £40,000 into a life annuity, this had ensured her an almost tax-free income in the high thousands. Enough, one would have thought, even for a Victorian old lady who liked to double the parson's stipend and to support charities with objects as diverse as the clothing of Esquimaux babies and the moral rearmament of Hottentot girls.

Moreover, when I had bought the annuity, I had made a very careful check of what money and securities were left, and the total was not far short of £20,000. Now, I could locate barely half of it.

Now assets cannot simply disappear. People talk about an inheritance melting away, as if it were a snowdrift when the sun comes out, but when brokers and bankers and agents keep accurate statements, and copies of those statements are sent to people whose job it is to understand them, the course of events is usually quite plain.

What seemed to have happened here was that my grandmother had sold off property and securities and had surrendered life policies, and the money she got for them had been credited to her current account at her bank. From there it had gone out, in very regular, substantial payments, to 'cash'. During the last two years of her life, these had never been less than £50, often as much as £100 a week.

On top of her annuity, these sums were wildly in excess of anything the old lady could have needed. So who had had them?

My first thoughts turned, I must confess, to Aunt Valerie. She, and her equally rapacious husband, had been assiduous in their attendance on Grandmother. At least once a month they had invited themselves down to Hambone Manor, sometimes taking George and Mary with them as an additional treat for their hostess. Had they, by pleading poverty, extracted a regular and secret tribute? I felt that they were quite capable of it; but that my grandmother was equally capable of saying 'No'.

Could she have been blackmailed? And, if so, who by, and on what score? Surely no more blameless life had ever gone into the books of the Recording Angel?

I was, incidentally, somewhat piqued by the fact that these transactions, many of which would have needed the attention of a solicitor, had not been referred to me, but must have been handled by a local firm. It almost seemed as though she had wanted to keep them secret.

All these speculations and suspicions were brought to a head when, about six months after my grandmother's rather sudden death, the agent sent me the catalogue of the contents of the Manor which he had prepared for auction. I rang him up at once.

'Why have you left out the Morland and the Etty?' I asked.

'I left them out,' said the valuer, 'because they weren't there.'

'Weren't there?'

'McGuffog sold them. About a year before Mrs Clatterwick died.'

It took a moment to get my breath back.

'*McGuffog* sold them?'

'On the old lady's instructions, no doubt.'

'No doubt,' I said, 'but it was McGuffog who arranged the sales?'

'I believe so, yes. The Morland wasn't signed, and it only fetched two thousand. The Etty went for one and a half.'

'And the money was paid to McGuffog?'

'So I understand.'

It was then that I decided that I must go down to Hambone Manor without delay.

Hambone Street lies in the miraculously still unravaged piece of Kent to the south of the A20. It has villages which still *are* villages, which possess things like village greens on which the local cricket team plays, village halls for the Women's Institute, and not fewer than three public houses for a population of four hundred and fifty. Lack of a rail service has helped to keep it the way it is, and I drove down by car, on a lovely autumn morning, when the leaves were just beginning to turn. I found the Manor in sad decline. The grass was uncut, the hedges were straggling, and there were unfilled potholes in the drive. This was disappointing. The estate had continued McGuffog's salary on the understanding that he did some work on the grounds. It looked as though he had fallen down on it.

However, there was someone in the house. Smoke was coming from one of the chimneys and the front door was open. I found Annie, one of the two dailies from the village, in possession. She had been told to keep the house clean and as dry as possible, and I could see she, at least, was making a job of it. When I asked her about McGuffog she looked startled.

'Didn't they tell you?' she said. 'He passed away. They should have let you know, sir. Certainly they should.'

'I'm terribly sorry,' I said. 'When did it happen?'

'Two weeks ago it was. They laid him to rest on Sunday. A *nice* service. Vicar's been very helpful, too. He left no family, you see. Only a cousin, or some such, who lives over in Essex. If you'd like a word with Mr Stacey, I saw his car in the yard. Likely he'll be over there now.'

I walked across to the stables and introduced myself to the Vicar, who was coming down the stairs which led to McGuffog's flat. He was a cheerful young man with the well-scrubbed face and no-nonsense look that theological colleges turn out nowadays. He said: 'I'm glad you're here. I thought of getting in touch with you. Not that there's much for a lawyer to do. All the stuff in the flat was borrowed from the house, you know. With Mrs Clatterwick's agreement, of course. But it belongs to her, not to McGuffog. Almost the only things he left were the clothes he stood up in. Oh, and the remains of the wine.'

'The remains?'

'He seems to have got rather fond of it. Rather too fond, perhaps.' The Vicar gave an unclerical chuckle. 'People in the village used to hear him singing. Fortunately they couldn't make out the words, so they assumed it was Gaelic.'

'*Can* you get drunk on raspberry wine?'

'I expect you can get drunk on anything, if you try hard enough. McGuffog certainly put his back into it. He took over nearly two thousand bottles of it . . .'

'Nineteen hundred and eighty-four,' said Annie who had joined us. 'I helped him store them in the hay racks in the stable. It took a whole afternoon.'

'When he died there were just about fifteen hundred left.'

I did some mental arithmetic. The period between my grandmother's death and McGuffog's was not much more than twenty weeks. Call it a hundred and fifty days. At three bottles a day he could just have done it.

Annie said, unexpectedly: 'I reckon he looked on it as a duty.'

We both stared at her. She blushed and then said, rather defiantly: 'Well, there's no harm in me telling you. They've both gone now. But they sometimes used to share a bottle in the evenings. I know, because I came back once and saw them. There was a bottle of raspberry wine on the table, and they were taking a glass each. I reckon they used to do it most evenings, when they were alone. Being home-made wine seemed to make it all right. It wasn't really *drinking*, you see.'

I saw exactly what she meant. If it had been real drink, it would have been an orgy. As it was elder-flower champagne or plum cordial, it was simply a charming, old-fashioned ritual. I said: 'I think it's a beautiful idea. You mean that McGuffog had such pleasant memories of these evenings with my grandmother that he thought it was his duty to finish off the whole stock rather than let it fall into the hands of uncaring outsiders.'

'Death cut him down before he could accomplish it,' said the Vicar. 'Sad.'

'Talking of outsiders – what have you done with the balance of the stuff?'

The Vicar said: 'The cousin from Essex suggested that we give it to the Women's Institute. They'll be selling it off at their jumble sale this afternoon. I was on my way there. Perhaps you'd like to come along.'

Whilst we were talking we had drifted into the stables; fine old-fashioned accommodation for eight horses, with deep hay racks. Annie spotted something in the corner. She said, 'There now. They've forgotten that one. It must have got hidden in the straw.'

It was a claret bottle of the green glass type used by some Bordeaux shippers for a few years after the war when supplies were scarce, but now uncommon. A label in Grandmother Clatterwick's spidery writing identified the contents as damson wine.

'Don't you think,' I said, 'that it would be a fitting gesture if we drank a last toast, a farewell salute, to a gallant old lady?'

'An excellent idea,' said the Vicar – adding: 'The later I arrive at that jumble sale the less I shall have to spend.'

Annie fetched glasses and a corkscrew. It was whilst I was in the act of drawing the cork that a great many questions were posed – and a few were answered.

The first thing that struck me was that the cork was remarkably firm. Amateur bottlers do not usually manage to sink the whole of the cork into the neck of the bottle. The next was that it was an old cork, stiff with age and impregnated with the lees of the wine. Now this really was curious. Not only was the cork clearly twenty to thirty years old, but it was equally clear that it had spent those twenty or thirty years *in that bottle*. I carried it to the door to examine it more closely. Imprinted into its side was the name of one of the four finest châteaux in the Médoc.

I went back, picked up the tumbler which Annie had filled for me, and held it up to the light.

The Vicar had already tasted his. 'Remarkable damsons,' he said.

I gave the tumbler a twist, and watched the thick dark red liquid cling to the sides of the glass and slide away. Then I tasted it, and all my suspicions became facts.

The Vicar, who had put his glass down, said: 'Hold on a moment. I wonder if this will help us . . .'

He went across to his car, and came back with an exercise book. 'I found it in McGuffog's flat. I was going to send it on to his cousin.'

I opened the book. The writing I recognised as McGuffog's. I only needed a single glance at it. 'When did you say that jumble sale was due to start?'

'It's started – half an hour ago.'

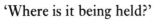

'Where is it being held?'

'Take you in my car. It'll be quicker than explaining.'

'Thank you,' I said. 'And if you'll excuse the expression, padre, drive like hell.'

There were half a dozen cars parked outside the Village Hall, a crowd of women, most of them with perambulators and push carts, and a lot of children skirmishing round the flanks. We pushed in, and the Vicar introduced me to a tweedy lady, whose name I never got. He said, 'This is Mrs Clatterwick's grandson.' I admired his tact. It was a better introduction than 'solicitor'. 'He's very interested in his grandmother's collection of home-made wines.'

The tweedy lady beamed at me. She said: 'I'd have recognised you anywhere. You've got the family nose. Yes. It was kind of McGuffog's cousin to think of us. We've been doing quite a brisk trade.'

My feelings must have been apparent. The tweedy lady said: 'There's a good deal left, though. I had them all put together over here.'

On and under the long trestle tables, normally devoted to village teas, the bottles stood, rank upon rank. 'I had intended,' I said, 'to make you an offer for the lot. As a single collection, you know.'

'That's a nice idea,' said the tweedy lady. 'This gentleman is old Mrs Clatterwick's grandson, Cynthia. He wanted to buy all the home-made wine. In memory of his grandmother. Has much of it gone already?'

Cynthia consulted a list. 'Mrs Parkin had a bottle, and Mrs Batchelor had two. Lady Lampeter bought a mixed dozen. And Colonel Nicholson took six dozen. His was mostly red currant wine. Oh, and there was a man – not very well dressed – I don't think he belongs round here. He bought a bottle of the elder-flower champagne, but I had to tell him that he couldn't drink it in here. He took it away with him.'

I was making a rapid count of the bottles, assisted by the fact that they were arranged in orderly groups of twenty-five. I said: 'That's right. Roughly fourteen hundred bottles left.'

'They took *hours* to arrange,' said Cynthia.

'What were you selling them at?'

'We had them down at sixpence a bottle,' said the tweedy lady. 'But we could give you a rebate if you really are taking the lot.'

'Far from it,' I said. 'A complete collection is always worth more than its individual parts.' I wrote out a cheque for a hundred pounds. 'Who shall I make it out to?'

'A *hundred* pounds,' said Cynthia, who had also been doing some arithmetic. 'But that's nearly three times...'

'I'm sure my grandmother – and Mr McGuffog – would have wanted it that way,' I said. 'I'll make all the arrangements for transporting it. Please don't think of disturbing it. Leave it just as it is. If you'll excuse me a moment...'

Outside the hall I spotted a chauffeur-driven Daimler reversing to get out. There was a grey-haired lady in the back, surrounded by her spoils from the jumble sale: pot plants, fruit, jam, and home-made cakes. There was a carton of twelve bottles on the floor by her feet.

Taking my courage in both hands, I introduced myself. I was far from certain whether what I was saying was being understood. Lady Lampeter had leaned forward when I started to talk and fixed me with the firm but abstracted look that members of the upper class assume when addressed by people to whom they have not been introduced.

When I had finished, she leaned forward even further and said: 'So you're Mrs Clatterwick's grandson.'

'That's right.'

'You must be Angus's son.'

'I am indeed. About that wine...'

'Of course you can have it. I only bought it as a kindness. Between you and me, I meant to pour it down the sink.'

'I'm thankful you didn't,' I said. 'I should have felt you were pouring away part of my grandmother. Thank you so much. No, don't bother your chauffeur, I can manage.'

My next step was to collar two intelligent-looking small boys. I said: 'Would you like to earn half a crown?' The less intelligent boy nodded at once. The brighter one said: 'What for?'

'One of you find Mrs Parkin, and one of you find Mrs Batchelor – do you know them?'

The boys said, yes, they knew them.

'I want to buy back the bottles of home-made wine they bought here this afternoon. Here's five shillings each. See how cheaply you can buy them back – you can keep the change.'

The two boys scudded off. I went to look for the Vicar.

'Last lap,' I said. 'Can you take me to Colonel Nicholson's house?'

'Almost as quick to walk,' said the Vicar. 'That path through the spinney there will bring you out on to his back lawn. Watch out for his dog, though. He's quite all right if you don't make any sudden movements.'

Halfway up the spinney a middle-aged tramp was sitting with his back to a tree. I saw what Cynthia had meant about his clothes. He was eating a late lunch out of a spotted handkerchief, and a tall, narrow-necked bottle stood

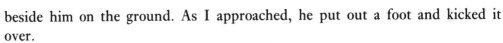

beside him on the ground. As I approached, he put out a foot and kicked it over.

I watched, fascinated, as the golden liquid ran out over the soil and leaf-mould, spread, soaked away, and disappeared.

'Didn't you like it?' I said.

'Waste of sixpence,' said the tramp, 'like lemonade, with too much sugar in it. I never could stomach sweet drinks.'

I picked the bottle up. It was still about half full. 'I'll buy what's left,' I said.

'It'll cost you threepence.'

'That seems fair,' I said.

I arrived at the Colonel's front door followed by a Dobermann-pinscher. I refrained from making any sudden movements, and rang the bell. It was the Colonel himself who opened the door. No doubt about that. A tall man with guileless light blue eyes and a silky white moustache. When I had introduced myself he said: 'Ah, yes. Come along in. I was half expecting a visit.'

He led me through into the dining room. An agreeable apartment, full of polished mahogany and sparkling glass and shining silver. One of the bottles I had come for was standing on the sideboard. The cork had been drawn, and there was a glass beside it.

'I don't normally drink wine at four in the afternoon,' said the Colonel. 'But this was by way of being an experiment.' He brought out a second glass from the cupboard, and filled them both. I was glad to see that he did this properly, tilting the bottle slowly, but firmly, with no sudden movements. The Dobermann-pinscher would have approved.

He said: 'About nine months ago, it would have been around the turn of the year, I had the pleasure of going to dinner with your grandmother. It must, I suppose, have been one of the very last dinner-parties she gave. We drank a *remarkable* red currant wine. I made up my mind that I must at all costs obtain the recipe, from her, or from her man, McGuffog, who had, I was told, assisted her to brew it.'

His eyes twinkling frostily, the Colonel picked up his glass, sniffed at it, tilted it delicately, and took a sip. I followed suit.

'Unfortunately she died before I could do so. And I did not like to intrude on McGuffog who seems to have led a somewhat hermit-like, if happy, existence for the last six months of his life.'

'Musical, too,' I said.

We drank again, and the Colonel continued. 'When, however, I learned that the wines were for sale, I hurried down and purchased a sample package. I

fully intended, if they came up to my expectations – as, indeed this one does – let me refill your glass – to go back and make an offer for the lot.'

'Too late,' I said. 'I've bought them in for the estate.'

'I feared as much.'

'And I'd like to buy back the six dozen you have.'

The Colonel considered the matter, stroking his moustache delicately with the tip of his little finger. Then he said: 'I'll do a deal with you. You can buy back five dozen, at the price I gave for them, which was thirty shillings. I'll keep the last dozen, as a memento, and you'll tell me the whole story.'

'I'm not sure that I know the whole story,' I said. 'A lot of it will be guessing. What I *think* happened is that my grandmother and McGuffog, both rather lonely people by that time, got into the way of splitting a bottle in the evening. But in order to avoid offending my grandmother's rather strict sense of propriety, it had to be something which sounded harmless and old-fashioned.'

'Raspberry cordial?'

'Exactly. Unfortunately, the only thing they both liked and appreciated were good French and German wines.'

'I wouldn't call it unfortunate,' said the Colonel, refilling both our glasses. 'Was it all as good as this?'

I took the exercise book from my brief case and showed it to the Colonel, who thumped through the pages.

'Glory be,' he said. 'It must have cost a fortune.'

'Not a whole fortune. Nine or ten thousand pounds.'

'There's a page of *trockenbeerenauslese* hock. That must have set them back fifteen pounds a bottle. What did they call that?'

'I think that was elder-flower champagne.'

'They seem to have chosen their stuff very well. I see they avoided the '47 clarets and stuck to the '45s and '49s. Sound judgement that.'

'It would be McGuffog who did the buying. He's had a good deal of experience.'

'Ah,' said the Colonel. '*That's* what I was looking for. Domaine de la Romanée Conti. They've got some of the Richebourg '29. Do you think that could possibly be what we're drinking now?'

''Twenty-nine or '34,' I said. 'This is certainly one of the finest burgundies I've ever tasted.'

The third glass of a triumphant burgundy induces contemplation and dispenses with the necessity for small-talk. As we drank in silence I reflected on the real motives behind that curious conspiracy between Grandmother Clatterwick and Mr McGuffog. Undoubtedly they both liked good wine. And un-

doubtedly re-labelling of a princely claret as raspberry cordial, and watching my Uncle Moffat turn his nose up at it, must have appealed sharply to their sense of humour. But I felt there was more to it than that. Like most very old and fairly rich people, my grandmother must have been conscious of her next of kin sitting round her like jackals round a dying lion, licking their chops and waiting to get their teeth in. As each night the log fire flickered in the grate and another great wine sank in its bottle, must there not have been a feeling akin to triumph? Another ten pounds salvaged from Gertrude, Valerie and Alexandra. Another crust out of the mouths of little George and Mary.

A further thought occurred to me. Might this not account for the heroic efforts of McGuffog after her death? His sensibility would not, of course, have allowed him to destroy such wine, but if it could all be consumed . . .?

The Colonel seemed to have read my thoughts.

'I'm told,' he said, 'that McGuffog was averaging three to four bottles a day. I suppose that's really what finished him off.'

'I fear it must have been.'

'What a *wonderful* death.'

© *from* THE COMPLEAT IMBIBER 12, 1971

The Siren s Gift to Men

NORMAN DOUGLAS

Come, let us discourse beneath this knotty carob tree whose boughs have been bent earthward by a thousand gales for the over-shadowing of the Inspired Unemployed, and betwixt whose lustrous leaves the sea, far down below, is shining turquoise-blue in a dream of calm content – let *me* discourse, that is – for if other people are going to talk, as Whistler used to say, there can be no conversation – let me discourse of leisure, the Siren's gift to men. But, first of all, pass nearer those flasks. They contain the closest approximation to that 'gold of Sant' Agata' – *oro stravecchio, oro del padrone* – the formula of whose composition was peevishly thrown away, like any ordinary Great Seal of England, what time the inn became a menagerie. Its label alone may be read on some bottles which need not be uncorked. 'Never,' said an august personage long ago to me, 'never give a man cigars, wine, or food above ten per cent better than what he gets at home. Never.' The serpent's wisdom! On this principle these caravanserais are worked, and all we can do is to seek our 'gold'

elsewhere. Meanwhile: your health! Drink, my friend, and let me see that smile of yours; soon enough, I daresay, neither of us will smile any more, though we may grin for all ages to come, if the soil is dry. . . .

A sorry preamble, this; not exactly a 'captation of benevolence' in the Ciceronian style. But what matters the exordium, if the *oro* is to our liking? Let us drown it in four inches, and begin again.

They had no *oro* in those times. Cicero's son, that ineffable drunkard and vagabond, knew this right well; if he had lived a little later, he might have found a substitute in the pages of Athenæus. But he was born before his time, like all great men. For where the *oro* now grows were forests; Pollio built his temple with their beams and the Amalfitans their fleets, and at their feet grew the wine of Sorrento, which Caligula called 'a respectable vinegar'. A dangerous liquor, by Hercules: did not doctors recommend it to their patients? In those days, the boughs of the grapes at Sorrento waxed so high and mighty that labourers were wont to insure their lives before climbing up to gather them.

Be prepared, under such a mere boughing acquaintance, for indifferent wine; like that inky fluid of the Naples Campagna where the grapes likewise clamber up to heaven out of sight of the peasant, who periodically forgets their existence and plants hemp and maize in their earth. No vine will endure this treatment; personal contact is the first requisite for good results. Where is that 'master's eye'? He would need a telescope to see his progeny. And the cultivator must also be a man of feeling, for there is a communion between the vine and him who tends it more subtle than between master and dog or lover and his beloved, and, bless you, more enduring. They end in resembling one another. Think of the priest-ridden Niederoesterreicher and his sour vintage! Then wander through golden Provence, wander to the Mainthal and Deidesheim of old romance, where the farmer loves his vines as children, and tell me if the liquor does not reflect the man? The taste of the wine depends upon the heart of the vintner.

And leisure is the *primum mobile* of the universe.

Without leisure, the sun, moon, and stars would not have been created, for it stands to reason that the Creator could not have carried out this idea if He had been busy at the time. Are not mankind and all the beasts of the field also products of leisure moments?

The wine of Capri used to be famed throughout Italy. It has now become a noisome sulphur-and-vinegar compound that will etch the bottom out of a copper cauldron; and though the natives still drink it by the gallon – what older travellers tell us of the sobriety of the Capriotes is hard to believe – yet, in the interests of public health, it would be better if the manufacturers of *vero vino*

di Capri were confined to the distillers of the relatively harmless Neapolitan preparation which goes by that name. Montesquieu lodged with the Carthusians on Capri and praises their wine in his journal. This shows that the exigencies of French politeness are not necessarily at variance with truthfulness: no man of the world will sniff at monks' liquor. But the amiable monarch Ferdinand, whom the Capriote Arcucci used to entertain for weeks at his house with 'Tears of Tiberius', a self-coined and self-manufactured native wine of noble pedigree, hit upon a more original way of showing gratitude, for he hanged his good host in 1799 – hanged him, that is, after the Christian Bourbon fashion, when white-haired patriots and delicately nurtured women and mere lads of sixteen were attached by the neck to tall gibbets, and while one fiend in human shape, called *tira-piedi*, clung to their feet, the executioner climbed up from behind and seated himself firmly, like the Old man of the Sea, upon their shoulders, where he was swayed to and fro by the victim's convulsions till at last the vertebræ were broken – all this, amid the shrieks of ten thousand ruffians, applauding the wit and wisdom of their lazzarone-king. It is well to bear these things in mind when one hears so much, even at Naples, of the good old times. Murat, the royal *tartarin*, had a finer conception of humanity; instead of murdering his benefactors, he planted French champagne grapes upon the heights beyond Naples, out of which they still extract a drinkable stuff called Asprigno. Try it, when you have the chance.

Another bottle?

So be it.

Now, leisure should be spelt with a capital 'L', otherwise it runs the risk of becoming materialized, like many similar things which have ceased to be abstractions. This is what they call 'treating a concept as if it were an entity'. *The Unknown*, for instance. I have passed that stage: the *Hibbert Journal* stage. We create a word for our convenience and forthwith, unless we are on the look out, there comes over it a horrid change. The word was made man. It puts on flesh and blood and begins to give itself airs. Soon enough, it stares us in the face, as though we were total strangers. 'Know you?' it jeers. 'Know you for a fool!' Many respectable men have been eaten alive by the words of their own creation, for their appetite exceeds that of Frankenstein's healthful monster, and I have reasons for suspecting that, like the ferocious Scythians of old, they only drink milk.

Milk! That explains everything.

Try, also that of Ischia. As a *vino da pasto*, it is surpassed by none south of Rome; indeed, it is drunk all the world over (under other names), and a pretty sight it is to see the many-shaped craft from foreign ports jostling each other

in the little circular harbour, one of the few pleasing mementoes of Bourbonism. Try it, therefore, through every degree of latitude on the island, from the golden torrents of thousand-vatted Forio up to the pale primrose-hued ichor, a drink for the gods, that oozes in unwilling drops out of the dwarfed mountain grapes.

Large heart in small grape.

Try also the red kinds.

Try them all, over and over again. Such, at least, was the advice of a Flemish gentleman whom I met, in bygone years, at Casamicciola. Like most of his countrymen, mynheer had little *chiaroscuro* in his composition; he was prone to call a spade, a spade; but his 'rational view of life', as he preferred to define it, was transfigured and irradiated by a child-like love of nature. 'Where there is no landscape,' he used to say, 'there I sit (i.e. drink) without pleasure. Only beasts sit indoors.' Every morning he went in search of new farm-houses in which to *sit* during the afternoon and evening. And every night, with tremendous din, he was carried to bed. He never apologized for this disturbance; it was his yearly holiday, he explained. He must have possessed an enviable digestion, for he was up with the lark and I used to hear him at his toilette, singing strange ditties of Meuse or Scheldt. Breakfast over, he would sally forth on his daily quest, thirsty and sentimental as ever. One day, I remember, he discovered a cottage more seductive than all the rest – 'with a view over Vesuvius and the coastline – a view, I assure you, of entrancing loveliness!' That evening he never came home at all.

© *from* SIREN LAND, 1911

Old Brompton Road Pub

DIANA MORGAN

Trying to look like members of Boodle's,
The near-gentlemen come with their women and poodles;
Their bowlers angled *à la* the Brigade,
Their Old School Ties very much displayed
(Dean Close, Dulwich, Canford, Aldenham):

Arriving in second-hand souped-up chariots,
With a gaggle of Sarahs, Carolines, Harriets
(Actually Jennifers, Maureens, Valeries),
They hope they look Lloyd's and very high salaries
(Dentistry, Accountancy, Auctioneering):

Greeting the barman by name very proudly,
Ordering Guinness, and name-dropping loudly,

VINTAGE TALES

Near-gentlemen bask in their brief Mayfly glory –
For soon, all too soon, comes the end of their story.

(Yes, soon will come marriage,
The rush back to dinner
To 'my house in the country' –
A mile out of Pinner.
An un-souped-up Austin,
A gnome in the garden,
A wife who likes gâteaux,
A child who says 'Pardon';
Ah, how brief was the sunshine,
The power, the glory
Of this middle-aged husband,
Father and Tory.)

Trying to look like Hambros or Couttses
The near-gentlemen come with their poodles and tootsies....

© *from* THE SPECTATOR, 5 July 1963

"Charles decided to lay it down as an investm...."

Punch, 3 April 1974

[194]

From Cork to Claret:
the Irish Cousins in the Médoc

C Y R I L   R A Y

I used to congratulate myself smugly on being acquainted with, and admiring, not only those dashing foxhunting stories of Somerville and Ross that deal with the adventures of the Irish resident magistrate, and Flurry Knox, M.F.H. (who 'looked like a gentleman among stableboys, and a stableboy among gentlemen'), but their less well-known and much more sombre novels of Irish life.

Indeed, I was unreasonably resentful when not long after the war the Oxford University Press published in its World's Classics series the tragic *The Real Charlotte*, which I had been hugging to myself or, at any rate, condescending to share only with those of my friends whom I considered worthy. One can be more selfish in one's enjoyment of a favourite, little-known, book than in any other pleasure: every bottle of wine is meant to be shared – which is why a wine-bottle is the size it is – but not every book.

I should not have been so complacent. If I was knowing enough to have on my remoter shelves, safe from the casual caller, *An Irish Cousin* and *Naboth's*

Vineyard, The Real Charlotte and *The Big House of Inver,* how could I have been so ignorant – I, who had lived for weeks at a time in the Médoc, and written for years about claret and its growers – how could I have been so ignorant for so long of *In the Vine Country?*

How was it, come to that, that none of my hosts in those parts had ever mentioned it to me?

It is only during the last couple of years, when I read, in rapid succession, first Mr Maurice Collis's and then Lady Violet Powell's biography of Edith Œnone Somerville and 'Martin Ross' (Violet Martin), that I have discovered that this strange pair of female, fox-hunting cousins, the closest of collaborators in authorship (and, it is clear, lesbian lovers of a sort), had travelled eighty years ago through the claret country and set down their experiences in a book that has long been out of print but is still far from unreadable. The title, *In the Vine Country,* refers not (as I had perhaps supposed, in ignoring it) to the country hunted by the noted north-Hampshire pack, as they might have written, say, *In the Quorn Country,* or being Irish, *In the Galway Blazers' Country,* but to the country where the vine grows, and is transmuted into claret.

Indeed, Violet Martin's first proposed title for the work was *From Cork to Claret,* the book beginning, typically enough, with a disastrous early-morning's cub-hunting in the county Cork, but the publisher thought it too subtle a title for the book-buying public, the authors' previous travel book having been burdened with no more allusive or recondite a name than *Through Connemara in a Governess Cart.*

Both the Connemara and the claret book were collections of articles reprinted from *The Lady's Pictorial,* the editor of which paid the two young ladies (though as Edith Somerville was thirty-three in 1891, and her cousin almost thirty, it is likely that they were thought of at the time as almost middle-aged spinsters) three pounds an article and expenses for a series on a tour of the vineyards. Not a vast amount, even in those days, for this was to include drawings in wash and line by Edith ('improved' for publication by F.H. Townsend of *Punch*), and the cousins were already established journalists and successful novelists, though success had not yet made them rich. Far from it, if we are to judge by Edith's diary entry, a week before they sailed for France: 'Took out of the bank all the money I have bar 3 pence – viz £10.' All the same, Miss Somerville of Castle Townshend and Miss Martin of Ross had hardly been starving in garrets: there was more than a tenner behind an Anglo-Irish ascendancy horse-Protestant lady of the time, even if it was not in her own private bank account.

By train to Dublin, passing pathetic groups of emigrants at the little stations on the way, waiting for the down train to Cork; a bad crossing by steamboat to

Holyhead; a night train to London for three days of shopping; another train to Dover, now laden with 'two portmanteaus registered to Bordeaux' and a 'cumbrous row of hand packages'; yet another steamboat journey to Calais – this time, though, 'in the most brilliant of sunshine and the most refreshing of breezes'; a train to Paris and a flea-bitten night in an hotel bedroom there as big as 'a good-sized opera-box'; and an eleven-hour train journey to Bordeaux next day. I write as a working journalist who also occasionally makes the journey to Bordeaux in the service of his paper (though at rather more than three pounds an article) when I express the hope that these predecessors of mine fiddled a bit on their expenses.

What I envy is their journey from Bordeaux itself to Pauillac – not, as now, a boring fifty or sixty minutes by motor-car along D1 or D2, but by the steamer 'that plies between Bordeaux and Royan, calling *en route* at several dozen places on the Garonne and Gironde', affording in those days a view of the Médoc that prompted the observation, 'the best wine in the world is made in places where there is no tall chimney or hideous range of manufactories'. Every château-owner of Pauillac ought to read these words at a window looking out on to the oil refinery that Shell should never have been permitted to extend to its present monstrous size.

Somerville and Ross must have boarded the steamer after office hours, for there is mention of the Bordeaux merchants and bank clerks returning 'by scores to the bosoms of their families', to be 'no doubt epigrammatic at dinner on the subject of the two absurdly emancipated *Anglaises*, with their sailor hats and brown shoes'.

Emancipated, certainly, but rigidly insular, these two *Anglaises*, the one with

her sketch-book, the other with her Kodak ('a photographic camera of the kind that is to the ordinary species as a compressed meat lozenge to a round of beef'); with their hold-all containing 'a spirit kettle, a teapot, and half a pound of English tea' for brew-ups in hotel bedrooms, with their noses turned up at 'grease and garlic' and the smell of 'the mysterious compound known to the French middle classes as tobacco'.

Though I wonder how much of this was genuinely felt, and how much was put on for the benefit of the readers of *The Lady's Pictorial*. Edith Somerville had lived in Düsseldorf, for the sake of the art school there, and then in Paris, working at Colarossi's studio in the Rue de la Grande Chaumière. It is hard to believe that the smell of garlic was all that shockingly unfamiliar, or that the sometime Paris art student, who had shopped and cooked for herself, spoke and understood French so badly as she made out (she knew it well enough to try to indicate in the book how the accent of the Bordelais differs from that of Paris). And Violet Martin, though she had not experienced *la vie de Bohème*, had been taught French, German, and Greek, drawing, music and dancing, and knew at first hand both high life in Dublin and how cottagers lived on her family's estate in Connemara. One of the two, what is more (the book does not specify which), had had a French governess, and one who came from Bordeaux, at that. Not in any sense of the word were the two cousins innocents abroad.

Still, the Somervilles and the Martins were not Anglo-Irish of the hard-drinking sort, and their families were not even great amateurs of claret, as were many of their kind, so the writers were not perhaps putting it on too much when they wrote that 'we felt a secret scepticism as to our fitness for this large and yet delicate mission', though it is hard to believe that before the journey Miss Somerville knew nothing of 'Château Lafite or Mouton Rothschild, except that a glass and a half of the former had once compelled my second cousin to untimely slumber at dessert'. Those who know such noble names and their significance are unlikely to be put to sleep by a glass and a half of the finest claret.

What was undoubtedly new and strange for them, though, was to see wine actually being made, and when they made their first excursion from Pauillac to a *pressoir* in the little neighbouring village of St Lambert.*

> ... It must be admitted that we found it startling. In the mouth of the archway was a broad and shallow wooden receptacle, called the *pressoir;* heaped up in it were mounds of grapes, all black and shining, with their splendid indigo bloom gone for

*There are many references in the book to Château Grand-Saint-Lambert, which is listed in Larmat's *Atlas de la France Vinicole* as a principal growth of Pauillac, but does not appear in the latest edition of Cocks et Feret. Can anyone tell me what has happened to it? C.R.

ever, and, splashing about amongst them, bare-footed, and ankle-deep in the thick magenta juice, were the treaders of the winepress. It was those bare feet, crimsoned with juice, that took our whole attention for the first few minutes. We had been given uncertain warnings as to what we might or might not see, but we had always hoped against hope for *sabots*. I think the proprietor felt for us – not sympathetically, of course, but compassionately. He hastened to explain that the fermenting process purified everything; the old plan had been for the men to join hands and dance round and round the *pressoir*, trampling the juice out of the grapes, and singing a little sacrificial vintage song, but now nothing like that obtained. All this was very consoling and nice, but it did not in the least mitigate the horror that fate had in store for us.

We had watched the carts unloading the big *douilles* packed with grapes at the mouth of the archway, and had heard, and straightway forgotten, how many *douilles* were yielded by an acre. We had seen with considerable repugnance the wiry and handsome little blue-clad workmen scrub the berries from the stems on the *grillage*, a raised grating that let the bruised grapes fall through, while the stalks remained on the top. We had watched them shovel the grapes in dripping shovelfuls into a small double-handled barrel, which was then snatched up by two of them, who, with it on their shoulders, would trot across the dusty floor of the *cuvier*, up two ladders that leaned side by side against a tall vat, and, having emptied their load into this immense maw, would trot back, and jump into the *pressoir* again. Through all these things we clung to the beautiful, purifying thought of the fermentation, and said to each other that when we ordered our bottle of Grand St Lambert at our English hotel we should see that we got it, and would think fondly as we drank it of that good, comforting process. At this juncture one of the barefooted and blue-clad workmen approached with a small tumbler in his singularly dirty hand.

'These ladies would like to taste the *moût*,' he observed, dipping the tumbler in a tub half full of the muddy juice that was trickling out of the *pressoir*. He proffered us the tumbler with a bow, and we looked at each other in speechless horror.

Bless them both, they drank it. Anyway, they must have eaten worse things in their time in cabins in Connemara.

There is no treading of the grapes now in the Médoc – precious little anywhere in Europe that I know of – and no reason nowadays for anyone to be so excessively ladylike about tasting the *moût*.

But – to turn from liquids to solids – there are plenty of *cèpes*, still a great Bordelais delicacy, and although I do not care for them myself, I think that Somerville and Ross made too much of their own repulsion.

They had been enjoying a Médocain dinner at the house of one of the peasant women who in those days fed the *vendangeurs*. They had been shown how to mop up

...the rich sauce of our delicious *ragoût* with pieces of bread ... Everything was going on velvet, when, after the *ragoût*, the smell of fried oil became apparent, and

from a covered-in pan Suzanne helped us each to a large piece of something that resembled sweetbread, and cut rather like a tough custard pudding. It was fried bright brown, but the inside was yellowish white, and the whole thing was swimming in hot oil. We asked nervously what it was. '*Mais, mangez-le donc,*' responded Suzanne, as she reversed the frying-pan to let the last drops of oil run on to our plates. '*C'est biang bong! C'est du cèpe – du champignong, vous savez*', seeing that we did not seem much enlightened. Here was local colour with a vengeance! The situation, however, did not admit of retreat. And we attempted none. The mushroom, or fungus, whatever it was, had a dreadful taste, as though rotten leaves and a rusty knife had been fried together in fat. Moreover, it was patent to the meanest intelligence that, whatever its taste might be, no digestion save that of a native or an ostrich could hope to compete with it. We each swallowed two lumps of it whole, and then my cousin looked wanly at me and said, 'One more, and I shall be sick.'

Next day, though, came visits to the grandest châteaux of the Médoc. The Irish ladies seem to have misunderstood the significance of one of the lordliest names –

> ... It would be neither kind or clever to call a newly-built house in the neighbourhood of Limerick, Pig Robinson or Pork Murphy; but in France, Sheep Rothschild is a very different affair ...

and they were suitably impressed by what, even before our own Baron Philippe's time, was

> one of the great fermenting houses of the Médoc. Right and left stood the huge barrels on their white stone pedestals, belted monsters, spick and span in their varnished oak and shining black hoops, with a snowy background of white-washed wall to define their generous contour, and a neat little numbered plate on each to heighten their resemblance to police constables. This was an *édition de luxe* of wine-making – at least, so it seemed to us after what we had seen of dingy sheds, wine-stained barrels, and promiscuous rubbish, with magenta legs splashing about in juice, and split dregs as a foreground.

Baron Philippe would not be pleased, though, to be told that the authors found that

> ... it is not only in wine that Mouton Rothschild is beaten by its nearest neighbour. In the matter of a *château*, Lafite scores still more decidedly; of that no one could have any doubt who saw this old country-house, with its pointed towers, its terraced gardens with their ambushed perfumes that took the hot wind by surprise, its view over the soft country to other *châteaux*, and its delightful wood, where grassy walks wound away into the shadows. After these things, going to see the *cuviers* and the wine-making was like beginning again on roast beef after dessert; but the appetite came in eating. It was Mouton Rothschild over again, only more so ...

It is odd that the two Irishwomen did not visit Château Langoa-Barton, which in 1891 had already been in the possession of fellow-countrymen of theirs for more than half a century, but after expeditions to Libourne and the St Emilion country (and, on the way, to the Bordeaux market – then, as now, 'a great iron tent, filled with the most variegated colours, voices, and smells') they were taken to spend a few days at the Gilbeys' Château Loudenne, in time for the end-of-vintage dance.

This is the climax of a book that is still engagingly readable to those who know the Médoc of today, though its naïveté, as I have already suggested, does not always ring quite true to those who have read about the cousins' background.

But there is no doubt about their having been enthralled by the dance and the dancers at Château Loudenne. They joined in themselves, 'till our legs ached and the cement floor wore holes in our shoes', and

> ...as we went back in the darkness to the *château* we felt as if the music had gone to our heads; and when I lay down under my mosquito curtains, the dark figures whirled and swung giddily before me, as if the spirit of the Médoc had been expressed in them as intoxicatingly as in its wine....

That, though, was the only form of intoxication: for it was already on record, in the account of the dance, that

> ...not one of these peasants of the most wine-making district in the world owed any of their hilarity to the claret in which they lived, moved and had their being; in fact, not once during our fortnight in the Médoc did we see any man who had taken more than was good for him....

Perhaps this was what had impressed the *Irlandaises* most of all: it was a far cry to the claret country from the county Cork, where a dance given by the Curranhilty Harriers ends with Flurry Knox's introducing a pack of hounds into the drunken Tomsy Flood's bedroom to convince him that he really has got the horrors, and Dr Hickey's tastefully arranging mule meat from the kennels around Tomsy's breakfast plate to accentuate his hangover.

It must have been a blessed relief for the fox-hunting ladies to escape, if only for a fortnight, from that island of saints and scholars even to a land deprived of tea and redolent of garlic.

© *from* THE COMPLEAT IMBIBER 12, 1971

A Rude Word in Crete

JOHN SILVERLIGHT

Almost in the middle of Crete, some twenty miles from Rethymnon as the crow flies, more like forty as the mountain road winds, is the village of Ano Meros.

There is not much to it: a few hundred souls living in white houses that cling to the side of Mount Kedros; two or three cafés; a church – and mulberry trees. It was the trees that had brought me there, or rather, the liqueur distilled from their fruit.

Some years ago I read in James Bowman's excellent *Travellers' Guide to Crete*: 'Ouzo is made by distilling the crushed mash after the wine juice has been pressed from the grapes, with anisette added to provide a slight flavour.

'On Crete the men are distinguished from the boys by drinking *raki*, a stronger, unflavoured version (and known in some parts as *tzikoudhiá*). An even stronger spirit is *mournoúraki*, made from mulberries and a speciality of Rethymnon.'

A Rude Word in Crete

It sounded interesting, but in Crete I drew a blank. *Raki*, yes, but not *mournoúraki*, which only increased my curiosity.

A Cretan acquaintance in London had given my wife and me introductions to friends and relatives. One relative was a lordly, almost feudal character in the east of the island. On learning of my quest he summoned a retainer, who brought a bottle and some liqueur glasses on a tray. '*Mournoúraki*,' he said.

Raki is a bit like *marc* (also made from grape mash) but with less character. This drink was different. Although less subtle, it called to mind what is to me the greatest of all *alcools blancs*, Framboise, in German *Himbeergeist*: Spirit of Raspberries. 'You will find *mournoúraki* only in Rethymnon,' said our host.

So to Rethymnon, where I went to twenty or thirty shops that sold drink. No *mournoúraki*. In the last one I said despondently, 'I don't suppose you sell *mournoúraki*,' and left without waiting for an answer.

After walking some distance I was aware of being shouted at: it was that last shopkeeper, who filled a small glass from what looked like a five-gallon petrol container: it was indeed *mournoúraki*. I made a bottle last fifteen months.

Last year we went back. My *mournoúraki* man had it in stock, but I wanted something more. Could he tell me how to get to a village that produced it? He pointed out Ano Meros on the map and we set off in a hired car.

In Ano Meros, outside a café, we found a lady who greeted us in English. In the café we ordered some wine and I explained my mission. Yes, they did make *mournoúraki*, but there was none to be had just then. It was mid-October and distilling would not begin for some weeks. No matter, what I really wanted was to see where it was made.

As we talked I became aware of slightly amused embarrassment. Eventually the lady said gently, 'You are using rather a rude word.' Though shaken, I pressed on. Could I see a still? 'This gentleman,' said the lady, indicating a small man sitting in the corner, 'distils *mournoúraki* from the fruit of his mulberry trees.'

I accompanied him up a steep slope to his house. Inside, up some steps, was a stone trough about 8ft long, 4ft wide and 4ft deep with, in the middle, a metal cylinder 6in wide and $4\frac{1}{2}$ft high. Next to the trough, sunk into the dirt floor, was a stone- or concrete-lined cavity, in which the mash is heated by wood fed into a hole I had seen outside. The vapours, I gathered, mount inside the cylinder and, on cooling, collect in the trough.

My guide's wife appeared and beckoned us into her kitchen, where she peeled an apple and handed slices to me and her husband. To share an apple with a guest, I learnt later is traditional rural Greek hospitality.

In Rethymnon I asked a young Greek couple, 'What was I saying that was

so rude?' The girl leant over and whispered in my wife's ear. Later she told me, 'You were saying: "I am an English journalist and I have come to Ano Meros in search of the female organ."' Apparently I was mispronouncing '*mournoúraki*' and the word I was using, so an old Greek hand tells me, is more opprobrious in Greek than it is in English.

The embarrassment still lingers, but it will pass. The memory of the shared apple will remain. And my *mournoúraki* is delicious.

© *from* THE OBSERVER, 12 December 1982

To Thea, at the Year's End:
with a Bottle of Gewürztraminer

P. M. HUBBARD

I have no fancy to define
   Love's fullness by what went before;
I think the day we crossed the line
Was when we drank the sea-cooled wine
   Upon a sun-warmed shore.

The sun in sudden strength that day
   Inflamed the air, but could not reach
The steel-sharp sea of middle May
That brimmed with cold the breathless bay
   Below the sun-drowned beach.

The sun's heat laid its heavy hand
   On unaccustomed skins as we

VINTAGE TALES

Went tip-toe down the tilted strand
And set our bottle on the sand
   To cool it in the sea:

And watched as, where the sea-surge spent
   The last of its quiescent strength,
Stone-cold and circumambient,
The intermittent water went
   Along its polished length.

The bottle took the water's cold
   But did not let its wetness pass;
Glinting and green the water rolled
Against the wine's unmoving gold
   Behind its wall of glass.

We cooled it to our just conceit
   And drank. The cold aroma came
Almost intolerably sweet
To palates which the salt and heat
   Had flayed as with a flame.

We swam and sunned as well as drank,
   And found all heaven in a word;
But, dearest Thea, to be frank,
I think we had the wine to thank
   For most of what occurred.

And now the winter is to waste,
   I bring a bottle like the first;
And this in turn can be replaced,
As long as we have tongues to taste,
   And God shall give us thirst,

Lest with the year our love decline,
   Or like the summer lose its fire,
Before the sun resurgent shine
To warm the sea that cooled the wine
   That kindled our desire.

© *from* THE COMPLEAT IMBIBER 8, 1965

What Claret had John Keats?

MARGHANITA LASKI

O for a draught of vintage! that hath been
   Cool'd a long age in the deep-delvèd earth,
Tasting of Flora and the country green,
   Dance, and Provençal song and sunburnt mirth!
   O for a beaker full of the warm South,
   Full of the true, the blushful Hippocrene,
     With beaded bubbles winking at the brim,
     And purple-stainèd mouth;
That I might drink, and leave the world unseen,
   And with thee fade away into the forest dim:

As with so much poetry, this second stanza of John Keats's *Ode to a Nightingale* of 1819, effortlessly accepted as beautiful and meaningful, becomes more and more difficult the more one looks into it. And not the least of its difficulties is that of discovering just what kind of drink Keats was thinking of.

Ostensibly, of course, he is talking about Hippocrene, the water of the Heliconian spring, the draught of which traditionally brings poetic inspiration. He has spoken of it before in his poetry, though not under the specific name of Hippocrene. In his sonnet of 1817 to that over-inspired painter, Benjamin Haydon, Keats expresses his wish to follow Haydon, had he strength enough, 'even to the steep of Heliconian springs', and in 1818, in *Endymion* (II.715 *et seq.*) he wishes that 'Old Homer's Helicon' might 'spout a little streamlet o'er These sorry pages.'

In these earlier examples there is no indication that the Heliconian spring is spouting anything but pure if magical water. But it is not water that the poet seeks in the second stanza of the Nightingale Ode. Here, the *true* Hippocrene is wine, and this is not the first time that Keats has associated Helicon's draughts and wine, for in an early poem, the *Epistle to Charles Cowden Clarke* of 1816, he has contrasted the poor wine of his own inspirations with the 'sparkling Helicon' of Clarke's. And, again in *Endymion* (II.441-4), a straightforward description of wine leads usefully to that of the Hippocrene of the Ode:

> – Here is wine,
> Alive with sparkles – never, I aver,
> Since Ariadne was a vintager,
> So cool a purple...

The draught of the Ode is even more specifically if somewhat conflictingly described. It is a crimson ('blushful') even a purplish wine ('purple-stainèd mouth'). It is sparkling ('beaded bubbles'). It has a fruity bouquet (I think a fair inference from 'Flora' – and see below) together with a certain crudity (I think a fair inference from the 'country green', etc.). It has been chilled (i.e. 'cool'd a long age in the deep-delvèd earth'). What was it?

Now Keats did, as we know, drink rather too much – or at least rather more than was good for him. 'Keats is much better, owing to a strict forbearance from a third glass of wine,' wrote Charles Brown in January 1819, and Keats confirmed this in a letter to his brother George in February of the same year: 'I never drink now above three glasses of wine – and never any spirits and water.' But if even his 'strict forbearance' was rather more flexible than Brown supposed, before this partial reformation he had drunk whatever was going. On his tour of Scotland of 1818, hardly a letter home but contains some happy reference to whisky, for instance:

> 'We have now begun upon whiskey, called here *whuskey*, very smart stuff it is – Mixed like our liquors with sugar and water tis called toddy, very pretty drink...'

Climbing Skiddaw, he was refreshed by rum and mountain-water, and, later in the same tour, he and his companion split 'a small chicken and even a bottle of Port.'

But his favourite drink had always been 'claret' – the reason for the quotation marks will emerge. In a letter to the George Keatses of 1818 he describes a vision of perfect happiness with

> 'the most beautiful Creature... waiting for me ... the Carpet ... of Silk, the Curtains of the morning Clouds; the chairs and Sofa stuffed with Cygnet's down; the food Manna, the Wine beyond Claret ...'

Claret is the proper accompaniment to a merry evening with a couple of friends:

> 'I pitched upon another bottle of claret – Port – we enjoyed ourselves very much were all very witty and full of wine –' (5 January 1818)

and even after his reformation claret still seduces him, for the same letter which announces his renunciation of spirits, his partial abstinence from wine, goes on:

> '– now I like Claret whenever I can have Claret I must drink it. 't is the only palate affair that I am at all sensual in. Would it not be a good Speck to send you some vine roots ... If you could make some wine like Claret to drink on summer evenings in an arbour! For really 't is so fine – it fills one's mouth with a gushing freshness – then goes down cool and feverless – then you do not feel it quarrelling with your liver – no it is rather a Peacemaker and lies as quiet as it did in the grape – then it is as fragrant as the Queen Bee; and the more ethereal Part of it mounts into the brain ... Other wines of a heavy and spirituous nature transform a Man to a Silenus; this makes him a Hermes – and gives a Woman the soul and immortality of Ariadne for whom Bacchus always kept a good cellar of claret –'

His most significant letter in this context is however that of 1 May 1819, written at almost the same time as the Nightingale Ode:

> 'please heavens, a little claret-wine cool out of a cellar a mile deep – with a few or a good many ratafia cakes – a rocky basin to bathe in, a strawberry bed to say your prayers to Flora in ...'

From this we may reasonably assume that the taste of Flora was a somewhat fruity if not strawberryish taste. And, further, we may be very nearly sure that the true, the blushful Hippocrene was no other than a claret. But *what* claret?

As Keats describes his ideal drink, in the letters, in *Endymion* and in the Nightingale Ode, what we have to infer is a purplish, fruity, sparkling claret, served chilled or at least at cellar temperature. Is this reasonable?

Purplish wine implies young wine, and this we may accept. Keats and his friends were poor, often very poor indeed. Young wine was almost certainly all

they could have afforded, and if Keats never knew any better (and later I will try to show that he did not) then he may well have accepted a purplish colour as normally characteristic of his favourite wine. The fruitiness too, even the strawberryishness, not a usual term of praise for good *old* claret, fits this picture.

Nor need the chilling give us pause, for it was usual then, as much later, to chill red wine. Peacock refers to the practice in his *Gryll Grange* of 1860, and Browning in *Bishop Blougram's Apology:*

> '... try the cooler jug –
> Put back the other, but don't jog the ice'

And Saintsbury, in his *Notes on a Cellar Book* (1920) refers to what he calls this 'barbarous' practice; some people, he adds, may remember 'marsupial' claret jugs with a pouch for ice.

The sparkle of the wine, if it was indeed claret as we know it today, is much more difficult. It is of course possible that Keats drank his claret diluted with seltzer as Byron drank his hock, but he never says that he does, and, aesthetically speaking, bottles of seltzer fit as ill with Endymion as they do with Keats himself listening to the nightingale in the Hampstead garden. That he drank whisky, rum and spirits diluted with water we know; but he never mentions seltzer or any dilution of wine.

There is of course that old scandal, put about by the egregious Haydon, long after Keats's death, that Keats in vinous orgy 'once covered his throat and tongue as far as he could reach with cayenne pepper in order to appreciate the "delicious coldness of claret in all its glory" – his own expression.' But though we might tentatively take this as evidence of Keats's liking for a prickling in his wine, even Haydon does not claim that Keats sought this particular excess of *pétillance* more than once, and Charles Cowden Clarke, Keats's close friend, attacked all Haydon's recollections of Keats and this one in particular. Clarke denied vehemently that Keats was 'so far gone in sensual excitement' as to try this 'stupid trick', and stated further that he had never known Keats purchase a bottle of claret (Can this be true? Did he always drink other people's?) or seen in him any tendency to over-indulgence.

Clarke, perhaps, protests too much towards the end. But – if not pepper, if not seltzer, then what? There was not then or ever has been since any such thing as sparkling claret. There is not even any evidence of the existence of sparkling *red* burgundy in 1819, though there were already sparkling white burgundies and Loire wines.

It is however possible that when Keats spoke of claret, he did not mean a wine from the Bordeaux district of France, and the historical use of the name

justifies this possibility. André Simon, in his *History of the Wine Trade in England*, writes of

'a wine known in England as *claret* as far back as the thirteenth century, but this denomination did not apply to the product of the Bordeaux vineyards, and probably meant a sort of blend of red and white wines.'

Indeed in 1562 William Bullein, in his *Bulwarke of Defence against all sicknesse*, wrote of 'pure claret, of a cleare Iacent [jacynth] or Yelow Choler' and, in 1600, Markham's translation of Surflet's *Maison Rustique* spoke of wines 'of a deepe yellow, commonly called clarets'. By Keats's day however the name was commonly applied to any red wine. A vocabulary of 1825 gives '*Claret*, any sort of foreign red wine' and in 1833 C. Redding, in his *History and Descriptions of Modern Wines*, writes 'There is no pure wine in France like that which is designated claret in England. This wine is a mixture of Bordeaux with Benicarlo [a Spanish wine] or with some full wine of France.' And as recently as 1965, in the latest edition of *The Plain Man's Guide to Wine*, Raymond Postgate writes:

'Claret in English means any light, clean red wine. By itself, the word "claret" should mean red wine from the great district around Bordeaux... but it is also correctly applied to any red wines of the same kind in the whole world – Australian, Chilean, New York State, or what you will.'

Against this we have to set the fact that by Keat's day connoisseurs at least *were* confining the name to Bordeaux wine. Already in 1707 we find an advertisement in the *London Gazette*: 'To be sold an entire Parcel of New French ... Claret ... being of the Growth of Lafitt, Marguize, and La Tour.' The question is, what was Keats's own usage?

In the first place, Keats certainly did not use the name *claret* for *any* red wine. When he drinks port, he so names it. Nor does he confuse claret with burgundy as his *Song* of 1818 makes plain – 'Hence Burgundy, Claret, and Port ...' More, he does seem to have believed that his favourite drink came from France, for in August 1819, the period when his eulogies of claret were at their most enthusiastic, he wrote, 'Give me Books, fruit, french wine and fine whether [*sic*] and a little music out of doors; and I can pass a summer very quietly.'

But though we must, I think, accept by elimination that when Keats drank claret, he believed he was drinking a French wine from the Bordeaux region, it also begins to be apparent that he was almost certainly deceived. Then as now, more wine was yearly labelled as from the Bordeaux region than ever was grown there, and it is surely significant that in all his rhapsodies over claret Keats never names a château wine. If he had ever tasted 'the Growth of Lafitt, Marguize, and La Tour', he could hardly have failed, inveterate and enthusiastic

letter-writer and drinker that he was, to have told someone about it. We cannot but conclude that what poor Keats, poverty-stricken Keats, drank for claret was then, as it might well be now, some young fruity blended wine, or even quite another wine from quite another region, passing itself off.

And does the sparkle on which he is so insistent give us a clue as to what wine it could have been? Might it have been – remember this was just after the Napoleonic Wars – a red *vinho verde* from Portugal the *pétillance* of which could have led Keats to suppose that claret was, of its nature, sparkling?

Poor Keats indeed. In the end, even his claret, whatever it may have been, failed him, and in an agonized letter to Fanny Brawne of February 1820, he wrote:

> 'Like all Sinners now I am ill I philosophize aye out of my attachment to every thing. Trees, flowers, Thrushes, Spring, Summer, Claret –'

But it had pleased him nearly to the end. 'My friends should drink a dozen of Claret on my Tomb' he had written to Bailey the year before – and so we may, though, we hope, of a more authentic claret than had John Keats.

© *from* THE COMPLEAT IMBIBER 9, 1967

The Growth of Marie-Louise: a Story

John le Carré

I was not, in my youth, fortunate with women. The point needs little elaboration. They found me either cold and wary, or over-attentive to their wishes. wishes. They cast me, I had the impression, midway between Cardinal Richelieu and an Italian head waiter. From time to time, because of this curious fusion of withdrawal and what the smart ones call empathy, I was challenged as a homosexual. The charge was false; my wishes were frank and uncomplicated: I longed for women, all women, and rejoiced in their embraces. Unfortunately, despite good looks, a fair wit and a reasonably charitable nature, I had little occasion to rejoice. In my childhood, women scolded me a great deal, and I learned quickly to obey them. It still came hard to me, in later years, to play a more masterful role. The psychiatrists may have their sport with me: my predicament was simple. I wanted women and won them seldom. It was a predicament in which (as I have since learnt from my contemporaries) I was not alone.

My needs were never more pressing, or more painfully frustrated, than in

the little Provençal town of Etrouille-sur-mer, in the year 1954. The date is relevant; for the people of Etrouille-sur-mer, 1954 is the *annus mirabilis*. In the preceding year, the small and normally unrewarding vineyards on the southern slopes, which hitherto had produced only a thin and disagreeable *rouge* –in its poorest years it was more like a blushing *rosé* – known throughout Provence as *le pipi d'Etrouille*, yielded providentially and with only the smallest encouragement from the dispirited inhabitants, a truly remarkable growth. The grapes, until then pallid and limp affairs, were bursting and erect; the vines, known everywhere for their frail and inhibited appearance, for once held their rich burden sturdily. Etrouille-sur-mer, barren for a decade, had borne Bacchus a child of delight. As for her inhabitants, filled to the brim with the new wine, they were as proud as if he had slept with every one of them; their skins swelled and coloured like the skin of their grapes; their eyes sparkled like the light in their vats; and none was more positively affected than my own Marie-Louise, employee and principal attraction at the Auberge de la Domaine where I myself, as a student awaiting admission to Oxford, had accepted service – need I say it? – as a waiter.

I will not say I loved her; I desired her. I wanted her with a physical pain known only to those who are accustomed to failure; I was her servant. Whatever strategy I had learned at the hands of the English girls in the meagre neighbourhood where I grew up was as useless as a toy pistol before her sexual armoury. At night I lay awake, constructing fine phrases, devising opportunities, hotly dreaming of her rich hips and thighs, her plump lips and dancing breasts; I stripped her, kissed, caressed, penetrated and amazed her, all in my imagination; but by day I was as cumbersome, as ineffectual, and as inwardly agonised as on my first day of puberty. I watched her, as I cleared away the empty glasses she had so provokingly replenished; I watched her as she lowered her black-fringed eyes at the brown peasants from the vineyards; I watched them lust for her blandly with their clean, outdoor, uninhibited gaze; and I hated her, as the jealous do, for the small favours she occasionally granted me. A kiss, a dance, a squeeze of the hand, even a consoling, playful pat upon the backside: what were these sweetmeats handed to the children while the adults glutted themselves on stronger fare? Even the carafe of new wine, the bowl of apples, which she occasionally left in my room, the small keepsakes she brought me from the town when she rode with the peasants to the *coopérative*, were nothing but salt in the wound. Now and then, I had no doubt, a certain maternal affection overcame her for the impoverished English boy who skulked so incongruously at the edge of their carefree lives; but I did not want a mother, I wanted a mistress, and to my aching envious heart, these moments of generosity were no more than the *coup de chapeau* of a wanton girl to the life she had left behind. In all Etrouille, I was convinced, I was the one man who had not enjoyed her charms. How she tantalised me! I remember still how at night, late at night, when we had swept away the last débris, counted the money, set the chairs upon the tables and sprinkled the wet sawdust on the wooden floor, she would even take my hand, and lead me upstairs, softly past her parent's door, would sit on the bed with a small and wistful sigh and – still without relinquishing my hand – shake her head so that the long ears of black hair fluttered like silk curtains over her retreating face.

'*Poor* one,' she would say, '*poor* one, you want me so much,' as if lust were a condition to be pitied in a person so far removed from the easy, primitive way of life. And then jump up, angry with me, toss her head, riffle through my books and papers.

'It is interesting?' she would ask in English. 'It interests you?' I could speak French to anyone but her. 'Tell me please about the world of the mind.' I forget what answer I gave, but inwardly I knew but one. 'Marie-Louise, Marie-Louise,' my heart cried, 'the mind has no meaning if it is not implanted in the flesh!'

I was even sorry for her then, sorry for the emptiness that awaited her, when her ripe body was past its year, her vintage beyond the caprice of man's enjoyment. And lifting my glass to her departing footsteps, I drank from the carafe she had brought me, drank until I fell asleep, drank the rich fruit of last year's miraculous vintage, promising myself that one day, when the turbulence of Marie-Louise's youth had worn itself out, and the *pipi d'Etrouille* was once more equal to its pathetic reputation, I would return, rich and wise and forgiving, to care for the twilight of her life, though she had scorned the dawn of mine.

It had a curious flavour, that great wine, even when it was new; it is with me still as I write. I knew nothing of wine in the general way; the cult bored me. Neither then nor now could I be relied upon to detect a great year from an indifferent one. But the wine of Etrouille, harvested in 1953 and first enjoyed (prematurely) in 1954, is like the one tune in the memory of a deaf man. It was constructed like the act of love itself. At first taste, it promised and withheld itself; it lay trembling upon the tongue, begging the reassurance of a kindly palate; this granted, it gently opened, responding to the new, internal intimacy, and suddenly the ecstasy was upon you: a strange but brilliant odour filled the nostrils, infused the palate; the liquid swelled and broke upon the senses; and thus, at last, but slowly, it sank little by little into the perfect languor of a protracted afterglow. I did not by any means wholly enjoy it, for we are not always generous to those who stir us from our apathy, or lull us away from our desires; but I could no more forget it than my first conquest in the field of love. They named it *la Cuvée Marie-Louise* after the girl they had all enjoyed; the outside world saw little of it. Only a few bottles, they say, found their way to the tables of the connoisseur; the lion's share remained in Etrouille, and was quickly consumed by greedy natives before it even had time to mature.

I left Etrouille in March, a few hundred francs the richer; I had nowhere particular to go. My tutors would accept me, but not immediately. But I could not endure the thought of living in Marie-Louise's presence a second time while the valley woke to the fertilities of spring. I took one job with the Post Office in St Albans, and another with a large store in Watford. Sometimes I wrote to Marie-Louise; sometimes she wrote to me. Once she sent me a rather pathetic parcel. It was my birthday, I suppose, for she was always sentimental about birthdays. There had not been a peasant in Etrouille whose birthday she had not remembered with a free bottle of *la Cuvée*. She sent me a tin of home-made pastries – they were salted things which she made herself and served free to regular customers – but they had crumbled during the journey and all that was left was a sort of cheesy shrapnel which I fed to the swans at Bushey. A week after Christmas I received a terse note from the Customs advising me that two bottles of 'dutiable wine' had been sent to me from Etrouille-sur-mer. But like the biscuits they had arrived broken. I wrote and thanked her all the same, but her letter was returned to me by her mother. Marie-Louise had vanished.

She had waited for me for over a year, her mother said, and surely that was long enough for any girl? She had eloped with a school-master, her mother said, an *assistant* of no fortune or prospects, a *Lyonnais* quite incapable of making her happy. Her father was furious, her mother said, and would have no part of it; the *assistant* was a prig, he had declared, a religious fool, and worst of all a non-drinker; he came from a family of notorious teetotallers. The child, in his frank opinion, had thrown herself away. She could come back any time but not with her damned *assistant*. Let her get the Englishman if she wanted something exotic. At least the Englishman drank... Her mother finally was extremely apologetic, but, she said, I must understand that young girls these days cannot wait for ever; Marie-Louise, though she had never broken faith with me, was of an age where she needed a man; she had always dreamed of marrying a schoolmaster, an academic, she was a passionate reader and at school she had taken the first place; though she had the instincts of a woman, her first ambition had always been in the spiritual direction...

I could bear no more. I tore the letter in pieces and withdrew, a broken man, to the bachelor seclusion of an Oxford college. I worked like a madman. The harder the memory of Marie-Louise oppressed me the more furiously I fought

it away with ruthless disciplines of intellectual abstrusion. Only once did I allow myself the pleasures of the body, and the result was a disaster. Under heavy pressure from my colleagues, I agreed to attend some wretched celebratory dinner. Our master of ceremonies, charged with arranging the menu, served a particularly foul *rouge* overpriced at twenty-two shillings, too thin to be taken for anything but a *rosé*, and distributed under the title of Merveille d'Etrouille. Even my colleagues found it undrinkable. The master of ceremonies, who was an idiot, refused to apologize. He had consulted written authorities, he explained, which spoke of the the Etrouille crops with the deepest respect; in nineteen fifty-three the southern vineyards of Etrouille had produced a wine... Later, having railed him, they threw him in the pond, and having given them every assistance I returned to my studies.

I suppose, nevertheless, that I owe my success in the examination to my poor Marie-Louise. The thought of her in the arms of her mean and cheerless academic drove me again and again to my desk. It was no longer the *Cuvée Marie-Louise* which lulled me into a giddy sleep, it was the ashen dullness of Kantian dialectic, the critique of pure reason, the observation of minds in flight from the flesh. Yet at heart I was not deceived by these stern philosophies. I had no taste for the disembodied mind; the abstractions of German philosophic verbalism were like a musical score that would never be played. I took high honours and was offered a fellowship. Thus, though the academic life drew me inevitably, I entered its gates as a prisoner, but not as a penitent. At least Marie-Louise, I thought, had she but known, would have been proud of me. I was not proud of myself.

The academic reputation of the provincial French University of Félon was in those days, heaven knows, not exactly high. Félon is a fortress town not far from Avignon; behind its redoubtable walls, five hundred years ago, a band of monks elected to subsidise their living by imparting secular knowledge to the sons of merchants. Neither the standard of instruction nor the pace of everyday life, it is often said, have been much altered by the intervening centuries. But academics, like the rest of the world, find their stars in strange places, and it was in

Félon, for all its somnolence, that they found du Chêne. All of a sudden, in the tiny world to which I now belonged, du Chêne was the arbiter of intellectual fashion. It is not much, I know, but the fact remains: from Uppsala to Berkeley, there was not a Germanist who ventured into print on the subject of the nineteenth-century thinkers without reckoning with the judgment of du Chêne. The merest hint of fantasy, the smallest leap into unfounded speculation, and in a dozen learned journals his pen struck like a whip. For du Chêne was not merely our star, he was our abbot, and the scourge of all untidy thinking; and it was in Félon, of all places, that he had made his home. It was with uncommon pride, therefore, that I accepted his invitation to address the Faculty. Not only had du Chêne been gracious enough on a number of occasions to give favourable notice to my work: the University of Félon was famous for its hospitality.

Du Chêne and I shared, I liked to think, a mutual regard. He had written warmly of my re-appraisal of Schiller's interpretation of the naive; I had been much excited by his observations on the inductive nature of Kant's logic. But his invitation, extended in the name of his colleagues, overwhelmed me with its generosity. '*Your diligence,*' I read, '*Your perseverance in the noble search for spiritual and intellectual enlightenment ...*' It was a citation. I replied the same morning: I would be proud, I said, to address the Faculty, and delighted to attend a dinner afterwards in my honour. The same afternoon I made a special journey to Low's in Hatton Garden. I bought an eighteenth-century bon-bon dish for the Professor's wife; the Professor should know that I did not take his invitation lightly. Du Chêne, to my delight, was to meet me at the station. I know precisely how I expected him to look: massive and oak-like, a Jung-like aristocrat, as rigorous and austere as his writings. I imagined a generous man, but stern, who strode firmly but not (since he admired me) uncharitably across the earth: I dressed him in a suit of dark grey, clean but rubbed shiny at the elbows by the rich teak of an ancient roll-top desk; and I fancied a large and cumbersome motor-car parked in a privileged place, and a loyal driver waiting at the wheel. So that when the freckled clerk in the English blazer approached me at the barrier, a grubby Bon Marché carrier bag dangling from his left hand, I assumed that du Chêne had been detained for reasons of state, and had sent his acolyte instead.

'Du Chêne,' he said, hissing like Kaa, while his upper lip rose in a sneer, as if names were a subject he had yet to write about, and with the contempt they deserved. I did not realise at first that he was introducing himself. I thought he was making an apology on behalf of an absent master, and that du Chêne was the subject of an unfinished sentence. But he had taken my hand in his by then, and was feeling the flesh with disapproval. We had a couple of hours to kill, he explained, before my lecture; had I eaten on the train or would I care for a sandwich?

My spirits were at a low ebb by the time my lecture began. I had gone to some lengths, in my paper, to pay tribute to my great patron, and by the time I got to the rostrum I was beginning to feel I had rather overdone it. It had occurred to me, as I listened to his unbroken monologue in the dingy bar where we drank our coffee, that du Chêne's ideas were not ideas at all, but attitudes of scorn conveyed by a sharp but barren mind, I had thought of him as breaking new ground, but now that I had listened to him, I knew that he was merely retracing old paths, and beating down the bushes to either side. I tried to remember what he had praised in my own work, and I realised for the first time that he had only sided with me where I had questioned the work of others; and as I watched him, perched on that bar stool and fluttering his hands about like any second-year undergraduate laying down the law in the bar of the Union, I wondered how on earth I had been taken in by him, and how his colleagues – who were now to form the nucleus of my audience – could tolerate the dictatorship of such a shallow, bitter and ungenerous intellect. I was soon to know the answer.

Du Chêne himself had decided to introduce me.

We would all be familiar, he said, with the rich contribution which our guest had made to his chosen field of study. Du Chêne himself had had occasion to be grateful for several stimulating suggestions. He referred in particular to my paper on the Schillerian distinction between naive and sentimental. Personally – the upper lip trembled – du Chêne was inclined to question whether Schiller was a philosopher at all. The word *Dichter* in German covered a multitude of confusions; he had noticed, in his recent readings, that the *literati* tended to speak of Schiller as a philosopher, while the philosophers spoke of him as a poet . . .

It was while he was making this tired joke that I woke to the reaction of the audience. It was one of unmixed loathing. They followed him as racegoers might follow an unpopular winner, longing for him to fall, yet knowing there was little hope. Some had lowered their heads and were staring miserably at their hands; some had turned their eyes glumly to the high dusty windows, but God was hidden behind a black and stormy sky that day and they had no comfort there. A few – they were the younger men whose nerve perhaps was stronger, and whose aspirations had not yet died – these few stared at him with passion burning in their Gallic gaze, each one a Cassius to this precocious, usurping Emperor; and I knew they hated me also as his protégé.

Du Chêne must have been nearly done, for he was talking now of my own person. We all looked forward, he said, to the privilege of a closer acquaintance at the Faculty dinner tonight; it was not often that they had the pleasure of receiving a *gentleman of Oxford* in their midst. Speaking for himself, du Chêne said, he had a warm affection for Oxford: he had spent a term at St Peter's Hall while still a student. *In vino veritas*, he had learned, was the Oxford motto; it was a nice thought, for those of us who enjoyed the pleasures of the table (the upper lip made it clear that he was not among them) that today an Oxford man was supplying the truth, and that Félon was supplying the wine.

I spoke appallingly. I departed from my text, I skipped, at random, long pages of eulogy of du Chêne, and the whole fabric of my thesis collapsed. I extemporised, and could not find the words; I made awful jokes and no one laughed; I apologised and no one pitied me. I spoke of the great French institutions of learning, of hands clasped across the Channel; but all I felt was the smouldering hostility of an alienated audience. And all the while, through the mist, du Chêne's gleaming eyes watched me like prison lights from which there was no shade and no refuge.

I think that in a way, they actually quite liked me. Du Chêne, after all, had raised me. Du Chêne, after all, had brought them here to listen to me; they expected a destructive robot of du Chêne's own school. Instead, they had watched me fail, and fail royally. The apprentice had disgraced his master; the day was not wholly the enemy's. When it was over, they shook my hand quite kindly. An older man – I had seen him earlier appealing to God – actually patted my arm. He had gained *much* from my lecture, he said; it had been a very *human* lecture. Humanity these days – here a small glance in the direction of du Chêne – was often in rather short supply at Félon, particularly among the *young*, he said; there was such a premium on youth these days. But tonight, he added with a parting smile, tonight they would do justice to my humanity. 'We bring our wives,' he explained, quoting John Gay to me. 'They unbend the mind,' he said. 'They unbend the mind.' He was an anglicist, I learned later, with a gift for apt quotation.

They had taken a private dining-room at the inn where I was staying. The french windows gave on to a courtyard planted with trees. The branches had been trained over a pergola, and the lamps shone downward through the leaves. I was reminded, a little sadly, of Etrouille.

Alone in the dining-room, I waited for my hosts to arrive. Du Chêne had gone home to collect his wife, and I knew at once that I would be facing him down the length of the table, for while every other place was set with a cluster of wine glasses, du Chêne's was provided only with a tumbler, a clouded, drab-looking tooth-mug which I am sure the *maître d'hôtel* had chosen personally as his emblem of contempt. I remained there sadly, listening for the first car to arrive. A waiter had entered, quite a young man, a student perhaps, filling in time before beginning his studies. He smiled at me pleasantly, and offered me an apéritif. I was enjoying my stay? I was enjoying it very much, I replied; I was overcome with hospitality, I was enchanted by the town; and I might have added, if I had not heard a car drawing up in the courtyard, I might very well have told him that I envied his estate, and wished to heaven I had never renounced it in favour of the hollow triumphs of an academic discipline.

I composed myself suitably, waiting for the door to open. It is a silly game one plays at such moments of nervousness. The hand before, or the hand behind? Should one be turned expectantly to the doorway, or allow oneself to be discovered unawares? It was the du Chênes; I actually caught a few words as he settled with the taxi-driver; a month ago, he was saying, the fare had been four francs sixty; now it was four francs eighty. The driver answered wearily: they were held up at the lights, the meter was controlled by a combination of time and distance; he could not be responsible for the meter. I heard the rustle of crinoline and a light, feminine step, and I saw in my mind's eye the pinched, sallow wife he would have, the mother-of-pearl handbag and the poor raincoat covering the black *crêpe*, and I was in the act of thanking God that I had not parted with the silver bon-bon basket as Marie-Louise walked in on the arm of du Chêne, her black hair brushed over her lovely shoulders, and her eyes turned down, so that I knew that she expected me.

Du Chêne was introducing us; I touched her hand, reaching towards her tentatively, a blind man reaching for the brush-strokes of a canvas. She gripped mine as if I would save her from drowning.

'Pierre has spoken constantly of you, monsieur,' she murmured, 'I do not understand all, but I admire you immensely.'

'Our work goes far over her head,' du Chêne remarked indifferently. 'But for some reason she has always been interested in your writing. Your style is very simple.' He turned his back on her in order to present to me another guest, who mercifully had just entered. Soon they were arriving in numbers, their faces bright with gastronomic anticipation. Rich smells preceded them from the hallway; they greeted me with pleasure, recognising, I am sure, the light of humanity and the dash of colour which now redeemed my features. Somewhere I heard music playing, though Marie-Louise has since assured me there was none. But a man who is on the edge of paradise hears his own sounds, and no one, not even Marie-Louise has the right to dispute them.

We were eighteen at table; Marie-Louise sat on my left. She sat very demurely, talking most of the time to the elderly anglicist, unbending his mind and almost unhinging mine, for her foot was resting against my ankle, and our hands had intertwined beneath the immaculate tablecloth. She was more beautiful than ever, but more assured. I read her afresh, and I read her accurately, with an eye sharpened by love and a mind improved by years of agonised reflection. She was lost, but not forfeit; disappointed but not despairing; she had made a mistake and had seen where it could lead, and she proposed to rectify it at the earliest opportunity. Her very body was a body in waiting; I was certain she had quickly determined not to waste it on du Chêne. She had had a lover – several – and some no doubt (it was in the air) were at this very table, but the lovers were to cover the mistake she had made six years ago, and now she faced a clear sea and meant to sail her own course. There was no flirtation between us; the pact was concluded with that first handshake. Our relationship was resumed where it had left off, but it was informed with the wisdom of the intervening years. We were lovers before the act, and the act – as our secret caresses now declared – would be taken care of at the earliest possible opportunity.

There are clichés about the arts of love and the art of cooking which I have never subscribed to. The French delight in them less than we suppose, but they are victims of their reputation. There are those, without a doubt, who could recite to this day the list of superb dishes that were put before us. And Marie-Louise, in any event, is in a special position to do so, since it was she, my deputed hostess, who had ordered them. We ate, and talked and drank, each with greater liberality as the evening proceeded. I have never been so entertaining. I made jokes, and the jokes were funny; I regaled them with small gossip from my arid Common Room, and they laughed out loud, rejoicing in my frankness. I even chose a moment to criticise my own lecture of that afternoon. I had thought about it too much, I said; I had been overawed by the honour of the occasion; but they would hear no wrong of me, shouted me down, lifting their glasses to me and assuring me that every word I spoke had been a jewel of wisdom. Opposite me, at the far end of the table, already out of focus, du Chêne sipped darkly at his tooth-mug, forgotten or ignored.

Who spoke first of producing a special wine? Marie-Louise assures me to this day that it was the old anglicist on her left, but if that is so, then Marie-Louise implanted the notion in his mind. The movement began with a conference from which I was excluded; a muddle of excited murmurs at the centre of the table, a short dispute followed by universal agreement, and the waiter, the young waiter, was summoned and addressed in terms near to reverence. The bottles should be decanted, they said; they should be uncorked now and allowed to breathe; no, they should be uncorked later. The dispute broke out again afresh, and this time it was Marie-Louise who quelled it. This wine, she said simply, should be drunk directly from the bottle and uncorked only at the last minute. The waiter returned with a colleague. The bottles they carried were wrapped in linen napkins. Silence descended on the company. Only du Chêne, sensing an irregularity, his rimless spectacles glittering unpleasantly in the candlelight, chose to speak.

'What ritual, may I ask, is being observed tonight?'

Not a head turned. It was the anglicist who finally replied.

'We are making a bridge,' he explained (I think he was holding Marie-Louise's other hand, for I felt a surge of warmth for him that was like an electric reaction), 'between the naive and the sentimental. Between the intellect and the body.'

'More like a river,' du Chêne retorted sullenly, regarding the little row of white-clad bottles which stood like virgins before their first communion, but the day was undoubtedly the old professor's and had been from the beginning.

'And since your guest,' the professor continued, '*our* guest, has taught us that life is not only to be contemplated but enjoyed, we propose to ask him' – here he glanced at Marie-Louise as if she were at least party to the notion – 'to ask our guest to sample a wine we have chosen in his honour, and to give us the advantage of his valued academic judgment.'

I protested, but only feebly. I was no connoisseur, I said, but again they shouted me down. All my reserve had left me. I am no musician, but if they had put a grand piano before me that night, I could have played them a Beethoven sonata with the confidence of a master.

The young waiter's hand trembled a little as he poured. He had put a new glass before me of the classic, balloon shape, and the whole table watched in silent rapture as the red wine spread like a stain over the broad base.

The glass had not reached my lips before I heard the raucous chatter of the peasants in the *bistro* below my bedroom; I smelt the wet, sweet scent of the vine-leaves on the southern slope of the valley and heard the cracked, irreverent chime of the little chapel summoning the heathen Gauls to worship some other God but Bacchus; I saw Marie-Louise lean back a little in her chair, as she had lain so vainly on my little bed. At last I drank. The liquid swelled on my tongue; its aroma infused my nostrils, turned my head . . .

For a moment, I feared I had lost altogether the power of speech: for not even the great *cuvée* could wash away the lump in my throat, or keep back the

tears which crowded my heated eyes. My first words, I think, were inaudible to all but those closest to me:

'It is the finest of all French wines ... I had thought it was lost to us for ever ... a wine as rare and as rich as happiness itself ... of multiple and mysterious tastes, a wine of the mind and of the body ... it was found once only' – my voice gathered strength – 'for those of us at this table, it will not be found again in our lifetime ... a gift of God to a barren valley ...' I named it, but not at once, for I had du Chêne in mind. Even in that moment of ecstasy, with Marie-Louise's little hand resting coolly on my thigh, cunning was my ally. The year was fifty-three, I said; the wine was first enjoyed (prematurely) in fifty-four; the valley was remote and even despised by those who thought they had experienced the best Provence could yield ... They were applauding, but I barely heard them. Someone was clapping me on the back, someone else was embracing me, but I saw only Marie-Louise and the sweet tears running down her cheeks ...

Du Chêne had made it a rule to retire at eleven. He liked to rise early, he explained in a metallic voice, in order to arrange his correspondence. I thanked him for his generosity. No, I said; I would make my own way to the station; he had done enough for me already. The anglicist promised to bring Marie-Louise home – she was, after all, the hostess and obliged to remain – and when du Chêne had left she gave him a little kiss which he seemed to understand.

We took the midnight train to Etrouille, changing at Avignon. I have altered the name, for we do not care for visitors in the valley. There are a few dozen bottles left in the cellar of the Auberge de la Domaine, and we like to use them sparingly. The bon-bon dish sits resplendent on our dining-table; Marie-Louise fills it from time to time with savoury pastries of her own manufacture. The quality of the *Cuvée Marie-Louise* has, if anything, improved; not even its most ardent admirers had dared to expect such a maturity in the flavour. The after-glow is particularly rewarding.

© *from* THE COMPLEAT IMBIBER 10

The Cocktail Classic

CYRIL RAY

There is something about a Martini,
A tingle remarkably pleasant,
A yellow, a mellow Martini;
I wish that I had one at present ...

So sang Ogden Nash, and so do I, obliged to write a thousand words or so on the most classical of classic cocktails. The noblest, too, for it boasts the longest lineage: a 'Martinez' cocktail was contemporary with the Connecticut Eye-Opener of the American Civil War and the Alabama Fog-Cutter of the War Between the States, though it was a sweeter drink than we know today, comprising maraschino, sweetish gin ('Old Tom') and sweet vermouth. No doubt Cuckold's Comfort had to be sweeter still ...

Half-way between then and now, in the so-called 'cocktail age' of the 1920s, the Martini was already firmly established – and still remembered as the Eye-

Opener and the Fog-Cutter and the Cuckold's Comfort are not, though some also old enough to remember the cloche hats and the Charleston, the short skirts and the long strings of beads, have long forgotten the other cocktails of the time – Monkey Gland and Mah Jongg, Between the Sheets and the Bosom Caresser.

It was the simple Martini in those days, though: the Dry Martini was only slowly emerging. According to the only book devoted to a single cocktail, John Doxat's classic *Stirred – Not Shaken*, it was not until after the First World War that the ratio of one-to-one gin and vermouth began to vary, and I, too, recall that a Martini was half-and-half (otherwise known as gin-and-French: a gin-and-It, also half-and-half, was sweet, and sported a maraschino cherry on a stick) whereas a Dry Martini was two of gin to one of dry – in those days necessarily French – vermouth.

I was once told by Alec Waugh, the best-selling but not now so well-remembered elder brother of Evelyn, and a greater authority on liquor and on ladies, that mixed drinks, if they survived at all, become stronger as the years go by – the Dry Martini, he said, one part drier every thirty years. He underestimated the rate of progress – or moved in his old age in sedater circles than had been his wont – for now, only half his suggested thirty years on, one hears of keeping the vermouth in a separate room and bringing it within three feet of the gin at cocktail-time. (An old friend once objected that this was not a Dry, but a Naked Martini, or Streaker.)

American officers I met during the war were already downing potent seven- or eight- or ten-to-one jobs, and the colonel who is the central figure in Hemingway's *Across the River and into the Trees*, calls at Harry's Bar in Venice for 'two very dry Martinis: Montgomerys – fifteen to one,' a calculated sneer at a better soldier than he ever was, who was determined that no British army under his command should suffer the losses it had sustained in World War One.

This apotheosis of the Martini into the driest of Dry Martinis explains The Lady's Lament, of which one version is:

> *I like a Martini, said Mabel,*
> *But I've learned to take two at the most,*
> *For with three I am under the table –*
> *After four, I am under my host ...*

In the interest not only of ladies who value their virtue but also of gentlemen who prefer to wreak their wicked will by more subtle means, I have put myself to the trouble from time to time to seek out what seems to me (not everyone will agree) the perfect Martini – which must mean, these days, the Dry Martini.

I must explain, first, that a Martini need not be made with Martini vermouth – it takes its name from that of a New York Waldorf-Astoria barman of many years ago, and the drink became a Martini by natural confusion with the vermouth – and what a stroke of luck for the firm!

Nevertheless, it seemed appropriate, when I began my scientific research some years ago, to sit at the feet of Jimmy, a barman for fifty years, first at the American Bar of the old Carlton Hotel and then, on the very same site, mixing Martinis with Martini vermouth on the Martini Terrace for the Martini firm.

What he offered, and what I gladly accepted, was the classic two-to-one – in this case, two of Booth's High and Dry, to one of the Martini dry. He poured this over broken ice and then stirred, not shook, the mixture quickly into a glass before it could be diluted by melting ice. Over this, Jimmy held a sliver of the zest of lemon – no pith, which is bitter – giving it a deft twist so that the essential oil of the lemon-peel sprayed into the glass before he dropped it in. An olive was optional, but a pearl onion turns a Martini into a Gibson, and is frowned upon by purists.

That long-ago demonstration by Jimmy was repeated in essentials only the other day by Giuliano at the Terrace Bar of the Dorchester Hotel. Three-to-one, though, this time – Tanqueray gin, as being export strength compared with its famous stable companion, Gordon's, and again the Martini dry vermouth.

Giuliano agreed with Jimmy about stirring, not shaking – only cocktails involving fruit juice or sweet liqueurs should be shaken, whatever James Bond may have said. (His creator, Ian Fleming, was Foreign Manager of the *Sunday Times* when I was its Moscow correspondent, and I can vouch that he knew less about drinks than he pretended James Bond did: he didn't know the difference between a hock and a Moselle, and he got his champagne vintages wrong.)

Like all good barmen, Giuliano will mix his Martinis any way he is asked, and recognises that Americans like them drier than the British do: he keeps vermouth in a drip-bottle (in the fridge, along with the glasses) like those that dispense chilli-vinegar in oyster bars, so that he can add a mere few drops to a very Dry Martini indeed, though some ask for Plymouth or Bombay gin instead of London as giving that little extra flavour not provided by vermouth.

Giuliano's choice, and mine, is to have the drink 'straight up' rather than on the rocks – no danger of dilution that way. He likes the cocktail glass of forty years ago, triangular in section, but I prefer the medium-sized sort of wine glass often used for white wine – it leaves room to put your nose into the glass before raising the glass to your lips: part of the fun is to sniff at the life-

enhancing liquor that is just on its way, and there must be at any rate a little vermouth to add to the fragrance, even if as Ogden Nash decided (and when you come to the fourth line remember that he pronounced 'vermouth' in the American way, which is only proper, for not only was the poet American by birth but so is the potation):

> *There is something about a Martini,*
> *Ere the dining and dancing begin,*
> *And to tell you the truth,*
> *It is not the ver*mouth –
> *I think that perhaps it's the gin.*

Or, as Mabel might have put it, gin and bare it ...

Wine, Women, Food, and Song

PETER DICKINSON

(Suitable for singing at almost all dining clubs)

Why are the songs of men who dine
Exclusive to the fruitful vine
  Or else the fruitful female
(As if Man needs a vocal line
  To prove himself a he-male)?

Our founding fathers, gentlemen,
Possessed a normal, healthy yen
  Not just for beer and Skittles
(If Skittles still was active then) –
  They also liked their victuals.

They swilled the white, they sloshed the red,
They whizzed about from bed to bed,
    Then sang in manly basses
About their sins. But when they fed
    Sat mumchance in their places.

Ah! What avails the artichoke,
What use to marinade and soak
    And run up luscious mushes,
When all the Muses are bespoke
    By lechers and by lushes?

'Tis time to set the matter right.
I hymn the joys of appetite.
    Why, of all men, should *we* shun
The task of bawling through the night
    The pleasures of repletion?

The man who drinks but does not eat
Reels out obnoxious to the street
    And tries to bash his fellow.
The man who takes his wine with meat
    Grows, glass by glass, more mellow.

How pale the skin, how sunk the eyes
Of him who hopes to womanise
    On too exiguous rations.
Statistics show he often dies,
    The victim of his passions.

By contrast, how serene the views
Of him who eats but does not booze,
    Nor thinks all women beddable:
He's time to *think* while as he chews:
    His exploits, too, are credible.

So drink you gin or orange juice
And be your life a trifle loose
    Or chaste as any freezer,
If you can eat your half a goose
    You are the man for me, Sir!

Wine, Women, Food, and Song

For Gluttony's the noblest far
Of all the Deadly Sins there are,
  And who is not a sinner? –
Though Sloth thereafter does not mar
  A decent little dinner.

© *from* THE COMPLEAT IMBIBER 9, 1967

'Very Good for the Kidneys'
also known as
'Music by Moonlight'

SOMERSET MAUGHAM

We finished ' ~heon and coffee was served. The wine waiter came up and asked whether we wanted liqueurs. We all refused except Gray, who said he would have a brandy. When the bottle was brought Elliott insisted on looking at it.

'Yes, I can recommend it. That'll do you no harm.'

'A little glass for Monsieur?' asked the waiter.

'Alas, it's forbidden me.'

Elliott told him at some length that he was having trouble with his kidneys and that his doctor would not allow him to drink alcohol.

'A tear of zubrovka could do Monsieur no harm. It's well known to be very good for the kidneys. We have just received a consignment from Poland.'

'Is that true? It's hard to get nowadays. Let me have a look at the bottle.'

The wine waiter, a portly, dignified creature with a long silver chain round his neck, went away to fetch it, and Elliott explained that it was the Polish form of vodka but in every way superior.

'We used to drink it at the Radziwills when I stayed with them for the shooting. You should have seen those Polish princes putting it away; I'm not exaggerating when I tell you that they'd drink it by the tumbler without turning a hair. Good blood, of course; aristocrats to the tips of their fingers. Sophie, you must try it, and you too, Isabel. It's an experience no one can afford to miss.'

The wine waiter brought the bottle. Larry, Sophie and I refused to be tempted, but Isabel said she would like to try it. I was surprised, for habitually she drank very little and she had had two cocktails and two or three glasses of wine. The waiter poured out a glass of pale green liquid and Isabel sniffed it.

'Oh, what a lovely smell.'

'Hasn't it?' cried Elliott. 'That's the herbs they put in it; it's they that give it its delicate taste. Just to keep you company I'll have a drop. It can't hurt me for once.'

'It tastes divine,' said Isabel. 'It's like mother's milk. I've never tasted anything so good.'

Elliott raised his glass to his lips.

'Oh, how it brings back the old days! You people who never stayed with the Radziwills don't know what living is. That was the grand style. Feudal, you know. You might have thought yourself back in the Middle Ages. You were met at the station by a carriage with six horses and postilions. And at dinner a footman in livery behind every person.'

He went on to describe the magnificence and luxury of the establishment and the brilliance of the parties; and the suspicion, doubtless unworthy, occurred to me that the whole thing was a put-up job between Elliott and the wine waiter to give Elliott an opportunity to discourse upon the grandeur of this princely family and the host of Polish aristocrats he hobnobbed with in their castle. There was no stopping him.

'Another glass, Isabel?'

'Oh, I daren't. But it is heavenly. I'm so glad to know about it; Gray, we must get some.'

'I'll have some sent round to the apartment.'

'Oh, Uncle Elliott, would you?' cried Isabel enthusiastically. 'You are so kind to us. You must try it, Gray; it smells of freshly mown hay and spring flowers, of thyme and lavender, and it's soft on the palate and so comfortable, it's like listening to music by moonlight.'

© *from* THE RAZOR'S EDGE, 1944

Let's Parler Franglais

MILES KINGTON

Drawings by Merrily Harpur

Dans le Cocktail Bar

Barman: Bon soir, monsieur.

Régulier: Bon soir, Harry.

Barman: Monsieur prend un Harvey Wallbanger?

Régulier: Un Frappemur de Harvey? Non. C'est démodé.

Barman: Un Tequila Sunrise? Une Pina Colada?

Régulier: Non plus. Ils sont tous yesterday's drinks. Les clichés du folk beautiful.

Barman: Alors, un Confort du Sud?

Régulier: *Un Southern Comfort?* Harry! Vous me choquez. C'est le drink du year before yesterday.

Barman: Peut-être qu'il soit due pour revival.

Régulier: Hmm. Non, mais nice try. Harry, pour une fois dans ma vie je veux être en avance de fashion. Je veux être un trend-champion!

Barman: Eh bien, monsieur, j'ai un petit secret. J'ai inventé en 1968 un drink que je n'ai jamais divulgué. Je

[234]

suis le seul à savoir. Son nom est le 'Garter Strangler'.

Régulier: Garter Strangler? Like it! En quoi ça consiste?

Barman: Rhum, grenadine, schnapps, un peu de café, jus de citron, vodka et . . .

Régulier: Et?

Barman: . . . et deux aspirines.

Régulier: Mon dieu. Et vous buvez cela, vous?

Barman: Non. Je l'emploie plutôt pour le shoe-cleaning. Mais c'est tout-à-fait potable. Du moins, ce n'est pas toxique.

Régulier: OK. Un Garter Strangler, s'il vous plaît!

Barman: Coming up, monsieur. (*Harry commence à mesurer et mixer*).

Régulier: By the way, où sont les autres, le crowd usuel? Ils font le roller-skating?

Barman: Non, je ne crois pas. On me dit que le rollering est maintenant passé, along avec windsurfing, la cocaine et les ear-rings. Et, voilà! Votre Garter Strangler.

Régulier: Essayons. (*Il introduit ses lèvres dans le verre.*) Holy Thatcher! C'est dynamite.

Barman: C'est fruity avec un kick de mule.

Régulier: Vous pouvez répéter cela. Still, je suis enfin ahead des trends! C'est moi seul qui connais ce drink. Quel moment! (*Entre le crowd usuel.*)

Crowd Usuel: Allo, Arry! What ho, tout le monde! Ciao, chaps! Et huit Garter Stranglers, s'il vous plaît.

Régulier: Huit Garter Stranglers?

Crowd Usuel: Vous ne savez pas? C'est l'in drink! Tout le monde le boit.

Régulier: I give up.

Dans le Pub

Landlord: Vous désirez?

Punter: Oui. We've got deux pints, un demi de lager, un Campari et soda, un Bloody Mary et un Scotch.

Landlord: Je regrette, nous sommes right out of Campari.

Punter: Oh. Hold on un moment. Il dit qu'il est right out of Campari. . . . Right, maintenant nous avons trois pints de Guinness, un demi de lager, un Pimms No 1, et pour moi un Screwdriver.

Landlord: C'est-à-dire, le Pimms No 1 . . .

Punter: Vous n'avez pas de Pimms Numéro Un?

Landlord: Si, si, mais aujourd'hui le cucumber est un peu floppy.

Punter: Dommage. Il dit le concombre est un peu flaccide.... OK, d'accord. Alors, c'est maintenant cinq Dubonnets et un pint de Guinness.

Landlord: OK, cinq Dubonnets. Mais le Guinness, euh, il faut vous aviser que c'est un peu heady à ce moment-là. Si vous pouvez attendre un quart d'heure....

Punter: Oh, la, la. Il dit maintenant que le Guinness est dans un froth situation.

Landlord: C'est à cause du temps qu'il fait.

Punter: Dans un meteorological froth situation.... OK, ça va. Nous désirons maintenant six verres de vin. Vous avez du vin, peut-être?

Landlord: Mais oui! Toute sorte de vin!

Punter: Six verres de rosé.

Landlord: Toute sorte avec l'exception de rosé. Je pourrais toujours mélanger le rouge et le blanc.

Punter: Non, je crois pas....

Landlord: Je n'ai pas d'objection si vous sortez pour acheter une bouteille de rosé et puis la boire ici.

Punter: Parfait!

Landlord: Il y un off-licence, seulement deux kilomètres d'ici. Et le corkage est £1.

Punter: Sod that. Six pints de bitter, s'il vous plaît.

Landlord: Voilà.

Punter: Et six packets de crisps, fromage et oignons.

Landlord: Je regrette, ils sont épuisés.

Punter: Il dit que les cheese'n'onions sont exhausted ... OK, un paquet de streaky bacon, un paquet de prawn cocktail flavour....

Le Hangover

Mari: Oah. Oah.

Femme: Quoi?

Mari: Oh. Ouf. Oah.

Femme: Comment, oh, ouf, et oah? Tu n'aimes pas les cornflakes?

Mari: Non, je n'aime pas les cornflakes. Ils font un bruit comme une division de Panzers.

Femme: Ah! Tu as un hangover!

Mari: Ce n'est pas seulement un hangover. C'est la fin du monde. Il y a un petit homme dans ma tête, qui fait le démolition work. Je crois qu'il est irlandais. Je suis dans un passing away situation. On me démolit pour l'érection d'un homme plus moderne.

Femme: Pauvre toi. Et pas de *Times* pour l'obituary: 'Après un short hangover, bravement supporté ...'

Mari: Ne te moque pas des mentally handicapped, je t'en prie. Ouf. Aouah.

Femme: J'ai lu un article très intéressant par Kingsley Amis sur les cures de hangover.

Mari: Ah, oui? Quand?

Femme: Chaque année dupuis 1968.

Mari: Et son verdict?

Femme: Que toutes les cures de hangover sont inefficaces. Inutiles. Un dead loss.

Mari: Merci.

Femme: Mais tu peux essayer un Super Prairie Oyster Special.

Mari: En quoi ça consiste?

Femme: Lea et Perrins, oeuf raw, poivre, garlic, Horlicks, cognac, baking powder, radish de cheval, aspirin . . .

Mari: Non, cesse, je t'implore. Ce n'est pas un pick-moi-up, c'est un embalming.

Femme: Alors, un poil du chien? Un petit pick-moi-up? A propos, qu'as-tu bu hier soir?

Mari: Où étais-je hier soir?

Femme: A la partie de bureau.

Mari: Ah, oui. Eh bien, j'ai commencé avec deux petits whiskys, puis quelques verres de vin rouge, puis, trois pints de Theakstons Vieux Bizarre, et après . . .

Femme: Et après?

Mari: Et après, la partie a commencé.

Femme: Mon Dieu. En ce cas, je recommande un bumper de potassium cyanide.

Mari: Il y a une chose. Nous avons un jour tranquille aujourd'hui. Pas de visiteurs. Je peux mourir en paix.

Femme: Tu as oublié?

Mari: Oublié? Oublié quoi?

Femme: Les in-laws arrivent ce matin. Et ce soir, un lovely family outing de dix-huit personnes à la pantomime.

Mari: Soddez–cela pour une alouette. Quelle pantomime?

Femme: Sleeping Beauty.

Mari: Bonne idée. Au revoir. Eugh. Ouaoaoah . . .

Let's Not Parler Franglais!
Every Picture Tells a Story

BERTALL

It was for a book on Château Lafite, published in 1968, that I first drew upon Bertall's *La Vigne: Voyage Autour des Vins de France* (1878) to provide chapter-headings, tail-pieces and suchlike, going on to raid the same treasure-house for later works. I seem to have set something of a fashion, for I began to find the same material in other works, notably in various wine-merchants' lists, not to mention Christmas cards. There are pretty little pieces from the same source in this very book but also – for the first time anywhere, I think, since 1878 – Bertall's illustrated Travelogue of the toper's progress.

I had thought to provide captions in English, but who am I to translate *dans les brindzingues*? I cannot even pronounce it … Anyway, the pictures speak for themselves, though the gentle reader may choose to while away an idle hour in trying his own versions. No prizes are offered.

'Bertall' is an anagram, or very nearly so, of one of the forenames of Charles Albert d'Arnoux (1820-1882), adopted as a pseudonym at the instance of Balzac,

[238]

who was an early admirer of d'Arnoux, to whom he gave some of his work to illustrate.

D'Arnoux was a prolific illustrator, especially of children's books, but he produced at least two works – *La Comédie de Notre Temps* (1874) and the similar *La Vigne* – that he not only illustrated but wrote, proving that his pen was as lively as his pencil. He was a younger contemporary of Constantin Guys, Gavarni (with and for whom he worked) and Daumier. He is a lesser draughtsman, but shares something of their style, in economy of line and feeling for movement. In 1871 he was an anti-Communard when better artists than he – among them Courbet and Pissarro – sought to cherish, on the other side of the barricades, what the greatest of them all, Renoir, recognized as 'that little flame that never dies'.   C.R.

On est bien.

On est gai.

[239]

On est lancé.

On est parti.

On est rond.

On est piqué. Dans les classes souffrantes, on dit: Je me suis piqué le nez dimanche, et j'ai mal aux cheveux lundi.

On est gris.

On est soûl, on a son jeune homme, on a son casque, on a son plumet. On est pochard.

On est dans les brindzingues.

On est paf.

The Kernel of Truth: a Story

MARGERY ALLINGHAM

Alfred inherited the recipe for Prior's Punch (whose other name in the lost archives was *Liquor of Happinesse*), and the *Jardin des Enfants Douces* in Siddon's Street, Soho, almost on the same day; and, since his was an essentially practical disposition, both were in the nature of a responsibility to him.

Des Enfants was out of favour with the Bohemians, who at that far off time could make or break any eating establishment, the chef was erratic to the point of being a visionary and the interior was badly in need of regilding. Alfred's father had never been remarkable as a restaurateur save in the single particular that he was an Englishman, and one day he gave up his good-natured muddling and stepped out of one garden into another, so to speak, where, no doubt, the indefatigable Frenchwoman who had been Alfred's mother was awaiting him on the lawns of Paradise.

A little later in the same week, far down in the country, there died also the fabulous great-aunt of whom Alfred had heard so much. In her time she had

cooked at a great house where Royalty had visited and had spent the remnant of her days in a tied cottage on a fast-dwindling estate. Alfred was her sole remaining relative and might, had he been of a less prosaic mind, have hoped for a share of the munificence of princes, but his inheritance, when it arrived in a registered envelope forwarded by the vicar of the parish, consisted of but two treasures. One was a button cut from Buonaparte's coat by an ancestor of the old lady's who had been in service with the Governor of St. Helena and the other was a sealed package, labelled simply, '*Itt.*'

Alfred had no doubt that this was the recipe for the Punch. He opened it and spread the tattered piece of sermon-paper (or its vellum equivalent) on the cash desk of *Des Enfants*. He had heard so much of the famous draught and its extraordinary properties that even he, for all his lack of romantic feeling, could not escape a thrill of anticipation as he saw the mystery set forth at last in a bold and clerkly hand.

Unfortunately the first item set his feet back firmly on the ground.

'*One. Take of finest French brandy 30 years in cask two full quarts and toss itt in a silver bowle made hot.*'

Alfred sighed. As he had feared, the Liquor of Happinesse had no great commercial possibilities.

He folded the parchment sadly and placed it with the button, which looked like a medal and had a note with it to say that anyone who wore it would 'achieve dominance,' in the secret drawer of the desk where the details of his overdraft lay.

However, after a spring in which *Des Enfants Douces* might well have been *Des Guttersnipes Revolting* for all the notice anyone took of it, the maternal relatives of Alfred, of whom there were several dozen in the immediate vicinity, made a fateful decision for him, and Augustine appeared.

In this important matter Alfred's practical disposition was a great comfort to him, for at first sight Augustine at twenty-eight was not a vision to quicken the blood. She was thin and sallow with a strong nose, a decided chin and little black eyes like sequins. But she brought a *dot* which was timely rather than sizeable and her parents, who kept *The Chicken on the Hearth* in Caroline Street, were sorry to part with her ... save, of course, for her tongue.

The miracle occurred at the actual wedding. After the ceremony at the breakfast, when there were thirty-five relatives of each family assembled and Augustine, wearing the button of Buonaparte which had been made into a brooch for her, was sitting in the centre of a smugly speculative throng, Alfred made the *Liquor of Happinesse* for the first time.

He made a half quantity only because, great though the occasion was, there is a difference between generosity and sheer prodigal extravagance, but there was no tampering with the ingredients. All was as laid down. Even the bowl was solid silver. Mr. Rubenstein from the corner, who lent the vessel, came with it of course but he had a charming character and a fund of the most delicate and suitable anecdotes and could almost have merited an invitation anyhow.

For Alfred the first intimation of the experience to come – the first few notes on the harp, as it were – began when he first poured the pint of Demerara rum into the quart of tossed brandy and a thin blue air, too rare to be called a fume, arose from a mixture, brown and soft as a passionate eye, in the soft, white metal of the bowl. Immediately a strange new sense of well-being stole over him and, for the first time, he saw the broad flat face of his mother-in-law without any unease whatever. He added the ten lemons one by one, rejoicing in their exquisite ripeness and the way the juice hung like mist swirls in the mixture. The powdered white sugar had seemed to him to be too lavish when he had first read the recipe, but he used the full half-pound and, as he breathed the now powerful fragrance, he began to smile and the worries of the past and the apprehensions of the future began to fade.

With the mace and the cinnamon – one penny-weight of each – he began to think of *Des Enfants* as a magnificent possession and, by the time he had added a trace of allspice, the pathway of his life had taken on a certain splendour unobserved by him before.

At this point the recipe ended, save for the direction concerning boiling water ('one gallon drawn from a fair spring'), but there was a single line of writing below so faint as to be indecipherable. Alfred gave up trying to read it and added the water which had just come to the boil in a coffee urn. At once the full melody, as one might say, of the beverage poured out beneath his nose in a glorious crescendo.

At that precise moment he caught sight of his bride and at once noticed something delightful about her which he had never seen before. Her long spice-brown hair, drawn back with a comb set high on the back of her head, had an undulation in its strands which touched his heart and reminded him of something pleasant and familiar. He stood looking at it open-mouthed, and absentmindedly his fingers strayed towards the spice tray where a packet of nutmegs nestled. Still absorbed by her hair, so like the brown fruit in his hand, he grated a whole small nut into the brew *after* – and this, as it happened, was important – the water had been added.

The rest of the evening was pure magic.

The gathering, made up of experts, was not an easy one to impress or to

soften, but the things that happened that night made talk among them for a decade. Men saw new beauty in the wives of twenty years; children confided in their parents; Mr. Rubenstein was actually prevented by the mother of Augustine from presenting the happy couple with the valuable bowl; and an obscure and hitherto neglected uncle sang a song of a far country which no one had ever heard before or could remember afterwards, but which was so beautiful that everyone who spoke of it sighed gently and made somebody else a small gift.

That was the first time Alfred made the *Liquor of Happinesse*, and for a very long time he thought it was also the last.

He brewed the Punch from the recipe, of course, a number of times, for in one sense he prospered. Augustine, with the sign of the dominator, blue and gold, upon her bosom, was the sort of woman who did not countenance failure

and *Des Enfants* waxed in popularity as their joint efforts were poured ruthlessly and untiringly into it. Alfred made the Punch a score of times throughout the years. It shed a scented benison at the christenings of each of his children. The heads of Alfred junior, of Ernestine, of Cecile, of Paul, of Tony, of Bettine and Josef were all wetted at the conventional times with no less a draught, but never once did it achieve quite the same unearthly potency as had been observed upon the first occasion. It was always remarkable, always admired, but the highest note, the sweet, shrill echo of the peace of the heart was never reached again until . . . very much later.

It was after the war. Alfred and Augustine were no longer young. The darkness and the banging and the tragedy and the labour had left their mark

upon them. Paul and Alfred Junior had left home to return no more. The *Des Enfants* itself had sunk in black ashes one summer's night and, but for Augustine's thrift, prudence, and indomitable courage, might never have risen again. But one Sunday in the early nineteen-fifties, in the new *Des Enfants*, recently enlarged, white walled and decked with blushing napery, Alfred made the Punch again.

The occasion was his silver wedding and there were a great many guests. He stood behind the table with the pink cloth on it and with a delicate hand poured four bottles of *fine* into his own silver bowl. Ernestine, Cecile and Bettine waited upon him and, far across the graceful room, Augustine sat stiffly among her guests, the Button of Buonaparte her only jewel.

In many respects it was a splendid affair and most eyes in the assembly were envious, but Alfred, catching sight of himself in a looking-glass, was full of vague resentment. He saw a fat man with a short neck and insufficient hair. It was only to be expected he told himself sensibly, as he stirred in the sugar and took up the small wooden box of powdered allspice. Life had been hard and Augustine's tongue one of its many scourges. Youth had come and looked at him and sighed and gone away.

It was sad, he reflected, sad but inevitable. He glanced across at Augustine and frowned. She was a remarkable woman, indefatigable and, but for her failing, a good enough sort, but she had never had beauty. Now, with her sallow skin, dusted with a powder too pale for it, her little eyes and her wrinkles, she looked like nothing so much as a nutmeg.

He was so struck by the similarity that he took one from the box without realizing it and grated nearly the whole of it into the Punch before he knew what he was doing. The bitter flakes lay on the steaming surface of the pool like dust on mahogany. Startled, he stood back hastily and nodded to his elder daughter to begin to serve.

The miracles of middle age happen slowly. The proprietor of *Des Enfants Douces* had reached the bottom of his first rummer before it occurred to him that something very remarkable had taken place. He observed the phenomenon when on looking in the glass he saw not a fat man but a stalwart one of becoming dignity, interestingly grey.

As he lifted his head he heard for the first time in twenty-five years a deep warm note in the chatter about him and his heart leapt. Bettine, who was in love as well – with Jules, the new *sommelier* – achieved beauty quite suddenly. It blossomed before her father's astounded eyes like a Japanese paper flower unfolding in a glass of water. Even Ernestine, who resembled her mother's family, had a radiance Alfred had never seen before.

The entire company underwent a strange, unforgettable experience in which only the very best in the nature of each enjoyed a sweet liberation, and later on in the evening someone sang a song everybody remembered hearing long ago but no one knew when or where. It had happened again. *The Liquor of Happinesse* had been achieved a second time.

Even the next day when, in the break after their late luncheon in a corner of the deserted restaurant, Alfred and Augustine discussed it, the affair appeared slightly uncanny. Alfred was inclined to put it down to the quality of brandy, but when they sent for a bottle of the same brand it was no better and no worse than the *fine* they had used so many times before.

'Think,' commanded Augustine, her sharp eyes earnest. 'Without doubt it is a matter of mixing. Think. First at our wedding and now again last night.'

Alfred allowed his practical mind to dwell upon the two occasions.

'Wait,' he said suddenly. 'That's right. It's something to do with you. Each time at the very end of the business, after the water had gone in, I caught sight of you and . . .' He paused abruptly.

His wife stared at him.

'Perhaps you have been drinking?' she suggested coldly.

'No.' Alfred was on the right tack but he perceived a difficulty. 'No, my dear. It's a fact. That's the only difference. On each of these special occasions, just as the stuff was ready, I looked over at you and – er – something happened.'

Augustine flushed and her sequin eyes grew ever brighter.

'Idiot!' she said, but she was very pleased and when she got up to go over to the account books she let a brown hand rest for a moment on his collar caressingly.

'The mother of Jules is coming to speak to you to-night about Bettine,' she murmured. 'He is a good worker. Let us hope they are as happy as we have been. "The look of love" eh? You old *blagueur*! That was the secret, was it?'

She went off laughing, and left to himself Alfred took a small glass of the *fine* to settle his digestion.

He reflected that Augustine was a good woman and the best wife in the world – but for her failing. Her last words were still in his ears and he answered them under his breath. He was a kindly man if a practical one.

'It wasn't, you know,' he said to himself. 'It was the nutmeg.'

© *from* THE COMPLEAT IMBIBER I, 1956

Wine, Nothing Much in the Way of Women, But a Certain Amount of Song ...

CYRIL RAY

Noah was not only the first man, according to the good book, to plant a vineyard: he was also the first drunk.

There is an early fifteenth-century carving on a corner of the Doges' Palace, showing the old fellow half-seas over, to which I touch a metaphorical forelock whenever I am in Venice, in tribute to his labours and in fellow-feeling for his lapses.

If I knew of a statue to the first man (or woman) who sang the praises of the grape I should do likewise. When, as the Governor of North Carolina, Edward Dudley, said to the Governor of South Carolina, Pierce Mason Butler, in 1838, it is a damn long time between drinks, it can be soothing to the spirit, even though not quenching to the thirst, to recall some pregnant line as a reminder that other men have found consolation in the bottle and, where you or I might hiccup, have committed literature.

I have admitted to a fellow-feeling for Noah, stewed for ever in stone, on the banks of the Grand Canal: so, too, for Omar Khayyam:

> *Drink! for you know not whence you came, nor why;*
> *Drink! for you know not why you go, nor where.*

I have small Latin, and less Greek, and few fugitive lines from the classics find refuge, untranslated, in my mind. Horace's *nunc est bibendum* might well have been my chosen family motto; it shall be my instruction to my mourners from beyond the grave, along with enough *denarii*, to buy them all a modest quencher. That is very nearly as far as my Latin takes me, in the original, save for some barely relevant impudicities from Catullus . . .

These days I must seek my Horace in translation – James Michie's for preference – and it is worth the seeking, for no poet has written more about wine, its dangers and its delights.

And did I detect a Horatian echo in Gavin Ewart's

> *A remarkable thing about wine,*
> *which we drunkards and lechers all bless so,*
> *is the way it makes girls look more fine –*
> *but ourselves, on the contrary, less so?*

I see that I have promised my heirs 'a modest quencher' – the phrase is Dick Swiveller's, but it floated into my mind from Calverley, who quoted it in his paean to beer: no lines are to me more memorable than those of the lighter-hearted versifiers. Milton eludes my memory, and yet I could quote A.P. Herbert without the burden of checking my references (save that I always check my references):

> *Start her on champagne, boy, but break her into hock –*
> *That's the only rule of life that's steady as a rock . . .*

Not that I have the late Duff Cooper's memory: it was to him that Hilaire Belloc dedicated his great *Heroic Poem in Praise of Wine*, and it was he who, coming straight from a debate in the House of Commons to a dinner of the Saintsbury Club, (or so Vyvyan Holland recorded) recited from memory and without a slip all two hundred and more lines of it:

> *To exalt, enthrone, establish and defend,*
> *To welcome home mankind's mysterious friend:*
> *Wine, true begetter of all arts that be . . .*

– a poem that, to my mind, more than makes up for all those boozy, back-slapping, cannikin-clinking jingles about beer, Burgundy and the Blessed Virgin

[250]

Mary that Belloc and his fat friend Chesterton were guilty of when they were not busy clobbering the Jews. (Noah was a Jew, damn it, and I have no doubt that Pussyfoot Johnson was a Gentile, to say nothing of Father Mathew's having been a Catholic . . .)

Not only light verse, but bad verse tickles my fancy, especially bad verse about bad wine. Henry Wadsworth Longfellow, for instance, on a wine from the state of Ohio:

> *Very good in its way*
> *Is the Verzenay,*
> *Or the Sillery, soft and creamy;*
> *But Catawba wine*
> *Has a taste more divine,*
> *More dulcet, delicious and dreamy . . .*

Good poets, in any case, can be bad guides. Keats, you will remember, liked his claret cold: when he was asking that 'the true, the blushful Hippocrene' should have been 'cool'd a long age in the deep-delved earth', he was writing as well to a friend for, 'please heavens, a little claret-wine cool out of a cellar a mile deep', and sweet ratafia biscuits to go with it.

Browning, in *Bishop Blougram's Apology*, asks for the cooler jug of claret with admonitions not to jog the ice, and Thackeray drank red wine with fish soup, and more than one, as his *Ballad of Bouillabaisse* shows: first, 'the Chambertin with yellow seal', and then:

> *Good Lord! the world has wagged apace*
> *Since here we set the claret flowing,*
> *And drank and ate the Bouillabaisse.*

Which is no odder, though, than Arthur Hugh Clough's

> *After oysters, sauterne(s); then sherry, champagne,*
> *Ere one bottle goes, comes another again;*
> *Fly up, thou bold cork, to the ceiling above,*
> *And tell to our ears in the sound that they love*
> *How pleasant it is to have money, heigh-ho . . .*

Robert Nichols, that unjustly forgotten Georgian poet, wrote too, between the wars, of the bold cork that flies to the ceiling above, hitting exactly the right sort of mock-heroic elegance that champagne seems to call for in his,

> *O Widow Clicquot, Widow Clicquot, queen*
> *Of all nymphs potable save the Hippocrene . . .*
> *Who twice as gay makes fluttering candlelight*
> *Where the jazz croons the lifelong summer night . . .*

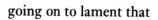

going on to lament that

> ....*Alas, the nights whereon*
> *Venus was kind to me are long since gone,*
> *As are the strains that filled the lighted house –*
> *Der Rosenkavalier and Fledermaus*

so that

> ....*no longer I upon the nose*
> *Of Laura, Averil, Imogen or Rose*
> *Undeftly plant the not-unlooked-for kiss*
> *Yet am I faithful to your mysteries*

and visualises a night of moonlit memories, and

> *On such a night, I say, I deem it due*
> *To keep, dear Madame Clicquot, tryst with you.*
> *Come then, brave bottle of the cheerful top,*
> *A wrench, a twist and – mind your eye, lad – POP!*

A near contemporary of Nichols's, Martin Armstrong, also sang of how

> ....*Golden wine*
> *Brims every glass. Seen through each crystal pane,*
> *In tall straight jets or whirled in spiral twine*
> *The hurrying air beads to the surface strain*
> *An April shower of bright inverted rain.*

Of Armstrong's other verses on wine and suchlike I like his lines to the un-known genius who first distilled wine into cognac –

> *In whose eye a subtle topaz gleamed,*
> *Then in an oaken cask of portly shape*
> *He stored the subtle spirit and darkly smiled,*
> *Knowing that he had craftily beguiled*
> *The Essence of the Essence of the Grape.*

After quoting which, never mind after drinking which, I cannot but recall some verses that a near contemporary of my own – a scholar of my own college, a fellow-contributor to *Punch*, and (this is where he left me standing) a winner of the Newdigate, no less – once wrote for *The Compleat Imbiber*, which I edited throughout its brief lifetime.

A Faint Drinking Song from Under the Table, Philip Hubbard called it, and the first and last verses ran:

Wine, Nothing Much in the Way of Women, But a Certain Amount of Song

> I have no head at all for drink;
>   You all have better heads than I.
> You gather strength as I get weak,
> Grow loud as I fall silent, speak
>   Large words when I can barely think
>   And stand when I must lie.
>
> So let me lie, my friends, and so
>   Have truth before my inward eye,
> While you regardless go your ways
> To worship gods less worthy praise.
>   But tell the waiters, when you go,
>   To leave me where I lie.

C. R.

Remembrance of Meals Past:
A Glance at Food and Wine in Proust

ANTHONY POWELL

I should prefer glycerine – yes, hot, excellent.' Marcel, dining with Saint-Loup in a Paris restaurant rather later than usual one foggy night, was horrified to hear these words spoken by a guest sitting behind him, instead of what was apparently the normal order: 'Bring me a wing of chicken and a glass of champagne – not too dry.'

The statement turned out less daunting than at first appeared, being merely uttered by a doctor using the first-person singular in reply to an acquaintance, who, seeing his physician at one of the tables, had hoped to get some free medical advice. All the same, as the shadow of the sick-room hangs over so much of *A la Recherche du Temps Perdu*, one would not be altogether surprised if Marcel himself had indeed, even if apologetically, made glycerine his appetiser that evening. *Tisanes* and orangeade were more in his line than aperitifs and *vin ordinaire*. The gourmet, especially the amateur of wine, who hopes to be provided by Proust with the same subtleties on the subject of eating and drinking

which he finds about, say, love, friendship, social life, writing, painting, music, will be disappointed. Nevertheless, investigation of their treatment is of interest, even when negative. We may regret that the local wines of France do not receive the attention devoted to place-names and their origin, churches and their architecture, but what is recorded about food and drink is well worth considering. I shall do no more here than indicate the lines along which an ambitious student might gain a Ph.D.

The classic mention of wine in the novel is, of course, Swann's gift of Asti Spumante to Marcel's aunts Céline and Flora; his grandfather's uneasiness that these ladies offered no apparent thanks for the present; the aunts' own self-satisfaction in having expressed their gratitude obliquely by reference to 'some people having nice neighbours'. Cyril Ray, in *In a Glass Lightly*, records his surprise – which many must have shared – that a connoisseur like Swann should have presented an Italian wine, and especially Asti, even to a couple of elderly provincial maiden ladies. Mr Ray goes on to say – quoting among other authorities the *Pink 'Un's* Dwarf of Blood and his collaborator Algernon Bastard in *The Gourmet's Guide to Europe* – that France was then, and still remains, Italy's best customer for sparkling wine. Swann was to be relied upon to produce just what was required, and it would certainly be true to say that Asti has something of its own in bouquet compared with even the sweetest French champagne.

A warning note is struck early in Proust's book by the fact that Marcel's grandfather is not allowed to drink liqueurs. On account of this, his great-aunt – to tease her sister-in-law – used to persuade him to take a few drops of brandy after dinner. This habitually upset Marcel's grandmother. However, the emphasis is on the pain caused to her, rather than on the quality of the brandy, about which we are told no more than that only very little was consumed, and it did not do the slightest harm.

Where food was concerned in Marcel's home at Combray, the presiding genius was their cook Françoise, one of the great figures of *A la Recherche*. She had come there from Aunt Léonie's, where she played an important rôle in discussing the neighbours, with special reference to such matters as who had been able to buy the largest branches of asparagus. Françoise, like most good cooks, was inclined to become bored with the uneventful routine of family cooking, and *bœuf à la casserole* seems to have been a fairly frequent item on the daily menu. Such humdrum dishes were varied, not only by the march of the seasons, but also by the moods of Françoise herself, who would serve up brill, 'because the fish-woman had guaranteed its freshness'; a turkey, 'because she had seen a beauty in a neighbouring village'; cardoons (a vegetable like the artichoke) with marrow, 'because she had never done them before'; roast leg of mutton, 'because the cold air makes one hungry'; spinach, 'by way of a change'; apricots, 'because they were hard to get'; gooseberries, 'because in another fortnight they would be over'; raspberries, 'which Monsieur Swann had bought specially'; cherries, 'the first to come from the cherry tree which had not yielded for two years'; cream cheese, 'because Marcel was extremely fond of it'; almond cake, 'because she had ordered one the evening before'; *crème chocolat*, 'because it was one of her specialities'.

As a boy at Combray, Marcel was usually sufficiently interested about dinner to go down to the kitchen beforehand to find out what was 'on'. Exciting arrangements of vegetables were always to be found set out there. The kitchen was also, of course, the scene of that 'solemn passover', the servants' mid-day dinner, though this is only referred to after the family had come to live in Paris in the house where they shared a courtyard with the Guermantes. Not even Marcel's father would have dared to ring during the celebration of that sacred congress, and, had he so far forgotten himself as to have done so by mistake, no one would have taken the slightest notice. The rite ended with Françoise undoing the napkin from round her throat, after which she wiped away the last traces of watered wine and coffee. So far as wine went, Françoise would always accept a glass offered between meals from time to time, by Jupien, – not yet revealed to Marcel in his intimate role vis-à-vis Monsieur de Charlus and others – social occasions that also required a longish talk. At those awkward moments when Marcel inadvertently entered the kitchen to find Françoise entertaining her daughter to a complicated spread, this was always designated by her as 'just having a scrap'.

However, the great set-piece for a meal at Marcel's home is undoubtedly the dinner to which the former Ambassador, Monsieur de Norpois, was invited: partly to advise Marcel on the choice of a career. The *pièce de résistance* was *bœuf en daube*, that is to say cold beef spiced with carrots, 'lodged by the Michael Angelo of our kitchen upon enormous crystals of jelly, like transparent blocks of quartz'. M. de Norpois was delighted with the manner in which the beef was cooked:

'You've a chef in the top class, Madame,' he said. 'That is not an easy thing to achieve. I myself, when I was living abroad, had to maintain a certain style in entertaining, and I know how difficult it is to find a perfect master in the kitchen. This is a veritable banquet you've set before us.'

M. de Norpois uses the characteristically carefully selected term *agapes*, meaning a love-feast held by the early Christians:

'This is the sort of thing you can't get in a tavern, even the best of them,' he went

on. 'A *daube de bœuf* in which the jelly doesn't taste of glue and the beef has caught the flavour of the carrots. It's admirable. Invite me please again.'

At this point he made a sign to show that he wanted more jelly. 'I should be interested to see how your Vatel would manage a dish of a different sort,' he said. 'I should like, for instance, to see him tackle *bœuf stroganoff*.'

Bœuf stroganoff (mushrooms, sour cream, olives, onions, lemon) gives us further insight into M. de Norpois's tastes, though he was not always prepared to reveal these. For example, Marcel's mother was hoping for praise for the pineapple-and-truffle salad, but the Ambassador, 'after fastening on it for a moment the penetrating glance of a trained observer', ate it 'with the inscrutable discretion of a diplomat', without disclosing his opinion. However, a moment later he could not prevent himself from exclaiming: 'What do I see? Nesselrode pudding! After a Lucullan feast of this sort I shall have to take a cure at Carlsbad.'

Afterwards, when congratulating Françoise on the dinner (they never seem to have admitted to M. de Norpois that their cook was a woman), Marcel's mother said: 'The Ambassador assured me that he knows no place where he can get cold beef and *soufflés* such as yours'; so presumably a *soufflé* was also one of the courses of the dinner. It is, however, notable – and very regrettable – that we are told nothing of the wine given to M. de Norpois, who might be expected to rise to great heights of praise or sink to depths of blame, when speaking of vintages he had enjoyed or execrated.

The question why Françoise made better jelly than that supplied at the great restaurants opens up an interesting list of names. Her own explanation of the restaurants' relative failure in this direction was that they 'do it in too much of a hurry', though she was prepared to admit that she could mention 'one of those cafés where they knew a bit about cooking'. The ideal to be aimed at she described as beef that was 'like a sponge' and mopped up the juice. Marcel's father, who had joined the discussion, asked if the restaurant to which Françoise allowed this claim was Henry's in the Place Gaillon, where he regularly attended *repas de corps* – club dinners:

'Oh, no,' said Françoise, evidently feeling some contempt. 'I meant a little restaurant. Henry's is more like a soup-kitchen.'

'Weber's, then?'

'Oh, no, sir, I meant a good restaurant. Weber's, that's in the Rue Royale, that's not a restaurant, it's a *brasserie*. I don't even know if they serve you there. I don't think they have any table-cloths, they just throw it in front of you anyhow.'

'Ciro's?'

'Oh, there I should think the cooking's done by *dames du monde*' – meaning ladies of the *demi-monde* – 'they need that to get the young men in! No, I mean a restaurant where they have a good little *cuisine bourgeoise*. That's what brings the money in. Madame knows it, right along the *grandes boulevardes*, a little way back.'

This restaurant finally turned out to be the Café Anglais.

At about the same period as this, Marcel was receiving invitations to Swann's house, but we are told little about the food there. Odette's anglomania caused her to provide Christmas pudding at the appropriate season, and certainly on one occasion there was lobster *à l'Americaine*. One might have expected here a dissertation on the question whether this manner of cooking had not once been *à l'Armoricaine* – in the Breton way – but Proust does not tackle the issue. Incidentally, in Madame Prunier's Cookery Book, the 'Armorican' version is different from the 'American', though only very slightly, the sauce of the former being bound with egg yolks and cream before being poured over the lobster.

This brings us to the Grand Hotel at Balbec. Madame de Villeparisis, a great epicure, thought the food there indifferent, although she recommended the oysters, the very thought of which made Marcel feel sick. Among the guests staying at the Grand, with his mistress, was a Frenchman who had proclaimed himself 'king' of one of the Cannibal Islands. His goings-on in general caused a good deal of offence to the more staid residents of the hotel, and, among other things, he always drank champagne at luncheon. On a later visit to the same hotel, Marcel found himself having to cope with the manager, who was famous for his malapropisms. Doing his best to offer everything at his disposal, the manager suggested that he should bring up some of the 'old wine' he had downstairs in a *bourrique* (she-ass), meaning a *barrique* (hogshead). He goes on to explain to Marcel that this wine is 'not Château-Lafite', but is almost as 'equivocal' (meaning 'the equivalent'), and, as it is light, would go well with a fried sole. Although the whole sequence is Proust in one of his knockabout moods, one knows pretty well what the wine would have tasted like.

It was also at the Grand Hotel that Monsieur Nissim Bernard, great-uncle of Marcel's friend Bloch, was 'keeping' one of the waiters. M. Nissim Bernard liked to lunch in the dining-room every day and watch the young man rush about with trays, a situation Proust compares to sitting in the front row of the stalls for those having an affair with a ballet-girl. This favourite waiter was only a *commis*, but owing to M. Bernard's influence with the management, was singled out for promotion. At one moment he was offered the job of *sommelier*, but M. Bernard made him refuse that post because its duties meant that too little would be seen of him. Instead of charging about in and out of the kitchen,

he would merely have approached each table discreetly with the wine-list. It is good to know that this reckless manner of appointing a wine-waiter was renounced from the start, if even for less than the best of reasons.

When Marcel lunched with Bloch's father, a 'light sparkling wine' was brought in a decanter, which purported to be champagne, but was decidedly not. In fact there seems to have been a strong tendency for champagne, or at least sparkling wine, to have been drunk in the middle of the day, and it seems surprising that the King of the Cannibal Islands should have made any impression, good or bad, by doing so. For example, on a day's leave from the garrison at Doncières, when he takes his mistress, Rachel, to Paris for luncheon, Saint-Loup drinks champagne. Indeed, he drinks too much of it, because Rachel irritates him by ogling the other men in the restaurant. Incidentally, at Doncières, the officers' mess was at the Coq-Hardi; the sergeants', at the Faisan Doré.

Marcel and Saint-Loup also drank champagne when they dined together at Rivebelle, near Balbec. Marcel, forgetting for once his grandmother and her anxieties about his health, apparently drank a lot of beer, as well as the champagne; also some port. The passage describing these potations is obscure, so that one is not absolutely certain that he did not actually add a few drops of port to the beer itself, since he says later that he could hardly taste the port. One hopes – indeed, it is much the most likely – that the figure of speech means merely that the port was taken as a digestive – rather than more normally in France as an aperitif – and that by that time it made little impression. In any case Marcel got rather tight. Here, again, the champagne appears to have been unsatisfactory, for several of the diners sent it away as 'not fit to drink', which for some reason gave positive pleasure to the young waiters.

When Albertine became part of Marcel's life, they used to tour the neighbourhood by car, looking at churches. To refresh themselves while doing this they would stop at farms and buy a bottle of 'calvados or cider'. The cider was always described as non-effervescent, but when opened would usually drench both of them from head to foot. Calvados, one feels, might be a little strong for such outings, and it is no surprise to learn that such powerful liquid restoratives ultimately suggested love-making. For shorter trips on foot from the hotel, they would take a bottle of champagne into the forest, or, on a fine evening, enjoy an alfresco no further away than among the dunes. Albertine was never easy to deal with, and, in spite of Marcel's dislike for oysters, always wanted to eat bivalves when she heard them cried for sale in the street. Marcel felt inclined to say that they would be better at Prunier's, but before he could give any such advice, she was tempted by other street-criers: shrimps, skate, whiting, mussels, mackerel. The vendor of the last of these announced his wares with the cry: '*Il arrive le maquereau!*', which always sent a chill down Marcel's spine – not merely because he disliked that particular fish.

Before we depart from the Grand Hotel, another friend of Marcel's must be called to mind in relation to Proust and wine. This is Monsieur Pierre de Verjus, Comte de Crécy, who turns out in due course to be none other than the former husband of Odette. Comte de Crécy was of very ancient family, related to the English bearers of that title (possibly the Cressys of Lincolnshire), though the connection is puzzling, as the Count's patronymic is later said to be 'Saylor'. He himself was extremely hard-up, living in fact on a pension paid by Swann. Comte de Crécy was also unusually good company, and, although modest about his own family, a notable authority on local pedigrees, also the gastronomic arts. Accordingly, Marcel used often to invite him as a guest.

The Verjus coat-of-arms, in punning reference to the name (it is not clear where 'Saylor' came in) was a *branch of verjuice slipped and leaved sinople* (one

translator renders this in English as *vert*, also meaning green, but Proust writes *sinople*, the rarer and more exotic heraldic term); though Marcel, no doubt rightly, judged that M. de Crécy would not have liked to be given verjuice (extract of sour grapes used for cooking) when asked out to luncheon or dinner. Indeed, so far was that from the case that the Count preferred only the most expensive wines in the list, about which he knew a great deal and for which he possessed a notable capacity. Here a real chance is missed of hearing what M. de Crécy ordered, preferably with the price. The suspicion that Proust himself was not deeply interested in wine is to some extent confirmed by the fact that he thinks it worth mentioning that M. de Crécy made the wine-waiter *chambrer* or *frapper* the wines, if so required, and always specified the date when he ordered port or brandy.

The Verdurins' table will be estimated later, but for the moment they are named only in connection with that party of theirs which Monsieur de Charlus attended as a consequence of his passion for the violinist Morel. M. de Charlus is a dominating figure from whom one might reasonably hope for a strong lead in the matter of wine, as on almost every other subject, but the incident in which he is first mentioned as selecting a drink is not encouraging:

'Have you tasted my orangeade?' Madame Verdurin asked him.
'No, I prefer its neighbour, the strawberry juice,' replied the Baron.

He said this in a voice so high that it once suggested his feminine side, even if the choice of beverage, in some eyes, might not have gone far towards prejudicing a reputation for masculine tastes. However, M. de Charlus somewhat redeems himself from the implication of liking sickly drinks on a subsequent occasion, when he is giving Morel dinner at a little restaurant at Saint-Mars-le-Vêtu on the Normandy coast; no doubt a contrast in price with the *Guillaume le Conquérant* at Dives, which Marcel thought very expensive; an opinion that half a century later I myself saw no reason to disallow. At the restaurant chosen by M. de Charlus the waiter brought them two glasses of frothy liquid:

'But I ordered champagne?' said M. de Charlus.
On this occasion, too, he spoke in an unusually shrill voice.
'But, sir ...'
'Take it away, this horror which has no connection with the worst known champagne. It is the emetic called *cup*, which is usually made of three strawberries rotting in a mixture of vinegar and seltzer water.'

M. de Charlus uses the English word 'cup', and he evidently felt strongly about it; as well he might. Later on in the meal he upset the staff of the restaurant again by saying fiercely:

'Ask the head waiter if he has a Bon Chrétien.'
'A good christian, I don't understand.'
'Can't you see we've reached the dessert? It's a pear.'

Morel was as much at sea as the waiter, and the Baron, after quoting the example of various members of the aristocracy who grew prize pears, together with references from Molière on the subject of the same fruit, tried to find out what was available in that line:

'Waiter, have you any Doyennée des Comices?'
'No, sir, there aren't any.'
'Have you Triomphe de Jodoigne?'
'No, sir.'
'Any Virginie-Dallet? Or Passe Colmar? No? Very well, since you've nothing, we may as well go. The Duchesse d'Angoulême is not in season yet; come along, Charlie.'

M. de Charlus's preoccupation with Morel eventually involved him in the question of fighting a duel, which, although something of a sham from the start, required a second. The Verdurin's friend, Dr Cottard, who had a great medical reputation, and had treated Marcel as a boy for his asthma, occupied this rôle. Cottard was, indeed, immensely excited about the duel. When it fizzled out, he and Charlus were left confronting each other with nothing to do but go home. The Baron took Cottard's hand – which filled the Doctor with fear that a sexual assault was about to be made on him – but all M. de Charlus suggested was that they should 'take something' together. 'What used to be called a *mazagran* or a *gloria*, drinks one doesn't find any more, like archaeological curiosities ... a *gloria* would be distinctly suitable to the place and the occasion.'

A *mazagran* (named after the once famous Café Mazagran) is simply coffee in a glass, but a *gloria* is coffee laced with brandy. Here, we may again invoke Mr Ray, who (in his section referring to 'Irish Coffee', mingled, of course, with whiskey) quotes Eliza Acton's *Modern Cookery* as to how to produce 'Burnt Coffee or Coffee à la militaire (*in France vulgarly called gloria*)'. Miss Acton (1799-1859), daughter of a brewer, which may have directed her mind towards food and drink, first published her *Modern Cookery* in 1845. She is probably better remembered for that work, or her treatise on bread, than for her fugitive poems. She never married, but whilst in Paris became for a time engaged to an officer of the French army, who perhaps taught her the term for – and the method of making – the drink that so much took M. de Charlus's fancy. However, Cottard disappointingly replied that he was President of the Anti-Alcoholic League, and that he could not risk some ass of a country doctor coming past and blaming him for not practising what he preached. In fairness

[262]

to Cottard, it should be remembered that he had ordered 'no alcohol' for Marcel's asthma, when other practitioners had recommended beer, champagne and brandy to produce 'euphoria'.

We must now return to the Verdurins, whose food and drink, as such, might almost be said to play the predominant part in the book. Madame Cottard, early on, had asked if one of their salads was a 'Japanese salad', but that was a joke with obvious reference to a current play by the younger Dumas. We know that they sometimes had bouillabaisse, because Monsieur Verdurin once said that 'the bouillabaisse must not be kept waiting'. Perhaps they rather went in for fish, since one of Monsieur de Cambremer's stock remarks, when an appropriately large one appeared on the Verdurin table, was to say: 'That fish is a fine animal.' He considered this comment sufficiently amusing and charming to absolve him from ever inviting the Verdurins themselves to eat in his own house.

At one of the Verdurin dinners, the Polish sculptor Viradobetski (who was always called 'Ski' because his name was regarded as too difficult to pronounce) asked: 'What is this pretty coloured thing we are eating?' Madame Verdurin replied that it was strawberry mousse.

'It's rav-ish-ing,' said Ski. 'You ought to open bottles of Château Margaux, Château Lafite, port.'

The thought of this prodigal outlay greatly alarmed Mme Verdurin, who at once pointed out that this reference to wine was a very good joke on Ski's part as he himself never touched alcohol. However, Ski was not to be laughed off as easily as that.

> 'But not to drink,' he said. 'You shall fill all our glasses. They will bring in marvellous peaches, huge nectarines, set out there against the sunset. It will be as luxuriant as a beautiful Veronese.'
> 'It would cost almost as much,' murmured M. Verdurin.
> 'But take away those cheeses with their dreadful colour,' said Ski.

He tried to remove his host's plate, who defended his gruyère with all his might. We must infer from this incident that the Verdurins' wine was nothing very remarkable, perhaps also in short supply. At the same time, in fairness to the Verdurins, the great Goncourt pastiche in which they appear, towards the end of *A la Recherche*, shows them in a rather different light. The reader must make up his own mind as to whether Marcel or the Diarist is to be believed.

Goncourt is fancied as recording that M. Verdurin dropped in to escort him to dinner, mentioning at the same time (something one forgets) that Verdurin was a former critic of *La Revue*, who had written a book on Whistler, and – how very up-to-date – was, or had been, a morphine addict. The 'Venetian'

wineglass in front of the Diarist at the dinner table, 'une riche bijouterie de rouge est mise par une extraordinaire Léoville acheté à la vente de M. Montalivet'. Montalivet (1800-1880) was a Minister of Louis-Philippe, who promoted museums and published a book of memoirs. One does not know the precise implications of a Léoville bought at his sale. The immediate thought is that the bottle might have been a bit on the old side, but the question deserves closer study, with more information. It should be borne in mind that the double-edged epithet 'extraordinary' is employed.

The food is described as an 'exquisite repast' and a detailed account is given of the crockery off which it was eaten. The menu appears to have included *foie gras* and turbot – the sauce a 'white sauce', not made like 'flour paste', but with butter 'costing five francs a pound'. When Goncourt remarked that her husband must be very proud of his beautiful china, Mme Verdurin replied in a melancholy tone:

> 'It's easy to see you don't know him,' she said.
> She described him as an absolute maniac, indifferent to these refinements.
> 'A maniac,' she repeated. 'Absolutely that, who would rather drink a bottle of cider in the rather degraded (*encanaillée*) coolness of a Normandy farm.'

The last two examples I chose of having a drink in *A la Recherche* are 'encanaillés' too, both scenes in houses of ill fame. The first was in the smart brothel a little way up the coast from Balbec, which so impressed strangers by its size and air of convenience that they supposed it would be a good hotel in which to stay. M. de Charlus went there with Jupien to spy on Morel. While he was waiting, a 'clever little lady' was sent to amuse him, and, to prevent her taking off her clothes, Charlus had to buy her champagne at forty francs a bottle. The second incident is when Marcel, quite by chance, found himself in the house of homosexual prostitution run by Jupien during the war; frequented, as it turns out, by M. de Charlus, in his more violently sado-masochistic interludes.

> 'Could somebody kindly tell me to whom to apply to get a room and have something to drink sent up?' asks Marcel, in all innocence.

After negotiation, the boss appears, carrying coils of ominously heavy chains. Marcel explains that he is not feeling well and would like something to drink. Sinister, even hair-raising, things are being said and done all round. The boss's order is something of an anti-climax. 'Pierrot, go down to the cellar and get some *cassis*. . . .'

© *from* THE COMPLEAT IMBIBER 11, 1970

Lickerish Limericks

Cyril Ray

with Filthy Pictures by Charles Mozley

Viva Italia

My God, he's an impudent fella!
—That girl that he showed round the cellar
Lost her *status quo ante*
Between the Chianti
And the magnums of Valpolicella . . .

(Which reminds me of Asti Spumante,
A wine that I'm more *pro* than *anti*—
The only thing is
That this fizz aphrodis-
-iac leads to *delicto flagrante* . . .)

C.R/C.M.

Dolce Fa Niente
or
Sweet Nothing Doing

I was sitting there, taking my ease,
And enjoying my Beaumes-de-Venise,
With a charming young poppet,
But she told me to stop it,
As my fingers crept up past her knees . . .

Vicarious Pleasures

No one could call me a prude,
But I *did* think it frightfully rude
Of the vicar's wife, Mabel,
To jump on the table
And perform a *pas seul* in the nude

(Except for the rose in her hair)
And what led to this sorry affair
Was the man she sat next to
(I'm afraid over-sexed) who
Plied her with J and B Rare . . .

[267]

All Very Fine and Large

I'm the victim of vile sabotage–
I'd set out for a day on the *plage*
And a picnic *à deux*
With some fruit and *Bresse Bleu*
(An especially fragrant *fromage* . . .)

And the prospect of gay *persiflage*,
But before I could cry, '*Soyez sage!*'
The girl I was keen on
Poured out some young Chinon
Instead of the old Hermitage . . .

On this tale I need hardly enlarge
—As you so rightly say, '*Quelle dommage!*'
For I needed *un vin*
That puts strength in a man
—And *esprit* and *élan* and *courage* . . .

So I went to collect my Delage,
Which I keep in a nearby garage,
Driving off in a huff
And proceeding to stuff
The cocotte on the second *étage* . . .

Stout Party

CYRIL RAY

'*Nice homely atmosphere this place has, Charlie.*'
Punch, 25 February 1953

HERE I am, then, in the land of saints and scholars, leprechauns and legends, by which I mean that I am in the Shelbourne Bar, on St Stephen's Green, with a glass of Guinness at my elbow, the only other occupant of the bar being an elderly gentleman, rather frayed at the edges, a pint bottle of the same within his reach, not simply talking to himself but, so far as I can tell, conducting a courteous two-sided argument.

I am no more well up on saints and scholars than I am on leprechauns, which means that I am not up at all, but I have been investigating a couple of the legends that attach themselves to Dublin's black wine, otherwise known as The Workman's Friend, my matutinal modicum of which is slowly sinking in the glass.

First, though, observe that I refer to a glass, not a half-pint, of the dark stuff. It was in Mulligan's of Poolbeg Street, many a long twilit Dublin evening ago, or it might have been in Madigan's, that I told my then host that I should like a half-pint, thank him very much, to be gently rebuked with, 'Pray remember that drinking in these parts is a manly thing, and it isn't manly at all to be *asking* for a half-pint, though a man may decently drink one, and no reflection on his virility.

'But there's a namby-pambiness about the word that makes it proper to ask not for a half-pint, straight out, but for a glass, which is the same thing, more magnanimously stated. And mind you,' he added, 'in as decent a place as this it takes time to draw a Guinness – time enough for us to have a bottle while it's drawn and the top taken off.'

Which reminded me that in the west of Ireland, which is draught-drinking country, the word for a half-pint of draught isn't, as in Dublin, a glass, but 'a bottle', so that in Galway, say, the man who so flies in the face of local feeling as actually to want a bottle, has to ask for 'a bottle bottle', which means a half-pint bottle, and what the Galway phrase is for a pint bottle, such as I see being slowly but relentlessly demolished by the frayed-at-the-edges citizen already mentioned, I have never got around to asking.

However, what I was saying before I interrupted myself – a habit one acquires in these parts – was that I would deal with a couple of the legends that attach themselves to the life-enhancing liquid.

One such is that the Guinness brewed in Dublin (I shall concern myself with the Park Royal product next week, if I am spared) is made with Liffey water, which it is not, and this news will bring relief to those who have smelled the Liffey, where it flows by the Guinness brewery.

No, the water comes, through filter-beds, from springs in the plains of Kildare and from springs the other side of the Curragh, by Pollardstown, piped by the Dublin Corporation, the Sheriff and officials of which, on 10 May 1775, laid claim to it, on the city's behalf, only to be met by the first Arthur Guinness in person, armed with a pickaxe he had wrenched from a workman and 'declaring with very much improper language that they should not proceed', since when there has been no such nonsense, and Arthur's descendants, quite properly, have been ennobled.

Although I express relief that malodorous Liffey water is not the basis of my modest glass I have it in mind that Dublin Bay prawns – the real thing, not frozen scampi – become fat and flavoury on the Liffey water that flows into the bay. By that time, these waters are charged with Guinness effluent – ah, how blessed, this city on the Liffey that takes the dark stuff in fluid and in fishy form!

© *from* PUNCH, 26 March 1980

A Pint of Plain – Une Pint' de Biere

FLANN O'BRIEN

'The name or title of the pome I am about to recite, gentlemen,
said Shanahan with leisure priest-like in character, is a pome by
the name of "The Workman's Friend". By God you can't beat
it. I've heard it praised by the highest. It's a pome about a thing
that's known to all of us. It's about a drink of porter.'

THE passage is from that remarkable, Joycean book, *At Swim-Two-Birds*,
which Flann O'Brien, who was also Myles NaGopaleen, who was also
Brian Nolan, wrote before the war, and had to wait a quarter of a century to
hear acclaimed as a twentieth-century classic, before he died untimely, in 1966.

Shanahan proceeds to recite a 'pome' that has been described as 'magically
banal' – not without such interruptions from his hearers as, 'Did you ever hear
anything like it in your life?' 'A pint of plain, by God, what!' 'There's one thing
in that pome, *permanence* ... that pome, I mean to say, is a pome that'll be

heard wherever the Irish race is wont to gather, it'll live as long as there's a hard root of an Irishman left by the Almighty on this planet ...'

And we give it here not only in its magically banal original, but also in Henri Morisset's translation into French, so that any reader, hard put to it to know how to demand his pint of porter in a Paris café, can learn to make his needs known, at length, and in a metrical version:

> When things go wrong and will not come right,
> Though you do the best you can,
> When life looks black as the hour of night –
> A PINT OF PLAIN IS YOUR ONLY MAN.

> When money's tight and is hard to get
> And your horse has also ran,
> When all you have is a heap of debt –
> A PINT OF PLAIN IS YOUR ONLY MAN.

> When health is bad and your heart feels strange,
> And your face is pale and wan,
> When the doctors say that you need a change,
> A PINT OF PLAIN IS YOUR ONLY MAN.

> When food is scarce and your larder bare
> And no rashers grease your pan,
> When hunger grows as your meals are rare –
> A PINT OF PLAIN IS YOUR ONLY MAN.

> In time of trouble and lousy strife,
> You have still got a darlint plan,
> You still can turn to a brighter life –
> A PINT OF PLAIN IS YOUR ONLY MAN.

> *Lorsque tout va mal et veut aller mal,*
> *Et tu as beau fair', ça ne va pas mieux,*
> *Quand la vie est noire ainsi que la nuit,*
> *UNE PINT' DE BIERRE EST TON SEUL AMI.*

A Pint of Plain—Une Pint' de Biere

Quand l'argent est rare et dur à gagner,
Quand tout s'est enfui, même ton cheval,
Qu'il ne reste plus qu'un gros tas d'ennuis,
UNE PINT' DE BIERRE EST TON SEUL AMI.

Quand le cœur va mal et le reste aussi,
Quand le docteur dit qu'il faut changer d'air,
Lorsque ton visage est pâle et blêmi,
UNE PINT' DE BIERRE EST TON SEUL AMI.

Quand ton ventre est creux et le buffet vide
Sans un brin de lard pour graisser ta poêle,
Quand tu dois jeûner ey que tu maigris
UNE PINT' DE BIERRE EST TON SEUL AMI.

Par les temps troublés et les luttes vaines,
Tu peux espérer une vie plus belle,
Il te reste encore un recours chéri,
UNE PINT' DE BIERRE EST TON SEUL AMI.

© *from* THE COMPLEAT IMBIBER 9, 1967

Napa, A Century Ago

ROBERT LOUIS STEVENSON

I was interested in Californian wine. Indeed, I am interested in all wines, and have been all my life, from the raisin wine that a school-fellow kept secreted in his play-box up to my last discovery, those notable Valtellines, that once shone upon the board of Cæsar.

Some of us, kind old Pagans watch with dread the shadows falling on the age: how the unconquerable worm invades the sunny terraces of France, and Bordeaux is no more, and the Rhone a mere Arabia Petræa. Château Neuf is dead, and I have never tasted it; Hermitage – a hermitage indeed from all life's sorrows – lies expiring by the river. And in the place of these imperial elixirs, beautiful to every sense, gem-hued, flower-scented, dream-compellers: – behold upon the quays at Cette the chemicals arrayed; behold the analyst at Marseilles raising hands in obsecration, attesting god Lyæus, and the vats staved in, and the dishonest wines poured forth among the sea. It is not Pan only; Bacchus, too, is dead.*

* Stevenson had just come to California from France, where the phylloxera was wreaking havoc.

If wine is to withdraw its most poetic countenance, the sun of the white dinner-cloth, a deity to be invoked by two or three, all fervent, hushing their talk, degusting tenderly, and storing reminiscences – for a bottle of good wine, like a good act, shines ever in the retrospect – if wine is to desert us, go thy ways, old Jack! Now we begin to have compunctions, and look back at the brave bottles squandered upon dinner-parties, where the guests drank grossly, discussing politics the while, and even the schoolboy 'took his whack', like liquorice-water. And at the same time we look timidly forward, with a spark of hope, to where the new lands, already weary of producing gold, begin to green with vineyards. A nice point in human history falls to be decided by Californian and Australian wines.

Wine in California is still in the experimental stage; and when you taste a vintage, grave economical questions are involved. The beginning of vine-planting is like the beginning of mining for the precious metals: the wine-grower also 'prospects'. One corner of land after another is tried with one kind of grape after another. This is a failure; that is better; a third best. So, bit by bit, they grope about for their Clos Vougeot and Lafite. Those lodes and pockets of earth, more precious than the precious ores, that yield inimitable fragrance and soft fire; those virtuous Bonanzas, where the soil has sublimated under sun and stars to something finer, and the wine is bottled poetry: these still lie undiscovered; chaparral conceals, thicket embowers them; the miner chips the rock and wanders farther, and the grizzly muses undisturbed. But there they bide their hour, awaiting their Columbus; and nature nurses and prepares them. The smack of Californian earth shall linger on the palate of your grandson.

Meanwhile the wine is merely a good wine; the best that I have tasted better than a Beaujolais, and not unlike. But the trade is poor; it lives from hand to mouth, putting its all into experiments, and forced to sell its vintages. To find one properly matured, and bearing its own name, is to be fortune's favourite.

Bearing its own name, I say, and dwell upon the innuendo.

'You want to know why California wine is not drunk in the States?' a San Francisco wine-merchant said to me, after he had shown me through his premises. 'Well, here's the reason.'

And opening a large cupboard, fitted with many little drawers, he proceeded to shower me all over with a great variety of gorgeously tinted labels, blue, red, or yellow, stamped with crown or coronet, and hailing from such a profusion of *clos* and *châteaux*, that a single department could scarce have furnished forth the names. But it was strange that all looked unfamiliar.

'Chateaux X – ?' said I. 'I never heard of that.'

'I dare say not,' said he. 'I had been reading one of X – 's novels.'

They were all castles in Spain! But that sure enough is the reason why California wine is not drunk in the States.

Napa Valley has been long a seat of the wine-growing industry. It did not here begin, as it does too often, in the low valley lands along the river, but took at once to the rough foothills, where alone it can expect to prosper. A basking inclination, and stones, to be a reservoir of the day's heat, seem necessary to the soil for wine; the grossness of the earth must be evaporated, its marrow daily melted and refined for ages; until at length these clods that break below our footing, and to the eye appear but common earth, are truly and to the perceiving mind, a masterpiece of nature. The dust of Richebourg, which the wind carries away, what an apotheosis of the dust! Not man himself can seem a stranger child of that brown, friable powder, than the blood and sun in that old flask behind the faggots.

A Californian vineyard, one of man's outposts in the wilderness, has features of its own. There is nothing here to remind you of the Rhine or Rhône, of the low Côte d'Or, or the infamous and scabby deserts of Champagne; but all is green, solitary, covert. We visited two of them, Mr Schram's and Mr M'Eckron's, sharing the same glen.

Some way down the valley below Calistoga we turned sharply to the south and plunged into the thick of the wood. A rude trail rapidly mounting; a little

stream tinkling by on the one hand, big enough perhaps after the rains but already yielding up its life; overhead and on all sides a bower of green and tangled thicket, still fragrant and still flower-bespangled by the early season, where thimble-berry played the part of our English hawthorn, and the buck-eyes were putting forth their twisted horns of blossom: through all this, we struggled toughly upwards, canted to and fro by the roughness of the trail, and continually switched across the face by sprays of leaf or blossom. The last is no great inconvenience at home; but here in California it is a matter of some moment. For in all woods and by every wayside there prospers an abominable shrub or weed, called poison-oak, whose very neighbourhood is venomous to some, and whose actual touch is avoided by the most impervious.

The two houses, with their vineyards, stood each in a green niche of its own in this steep and narrow forest dell. Though they were so near, there was already a good difference in level; and Mr M'Eckron's head must be a long way under the feet of Mr Schram. No more had been cleared than was necessary for cultivation; close around each oasis ran the tangled wood; the glen enfolds them; there they lie basking in sun and silence, concealed from all but the clouds and the mountain birds.

Mr M'Eckron's is a bachelor establishment; a little bit of a wooden house, a small cellar hard by in the hillside, and a patch of vines planted and tended single-handed by himself. He had but recently begun; his vines were young, his business young also; but I thought he had the look of the man who succeeds. He hailed from Greenock: he remembered his father putting him inside Mons Meg, and that touched me home; and we exchanged a word or two of Scots, which pleased me more than you would fancy.

Mr Schram's, on the other hand, is the oldest vineyard in the valley, eighteen years old, I think; yet he began a penniless barber, and even after he had broken ground up here with his black malvoisies, continued for long to tramp the valley with his razor. Now, his place is the picture of prosperity: stuffed birds in the verandah, cellars far dug into the hillside, and resting on pillars like a bandit's cave: – all trimness, varnish, flowers, and sunshine, among the tangled wildwood. Stout, smiling Mrs Schram, who has been to Europe and apparently all about the States for pleasure, entertained Fanny in the verandah, while I was tasting wines in the cellar. To Mr Schram this was a solemn office; his serious gusto warmed my heart; prosperity had not yet wholly banished a certain neophyte and girlish trepidation, and he followed every sip and read my face with proud anxiety. I tasted all. I tasted every variety and shade of Schramberger, red and white Schramberger, Burgundy Schramberger, Schramberger Hock, Schramberger Golden Chasselas, the latter with a notable bouquet, and

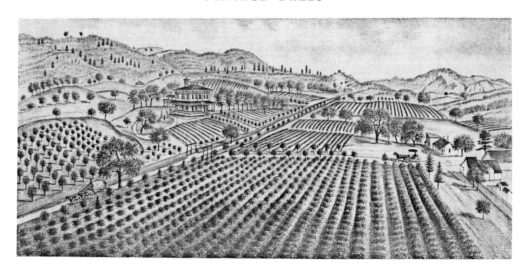

I fear to think how many more. Much of it goes to London – most, I think; and Mr Schram has a great notion of the English taste.

In this wild spot, I did not feel the sacredness of ancient cultivation. It was still raw, it was no Marathon, and no Johannisberg; yet the stirring sunlight, and the growing vines, and the vats and bottles in the cavern, made a pleasant music for the mind. Here, also, earth's cream was being skimmed and garnered; and the London customers can taste, such as it is, the tang of the earth in this green valley. So local, so quintessential is a wine, that it seems the very birds in the verandah might communicate a flavour, and that romantic cellar influence the bottle next to be uncorked in Pimlico, and the smile of jolly Mr Schram might mantle in the glass.

But these are but experiments. All things in this new land are moving farther on: the wine-vats and the miner's blasting tools but picket for a night, like Bedouin pavilions; and tomorrow, to fresh woods! This stir of change and these perpetual echoes of the moving footfall, haunt the land. Men move eternally, still chasing Fortune; and Fortune found, still wander. As we drove back to Calistoga, the road lay empty of mere passengers, but its green side was dotted with the camps of travelling families: one cumbered with a great waggonful of household stuff, settlers going to occupy a ranche they had taken up in Mendocino, or perhaps Tehama County; another, a party in dust coats, men and women, whom we found camped in a grove on the roadside, all on pleasure bent, with a Chinaman to cook for them, and who waved their hands to us as we drove by.

© *from* THE SILVERADO SQUATTERS, 1883

The Champagne Campaign

WYNFORD VAUGHAN-THOMAS

S ober military historians call it 'Operation Anvil'. To me, it will always be
the 'Champagne Campaign'.

I can see myself now – as dawn broke on that warm August day in 1944 –
crouching against the steel sides of a packed LCT, with recording gear fes-
tooned all over my ill-fitting battledress. We were racing for the shore in the
approved style for well-conducted amphibious assaults. The shells from the
fleet whistled overhead and burst with a roar on the enemy defences. Or we
hoped they did. The GIs around me swore like Norman Mailer heroes and
looked as if they were already signed up for Darrell Zanuck's *Longest Day*. Our
objective, of all places, was the sands at St Raphael in the South of France.

A thick smoke-screen drifted across the beach ahead. Our LCT grounded in
luke-warm water, down came the ramp and we splashed through the smoke to
the shore. The GIs prepared to sell their lives dearly and I prepared to record
them doing it. A whistle shrilled somewhere in the murk and we ran forward.

At any moment the machine-guns would be opening up. The light was increasing in spite of the smoke screen. Suddenly we were out of the smoke and blinking in the first sunshine of the day. Ahead of us, no German strongpoint but a Riviera villa which had escaped all our shells. The door opened, and an immaculately dressed Frenchman appeared. He carried a tray on which were ten glasses and a bottle of Veuve Clicquot '34. We stopped the war immediately and crowded around. Carefully he poured out the wine and handed glasses to the sweating and astonished GIs.

'*Messieurs les Americains,*' he said, '*Soyez les bienvenus,*' and then added, gently, 'even if you are a little late.'

He set the key-note for the stern days that followed. The experts still argue learnedly and acidly about the point of the Champagne Campaign. Perhaps after this long interval one needs reminding that it took place two months after D-Day in Normandy. The Americans under General Patch and the French under General de Lattre de Tassigny landed on the Riviera and swept up the Rhône valley to link forces with General Eisenhower's troops advancing across northern France. 'Vital to the task of smashing the Germans before they reach the Rhine', insisted Eisenhower. 'Fatal to our hopes of forestalling the Russians in the Balkans', lamented Churchill.

But time softens controversy, and the history of distant wars grows mellow like '49 burgundy. At last we can see ANVIL in its true perspective. It wasn't fought for military motives at all. One glance at the map and the route taken by the invading armies makes the *raison d'être* of the Champagne Campaign crystal clear.

Ahead of the advancing troops was grouped such a collection of noble names that the mouth waters as the hand types them: Châteauneuf du Pape, Tavel, Tain-l'Hermitage, Château Grillet, the Côte Rotie. And, beyond, the greatest objective of them all – Burgundy and the Côte d'Or!

Was it possible – when the German front had started to crumble elsewhere – that these œnological strong-points should be left at the mercy of the Nazis, especially with the vintage only a few months ahead? General Eisenhower and Sir Winston Churchill may not quite have appreciated the urgency of the situation, but there was one man who did. General de Montsabert was one of the most trusted generals of the new French army. He was a soldier of energy and resource but, more important for the future of France and for our own cellars, he was a lover of wine. He was in the centre of the planning of ANVIL. I need say no more.

I admit that I have no documentary evidence that the gastronomic general played the decisive role in swinging the invasion towards the threatened vineyards, but historians cling too readily to official documents. I prefer to trust the subtle hints that the General himself gave me when the Champagne Campaign was safely over and we were enjoying the grateful hospitality of the winegrowers of Nuits St Georges.

We were pouring out bottles of such quality that the General's usual sense of security became slightly less strict than usual. We fought all over again the campaigns we had covered together, and I broached the vital question, 'Why did we have to land in France? Would it not have been better to continue up Italy with full strength and with the Germans on the run?'

'My friend,' said the General, 'you do not sufficiently consider one great difficulty. In Italy we were fighting our way through an art gallery and a museum. It was no longer the Art of War but the War of Art. How could we deploy our full strength? The fifteenth century? I could not attack, but had to make an outflanking movement. The sixteenth? Then I permitted myself a little machine-gun fire. The seventeenth? Ah! now we could have artillery support. The eighteenth meant tanks and for the nineteenth, monsieur, I had no hesitation in calling in the air. If only Italy had all been built in the twentieth century we should be in the Alps by now!'

'And ANVIL?'

'Let us re-christen it "WINEPRESS". I admit it commanded my immediate support. In Italy all we could do was smash things and the outside world doesn't like to hear of works of art being smashed, even in the best of causes. But in this campaign we came as saviours of the greatest works of art in the world.'

'Works of art, *mon général?*'

'But certainly – the vineyards of Burgundy.'

So it was that the Champagne Campaign combined glory with pleasure in a way never before or since achieved in modern war. In the actual plan of the advance I detected the subtle thinking behind the scenes of a Man of Wine. Take, for instance, the lines of attack assigned to the different commands. The American army swung north from the Riviera through the rough country of the Basses Alpes, with the task of cutting into the German army retreating up the actual valley of the Rhône. Their job was vital and took them through superb country, but the vinously minded historian will note that it did not take them near a single vineyard of quality, with the possible exception of a slight reconnaissance towards Clairette de Die. Frankly, I cannot see Clairette de Die inscribed on the flags of General Patch's army as one of its notable battle-honours.

Now follow the advance of the French army. The soldiers of de Lattre de

Tassigny and of Montsabert took the valley and the left bank of the Rhône. Swiftly they possessed themselves of Tavel, and after making sure that all was well with one of the finest *vins rosés* in France, struck fiercely for Châteauneuf du Pape. Northward they raced for St Peray and Hermitage. The Côte Rotie fell to a well-planned flanking attack. It was then only a matter of days before the French were masters of the Mâconnais in every sense of the word.

On the surface all was going well, with the Germans on the run and the Americans racing through the Jura towards Besançon. But when I dropped into American HQ for a briefing on the general situation I detected a slight anxiety in the air. As a war correspondent I had become a connoisseur of briefings and had been fascinated by the differences in each Allied army's approach to this esoteric branch of the military art. Instinctively the British officer tends to avoid the vivid word, wisely feeling that he can minimise the horror of war if he can describe it in everyday terms drawn from the vocabulary of sport. If he is a senior officer that sport will be fox-hunting. When Field Marshal Montgomery told a group of Americans that his men had their tails 'well up', a puzzled colonel asked a British officer in the group, 'Excuse me – up *what*?'

I remember at Anzio listening to a British officer putting the Americans in the picture about a tank clash up the Albano road. He stood in front of a map on which every position was meticulously marked. 'Well, gentlemen,' he proceeded, 'our tins were hacking along the road with their swedes out of the lid when they got a bloody nose. The question is, shall we thicken up the party or do an Oscar? In any case we'll have to tie the whole thing up on the Old Boy net.' Said one American anxiously to me, 'Thomas, are we advancing or are we retreating?'

The French method was in complete contrast. It naturally derived from the Napoleonic communiqué. Every statement had to be '*court, energetic et decisif*'. General de Lattre, standing before the flag of France but with no map, explained how he pierced the Gap of Belfort. 'First it was the optimism of the morning. Then came the pessimism of the evening. And then, Messieurs de la Presse, we consulted the final reports and, *pouf, c'était la Victoire!*'

The Americans also believe in the swift punch-line. When I discussed the problems facing ANVIL with General Patch I asked him how he proposed to solve them. 'Sir,' he replied, 'we don't solve our problems, we overwhelm them.' The American briefers certainly overwhelmed me. I always came out from a session with them slightly dizzy but boundlessly confident. Men who could make wisecracks with such effortless ease were obviously men of resource. As the briefer told us before the Anzio break-out, 'General Mark Clark has got fifty-seven different plans and he's going to use every one of them!'

But on this occasion I detected a slight lack of the usual buoyancy in the air. General Patch might well have had fifty-seven different plans up his sleeve but clearly he was now a little uncertain about which one to use.

After the briefing, a colonel on the staff – an old comrade-in-arms of Anzio days – took me aside.

'You're going across to see the Frogs this afternoon, I hear?' I had, indeed, intended to go scouting through the vague no-man's-land of fifty miles which now separated the two armies.

'Well,' said the colonel thoughtfully, 'I wonder if you'd give me your private opinion, while you're there, on a little problem that's got us kinda worried. I've got a feeling that the Frogs are doing a little bit of a 'go slow' on us. I've got no proof. On paper, all's well. But in this game I've found that it's sometimes wise to back a hunch, and right now I've got a hunch that our friends are staying a little too long at this place Chalons something or other. Not like them, either. Those babies can move all right when they want to.'

Chalons something or other! Obviously this was Chalons-sur-Saône. I felt that I already had a shrewd idea why the 'Frogs were dragging their feet'.

That evening I presented myself at the field HQ of Montsabert and received the usual warm welcome. The Intelligence Officer took me to the map tent and we reviewed the situation. There was no doubt that the enemy was retreating but the point was – how fast was he moving? Was he prepared to fight a strong rearguard action before Dijon? 'I need hardly tell you,' said my friend, 'the terrible consequences of such a decision. It would mean war, mechanised war, among the Grands Crûs! Would France forgive us if we allowed such a thing to happen? We must not forget 1870.'

I confess that I had long ago forgotten what happened in Burgundy in 1870. But the Colonel swiftly reminded me that one of the last battles of the Franco-Prussian war took place around Nuits St Georges: 'Shells fell on Les Cras, the German reserves swept forward over La Tâche, Romanée-Conti and Richebourg. This must never be allowed to happen again.'

We both looked thoughtfully at the Colonel's private map of the German positions. They were – quite properly – marked with care on the relevant sheet of Larmat's *Atlas Vinicole de la France*. There had been reports of a Tiger tank at Meursault and of demolitions prepared at Chassagne-Montrachet. There might even be a strong German rearguard assembled behind Beaune. A picture immediately leapt into my mind of air attacks on Chambolle-Musigny, of tanks rolling forward over the carefully tended vines of Vôsne-Romanée, of smoke rising from the burnt-out château of Clos de Vougeot.

Then occurred one of those dramatic strokes that are the speciality of the

French at war. A young *sous-lieutenant* entered, hurriedly saluted and, with a smile illuminating his face, declared, 'Great news, *mon colonel*, we have found the weak point in the German defences. Every one is on a vineyard of inferior quality.'

We both recognised that we had reached a turning-point in the battle. Said the Colonel, 'General de Montsabert must know at once, but he will give only one order, "*J'attaque*".'

Attack he did, and to such effect that in a matter of twenty-four hours the Germans were bundled out of Burgundy and the schedule of the French advance jumped boldly ahead of the Americans. None of us can forget the glorious days that followed. *Les Trois Glorieuses* are celebrated every year at Dijon and in the Côte d'Or as a feast of wine and gastronomy. It has been my pleasure and privilege to attend the sale of wine at the Hospices, the feast of the Confrérie du Tastevin at the Château of Clos de Vougeot and the 'Paulée' at Meursault. But none of them could ever rival those fabulous three days of the Liberation of Burgundy. For a brief moment the cellar doors of the Côte d'Or opened almost of their own accord. . . .

No wonder General de Montsabert's eyes sparkled as we raced up Route National 74 in his jeep, close on the heels of his forward tanks. A blown bridge here, a demolished house there – what could these matter beside the great, over-riding fact of the undamaged vineyards stretching mile after mile before us?

To our left rose the long line of the hills of the Côte; it was as if the Cotswold escarpment had been planted with vines and bathed in mellow sunshine. 'Decidedly,' said the General, 'in the matter of wine you must count me a Man of the Left.'

I must admit that, at this point, I lost touch with the advanced elements of the French army. A sound military maxim teaches the enlightened warrior that his first duty after victory is to make sure of his base. Accordingly I disappeared into the cellars of Beaune and Nuits St Georges to make sure that our objective had remained undamaged. To my relief, I found that the treasure-house of the Côte had been untouched through the trials of war. The great *négociants* have learned by the experience of 1914–1918. For that war, historians will recall, the wine-men of France had been inexperienced in the tricks of resistance. M. André Simon relates the sad story of a friend of his who was unpleasantly surprised to discover that the advance guard of the German army was rapidly approaching his priceless cellar. He made a quick decision. The only thing to do was to hide his great wines under the waters of the ornamental pond of the château. He had completed this hurried bestowal of his treasures to the lake when the enemy arrived. All went well until, one morning, the Germans walked out to the lake to find the surface of the water covered with floating wine-labels.

The Burgundians made no such mistake. They quickly spirited away their finest wines behind false walls in the depths of their cellars. A swift re-pasting of labels on inferior bottles convinced the ignorant conquerors that they were enjoying the great vintages of the Côte d'Or. The real treasure remained secure – until we arrived.

I have drunk great wines in many parts of France but never have I tasted such nectar as was offered to me during the early days of the Liberation of Burgundy. That whole enchanted period of my life is a symphony of popping corks, through which the voices of the Cadets de Bourgogne reach me, accompanied by the endearingly uncertain hunting horns of the Cor de Chasse de St Hubert singing the theme song of Burgundian Liberation:—

'*Toujours buveurs, jamais ivrognes!*'

But on the third day, as we tackled our twentieth cellar, my friend the Colonel of Intelligence suddenly recalled that the Outer World still existed. '*Les braves Americains,*' he declared, '*anciens camarades de la France. Il faut les envoyer quelque-chose!*' Quickly my jeep was filled with some of the rarer treasures of the Côte. Outside one of the noblest cellars a little ceremony of historic importance was performed. The guard of honour saluted the great bottles destined for American consumption.

I drove my precious jeep-load of noble bottles back over the bumpy roads of La Bresse to American HQ, now safely established in Besançon. Hurriedly I sought out my American contact and consigned the treasures to his care. All of them? Let me be honest: some of them, by an unaccountable chance of wartime transport, found their way into my cellar in the year after the war. Still, the bottles I handed over to the Americans were enough to make the fortune of any London restaurant in these over-priced years of the 1960s.

'These are the greatest wines of France,' I said with a flamboyant flourish. 'Guard them with care; rest them; and make certain that they are *chambré* before you serve them.'

'Don't worry,' the gallant U.S. soldier reassured me, 'the Doc knows all about this Frog liquor. And while we're about it, we'll invite them over to drink it.'

So it was that in a certain eighteenth-century palace at Besançon the ancient splendours of the *Belle Époque* were gloriously revived. The French guests advanced up flights of stairs lined on one side with Spahis and on the other with American military police – Snowdrops. The Americans awaited them in a salon worthy of the receptions of a Pompadour. Trumpets sounded, and a column of

waiters marched in bearing bottles on silver trays. My heart gave a warning thump – the bottles were from Burgundy, the noble gifts of the Côte and, horror of horrors, they were bubbling gently.

'We're in luck,' my American colonel whispered to me, 'the Doc's hotted this stuff up with medical alcohol.'

A look of incredulous horror flickered over the faces of the French. All eyes were turned to de Montsabert. He had led them through the campaigns of North Africa and across the snow-clad mountains of Italy. Faced with the greatest crisis so far in Franco-American relations – how would he behave?

He fixed his staff with a stern glare of command. 'Gentlemen, take up your glasses.' Reluctantly the French reached out their hands. 'To our comrades-in-arms, *les braves Americains*,' he ordered, in a ringing voice. He drained his glass with panache – every drop! Then in a quieter voice that only the nearest Frenchman could hear, he murmured: '*Libération, Libération*, what crimes have been committed in thy Name!'

© *from* THE COMPLEAT IMBIBER 6, 1963

M.A. Deira

ROBERT GITTINGS

When I first went to Cambridge Coll.
A Doctor of Divinity
Gave words of wis. that spoke a vol.
To those in his vicinity.
He cried: 'From all the history
Of our great Christian era,
Note down one-four-two-owe A.D. –
Discovery of Madeira!

Four centuries supremely good
This wine ruled England's salons;
In eighteen-twenty, imports stood
At half a million gallons.
O what a falling-off was there!

[287]

O tempora, o mores!
So you, young man, must now repair
Its fame, and sing its glories.

Come, praise this wine by night and day
To all your generation
Till once again our land is a
Madeira-drinking nation
And if they snidely ask you why
Your Muse such claims advances,
Come to the fount of learning: I
Will tell you all the answers!

Before and after dinner, you
May drink it with impunity,
Aperitif, dessert-wine too,
Both in one blessed unity.
As for that modern horror, which
(I hear) is called elevenses,
This liquor, golden, dry, yet rich
Puts one in seventh heavenses.

Who can describe it? Who can catch
Its flavour, brisk, volcanic?
Milton's great poem could not match
This Angel half-satanic.
From Sercial keen to Malmsey bland
It runs the palate's gamut.
Young man, you drink it! Understand! –
Or you'll be sent down, dammit!'

So spoke the sage. I meekly conned
The subject of his lecture,
Tried it, and found it true, beyond
All possible conjecture:
And now that Learning's door is shut,
And Age is growing nearer,
These letters to my name I put—
'B.A. and M.A.(deira)'.

© *from* WINE MINE, A FIRST ANTHOLOGY, 1970

[288]

No Wine for a Lady? A Story

ERIC LINKLATER

If you want delicacy you don't go to the Rhône or
anywhere in France below Gascony. But it was the
manliest French wine I ever drank.
          George Saintsbury, Notes on a Cellar-Book.

T wo hundred years ago, when refugees were still a minority in the world,
England was the universal roof for persecuted and unhappy men. It was
inevitable, therefore, that at some period in his life the much-loved and marvellously foolish philosopher, Jean-Jacques Rousseau, should arrive, curiously
clad, in the kindly streets of London; for no one has ever been more vulnerable
than he to imagined hurt or real hostility.

In the winter of 1765 he was subject to the animosity of both Church and
State – a church of some denomination, a state of some other – and from
possible danger and an ever-present unhappiness he sought escape across the
Channel. He had many friends, in whom he rarely trusted, but at that time he

reposed confidence in the Scottish philosopher David Hume, and relied on him for escort and guidance.

Hume was a philosopher of a sturdier sort than Rousseau. As a young man he had survived the world's indifference, and when his first book fell dead from the press he confidently began to write another. He ate well, and drank well, and by the age of fifty looked like a comfortable burgess who enjoyed his boiled fowl and oyster sauce, his claret, and his sirloin of beef. He was the most amiable of men, and when his employment in Paris, as secretary to the British ambassador, came to an end at the same time as Rousseau's unhappiness reached a climax, he readily accepted the responsibility of ferrying his distracted friend across the Channel.

It was fortunate for Rousseau that Hume could afford to hire a private coach for their journey to Calais. Rousseau's dog Sultan had to go with them, and a tiresome weakness of the fugitive philosopher's bladder compelled him to carry with his hand-luggage a chamber-pot. They made an oddly contrasted couple as they sat together in the jolting carriage that rattled so noisily over frozen roads, for Hume was plump and pink, Rousseau dark and pallid – Hume was robust and fatly fed and clumsy in movement, Rousseau delicate, handsome and hungry-looking, given to nervous gesture – and to aggravate the difference Hume was thickly but conventionally clad for a winter journey, while Rousseau wore his customary Armenian dress of fur cap and a long, warm, belted garment called a caftan. This enabled him to deal with his weakness more conveniently than breeches would have permitted.

Their journey lasted eight or nine days – the short grey days and bitter, protracted nights of January – but Rousseau's appearance of delicacy hid a tough, resilient frame, and he was less susceptible to icy draughts and winter skies than to wintry voices and cold comment. They arrived in London without mishap, and a lodging was found for the refugee in the house of Mrs. Adams in Buckingham Street which, from near Charing Cross, ran downhill towards the river. It was a street of small but elegant houses, and Rousseau took particular pleasure in the front room on the first floor, which was furnished in very good taste for all necessary comfort. His dog Sultan, however, was strangely excited by the foreign smells of England – an aroma of cooking, perhaps of cabbage, blew in on errant gusts – and Sultan, either critical or responsive to alien adventure, lifted his leg against a valuable escritoire.

Rousseau was sadly abashed, Mrs. Adams loudly indignant, and David Hume, interpreting for both, had to exercise all his charm and ingenuity to restore a friendly atmosphere. He was assisted by Rousseau's weakness, for he, untimely stimulated by Sultan's behaviour, had to retire to a nearby closet; and

Mrs. Adams, a kindly woman, was deeply influenced by Hume's eloquent description of her guest as the foremost man in Europe, but so sensitive that no living creature could show distress without his sharing it.

Rousseau returned, a maid with cloths and dusters was summoned, and Mrs. Adams was flustered but flattered by Rousseau's determination to kiss, not merely one, but both of her hands. Hume was eager to retire to his own lodging, in Lisle Street, but Rousseau would not let him go until he had been reassured, yet again, of the imminent arrival of his devoted friend, Thérèse le Vasseur, whom he had been obliged to leave behind.

'She is in good hands,' said Hume. 'Another honest Scot – '

'That young man!'

'It's true that I wouldn't be happy to leave my daughter, if I had one, in Jamie Boswell's care, but Mlle. le Vasseur is a woman of discretion – '

'Can that be said of any woman?'

'She is old enough, or nearly, to be Jamie's mother.'

'M. Boswell sent her a garnet necklace.'

'He is a generous creature, and a man of his word. He promised to bring Mademoiselle safely to England, and you can rest assured that he will do so. As you trusted yourself to me, so you can trust Mademoiselle to him.'

Hume took his leave, and Rousseau was left to speak seriously to Sultan and count the days and hours before he could hope to see Thérèse.

She had been his laundress to begin with – that was twenty years ago – but she had a sort of genius, she was dextrous in the house and a good housekeeper, she could cook and manage a kitchen as well as she washed a shirt and starched it; and by degrees she had assumed, in his household, certain emotional responsibilities. She had borne him five children, all of whom he prudently gave to a foundlings' hospital. He had never seen much reason to be faithful to Thérèse, but whenever he remembered her he called her his *gouvernante*; and in his voice there was gratitude.

Now in the latter part of the eighteenth century there were Scotsmen everywhere, and all of them distinguished by exceptional ability and a genius so persuasive that their superiority was universally recognized. In these circumstances, then, there was nothing to occasion surprise in young Jamie Boswell's timely appearance in Paris, and his ability to offer Thérèse the protection she needed for a foreign journey.

Boswell had paid his court to Rousseau at Môtiers near Neuchatel a year or two before, in what was then Prussian territory. He had arrived at a singularly inopportune moment, when Rousseau was suffering from a dilation of his erratically conditioned bladder; but Boswell, who had previously sent him a fragment of autobiography, was too intent on eliciting admiration of his essay to be much aware of his host's discomfort. Rousseau was hostile, Boswell insistently friendly. The egotism of the one met the egotism of the other – both talked portentous nonsense – and in the clash of loud and empty opinion they discovered a mutual, if shallow, liking. Rousseau was persuaded to a grudging hospitality, and Boswell ate greedily at a table well-furnished by Mademoiselle's skill in the kitchen. Mademoiselle, indeed, was much more friendly than her master, and after Boswell had reluctantly left them he sent Thérèse, from Genoa, a necklace of garnets that Rousseau, when asked to admire it, had examined with some suspicion.

So Thérèse, in Paris, greeted Jamie with manifest goodwill. Not everyone was inclined to see virtue in him, but surly, opinionated old Sam Johnson had lately admitted him to friendship, and Thérèse had been quick to perceive an essential quality in the ebullient young man with an eager voice, a brilliant eye, an impudently questioning nose, and a patent interest in her sex. He was temperamental, he could fall a sudden victim to frightful melancholy from the very alps of exaltation. But a recurrent enthusiasm would always lift him again, and no experienced woman of forty – or perhaps a little more – has ever been contemptuous of enthusiasm.

The frost had melted when, in the first days of February, they set out together, and a cold, sleety rain fell dismally as their evil-smelling coach lurched heavily out of Paris on the long road to England. They were thrown together in that ungainly vehicle – there were others who shared it – and the discomfort of their journey was ameliorated by the genial warmth of adjacent thighs. Many who have written in praise of her distinguished master have made slighting reference to Thérèse; but she was more agreeable, to touch and eye, than they suppose. She was small and neat, a trimly built woman, and the fact that she was nearly illiterate did not diminish the pleasing impact of her legs.

On their second night they came to an inn where, in the rude conditions of the time, Thérèse and Boswell, fellow travellers, were allotted beds in the same room. After supper, stammering a little in the urgency of his desire, Jamie said to Thérèse, 'If you will allow me certain favours, Mademoiselle – favours which I need not specify – well, I shall be much obliged.'

Thérèse put on an expression of modest disapproval, but offered no other objection, and Boswell, having undressed, sat in his shirt on the side of her bed and in the simplicity of his delight sang the song 'Youth's the Season' from *The Beggar's Opera*. He was much given to singing, and sometimes postponed lechery to enjoy a little music.

Another long, cold day in the coach followed their first night together, and they came to another inn. There, after some fondling, Boswell was sadly disconcerted by what Thérèse said to him.

'You are young and strong,' she said, 'and I like you. I like you very much. But you are uncouth, you lack grace and knowledge. You have not enough experience, and before we again sleep together I must talk to you. I must talk very seriously. I must tell you many things that you do not know, but if you listen to what I say, why, then we shall both enjoy ourselves much better than we did last night. You understand?'

Boswell, unhappily, did not understand. What on earth, he wondered, had Thérèse meant when she accused him of lacking grace and knowledge?

They had been given an expensive room in which a double bed stood in an alcove. Thérèse, who pretended to be tired, undressed, and Boswell went downstairs to ask the landlord for a bottle of wine. His landlord, a paunchy, genial man who came from somewhere near Tournon in the great valley of the Rhône, at once showed sympathy for a young man involved in a situation of not uncommon difficulty.

The inn-keeper said, 'Let us try, to see if you like it, a bottle of Hermitage, of which I have a few score in my cellar. It is, I must tell you, no older than last year's vintage, and there are many people who say that new wine is dangerous. This Hermitage, however, has an excellent flavour, a good nose, and you'll find it uncommonly robust and comforting.'

'Good indeed,' said Boswell as he sniffed his glass.

'I myself,' said the landlord, 'own a little vineyard near Tournon, and I drink all I grow. Now it is well known that we in those parts are not only men of great mental alertness, and of a profound moral rectitude, but also men who are uncommonly well-qualified to satisfy the inordinate demands on our virility which the exquisite women of our neighbourhood habitually make.'

'Give me another glass,' said Boswell.

'Most willingly,' said his landlord, and let him drink nearly two-thirds of the bottle that stood between them.

'What is the price of this wine?' asked Boswell.

'No matter,' said the landlord. 'It will be added to your bill in the morning.'

'Then give me another bottle,' said Boswell. 'I will drink a little more before I go to bed.'

He went upstairs, and Thérèse, from her pillow, said, 'Boswell! Why do you wait so long?'

'I have letters to write,' said Boswell, and in the far end of the room sat down at a table furnished, not only with ink and writing-paper, but with a well-shaped glass and his bottle of Hermitage. That supernacular wine, he found, was so benevolent as to inspire in him, not only a quiet and manly confidence, but a most civil recognition of his partner's claim to happiness.

In the morning he and Thérèse came down hand-in-hand, laughing and talking in the most amiable way, and before they took their places in the waiting coach – while the impatient horses stamped and fretted under the soft snow that fell from a viewless sky – Boswell said to the landlord, 'That Hermitage was the finest wine I have ever drunk. And now I am going to join, in London, the great philosopher M. Jean-Jacques Rousseau, whose name, I do not doubt, you hear with reverence.'

'With deep reverence,' said the landlord.

'Then let me buy another bottle to take to him, as a symbol of affection from all the better parts of France.'

He got his bottle, and through the whitened February air the coach drove off. He and Thérèse had a stormy crossing of the Channel, and it was not until they were in the coach from Dover to London that Boswell had leisure to reflect on his recent activities and speak seriously to Thérèse about their joint necessity for discretion. Their fellow-passengers, a man and a woman, fortunately understood no French, and could be ignored.

'As you know,' said Boswell, 'I am sincerely devoted to M. Rousseau.'

'Naturally,' she answered. 'He requires the sympathy of all who know him.'

'I value the thought that I am his friend.'

'There are many who think highly of him.'

'For me it would be a calamity if anything happened to mar our friendship.'

'That I can understand.'

'If, for example, Rousseau were to hear that you and I – '

'What should he hear?'

'You cannot have forgotten already!'

'I forget nothing, but I am not a young girl. I do not talk like a young girl, who tells everything to everyone.'

'Not to everyone – but perhaps to Rousseau?'

She turned to look at Boswell with scorn in her eyes; but changed her mind and said gently, 'He is not a priest, and I am in no danger of mistaking a bed for the confessional.'

'I have,' said Boswell, intent on excusing himself, 'a strange and difficult nature.'

But Thérèse was tired, and patting his hand said consolingly, 'You have a beautiful nature.' Then she went to sleep.

In London they drove to David Hume's lodging in Lisle Street. There they learnt that Rousseau, after three weeks in London, when he had been fêted by the fashionable world and applauded by the mob, had retired, exhausted, to Chiswick. Boswell, by now weary of Mademoiselle's company, persuaded the good-natured Hume to find her a bed for the night, and before leaving gave her the bottle of Hermitage that he had bought from the obliging inn-keeper.

'It is for M. Rousseau,' he said. 'Ask him to accept it, not only as a small tribute from a devoted friend, but as a symbol of the generous sympathy still felt for him in one of the noblest districts of France.'

Then, rather hurriedly, he left them and spent a talkative evening with his old friend William Temple in Cecil Street. On the following morning he was surprised by an urgent message from Hume, bidding him to come at once.

Hume met him with a bland smile and said, 'Our dear Jean-Jacques is suffering from the vapours, and I think you should go and console him.'

'To Chiswick? But today I am engaged with Dr. Pringle.'

'Last night he was in Chiswick, but early this morning he returned to Buckingham Street, where he wrote a letter which I received an hour ago. He is in a fever of anxiety about Mademoiselle. He had expected her to be in London before now, and he is beginning to wonder if you have failed in your duty to him, if not to her. He is, in short, almost persuaded that you have run off with her.'

'But Mademoiselle is here! Why did you not send her to him?'

'I thought it better that you should be her escort, and so relieve him of two anxieties. He will see that she is safe, and you can assure him that your conduct has been honourable. Or so I hope.'

'You need have no fear of that, but there is nothing to be gained by my going with her. It is she whom he wants to see.'

'It would be discourteous to send her alone. Mademoiselle is ready, and a post-chaise will be here in two minutes.'

Mademoiselle appeared calm and untroubled. She said she had slept well, and Boswell concealed, as best he could, a persistent feeling of unease.

On their short drive to Buckingham Street there was little conversation between Boswell and the companion of his journey. He did, indeed, with a pretended carelessness, say, 'I hope you will not forget – '

'Only yesterday,' she replied, 'you hoped I would not remember.'

'That is not what I said. My meaning was – '

'Whatever you meant, or did not mean, makes no difference to what you should know. I am not a fool, monsieur.'

At Mrs. Adams's house, in his front room on the first floor, they found a Rousseau pale and drawn; shrivelled, as it seemed, by the fever of anxiety. No one, indeed, could say much, or speak to any purpose, for Sultan, in a frenzy of excitement, barked continuously until Mrs. Adams led him away.

'I am very tired,' said Rousseau. 'They made much of me, here in London, they welcomed me like a hero. But were they sincere? That I don't know. I could not sleep, I had to go away. And still you did not come. Why have you been so long?'

'It is a long journey at this time of year,' said Boswell. 'You can't hurry the horses on winter roads.'

'It was to Mademoiselle I was speaking,' said Rousseau.

'Then I will leave you, sir, to speak to her alone. That you have much to say to her I can understand. I wish only to say that I have done what I was asked to do. I have brought Mademoiselle here in safety, and I expect no gratitude. I will wish you good day, sir.'

Boswell's high horse had come to hand most opportunely. Quickly he took advantage of Rousseau's discourtesy, became at once the young laird, the offended Scot of high lineage – and immediately seized the excuse to leave a discussion that threatened to be embarrassing.

Rousseau paid no attention to his departure, but Thérèse said, 'You should not have been rude to him. He has been very kind to me.'

'How far did you let his kindness go?'

'His behaviour was always correct. He is a "gentleman".'

'So! He has been teaching you English?'

'He is also generous. He bought this bottle of very good wine for you, and told me I was to give it to you with some expression of his regard. Let us drink a glass of wine together.'

She found a bottle-screw and glasses, but Rousseau made no response. He sat miserably on a sofa and looked at her with sad, suspicious eyes. Again she offered him wine, but he shook his head.

'My stomach is bad. I drink nothing, I can eat nothing. Sometimes a little toast in hot milk, with some caramel. Nothing else.'

'Shall I make you a toast in milk?'

'If you like. But I will not eat it.'

She went out to look for milk and bread, and when she returned Rousseau had gone. She shrugged her shoulders. She knew his weakness, she knew the effect on him of sudden emotion.

There was a fire in the room, and she set a little saucepan of milk on the coals. She cut bread, and drank one of the two glasses of wine she had poured.

It was a wine of wonderful, unexpected quality. How right Boswell had been to speak so highly of it! She sipped the other glass. She had no intention of drinking it. All she wanted was to taste it, to reassure herself that its flavour and bouquet were as exceptional as she thought. She sipped, and sniffed, and sipped again. The wine was irresistible, and before she knew what had happened, the second glass was empty.

She pulled a chair to the table and sat down. She had been tired after her long journey, but weariness was melting away, and into its place came slowly a little tide of well-being, of geniality and comfort. And as her body responded to the wine's beneficence, so did her mind become a receptacle for sympathy and tenderness and charity. That poor Jean-Jacques! How tiresome he was, but how deeply he suffered, and how much she owed him! But for him she might have been a village laundress still. She re-filled her glass, and wiped away a tear.

She drank slowly at first, and then, with a gulp, the glass was empty. She had come to a decision. She must be generous. She must be as noble in spirit as Jean-Jacques, as truthful as Jean-Jacques. True love could not live with dark deceit, so there must be no deceit. She must tell him all.

The milk boiled over, and she took the little saucepan off the fire. She returned to the table, and was surprised to see her glass empty. So she filled it anew, and was fortified in her resolution to tell him everything. But where was he? Where was Jean-Jacques?

She went to the nearby closet and beat on the door. 'What are you doing, Jean-Jacques? Come out! I have much to tell you.'

'Go away,' he answered. 'I am in distress.'

'Come out, come out! I love you, I want to tell you everything.'

'Not yet, I am in pain.'

She went back to her chair at the table. Sometimes he suffered in one way, sometimes in another. Incontinence was embarrassing, but retention torment. Poor Jean-Jacques! She must be patient.

But Rousseau was at her elbow before she had filled her glass again, and shrilly he demanded, 'What have you got to tell me?'

'It is because I love you. You understand?'

'You have been false to me!'

'No, no! You must not put it that way. I am going to be truthful and tell you everything, and you cannot be truthful and false as well. But Boswell–'

'He has been making love to you?'

'He is not so good a friend as you think. You are too kind and amiable, your friends are not worthy of you. Should you ask if Boswell has been false to you, I would have to admit it.'

'I have never trusted him! But if he was false, then so were you. Falsity of that sort is not a solitary act.'

'He is so young,' said Thérèse, 'and very strong.'

'He forced you? Against your will? You struggled?'

'Yes, I struggled.'

'So it happened once, and only once?'

Thérèse drank a little more wine, and again the nobility of that remarkable bottle charged her mind with the impulses of truth and goodness. 'It was more than once,' she whispered.

Rousseau, in a frenzy of rage, seized her by her well-dressed hair, and shook her violently.

'How often?' he demanded. 'If it was more than once, it was twice at least. Was it more than twice?'

Her voice was low but clear: 'More than twice.'

'Then how often? Tell me, tell me!'

Again he shook her, with all his strength, and still holding her hair, pulled her to her feet. She threw her arms round his neck, and whispered in his ear.

At what he heard, he started back and looked at her with incredulity so stark that his white face was like the bleached emptiness of a skull. But pain and anger quickly humanized his expression, and with a great shout of wrath he hurried from the room. She followed, and beat again upon the closet door.

'It is because I love you that I told the truth,' she cried.

'But it cannot be the truth, and I am in worse pain than ever. Do you still say he forced you?'

'I swear it!'

'To be raped once is a misfortune, twice a calamity, but thirteen times – oh, there is no word for that! And my pain is killing me.'

[298]

Mrs. Adams, alarmed by the noise of uncomprehended passion, had come to see what was amiss, and now stared in astonishment at the dishevelment of Mademoiselle's hair. She had many visitors from the continent, and spoke a little French.

'M. Rousseau is not well,' said Thérèse.

'Oh, I know! More than once, while he was here, I found him in great pain. That is why his friends persuaded him to go to Chiswick. They thought he would feel better there.'

'That place – where is it?'

'Chiswick? It is by the river. There are houses on the river-bank.'

'How far from here?'

'Well, I can't say exactly, but not far. Nine or ten miles, perhaps.'

'Then get a coach, we must go at once. It always does him good to live beside a river.'

Mrs. Adams, with a backward glance – still troubled, but fortified by her long acquaintance with foreigners and their curious ways – went on her errand, and Thérèse, kneeling at the keyhole, spoke urgently to the philosopher within.

Then, returning to the front room, she drank a little more wine and thought contentedly that she had done her duty, and soon all would be well.

The dog Sultan, released by Mrs. Adams, came bounding into the room, still excited by her return, and sniffed eagerly at the escritoire.

'Come here, Sultan,' she cried. 'Here in England it is necessary to behave with propriety.'

© *from* THE COMPLEAT IMBIBER 9, 1967

Vintage Years
in Wine, Cricket, Dress and Sardines

Wisden and Wine
TERENCE PRITTIE

'Of course', one or other of my German friends has said to me, 'you don't grow any wine in England, do you? And so ...' The line of thought is obvious – the English, living in a windswept, sunless island and on a soil which is usually chalk or clay, have neither right nor reason to know anything about wine in general, or German wines in particular. This line of thought *seems* rational.

It is, however, a fact – which is absolutely unknown to Germans – that an Englishman with a good working knowledge of *Wisden's Cricketers' Almanack* may have even a German wine-connoisseur at a disadvantage. For there is an uncanny connection between German wine years and English cricket seasons – uncanny, that is, unless one remembers that German grapes need the sun, and suffer very often from the same lack of it as English cricketers (the grapes of the 'Weinstrasse' in the Rhine-Palatinate are sometimes the exception, and I would always buy a Rhine-Palatinate in preference to a Moselle, Rheingau or Franconian in a poor year).

'Perhaps you have not heard of our 1911s?' a well-meaning, bespectacled and

somewhat intense German friend of mine once asked me. 'Ah, but then you would hardly have had the chance of drinking them. Those were "Jahrhundert" wines!'

One can safely let a remark like this pass. In the summer of 1911 the sun shone brilliantly in England. Plum Warner scored over two thousand runs in a season for the only time in his career, Patsy Hendren made the very first of his 170 centuries and Reggie Spooner was charming Old Trafford crowds that basked in a most unusual warmth. A German of this kind is bound to tell you next about the 1920s, and the 1921s (Charles Macartney made 345 in a single day off the Nottinghamshire attack in June 1921, and Philip Mead achieved his highest-ever aggregate of 3,179 runs).

This sort of German will throw in a reminiscence or two about the 1934s and the 1937s, and then begin to recount the glories of the post-war era – the distinctive 1945s and 1947s, the big 1949s and 1953s, the 1955s – which promised more than they fulfilled – the 1959s, which seemed to have everything. But he will not be telling the student of *Wisden's Cricketers' Almanack* anything that he does not know already. For all these wine years were fine cricket seasons. In 1947, for instance, Denis Compton made more than 3,800 runs – a record which may stand for ever – while in 1959 there were 23 first-class cricketers who scored more than two thousand runs, and many of them went more than sixty times to the wicket in that golden summer.

There is, indeed, no difficulty in taking on a German wine-drinker over very recent years or over the good years of the last half-century. And it is pretty easy to confound him over the bad years of the long-ago. Let him rhapsodize, and then fire in a below-the-belt question like 'What about the 1907s?' The odds are that he has never heard of them, but you (knowing your *Wisden's*) have. In 1907 two medium-pace bowlers, one spinning the ball from the leg and the other from the off, won an otherwise poorly equipped Nottinghamshire side the county cricket championship. Having Hallam and Wass in mind, it is perfectly easy to mark down the 1907s as undrinkable. They were.

Try your German on the 1923s. He may just remember that this was a wretched wine year. But throw in a 'And what a dreadful August!' and he may begin to register surprise. Follow up with a question about the August of the next year, and you should have him rattled. Can he possibly remember? You can, for in that miserable summer of 1924 the sun-starved South African tourists were at last able to begin playing cricket in August.

I have found that something like a *coup de grâce* can be administered by recalling August 1927. I was thirteen years old at the time and trying to play on the sands at Tenby. I was also a Middlesex supporter. Six Middlesex matches running were ruined by rain, and from August 5th to August 26th the sun scarcely shone. A sad holiday, less because of the lack of warmth at Tenby than because of the sheer frustration of reading the sports page of the daily paper.

So, when competing with the German wine connoisseur, mix the stuff you are bowling to him. See if he knows about the shocking setback of 1912 and the slight improvement of 1913. Test him on the mixed year in 1929 and see what he has to say about 1900 (Ranjitsinhji's greatest season, and a fine summer). Mix the ordinary straight up-and-down stuff with the occasional spinner and the ball out of the back of your hand. You will know as much about wine years as he, just as long as you study your *Wisden's*.

Vintage Dress and Vintage Drinking
JAMES LAVER

Is there any connection between women and wine? 'Tut, tut', I can hear the moralists say: 'Only too often'. But we are not here concerned with the ravages of alcoholism, or with the ruin that awaits those who love, not wisely but too well. We are concerned with women's outward appearance: with the clothes they wear. And it does seem, on looking back over the history of dress, as if Fashion, like wine, has had its vintage years. Cannot clothes, and the women who wear them, sometimes be described in the kind of language to be found in wine merchants' catalogues: 'good body', 'delicate', 'not too sweet'? Is there, by any chance, a connection between the years when the vintners could congratulate themselves on the quality of their wares and the years when clothes reached some special height of beauty and distinction?

As an historian of Fashion, I have often striven to find connections between dress and economics, dress and war, dress and female emancipation. But dress and drink! I was once frivolous enough to suggest that there seemed to be some connection between the shape of women's shoulders and the drinks they were fond of at any particular period: I hardly expected to be taken seriously. But vintages: that is another matter.

Let us go back a hundred and one years. The year 1863 was a happy and prosperous one for the whole wine trade in Britain. Gladstone had just reduced the duty on imported wines, and had allowed grocers and other traders the privilege of an 'off licence'. Consumption rocketed, particularly of sherry, which accounted at that time for forty-three per cent of all the wine drunk in England. The vintage at Jerez was excellent. Port, too, had one of its best years, escaping the excessive dryness and lightness of the previous four years, and being pro-

duced in considerable quantities. It was also a good year for champagne, but not for claret.

For women's dress, 1863 was certainly a vintage year. The crinoline had reached the very limits of its expansion, and fashionable ladies took up so much room in the world that it was impossible for two of them to sit upon the same sofa or enter a door side by side. The victorias in which they went driving became more saucer-shaped than ever to accommodate the billowing skirts. The supporting framework usually had nine hoops for day dresses and eighteen hoops of watch-spring for evening dresses, and the dress could be looped up over them, giving excellent glimpses of coloured petticoats and stockings with horizontal stripes of black and red.

Eleven years later there was a tremendous year for champagne; for many wines, 1874 was the last year free from the blight of phylloxera – and they rose to the occasion almost as if they knew it. The sherries of 1874 were generally sweeter, but lighter than those of the preceding vintage, and they showed extraordinary lasting qualities, being still drinkable seventy years later. There was some good vintage port, and splendid clarets. Professor George Saintsbury said of 74s that 'as long as they lasted nothing quite touched them'.

The world of Fashion had recovered from the setback of the Franco-Prussian War, and Paris was once more leading. It was the age of the bustle: not the mere binding-up of the back of the skirt (as if the dress-makers, having discarded the crinoline, were at a loss to know what to do with the quantities of material left over) but a series of horsehair pads to give the posterior protruberance which was so much admired. The striking thing about the dresses of this period was that they were often made of different and contrasting materials, the bodice being of a different colour from the skirt and the sleeves matching the trimming.

The year 1895 is not very helpful for our theory. We think of it as a striking year for Fashion: those immense balloon sleeves, those swirling skirts familiar to us in the lithographs of Toulouse-Lautrec conjure up a whole world of reckless gaiety – the Moulin Rouge, June Avril and Nini-*patte-en-l'air* – all the excitement of the Naughty Nineties! But alas, in wine it is another story. The champagne shippers were in despair; their wines threw a cloudy sediment which ruined their looks if not their taste (but, after all, it wasn't the 95s that the men-about-town were drinking in the Long Bar at the Cri). The clarets were poor, due to the drought which lasted from mid-August to mid-September. Only the Lafites came through really well. Sherry was ruined by the phylloxera, which appeared for the first time at Jerez. The experts describe the ports of '95 as simply 'a failure'. Eighteen ninety-nine was a good year for nearly everything,

but Fashion was passing through an indeterminate phase without any striking characteristics.

By 1906, the Edwardian Age was at its apogee – *la belle époque*, as the French call it, a period of 'fine women' with busts like the prow of a ship, women dripping with lace not only on the bodices, but edging the petticoats glimpsed with every movement. It was the age of frou-frou, extravagance – and champagne. And, as if in obedience to the Spirit of the Age, the wines of Épernay rose to new heights. They were described as elegant, fruity and luscious, and even fuller than the great 1904s. The Monarch himself liked them pink. Not only the champagnes were great in the happy year of 1906. Burgundy, Sauternes and hock were at their best and if sherry, port and claret were not outstanding they were good enough. Indeed, it is difficult to find any record of bad wines of the 1906 vintage.

Almost the same can be said of 1911. The champagnes of the year are

remembered as being very light in colour, very delicate and most attractive. Small quantities of port were produced, but the quality was excellent. Only the hocks of that year were a little uneven, owing to the extremely hot German summer. But the best were superb.

In Fashion, 1911 was certainly a vintage year. There had been a radical change in the silhouette. The bust was still big but no longer thrust forward and the skirts were tubular, narrowing at the hem – the hobble skirt, in fact. The hats were prodigious. Not since the years immediately before the French Revolution had they been so large. They had wide brims and were trimmed with ostrich feathers or wreaths of roses, small stuffed birds and imitation fruit. We read of tricornes and quatre-cornes, helmets, coal-scuttles and 'bizarre' toques with mountainous crowns of pure silk. Fashion certainly seemed to have gone to women's heads.

And then came the War, with its usual damping effect on Fashion. It was not until 1921 that the couturiers really recovered their nerve. Most people think that the dresses of the early 'twenties were short. They were not; they were quite long but strangely straight and tubular. And busts were definitely 'out'.

The experts ran out of words to do justice to the almost universally excellent wines of 1921. Some of the great clarets were described as 'freaks', so much did they exceed expectation in liveliness and richness. The vintages of the Rheingau, Rheinhesse and the Palatinate were thought to equal the greatest German wines of the previous century – those of 1857. Château d'Yquem also was at its best.

In 1928 claret swept the field, and had so much body that some of them may not have reached their peak even yet. Fashion, on the other hand, was timidly trying to escape from the tyranny of the short skirt and the cloche hat. Definitely, not a vintage year.

When we jump to 1947, we find an historic year for Europe's vineyards: almost every wine reached or neared its peak. And Christian Dior revolutionized Fashion with his 'New Look'. Have I succeeded in showing that there is an inevitable connection between vintage years in wine and vintage years in women's dress? Perhaps not! But it has been fun trying, if only to remind myself of some of the *toilettes* I have admired, and some of the wines I have drunk.

Sardines and Sauternes
VYVYAN HOLLAND

There is a public-house just behind the Palace Theatre, at the edge of Soho; this has now changed hands and has been renovated and brought up to date and made spacious and uncomfortable, but when my story starts – before the war – it was owned or managed by a Mr Moar, and was a small, comfortable, frowzy London pub.

At the back of Mr Moar's saloon bar, instead of the usual phalanx of undrinkable concoctions that accumulate in all bars when the publican is off his guard and is persuaded by some keen-eyed traveller to buy them – instead of these there were rows upon rows of sardine tins, all carefully labelled, and all the labels bearing dates. These of course intrigued me; I was a little nervous at first about enquiring about them, but I plucked up courage and asked Mr Moar what it was all about. I found that he was an enthusiast on the subject of old-landed sardines. Now I do not suppose that he was interested in anything but their age; to him a sardine was a sardine and olive oil was olive oil. All that he was concerned with was the age of the oil. He pointed out to me that a sardine which had been marinaded in olive oil for five years was much to be preferred to one that had only been in oil for a few weeks.

I pondered over this statement and wondered whether there was anything in it. And I decided to consult with Curtis Moffat, my guide, mentor and friend on matters gastronomic, and whose knowledge of food and wine was encyclopaedic and who was always enthusiastic about anything new. The same thought struck us simultaneously, 'Was there any connection between the vintage of olive oil and that of wine?' And with this thought the idea of vintage sardines came into being.

Here were the sardines, for the past twenty years at least, on Mr Moar's shelves, waiting for our experiment. The sardines were incidental; it is true that they contributed to the oil, which would hardly have been preserved but for them, in airtight tins. I am no ichthyologist, but I am pretty sure that the weather in the Mediterranean Sea and the Atlantic Ocean does not make much difference to the fish in them, and he would be a very clever naturalist who could distinguish the sardine of one year from that of another.

But the oil was another matter, and we reasoned that if the alternation of sun and rain could so affect the grape as to cause the wine made from it to be of really excellent quality or very poor, it might easily affect the olives as well. So we went to see Mr Moar and we each bought one tin of all the sardines available back to 1906. Mr Moar had only begun collecting them a short time before, so he had not got every year. I think someone must have given him the idea and helped him with his stock; still, we had enough to experiment upon and remembering a Spanish proverb which says that 'olive oil, wine and friends should be old', we opened a twelve-year-old tin. The contents surprised us; the oil had darkened with the years and had become largely incorporated in

the sardines; the backbones had dissolved and the skins had acquired a parchment-like quality and could be removed in one piece.

We now became more critical and we wondered whether the olive-oil harvest years followed the great years of any particular wine – Sauternes, for instance. This was a very interesting theory, but we were not going to become confused into wishful thinking and, proceeding on the principle that sardines tinned early in any particular year would have been put into the previous year's oil, we selected eight tins of the years between 1919 and 1930 and removed their dates, substituting signs by which we alone could know them. We then collected a symposium of gourmets, consisting of André Simon, Colonel Ian Campbell and Barry Neame and asked them to adjudicate.

I must say that a feast of sardines, particularly when helped down, as this one was, by Sauternes, sounds a little bilious, but we had selected men of strong stomach, particularly André Simon, who once confessed to me that he had eaten six dozen Colchester oysters with brown bread and butter and goblets of champagne as a preliminary snack before a city banquet. But that is another story. Anyway, they unanimously placed the sardines in the following order, with the rest nowhere: 1921, 1929, 1924, 1914; thus *exactly following the years of good Sauternes.*

We were now convinced that our theory was correct, and we set about forming a sardine cellar. At the beginning of 1938 we each bought a case of six dozen Rodel and Peneau. But wars destroy good resolutions. Curtis Moffat went to America, food became scarce and I ate my sardines, and Mr Moar retired from business, selling his carefully collected stock to Fortnum & Mason, who treated them as a gimmick for a short while, but made no attempt to replenish them. So the whole carefully devised plan went with the wind. It would be difficult to start a sardine cellar now, as any odd tins that one might find would be undated and unidentifiable, and it would be too much of an uphill fight. There may be someone somewhere who collects them, but if there is I do not know him. I still have a few tins which I have preserved, more out of curiosity and sentiment than as a serious collection. But I remember with delight and pride a 1906 Rodel which I ate in 1940; and at a Committee luncheon of the Saintsbury Club in 1943 André Simon asked me whether I had any sardines left and I produced my last 1908, which was ambrosial.

Perhaps it may be a little late to start now. Some enthusiast started Mr Moar and handed over his stock to him; the departure of Mr Moar and the distribution of his wares destroyed the small nucleus upon which a new gastronomic treasure might have been built up. But if any young man likes to start laying down sardines, here are a few instructions. I say any *young* man, because it may

be twenty years before he will reap the full benefit of his industry. Buy the best French sardines, Rodel, Amieux or Peneau. Get them in cases of six dozen, as they must be turned over every three months, and it is easier to do this if they are in their original cases. Keep them for some years in a cool place and eat them when you drink the Sauternes of their year – a Château d'Yquem, a Guiraud, a Climens or a Suduiraut, and you will find that your patience and your labour will be amply rewarded.

© *from* THE COMPLEAT IMBIBER 7, 1964

Imbiber, Beware!

JULIAN JEFFS

Every drinker of hard liquor faces a danger seldom heard of nowadays, a doom never even considered: death by spontaneous combustion.

Do not mock. There are many tragic cases on record; and if we may be momentarily sceptical, we should do well to remember that the boundaries of our comprehension are for ever being widened; that the horrors of boys' adventure stories are daily becoming realities; that often in the practical sphere of medicine those who scoff today eat their words tomorrow. Once we laughed at the natives for wrapping mould upon their wounds. Then we discovered penicillin.

The *locus classicus* of spontaneous combustion is Charles Dickens's *Bleak House*. Here the combustion was symbolic as well as actual, for it was not only the unfortunate Mr Krook, the 'Lord Chancellor of the Rag and Bottle shop', who perished, but the whole infernal institution of the Chancery courts. Despite Dickens, the courts continue, but they are not what they were.

As for Mr Krook, he was described as being 'continually in liquor'. His fate was the reward of his habits.

... It is a close night, though the damp cold is searching too; and there is a laggard mist a little way up in the air. It is a fine steaming night to turn the slaughter-houses, the unwholesome trades, the sewerage, bad water, and burial grounds to account, and give the Registrar of Deaths some extra business. ...

Mr Guppy has been biting his thumb-nail during this dialogue, generally changing the thumb when he has changed the cross leg. As he is going to do so again, he happens to look at his coat-sleeve. It takes his attention. He stares at it, aghast.

'Why, Tony, what on earth is going on in this house to-night? Is there a chimney on fire?'

'Chimney on fire!'

'Ah?' returns Mr Guppy. 'See how the soot's falling. See here, on my arm! See again, on the table here! Confound the stuff, it won't blow off – smears, like black fat! ...

'What, in the Devil's name,' he says, 'is this! Look at my fingers!'

A thick, yellow liquor defiles them, which is offensive to the touch and sight and more offensive to the smell. A stagnant, sickening oil, with some natural repulsion in it that makes them both shudder. ...

Mr Guppy takes the light. They go down, more dead than alive, and holding one another, push open the door of the back shop. The cat has retreated close to it, and stands snarling – not at them; at something on the ground, before the fire. There is very little fire left in the grate, but there is a smouldering suffocating vapour in the room, and a dark greasy coating on the walls and ceiling. The chairs and table, and the bottle so rarely absent from the table, all stand as usual. On one chair-back, hang the old man's hairy cap and coat. ...

'What's the matter with the cat?' says Mr Guppy. 'Look at her!'

'Mad, I think. And no wonder, in this evil place.'

They advance slowly, looking at all these things. The cat remains where they found her, still snarling at the something on the ground, before the fire and between the two chairs. What is it? Hold up the light.

Here is a small burnt patch of flooring; here is the tinder from a little bundle of burnt paper, but not so light as usual, seeming to be steeped in something; and here is – is it the cinder of a small charred and broken log of wood sprinkled with white ashes, or is it coal? O Horror, he IS here! and this, from which we run away, striking out the light and over-turning one another into the street, is all that represents him. ...

But the nineteenth century was inclined to rationalism, and critics proved sceptical. Dickens was particularly vexed by the strictures of G.H. Lewes, the paramour of George Eliot. In the preface that he wrote to later editions of the novel he defended the possibility of combustion, and was able to quote his sources, which were those cited in a scientific dictionary current at the time. His account of Mr Krook's tragedy was precisely in accordance with the records.

Imbiber Beware!

Many cases of spontaneous combustion have indeed been recorded. One of the earliest examples would appear to have been that of Abdallah-ben-Ali, a man who, contrary to the dictates of his religion, became strongly addicted to alcohol. Wakened by a smell of burning, his father found him suffering atrocious pains. He gave him a glass of water to drink and sprayed him with water, but it was without effect: he was quite burnt up.

In 1745, a number of papers on the subject were read before the Royal Society. The earliest case cited was in a pamphlet by one John Hilliard, entitled *Fire from Heaven burning the Body of one John Hitchell, of Holnehurst, within the Parish of Christ-Church, in the County of Southampton, the 26th of June, 1613*. Unfortunately, however, this is not a clear case, as the unfortunate carpenter (for such was his trade) caught fire whilst lying in bed during a thunder storm, and the storm, rather than strong drink, might have been responsible. Moreover, the style of his burning was quite different from that of the later victims. His wife

> ... dragg'd him out of the Bed into the street; and there, by reason of the Vehemency of the Fire, she was enforced, to her no small Grief, to forsake him; where he lay burning upon the Ground for the Space of Three Days after, or thereabouts. Not that there was any Appearance of Fire outwardly to be seen on him, but only a kind of Smoke ascending upwards from his Carcase, until it was consumed to Ashes, except only some small Shew of Part of his Bones which were cast into a Pit made by the Place....

In the majority of the reported cases the fire was much more rapid and dramatic. In 1800 Pierre-Aimé Lair published a valuable little book entitled *Essai sur les Combustions Humaines, Produites par un long abus des liqueurs spiritueuses*. The earliest case that he found occurred in Copenhagen in 1692, when a woman who for three years had made abuse of strong liquors to the point of taking no other nourishment, was totally consumed by fire during the night save for her skull and the extreme joints of her fingers. But this instance is also imperfect: she had been sleeping on a straw-filled chaise, and the combustion may not have been entirely internal.

An instance described by Le Cat in his *Mémoire sur les Incendies Spontanés* proved almost as fatal to the victim's husband as to the victim herself. It happened in Rheims, on 20 February 1725, when a drunken lady named Millet was found consumed in the kitchen, half a yard from the fireplace. Only a part of her head, a portion of her lower extremities, and some vertebrae escaped the conflagration. A foot and a half of floor under the corpse had been consumed, but items very near her were undamaged. Unfortunately, the deceased woman had a particularly pretty servant, and this almost proved her husband's undoing:

he was accused of causing the fire in league with the servant and of making it appear like an accident. In the court of first instance he was found guilty, but on appeal other similar instances of spontaneous combustion were brought to the notice of the judges and he was acquitted. It was too late: overwhelmed with grief, he spent his last sad days in hospital.

Nearer home, and rather more typical, was the case of Grace Pett, a fishwife of Ipswich who, on 10 April 1744, unfortunately drank a large quantity of gin to celebrate the return of her daughter from Gibraltar. In the middle of the night, having the urge to smoke her pipe, she went downstairs, carrying a candle. What happened next is unknown. Her daughter came down early in the morning to find her mother lying by the grate. There was no fire in the grate, but her mother appeared

> ... like a Block of Wood burning with a glowing Fire without Flame; upon which quenching it with two Bowls of Water, the Smother and Stench thereof almost stifled the Neighbours, whom her Cries had brought in; the Trunk of the Body was in a manner burnt to Ashes, and appeared like a Heap of Charcoal cover'd with White Ashes; the Head Arms, Legs and Thighs were also very much burnt. ...

The fire was entirely internal; a paper screen and some clothes which lay next to the body were unaffected. The most unusual aspect of this case is that the fire could be extinguished by water. Generally this proved impossible.

The *Annual Register* for 1763 includes a sad instance of the combustion of the Countess Cornelia Baudi, of Cesena, described by J. Bianchini, prebendary of Verona. This lady was in her 62nd year, and felt well all day until at night she began to feel 'heavy': after supper she was put to bed, and talked three hours with her maid; at last, falling asleep, the door was shut. In the morning, the maid, going to call her, saw her corpse in a deplorable condition. Four feet from the bed was a heap of ashes. Her legs were untouched, and her stockings were still on, but her head lay between them, her brains, half of the back-part of her skull, and the whole of her chin burnt to ashes. There were also three blackened fingers. All the rest was ashes, of a peculiarly disagreeable kind, that when touched left in the hand a greasy and stinking moisture. Soot was floating in the air of the room. A small oil lamp on the floor was covered with ashes, but the oil was all gone. The two candles on the table were strangely affected: the tallow was gone, but the cotton wicks were left, and there was some moisture around the feet of the candlesticks. The bed was undamaged, the blankets and sheets only raised on one side, as if the lady had just got out of bed, but the whole furniture was covered with moist, ash-coloured soot, which penetrated into the drawers, and fouled the linen. This soot even got into a neighbouring kitchen, where it hung on the walls and utensils. A bit of bread, covered with this soot, was understandably refused by several dogs. From the windows there trickled down a greasy, loathsome, yellowish liquor with an unusual stink. The floor was thickly smeared with a glue-like moisture, which could not easily be got off, and the stink spread throughout the house.

Ten years later the *Annual Register* published an account by one B. Wilmer, a surgeon of Coventry, of a typical case of spontaneous combustion that had occurred during the previous year in that City:

> ... Mary Clues, of Gosford Street, this city, aged 52 years, was of indifferent character, and much addicted to drinking. Since the death of her husband, which happened about a year and a half ago, her propensity to this vice increased to such a degree, that as I have been informed by several of her neighbours, she has drank the quantity of four half pints of rum, undiluted with any other liquor, in a day. This practice was so familiar to her, that scarce a day has passed this last twelve-month, but she has swallowed from half a pint to a quart of rum or aniseed-water. Her health gradually declined; and, from being a jolly, well-looking woman, she grew thinner, her complexion altered, and her skin became dry. About the beginning of February last, she was attacked with the jaundice, and took to her bed. Though she was now so helpless, as hardly to be able to do anything for herself, she continued her old custom of dram-drinking, and generally smoked a pipe every night. No one lived with her in the house. ...
>
> At half after five the next morning, a smoke was observed to come out of the window in the street; and, upon breaking open the door, some flames were perceived in the room, which, with five or six buckets of water, were easily extinguished. Betwixt the bed and fire-place lay the remains of Mrs Clues. The legs and one thigh were untouched. Except these parts, there were not the least remains of any skin, muscles, or viscera. The bones of the skull, thorax, spine, and the upper extremities, were completely calcined, and covered with a whitish efflorescence. ...

The conditions leading to spontaneous combustion were ably summarised by Lair, and are as follows: firstly, the people concerned made abuse, over a long period, of spirituous liquors; secondly, they were nearly all women; thirdly, they were mostly aged; fourthly, they were generally fat. When disaster overtook them, the extremities of their bodies were generally spared, and water, instead of putting the fire out, sometimes only made it more violent.

The description of the phenomenon as given by A. Devergie in his *Memoire sur la Combustion Humaine* (1851) corresponds closely with the account of Dickens. At the moment that combustion starts, a little bluish flame is seen, which extends very rapidly to all parts of the body. When someone touches a part that is burning, fat matter attaches itself to his fingers and continues to burn. At the same time, there is an odour of the strongest and most disagreeable kind, having something in common with burnt horn. A thick black smoke envelopes the burning body and clings to the furniture in the form of an oily and fetid soot. Complete combustion can take place in the space of an hour and a half, but objects in close proximity to the body are seldom burnt.

There are some who claim that the age of miracles is past, while others suggest that we are merely blind to them. Certainly our scientists have made sceptics of us, and we are very willing to disbelieve anything we are unable to explain. But the best scientists are those who make their observations with open minds and then seek to explain what their eyes have seen. One must admit that there have been no recent cases of spontaneous combustion, but that is a far cry from saying that there have never been such cases. The explanation may well be that we live in a better-governed age. Any fishwife feeling inclined to live on nothing but rum and aniseed would likely be restrained: she would be taken to a suitable hospital and given medical care.

But even now it is just possible that some inebriate may escape the well-meaning clutches of the welfare state. Be prudent. If you are a fat old woman with a taste for spirits, beware!

The solemn accounts of eighteenth-century observers are horrific enough, but let the last word, as did the first, rest with fiction. The following is from a nineteenth-century penny dreadful quoted by E.S. Turner in *Boys will be Boys:*

. . . Her face assumed a frightful colour.

She stretched forth her long talons, yelling in the fierce grip of delirium tremens, as she advanced to where Jack was, to fling him into the flames, shrieking –

'Now, boy, you shall be my victim. Ha! Ha! Ha!'

Hitherto he had stood horrified and fascinated.

But the instinct of self-preservation was strong within him.

He stepped back and drew his pistol to fire.

But there was no necessity for him to use his pistol: a sight which no pen can adequately describe greeted him.

The hag paused in her rush and pressed her hand over her breast.

Then the fearful sounds she was uttering came forth no more.

Their place was taken by a bluish lambent flame that came forth from her mouth and curled in fearful fantastic wreaths about her face.

The boy covered his face with his hands.

The sight was too awful.

Moments passed.

Again he ventured to look up.

She was still standing there but another change had come over her: now the features that had likened her to humanity had disappeared.

She was an incandescent mass of matter like a statue, burning and glowing like the centre of a fire.

He sprang forward.

Imbiber Beware!

There was some water in a bucket.

He seized it and poured it over what had once been a woman.

The water turned at once to steam and flew off. . . .

He sat down in sheer despair.

The fearful effluvia cast off by the burning made him ill.

And so he sat there sick with horror and watched the mass turn from red to dull blue and finally go out altogether.

© *from* THE COMPLEAT IMBIBER 10, 1969

Triptyque

THREE BRIEF ENCOUNTERS

Defeat of a Drinking Man

Alan Brien

One day in 1956, it reached the ears of the *Evening Standard* that Hemingway was in mid-Atlantic on the *Liberté*. And some officious desk-bound executive conceived the idea of sending me down to Plymouth to extract an interview as he passed within sight of the English shore. My journey down there was made miserable by the thought that I might have to scale some slippery, swinging rope-ladder, green with fear and sea-sickness, while the great man sneered from the bridge.

Needless to say, the operation which had been simply demonstrated in Shoe Lane by moving a nicotined finger across a tiny map of England turned out, when put into effect by a flesh-and-blood correspondent dealing with actual trains, motor-cars, boats and bureaucrats, to be an odyssey of snags and frus-

trations. Once in my compartment, I was seized with a fit of nervous amnesia and suffered from delusions that I should be going to Portsmouth or Southampton. The shipping line at Plymouth was shrouded in a pall of vagueness about the hour, or even the day, of the *Liberté*'s arrival. Some officials promised that I could travel out to its mooring spot on the luggage tender. Others insisted that the Customs authorities would not permit any visitors. The shore-to-shore radio telephone operator connected me with a laconic American voice that insisted that Mr Hemingway had failed to turn up in time for the departure from New York.

My only success was in hiring a miniature tug affair, steered by a Bogartian, unshaven salt in plimsolls and a yachting cap, for five pounds. That at least would give a professional look to my expense sheet. We seemed to spend hours circling the ship while the suitcases spilled out of some hole in its side like giant children's bricks, but no one resembling the great man peered out from among the faces along the rails. Once inside, not up a rope-ladder but across an almost equally vertiginous and shuddering ramp, I realised that I had not the faintest idea of where to start looking. It had never occurred to me that a liner could be so enormous and complicated – it was like being insinuated into the base of a bee-hive and told to have a word with the queen.

My deadline, which had once seemed so comfortingly distant, was now almost upon me. I started running the corridors shouting, 'Où est Monsieur 'Emingway? S'il vous bloody plaît.' Various steward figures in dazzling white ducks gave me cabin numbers, apparently at random, in French, and I plunged, sweating and Medusa-haired, into various wrong staterooms.

Twice I found bars tucked away in windowless metal caverns. The bartenders denied any knowledge of 'Emingway and suggested different bars. Other journalists, who must have been deposited aboard by submarine, appeared at the end of long carpeted vistas, pantomimed fury like the Demon King and contempt for rival papers, and made off at a trot.

Eventually, having traversed the ship a couple of times, I arrived back at one of the bars and discovered there a battered, burly figure humped on a stool. He didn't look like Hemingway so much as like an old, over-exposed, badly re-touched photograph of Hemingway. His hair and beard seemed to have been knitted on heavy wooden needles out of shiny, new, delicate barbed-wire. His face, such of it as was visible, was as bright as a peeled orange. And as he spoke tiny vessels appeared to explode across his cheeks like Very shells over a battle-field. 'Mr Hemingway,' he said, 'has nothing to say to the press, but I will buy you a drink.'

He spoke very slowly and carefully like someone counting out small change in a foreign currency and watching to spot the moment when he is being overcharged. I took the drink and poured it down into a stomach already distended by a queasy brew of ale and resentment. Now I was here I couldn't think of a single thing to say. A hasty rake over the surface of my mind produced a recent small news item – some bumptious tourist in Havana had taken Hemingway's place at a bar and been picked up and ejected by an indignant boozing crony. What was the use of Preaching about the True and the Beautiful and the Good and That's the Way It Should Be Among Men, I asked, if the preacher behaved like any Hollywood bum on a spree?

Hemingway punched himself in slow-motion on the ear as if annoyed that it should be transmitting such gibberish.

'You a drinking man?' he said.

'Yes,' I said.

'You have your favourite bar?'

'I suppose so,' I said.

'Then you have your favourite place in that bar. And that is your place. And they keep it for you.'

'No I don't,' I said, 'And no they don't.'

'Then it's not a real bar,' he said amicably. 'In a real bar, they keep your place where you put your back to the wall. That's all.'

'That's not all,' I said, stamping my feet. 'That's Warner Brothers gangster talk. How would you like it if I had you thrown out of my bar?'

Just then a fat Frenchman appeared. 'I think my seat, sir,' he announced.

Hemingway slid off like a boxer who hears the bell for the next round.

'Excuse me. Excuse *me*,' he said. 'Your seat, certainly.'

There was a longish pause and then we were both shaking with laughter until the counter rattled.

'To hell with newspapers,' he shouted. 'Come to France. We'll get off the boat and just drive into anywhere.'

I thought of the nicotined finger, the last edition, the pay slip, Lord Beaverbrook. 'Some other time,' I said. Back on shore I scribbled my newless story as I waited for the call to FLE 3000 to come through. At last it came – 'the office is closed for the day,' they said, 'try tomorrow morning.'

And that's the way it was.

© *from* THE COMPLEAT IMBIBER 8, 1965

Whisky and Nougat: Tea with Noël Coward

Edgar Lustgarten

In 1929 I was an undergraduate with a dominant ambition.
Not to get a First (I didn't). Not to get a Blue (I couldn't).* My ambition, my *idée fixe*, was to meet Noël Coward.

The gap between our ages was eight years. (It still is.) The gap between our achievements was enormous. (It still is.) He was world-renowned, as actor, dramatist, song-writer; had already among his credits – to use more recent jargon – *The Young Idea*, *The Vortex*, *Fallen Angels*, *Hay Fever*. To say nothing of the revues *On With the Dance* and *This Year of Grace*. All I had to counter this formidable hand was some success at the Oxford Union – a very minor card.

So my chance of meeting Noël Coward did not appear bright. Vaguely I worked out plans. Vaguely I thought up schemes. To no practical effect. I was forced to console myself with one slight contact I had made with him through correspondence.

That, at least, did not result from calculation. It resulted from uncontrolled enthusiasm.

During the curious process known as Eating Dinners – a compulsory ritual before Call to the Bar – I had escaped one night in time to reach the Playhouse Theatre where Noël Coward was starring in *The Second Man*. For the first time I saw and heard *him*, not only his work. For the first time – I lived in Manchester where we got a lot of highly sophisticated plays, but not a lot of highly sophisticated players – I saw great comedy acting in the modern style.

It was an occasion to be forever treasured. I longed to express my gratitude

*But he did become President of the Union. C.R.

in more individual terms than by anonymously clapping with the crowd. After much hesitation, and much more trepidation, I set out to compose a congratulatory letter.

I sweated blood over that letter. Vainly seeking the right words. Every draft depressed me. Either it was slushy, or inadequate, or both. Revised a dozen times, it remained a clumsy tribute. But it was sincere, and at last I sent it off. Noël Coward, Esq. Personal.

I would not have been at all surprised if it had gone unanswered. I knew the pressures on him, guessed the volume of his mail. An acknowledgement from a secretary would have struck me as most civil. To my astonishment, I received a reply in Noël Coward's own hand.

Not a formal reply, either. Not a reply that would have done for twenty thousand others. Nothing like 'Send a photograph' in 'Mad About the Boy'. Noël Coward had clearly read my letter; got the muddled message; expressed appreciation. I gasped. *He* was appreciating *me*.

That was my initial glimpse of a quality in Noël Coward that many have learnt to value second only to his genius.

Kindliness cohabiting with astringency....

Those letters were exchanged in 1928. Obviously self-sufficient, self-contained. No *reason* for him to write again. No *excuse* for me. My ambition – for what would now be called a confrontation – receded further from fulfilment than before.

I grew resigned. Perhaps when I'm Lord Chancellor? A nice chat on the Woolsack? Though we'd both be rather old.

Then C.B. Cochran announced he would present *Bitter Sweet* – Noël Coward's new, very hush-hush, operetta – at the Palace Theatre, Manchester, in 1929. (Goodness, is it all those years ago?)

Splendid. The North lit up with anticipatory glamour. Special house-parties were formed at Knowsley and at Chatsworth. Special trains were booked to bring celebrities from London. Special this and special that for everyone who counted. Like a Coronation. A Cup Final. A Durbar.

But what claim had *I* to any special treatment? Least of all, to reception at Supreme H.Q.

I don't know – even now. My relentless importunity? His generous indulgence? I only know it happened. Noël Coward invited me to tea. In his hotel suite. Just before the dress rehearsal.

I don't think I ever felt so nervous in my life. It was not simply the impact of the famous on the obscure. Baldwin, Churchill, the first Lord Birkenhead – at the Union I'd had the lot, sometimes more than once. And I'd never felt

that sort of nervousness with *them*. Perhaps because I'd never wanted to be another Baldwin. Never wanted to be another Churchill. Never wanted – well, not *much* – to be another Birkenhead. But I *did* want – desperately – to be another Noël Coward. Unattainable. Made you frightened of the prototype.

I tried to keep my head. To be observant and acute. To register a close-up mental portrait of the Master – a title, if not then conferred, fully merited – that I could recall for the remainder of my days.

My head swam. My reflexes worked automatically.

Dressing gown. Cigarette (no holder). High forehead. Eyes on the verge of twinkling. Mouth mischievous, amused.

'Now,' he said. 'You wanted to have a talk. What shall we talk about?'

That was an easy one.

'You,' I said.

'Certainly not. There are far too many people talking about me. Not invariably to my satisfaction. I have a better proposal. Let's talk about *you*.'

He leaned back with every sign of close attention. I gathered, as best I could, my scattered wits.

I told the Master I wanted to write. That I meant to write professionally. That I had no illusions – I knew the going would be tough. That the sole money I had yet earned by writing was a fee paid to me for an article on him. That it had been printed in a highbrow monthly (now defunct), edited by John Middleton Murry (now deceased). That Murry had sent me a strange note of acceptance. 'I regret to say I have never heard of Noël Coward. But I like your piece. I am sending you a guinea.'

'Did he send the guinea?'

'Yes.'

'You were gr-rossly underpaid.' That characteristic ripple. 'It was an admirable article.'

I preened myself. Though I doubted whether he had read the article. (I doubt whether he has read it now.) But he was giving me heart – from the goodness of his own. I wanted this conversation to go on and on.

'I predicted a great future for you,' I remarked insanely.

'Most encouraging.' Not a trace of ridicule, not a hint of sarcasm. Adding, 'You must guard, though, dear boy, against exaggeration.'

I silently vowed I would.

'My future,' said the Master, 'is a subject – to me – of inexhaustible interest. I would willingly hear you dilate on it for hours. But I have to be at the theatre before six. We must have tea.'

Tea. Of course. That was nominally our purpose – having tea.

[321]

I had not expected a cuppa. That would have been *mal à propos*. Crumbling an image. I hadn't bargained, though, for what I was hospitably offered.

A bottle of Scotch. Dry Gingers. Baby Sodas. Ice.

And a Lalique bowl full of succulent French nougat.

'Help yourself,' the Master said.

I did. So did he.

There are many drinks I like – ask my wine merchant, my local – but whisky (blame my lack of taste) has never been among them. There are many sweets I like – ask my home, my restaurants – but nougat (blame my lack of taste) has never been among them.

In combination, they were scaring. But I wouldn't succumb. I struggled.

'You wrote to me, didn't you, some time ago?' the Master said.

My head – which had steadied somewhat – suddenly got worse. My stomach gave warning that it might soon follow suit. I envied the Master's enjoyment of this exotic diet.

'Wrote? Yes.' I blinked to keep him in focus. 'Yes, I did.'

'About *The Second Man*.' He looked up seriously. 'Have you seen the Lunts?'

Lynn Fontanne and Alfred Lunt were then enchanting London theatre-goers in *Caprice*.

'No? A pity. If you had, you would class me in *The Second Man* as a mediocre pantaloon on the pier at Brighton.'

'Yes,' I said submissively.

The Master. The Lunts. Pantaloons. Brighton Pier. All perishing in the growing strain on my digestive organs.

'What are you going to do with your life?' inquired the Master, munching another chunk of nougat, taking another sip of whisky. 'Apart from writing – a commendable hobby – what are you going to do?'

'Be a barrister. To start with.'

'Dignified. Lucrative, too, I'm told.'

'At the top.'

'Yes.' He nodded. A nod conveying a wealth of meaning. Going to the Bar doesn't make you Norman Birkett. Any more than going on the stage makes you Noël Coward.

'Another drink?'

'Well ...'

He poured two fingers out for me. One finger for himself.

'More nougat?'

'No, thank you. No more nougat.'

'I've had enough of it, too.'

Could anyone be so calm at such a time? Not I. But then I couldn't have written, composed, directed, *Bitter-Sweet*. I found that reflection illogically comforting.

'It's been a pleasure,' said the Master, in courteous dismissal. 'But now I must go to work. And you to play.'

'To read Byles on Bills,' I said.

'The same thing,' said the Master.

Thus we parted, with what earlier writers used to call 'expressions of mutual goodwill and esteem' . . .

Absurd to pretend that ever since we have trodden the same path, or that our convergences have been other than occasional. Each, though, without exception, has been illumined by at least one flash of the Master's instant wit.

As when I mentioned a scruffy actor who posed as a country squire. 'I know him well,' the Master said. 'Every other inch a gentleman.'

As when he referred to a loquacious socialite whom he had escorted recently to the opera. 'A fascinating experience,' said the Master. 'I had never heard her before in *Lohengrin*.'

As when I met him before my school dinner and explained - rather sheepishly - that I was going to an 'Old Boys' Thing'. 'An interest in *young* boys,' said the Master, 'is understandable, and, I believe, prevalent. An interest in *old* boys savours strongly of perversion.'

All are vividly impressed upon my memory. But none quite so much as what I call privately The Manchester Encounter. When a great artist, at the very top of the tree, took time out from his own preoccupations at a crucial moment in his dazzling career to inspire confidence in a youth he did not even know and who had not yet even reached the lowest branch.

Oh - as Francis Thompson so very nearly wrote - Oh my whisky and my nougat long ago.

© *from* THE COMPLEAT IMBIBER 10, 1969

No ... er Crème de Menthe:
A Desperate Conversation with Evelyn Waugh

Oliver Knox

'That's Evelyn Waugh at the table over there,' said a friend with whom, some years ago, I was having lunch at Boodle's – the bow-windowed St James's club, accorded in *Officers and Gentlemen* the round, comfortable and unflattering *alias* of 'Turtles'. 'Why don't you introduce yourself? Really, you should. He'd like it.'

This seemed barely plausible. Certainly he had written the biography of my uncle, with whom, however, I had been on only remote terms, meeting him seldom and – probably quite unnecessarily – holding him in awe at rare family funerals and weddings. On the other hand, Evelyn Waugh's dislike of casual encounters, his stage-choleric objection to intrusion by strangers, was well-publicised enough for me to suppose it had some reality.

One of the – possibly rather feminine – characteristics of a certain type of old and close friend is delight in arranging improbable encounters, in order to witness the minor imbroglios that ensue. This social voyeurism is slightly embarrassing, but also rather flattering to its objects.

It took a single glass of port after lunch to inveigle me into walking across the morning-room to one of the half-dozen identical plum-coloured sofas on which Evelyn Waugh was sitting in conversation with his companion. I stood awkwardly in front of them both.

'I'd very much like to introduce myself, sir,' (slightly stammering). 'My name is Oliver Knox. I'm a nephew of Ronald's.'

He looked half up, and did seem taken aback at being accosted in a club – which is, it is true, a normally safe social sanctuary.

'RONALD WHO?'

Not for the last time I raised my voice – far too loud, I expect – and felt myself colour. I had forgotten that deafness was said to be another of his defences (or handicaps, or both).

'Knox. Ronald Knox.'

He stared at me for seconds, in silence. He didn't ask me to sit down, and I thought it forward to pull up a chair. The invitation which followed was unexpected and one I have never been proffered, before or since.

'Have a crème de menthe.'

Some openings don't help at all in building bridges, serving indeed – though not necessarily by intent – only to increase the gulf between people who are left stranded, on opposite shores of converse, all usual semaphore having broken down. This was one of those openings.

'No thank you. No . . . er crème de menthe.'

'You must be U oy's son.'

'I'm sorry. U oy. . . .?'

Who could U oy possibly be? Should I shout K–N–O–X? Surely Evelyn Waugh must be utterly familiar with the surname, totally unlike, even on the most incoherent of mumblings, U oy?

'This is ——, my publisher.'

Still puzzled by the identity of the gentleman whose son I was apparently taken to be, I in turn failed to catch the name of Evelyn Waugh's companion who rose, shook hands, and sat down again. I was still standing uneasily, half on one foot, *in statu pupillari* as it were.

'We're not members here. We're visiting from White's.'

This seemed to put Boodle's in its place. Meanwhile a light, similar to that experienced on solving at long last a glaringly obvious clue in a crossword puzzle, had dawned. It would have been better if I had then answered more straightforwardly. Perhaps I hoped to steal some small advantage in return for my – largely self-inflicted – discomfiture. If so, I was to be disappointed.

'We used to pronounce it E-V-O-E. To rhyme with "goddesses three". You know that song "EVOE, goddesses three" . . .?'

'No. It's U oy.'

'Anyway, I'm not Edmund's son.'

(U oy, Ἐνοι, or Evoe or Edmund Knox is another of my fairly famous uncles, editor of *Punch* for many years during the 'thirties and 'forties.)

'I'm Dillwyn's son.'

'Not an atheist like Dillwyn, I hope.' This seemed abrupt, though not said unkindly. My father had certainly been agnostic, but atheist implied more militancy than I, at least, had ever been aware of.

'No, an Anglican – a rather bad Anglican, I'm afraid.'

'Never mind, you're halfway there. What do you do for a living?'

This was a question I had foreseen, and rather dreaded. It is not that I am ashamed of my career in advertising – or rather, ashamed only to the extent of my shortcomings in the business itself – but rather that I was sure, whatever the arguments for such an occupation might be, they would not appeal to Evelyn Waugh. Certainly I had no wish to use the occasion to justify my job. Fascinating in their right place though, say, the intricacies of the budgerigar-seed market may be, I did not care for the prospect of elaborating on them just now, necessarily in a loud voice and to the possible disturbance of other members.

'Oh, business.'

It was no use. 'What kind of business?'

'Advertising.'

There was a rather long pause. Evidently he was considering in which direction this – possibly slightly distasteful? – topic should be pursued. The tangent he chose could not have been predicted.

'Have you ever read the life of your great-grandfather Bishop French . . .?'

The story of the ascetic Bishop French's mission in Lahore – his phantasmagorical latterday wanderings as a holy man to preach the gospel in the Sultanate of Muscat, the description of him as a protestant Charles de Foucauld – had been to me the most interesting chapter of Evelyn Waugh's *Ronald Knox*.

'. . . You ought to go and look him up in the D.N.B. Never know when it would come in useful in your advertising.'

The meaning of the latter suggestion (except in the most crudely, and indeed cruelly, sarcastic sense) continues to baffle me. Possibly it was a wild *non sequitur* induced by a mutual shyness and embarrassment. At any rate it had the merit of closing the topic of advertising, since neither of us was prepared to track down the – inconceivable – connection between the gaunt visionary's life in India and Arabia and his great-grandson's role in one of the most worldly of modern trades.

Conversational panic now set in, at least for me.

'I very much admired your biography of Ronald. Of course you knew him *far* better than I did. If I did have one criticism – if you will allow me to say so – you made so much of his life sound rather sad and damp, rather October-ish . . .'

He didn't reply. I thought he had stopped listening. There are moments when one longs never to have embarked on a conversation; but desperation, so far from imposing a merciful guillotine on speech, makes one splash and flounder on, sinking deeper.

'...My 7-year-old daughter Charlotte has just written a childish poem.'
(What *was* I saying? Why on earth should this interest him? Should I raise my voice?)

I am a dog	I am a dog
That's always fed,	That's never fed,
That's always met	That's never met,
By travelling dog	By travelling dog,
That comes my way.	That comes my way.

I was perceptibly sweating now. My voice seemed pitched rather high, too.

'You see, I thought you made Ronald sound rather like the dog that's never fed, never met....'

Evelyn Waugh's small, bright astonished eyes were now fixed on me. I expect he was as bemused as I had been by U oy and Bishop French's advertising relevance. He looked alert, still and ready to pounce.

He did pounce. He said, '*Very* remarkable. *Very*. Have you published it yet?'

At last I have.

© *from* THE COMPLEAT IMBIBER 10, 1969

The Sentinel's Story, 1805

CHARLES CAUSLEY

After the Battle of Trafalgar, the body of Lord Nelson was placed in a cask of brandy as the *Victory* made for Gibraltar. On the night of 24 October, owing to a displacement of air from the corpse, the lid of the cask burst open and the body reappeared. The rumour ran round the ship that the Admiral had risen from the dead.

Three days below Trafalgar
   Walking the western swell,
Where in the Shoals of Peter
   Many deep seamen dwell,
Our ship, wearing the weather,
   Taut as the travelling tree,
Now shook its shuddered branches
   On forests of the sea.

The Sentinel's Story, *1805*

The Captain in his cabin
 Slept in the walnut wood,
Jack Strop within his swinging bed,
 The nipper where he could.
Some slept above and some below
 The waving water-line,
But soundest slept the Admiral
 Buried in brandy-wine.

I saw the midnight turning
 That still, surrendered breath,
The good Lord Nelson burning
 Upon the reefs of death.
I saw him take the bullet
 Aboard his breast, his spine,
On his cocked coat of medals
 Spill the bright, bitter wine.

The marksman in his mizen
 Fifteen salt yards away
Saw good Lord Nelson strolling
 About his bloody day.
The gunners they stood naked
 Upon their deadly drill,
But Nelson, cased in the gold-lace,
 Was dressed to kill, to kill.

Around his throat his ribbons,
 His high-hat on his head,
Mates, in that tiddley uniform
 He was already dead.
His five of decorations
 He ferried on the flood,
The four all made of silver
 And one all made of blood.

The water, wine and lemon
 They carried to his bed,
They rubbed his chest, they rubbed his breast,
 They shot his sniper dead.

Don't throw me overboard, he cried.
    How dear is life to men!
He opened up his pearly eyes
    And shut them down again.

They cropped for Lady Hamilton
    The harvest of his hair,
They put him in his pusser's shirt
    Within the leaguer there.
Around the ripened hour
    They cut for him a cape,
Stitched with the sacred spirit
    That's gathered from the grape.

On the October ocean
    Loud blew the bucking gale
As south towards Gibraltar
    Now swam the wooden whale,
And in her level belly
    No shake Lord Nelson feels,
The new wine pouring at his head,
    The old out at his heels.

But with the marching midnight
    The good Lord Nelson stirred,
The breath within his body
    Burst in a long, last word.
The top leapt off the leaguer,
    He lifted up his head,
And pale as paint the seaman's saint
    Came driving from the dead.

O some were winding up their wounds,
    Some prayed, some played, some swore,
And some were saving up their strength
    For a dicky-run ashore,
But when the Lord High Admiral
    Came dancing through the drum
Every man in *Victory*
    Thought his hour had come.

The Sentinel's Story, 1805

We should have anchored, Hardy said.
   It was his last command!
I shouldn't be surprised, boys,
   If we never got to land.
But casting his caulked eye about
   His cold, his canvas crew,
Lord Nelson sank within his tank,
   The sailing storm hove to.

Now wheeled the white, the wandered moon,
   Now spun the little stars,
Soft as a wish flew the white fish,
   Now slept the steady tars.
Now ran our ruined vessel
   About the beating clock
And anchored with the weather
   Beneath the bully Rock.

So here's to good Lord Nelson
   Who got up from his grave
And called to wind and weather
   His sailors for to save,
And here's to the good brandy,
   Long may its blessings be
As on old England's seamen
   In the Spanish-speaking sea.

© *from* THE COMPLEAT IMBIBER 4, 1961

[331]

Vintage ffolkes

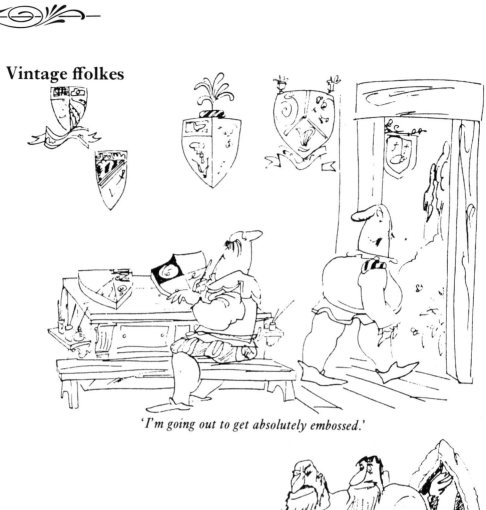

'*I'm going out to get absolutely embossed.*'

'*No, not Malmsey, I wouldn't be seen dead drinking Malmsey.*'

'...nheer Rubens, ...e gentlemen to see you.'

'...don't care how long he's been with us. Hollingsworth must go!'

'Ah, Count, a Jeroboam!'

'This has been fun. Why don't we get some more members and do the same thing next year?'

© *from* PUNCH 17 November 1976

How to Taste

J. M. SCOTT

I am always sorry to come up again from a cellar. Cellars have an architecture of their own, their own smell, temperature, light. They even have their own vegetation. There is a kind of fungus which sprouts from barrels, living exclusively on the fumes of good wine.

But we are not yet coming up from the cellar. It is during its schoolboy age – one, two, or three years – that the wine is judged and bought by the merchants. You too will be given wine to taste and judge; and the chief cellarman, not knowing how unimportant you are, will watch your face and listen to everything you say most seriously.

It takes twenty years of hard work to develop a discriminating palate for wine. Having been brought up on gin and beer and also being poor, I certainly will never know much more than that wine is good. But I must have tasted wines a score of times in the company of experts, and I developed a technique which deceived the most critical *maître de chai* or *chef de caves*. For what they are worth I will pass on my notes. (A *chai*, by the way, is a ground-cellar where barrels are kept; a *cave* is an underground cellar.)

The first rule is to say nothing. Actions and expressions are more significant and much safer than words. A mistake most amateurs make at first is to behave as if they were being judged by the wine and by the company. That may be true. But behave as if you were doing the interviewing – with dignity, courtesy, keen interest, and decision.

When the wine-glass is handed to you, do not take it by the stem but by the base, between forefinger and thumb. Bow to the man who gives it to you. Hold the glass up to the light, peer at it, frowning slightly and swilling the wine round and round in the glass. You must not spill it, of course, but it is most impressive if you can learn – with a glass of water in your bedroom – to make it swish round just below the rim, as fast as a motor-cyclist on the wall of death. Having done this, you study your wine-glass again, this time with the expression you might wear while reading small type. What you are looking at is the speed or slowness with which the last of the wine drains down the sides of the glass.

Then swish it round again and immediately afterwards cup your two hands about the bowl and bury your nose in it as if you were inhaling something for a cold. When you lift your face again the fumes of the wine, the bouquet at the back of your nose, will of their own accord have given you the right expression. But you may accentuate the effect by throwing up your eyes and then bowing your head. After this, swish the wine round the glass, frowning thoughtfully.

Now take a mouthful. A mistake most novices fall into is to take a sip, which gives them away at once. You must take a great hungry gulp of wine. But you don't swallow it, of course. You chew it. You push it forward through your teeth with the tongue and suck it back to the back-door of your nose. If the *maître de chai* is watching you at this time, as he certainly will be, make sure that all your facial muscles are working. But look at nobody yourself. Your eyes must be far away in the dim recesses of the cellar.

You should practise this chewing, for you must be able to keep it up for a long time without swallowing, which is not easy. Your face works more and more strongly. You have now appeared to appreciate the wine with all your sensory nerves. You have reached your decision. The moment of climax has come.

The climax is the spit. Again and again I have seen a good performance ruined by the spit. It is disastrous to bend down in a corner and merely open your mouth. It is little better to purse your lips as if you were getting rid of a cherry stone.

You have reached your decision, remember; so your spit must underline it. It must be as bold and emphatic as an exclamation mark. The way to do it is to draw your shut lips wide as if you were about to whistle for a taxi, and with a tremendous flick of the tongue send the stuff jetting out so that it strikes the floor like a fist banged on a table. Then look round at everybody happily and proudly, because you have been allowed to share in a tremendous secret.

If you are unable to perfect the spit, then swallow. But don't do it steadily. Do it as if carried away by passion, and afterwards slap your chest gaily to emphasize your independence. But there are disadvantages in swallowing if there are many wines to taste during the morning. There are always disadvantages about being carried away by passion.

All this, you notice, has been done without a word. Only at the moment of leaving the cellar need you speak. You step impulsively up to the *maître de chai* and wring his hand and mutter, '*Merci, Maître, merci, merci,*' then hurry out-of-doors.

In the sunlight there may be discussion about the wines. This need not alarm you, for your sense of hearing has been as busy as the rest and you have probably overheard some safe opinions. '*Très souple*' is generally a safe one. But unless asked a direct question, it is best to maintain a sphinx-like silence, smiling knowingly at the whole world from half-shut eyes.

Ⓒ *from* VINEYARDS OF FRANCE 1950

'Yes, I Think So...'

EVELYN WAUGH

One day we went down to the cellars with Wilcox and saw the empty bays which had once held a vast store of wine; one transept only was used now; there the bins were well stocked, some of them with vintages fifty years old.

'There's been nothing added since his Lordship went abroad,' said Wilcox. 'A lot of the old wine wants drinking up. We ought to have laid down the eighteens and twenties. I've had several letters about it from the wine merchants, but her Ladyship says to ask Lord Brideshead, and he says to ask his Lordship, and his Lordship says to ask the lawyers. That's how we get low. There's enough here for ten years at the rate it's going, but how shall we be then?'

Wilcox welcomed our interest; we had bottles brought up from every bin, and it was during those tranquil evenings with Sebastian that I first made a serious acquaintance with wine and sowed the seed of that rich harvest which

was to be my stay in many barren years. We would sit, he and I, in the Painted Parlour with three bottles open on the table and three glasses before each of us; Sebastian had found a book on wine-tasting, and we followed its instructions in detail. We warmed the glass slightly at a candle, filled it a third high, swirled the wine round, nursed it in our hands, held it to the light, breathed it, sipped it, filled our mouths with it, and rolled it over the tongue, ringing it on the palate like a coin on a counter, tilted our heads back and let it trickle down the throat. Then we talked of it and nibbled Bath Oliver biscuits, and passed on to another wine; then back to the first, then on to another, until all three were in circulation and the order of glasses got confused, and we fell out over which was which, and we passed the glasses to and fro between us until there were six glasses, some of them with mixed wines in them which we had filled from the wrong bottle, till we were obliged to start again with three clean glasses each, and the bottles were empty and our praise of them wilder and more exotic.

'... It is a little, shy wine like a gazelle.'

'Like a leprechaun.'

'Dappled, in a tapestry meadow.'

'Like a flute by still water.'

'... And this is a wise old wine.'

'A prophet in a cave.'

'... And this is a necklace of pearls on a white neck.'

'Like a swan.'

'Like the last unicorn.'

And we would leave the golden candlelight of the dining-room for the starlight outside and sit on the edge of the fountain, cooling our hands in the water and listening drunkenly to its splash and gurgle over the rocks.

'Ought we to be drunk *every* night?' Sebastian asked one morning.

'Yes, I think so.'

'I think so too.'

© *from* BRIDESHEAD REVISITED, 1926

Golden in the Glass

CYRIL RAY

Just as cognac does not improve in bottle so, by the same token, it does not deteriorate. Unopened, it does not matter how long you keep it, or whether it is kept in a hot cupboard or in a cold cellar. Nor does it mind, as a fine wine would, being shaken up in the boot of a car, or the hands of a clumsy wine-waiter.

Is it worth keeping bottles of brandy in the cellar, when we are told that it does not improve in bottle? Apart from the fact that it does not deteriorate either, it is well to remember that nothing ever goes down in price. Cognac is expensive now, but it may well become more so, and a bottle put away today may save a few pence or a pound or so next year. And Henri Exshaw, head of his family firm, which matures its cognacs in Bordeaux, once held forth to me on the subject, saying, 'Well, it doesn't actually *improve*, but it *does* settle down. Cognac is a blended product, and the longer the various elements are together the more completely they merge. Like an old married couple – neither may get

any better-looking with age, but they do get used to each other. In a good marriage, they get more like each other in habits and even in looks – same thing with the various elements in a good blend.'

The one thing to remember in storing bottles of brandy for any length of time is that, unlike bottles of wine, the corks of which must be kept moist to remain healthy, they must be stood upright: spirits attack cork and rot it.

As for bottles that have been opened, this is another matter. Cognac does not change in an unopened bottle because it is not exposed to the air: once the cork has been drawn and the cognac poured there is more, and fresher, air between cork and liquid, and this will have an oxidizing effect.

Such effect on a three-star brandy would be negligible for many weeks, for the brandy is young – indeed, what little change there would be is likely to be for the better.

But it was François Chapeau, the *maître de chai* at Martell, who pointed out to me that he and his peers in other great firms had blended their VSOP and older brandies to be just in balance when bottled, and that even a modest further oxidization would throw that balance out. His advice – and no one's could be more worth having – is that once a bottle of VSOP or finer liqueur brandy had been opened, the unconsumed contents should be decanted into smaller bottles, with as little space left as possible, though without contact, between cognac and cork. Otherwise, a liqueur brandy left for more than a few days with a considerable air space (what the wine-shippers call 'ullage') begins to lose life and flavour, though its acidity increases.

Mind you, this is a Frenchman speaking, and a Cognaçais at that. The loss of life and flavour he refers to may be related in some way to the softness that Englishmen find agreeable, and the French find mawkish, in brandies matured in wood in England – 'late-bottled' or 'early-landed' brandies. Perhaps there is room here for experiment – myself, I can never keep a bottle of liqueur brandy open for long enough without finishing it to be able to decide whether, after a time, it begins to resemble an early-landed brandy or not...

Virtually all cognac-lovers, and certainly everyone in Cognac, talks of three-star brandy as suitable only for mixing as a long drink. Ask in a café in Cognac for any brandy by name and you are automatically served with a VSOP. If you want a three-star you must ask for it specially.

Of course, a VSOP is preferable as a liqueur, but one can be too high-and-mighty about the three-star of a reputable house. I have finished off many a meal in provincial England with such a one, neat with my coffee, and been genuinely grateful. It is not that three-star is an inferior cognac: it is simply that the older ones are even better.

All the same, if cognac *is* to be mixed, then three-star is the quality for mixing: the higher ranks must be treated with greater deference, when drunk as what the French call a *digestif* after dinner.

Let an English novelist be our first guide:

Franklin Blake, whom I suppose to be the hero (unless I am doing an injustice to Sergeant Cuff, English fiction's first detective) of Wilkie Collins's *The Moonstone*, asks the butler whether on the night of the theft he could possible have been drunk.

Betteredge replies that as he looked wretchedly ill, he was persuaded to take a little brandy-and-water, and Franklin Blake says,

> ' "I am not used to brandy-and-water. It is quite possible..."
>
> ' "Wait a bit, Mr Franklin. I knew you were not used, too. I poured you out half a wineglassful of our fifty-year-old Cognac; and (more shame for me!) I drowned that noble liquor in nigh on a tumblerful of cold water. A child couldn't have got drunk on it, let alone a grown man." '

Here, then, is a lesson to us – our first lesson. It is shame upon us to drown in cold water what Betteredge the butler rightly calls a noble liquor. A liqueur brandy is to be drunk neat.

Wilkie Collins published *The Moonstone* in 1868, though it was set in the eighteen-forties.

Our second lesson beginneth with a novel published in the nineteen-forties, though here, too, the significant scene is earlier still.

It was, according to the plot, some time between the wars that Charles Ryder, in Evelyn Waugh's *Brideshead Revisited*, took Lady Julia Flyte's rich, hairy-heeled husband, Rex Mottram, to Paillard's in Paris for dinner. Mottram lit his first cigarette between the sole in a white wine sauce and the *caneton à la presse* – which meant also on this occasion between the 1906 Montrachet and the 1904 Clos de Bèze – and then:

> 'The cognac was not to Rex's taste. It was clear and pale and it came to us in a bottle free from grime and Napoleonic cyphers. It was only a year or two older than Rex and lately bottled. They gave it to us in very thin tulip-shaped glasses of modest size.
>
> ' "Brandy's one of the things I do know a bit about," said Rex. "This is a bad colour. What's more, I can't taste it in this thimble."
>
> 'They brought him a balloon the size of his head. He made them warm it over the spirit lamp. Then he rolled the splendid spirit round, buried his face in the fumes, and pronounced it the sort of stuff he put soda in at home.
>
> 'So, shamefacedly, they wheeled out of its hiding place the vast and mouldy bottle they kept for people of Rex's sort.
>
> ' "That's the stuff," he said, tilting the treacly concoction till it left dark rings

round the sides of his glass. "They've always got some tucked away, but they won't bring it out unless you make a fuss. Have some."

' "I'm quite happy with this."

' "Well, it's a crime to drink it, if you don't really appreciate it."

'He lit his cigar and sat back at peace with the world; I, too, was at peace in another world than his. We both were happy. He talked of Julia and I heard his voice, unintelligible at a great distance, like a dog's barking miles away on a still night.'

It will already, I hope, be clear to the reader what merit there must have been in that cognac that was first offered – 'clear and pale ... only a year or two older than Rex' (who was, I suppose, in his thirties). It was especially meritorious of Paillard's to have a cognac 'lately bottled' – late-bottled cognacs, as I have shown, are only fairly frequent in England, and rare indeed in Paris restaurants even of the noblest sort. (But Evelyn Waugh was right in referring to 'lately-bottled' and not to 'early-landed'. The terms are sometimes used indiscriminately, but a 'lately-bottled' cognac could be found in France, 'early-landed' only in Britain.)

So, too, was it praiseworthy to offer it in 'very thin tulip-shaped glasses of modest size'. Better men, and nicer men, than Rex Mottram have taken their brandies in balloons the size of their heads, but it is a mistake, none the less. Not that one advocates one of those piddling little so-called 'liqueur glasses' that have to be filled to the brim for one to enjoy even a modest mouthful, but one needs a glass big enough only to be filled one-third or one-quarter full when a decent measure of brandy (what an English pub would call a double, say) is poured in and, ideally, narrowing a little towards the top, so that the fragrance of the spirit is not only trapped, as it were, but directed and concentrated towards the nose.

At Lasserre – to me, it is perhaps the greatest restaurant in Europe – they serve their superb cognacs in moderate-sized, slightly tapering glasses very like sherry *copitas*(a), if not perhaps quite so narrow at the top, and this is the type most favoured in Cognac itself, whether in the tasting-rooms or at table.*

Virtually the only other shapes to be met with (though not so frequently) amongst the Cognaçais are what they call a tulip(b) and a very small *ballon*(c) of roughly the same capacity as either of the other two.*

I have never seen one of those big goldfish-bowl balloons in the hand of anyone who distils or blends or ships serious cognac.

All glass from which one drinks fine wine or good cognac should be thin, but there are many who will say that this is especially important in a brandy

* See illustration, next page.

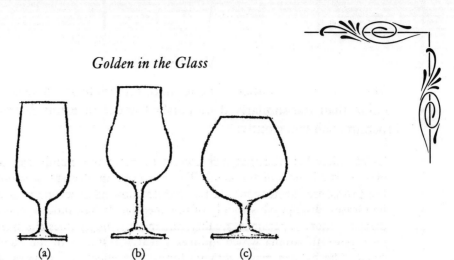

(a)   (b)   (c)

glass because the liqueur must be gently warmed by the heat of the hand. This is the view most generally held by amateurs, and advocated by most of the great cognac houses themselves. Indeed, the small *ballon* is meant to be of a size that can just comfortably be completely cupped in the hand.

Thus, Charles Walter Berry, a dedicated wine-merchant and a great lover of fine wines and brandies, who lived in the age of fancy writing on the subject, laid it down in his *Viniana* (1929) that:

'Liqueur Brandy ... should be served in suitable glasses, tulip-shaped and light in weight, not too large, and in no circumstances in those stupid oddities known as Liqueur Glasses. The stem should be slender, and when the priceless nectar has been served, the glass should be held in the right hand between the second and third fingers until such time as the Brandy has taken the warmth of the touch ...'

At first reading, I took the old boy to mean that the bowl of the glass was to be held between two finger-tips, but one has only to try that operation with the second and third fingers to realize its impossibility. What he meant, of course, was that the stem of the glass was to be slipped between these fingers: in other words, the glass was to be cupped in the palm.

He went on:

'– that is the ideal temperature. While it is being obtained, there need be no waste of time, *au contraire*, for the glass can be gently turned in the hand, this way and that way, and by thus enjoying the fragrance with its stimulating effect the senses will give timely warning to all the members of the body of what a treat there is in store ...'

And, similarly, Martell's handsome brochure advises, 'the glass should be warmed carefully in the palm of the hand and the aroma of a good Cognac will develop; it will even linger for a long time in the empty glass'.

But there are dissentients, none more forthright in advocacy of the opposite opinion than the similarly distinguished house of Rémy-Martin, who in their brochure maintain stoutly:

'It is widely believed that it is correct to warm the brandy contained in a balloon glass in the hollow of the hand. There is even an element of snobbery attaching to the procedure. Professional tasters, while allowing everyone to drink his brandy as he pleases, disapprove strongly of this method. It has, indeed, one serious disadvantage: the more superior its quality, the more strongly does the warmed brandy give off a powerful aroma which induces a real anaesthesia of the faculties of taste and smell. The balloon glass, with its funnel-like effect, accentuates still more this regrettable effect. Warming a balloon glass in the hollow of the hand is of use only to bring out the quality of second-rate brandies, from which an aroma may thus be forced.

'A good brandy like Rémy Martin's Fine Champagne VSOP contains subtle perfumes which can be inhaled and appreciated even when it is iced. And so we suggest to connoisseurs this test to genuine quality which consists of drinking brandy only in glasses the form of which has been chosen by professional tasters. These glasses are almost straight, and tall enough to be used only a third full, leaving the top free to collect the most subtle and gratifying vapours. The true-brandy lover, if he so wishes, may make a test by adding an ice cube in the glass, which will emphasize still more the incomparable fine quality of Rémy Martin Cognac.'

When experts differ so widely as this, we amateurs may surely regard ourselves as at liberty to go each our own idiosyncratic way. Myself, I am more – much more – for the hand-warming than for the icing, which to my mind numbs fragrance and flavour, but I agree whole-heartedly with Evelyn Waugh's implicit condemnation of the spirit-lamp. If one's taste is like mine, then the warmth of the hand is quite adequate for cognac, as it is for claret: warmed on a spirit-lamp the glass becomes too hot, and releases the fine fragrance of its contents too violently. And to burn methylated spirits in the presence of a fine brandy is, in any case, an act of consummate lunacy.

For further refinements – though few of us, I fear, are so dedicated as this – I commend those interested to the practice in the tasting-room at Hine (and, I am sure, of most other firms of the same meticulous sort, but it was at Hine that I recorded the details in my note-book).

The fine, thin Baccarat glasses are washed only in distilled water and are then hung upside down to drain themselves dry – never wiped, lest even the finest linen cloths impart a lingering flavour or aroma to the glass. The girls who sweep the floor are forbidden to touch the glasses (or the tasting bench, come to that: only a member of the Hine family may wash a glass, or clear the table), which are rinsed, inside and outside, in the cognac one is to taste before one tastes it.

The same sort of glass is used for the *trou charentais*, or *coup de milieu*, the glass of cognac served as a digestive and to give a breathing-space between the main courses of important public dinners in the region and at bucolic banquets, in the way that calvados is served as a *trou normand*, or that sedater folk serve a sorbet. But the custom is dying out: I have come across it only once myself. Even at French banquets, the courses are not so many or so heavy as they used to be.

There is no need to be so pernickety about what glass to use for cognac as a long drink, or as an aperitif, or, indeed, as medicine – the usual three-star, or similar quality and age, that is. Writing in his middle years of how, when he was eighteen, he had broken his bones and ruptured a kidney by jumping from a bridge on his aunt's estate and falling twenty-nine feet to the hard ground, the late Winston Churchill recalled* that Lady Randolph 'hurried down with energetic aid and inopportune brandy', but not the suitability or otherwise of the brandy glass.

(Unlike Bertrand Russell, who remembered all his long life how, as a boy of seventeen, in 1889, he chanced to be the only male member of the family at home when the eighty-year-old Mr Gladstone came to dine and stay the night. After the ladies had left the dinner table the boy waited – himself grandson of a prime minister – nervous but agog, for the pearls of wisdom that would surely fall from the aged statesman's lips. There was a silence, and then Mr Gladstone spoke:

'This is very good port they have given me, but why have they given it me in a claret glass?')

A tumbler, or what the Americans call a highball glass, is good enough for brandy and soda, and on the bridge of a destroyer in what was then Captain Mountbatten's Fifth Destroyer Flotilla of Js and Ks, under fire for the first time in what had hitherto been a sheltered life, I have drunk brandy-and-ginger ale from a chipped enamel mug and felt a little less cowardly in consequence.

The taste I then acquired has stayed with me sufficiently for it still to be my chosen tipple at theatre bars when I can fight my way to one at an interval. In other circumstances I now find the mixture too sweet, but it is no doubt the sugar in the ginger-ale that keeps one going from too early a dinner to too late a supper – sometimes even giving one the strength to battle one's way into that other kind of stall in a London theatre's invariably inadequate urinal.

* Churchill, *My Early Life*, London, 1930.

The first time I visited Cognac, many years ago, I was surprised and amused to find my hosts, distinguished distillers and blenders of brandy, taking Scotch-and-soda before dinner while their English guests politely took the cognac of the house with water – *fine à l'eau.*

That was *le snobisme* of the time – Scotch is selling more widely now in France and, in consequence, has lost its *chic.*

Now, it is cognac or champagne as an aperitif (pineau, or pineau with vodka, say, is less likely) – the cognac usually with soda or with a bottled table-water. But at the hospitable house of a Hennessy director during my latest visit I was offered a mixture new to me – *cognac-orange*, which consists of two-thirds fresh orange juice and one-third cognac, served on the rocks as an aperitif, a sort of supercharged Buck's Fizz, save that it reverses the proportions (Buck's Fizz is two of champagne to one of orange) and is a good deal more potent. But deliciously refreshing and bracing after a long hot day.

I have heard tell of Americans who take their cognac with tonic, a mixture I have not tried, and do not propose to. There may well be those who take it with Coca-cola, and I shall not try that, either.

As a long drink, I like brandy with soda, or with any sparkling table water, such as Perrier or Apollinaris (with the ice that I eschew with a liqueur brandy), and the French like their *fine à l'eau*, or brandy and tap-water, which I find a flat and mawkish drink. All the same, cognac served this way, with still or with sparkling water – or, indeed, with the orange-juice I have mentioned – makes a good aperitif because, being made from the grape, it is not going to quarrel with one's dinner-wine as whisky or gin or vodka can. Not that I am puritanical about mixing grape and grain, but like goes with like, and brandy seems to me to be more especially in keeping with wine, whether before or after, than other spirits.

'Fine' in a restaurant or a café, when one asks for a *fine maison*, *une fine*, or a *fine à l'eau*, does not mean what it is obliged to mean on a label: it is any house brandy. On the other hand, there is many a French cook and many a French housewife with recipes that require cognac in the sauce or the marinade or for a final flaming, and all such are worth serious attention.

It was one of the most distinguished of London restaurateurs who once told me, in a burst of confidence (which is why I do not give his name, or that of his restaurant), that what made even his luxurious *caravanserai* inferior to restaurants of similar rank in Paris was – to give an example, he said – that in his kitchen they used 'cooking' butter and 'cooking' brandy, because of the way his books were scrutinized by accountants and shareholders and the like, whereas in the kitchens of his opposite numbers in Paris, where even accountants and shareholders care as much about quality as about profit, they used the same brandy and the same butter for cooking that they served at table.

I did not take him to mean that it was liqueur brandy that went into the sauces in Paris, but that it *was* cognac, and not 'grape brandy'.

Does it make all that difference in the taste of a sauce? Perhaps not, but it makes an enormous difference to the moral of the chef and his *brigade*, and to their pride in their job.

This is not the place for a long list of recipes, whether for memorable dishes or for mixed drinks, but it would be remiss of me not to quote Eliza Acton's 1845 comment (remiss of me, because my wife edited Eliza Acton for readers of our own time*) that her 'Very Superior Whipped Syllabubs' are 'considered less wholesome without a portion of brandy', and her recipe for a sort of forerunner of Irish coffee, but without the cream: 'Burnt Coffee, or Coffee à la Militaire (in France vulgarly called Gloria): Make some coffee as strong and as clear as possible, sweeten it in the cup with white sugar almost to syrup, then pour the brandy on the top gently over a spoon, set fire to it with a lighted paper, and when the spirit is in part consumed, blow out the flame, and drink the *gloria* quite hot.'*

Nor can I forbear to mention here that it is the addition of brandy to a champagne cocktail (which in itself consists only of champagne poured over a lump of sugar on to which have been shaken three drops of Angostura, with a twist of lemon or orange peel added) that transforms it into a Maharajah's Burra Peg, which is worth knowing about for when maharajahs come to dinner.

For lesser mortals, it would be nice to revive one of the classic cocktails of the cocktail age – that period of cloche hats, Carpentier and the Co-optimists, Lenglen and the League of Nations, and of flat-bosomed flappers, between charlestons, gossiping over clover clubs or white ladies about the man that danced with the girl that danced with the Prince of Wales. All that is left to us is the dry martini, but the sidecar used to be regarded as the one mixed drink to take before a dinner at which fine wine was to be served, for it was brandy-based, with nothing more added than half as much fresh lemon-juice as brandy, and the same of any triple sec white curaçao, such as Cointreau, served ice-cold. Delicious!

Those who have wintered in Scandinavia must inevitably have come across Swedish glögg, for which I have seen many elaborate recipes. The simplest heats a quart of brandy into which have been put half a cup of sugar, a dozen cloves and a stick of cinnamon. When almost boiling a pint of sherry is stirred into the mixture, which is then served in warmed mugs in each of which are a

*Elizabeth Ray, *The Best of Eliza Acton*, selected and edited, London, 1968.

couple of raisins and of blanched, unsalted almonds. Port, madeira or claret can take the place of sherry, but nothing can replace the brandy.

Proportions may be altered, too, but it is as well to bear in mind the warning pronounced in 1862 by Jerry Thomas, the great New York bar-tender of a century ago, in writing about a similar concoction in his classic *How to Mix Drinks, or the Bon-Vivant's Companion*:

> 'This preparation is a very agreeable refreshment on a cold night, but should be used in moderation; the strength of the punch is so artfully concealed ... that many persons, particularly of the softer sex, have been tempted to partake so plentifully of it as to render them somewhat unfit for waltzing or quadrilling after supper.'

The Viennese *Lebensretter*, or life-saver, is nothing more (or less) than a bottle of port to half a bottle of brandy, sugared to taste, and served hot.

The good book in which I first came across this noble brew, (I think it was an American 'Old Vienna Cookbook', so-called,) said that it was efficacious as a remedy for fainting spells, and I can well believe it. The Wine Society calls it negus, and makes even more potent medicine of it, by recommending as much brandy as port, besides adding a splash of lemon-juice and a dash of spice.

But then, there is no end to the medicinal uses of the good creature.

My old, late, and much-lamented friend, Vyvyan Holland, who survived the savageries he suffered as a child, and wrote about so movingly in his *Son of Oscar Wilde*, to become a much-loved lover of life, used to tell of a great-uncle who kept a few fine bottles of rare old cognac for rare old friends. One day his house took fire and one fireman, in particular, behaved with great gallantry. The old gentleman could think of no more handsome gesture than to offer him a glass of his oldest and most noble brandy. The fireman, drenched by the hoses, sat down, took off his boots and socks and said, 'Thank you kindly, sir: a very happy thought. I'm a teetotaller myself, sir, but I've always found that there's nothing like brandy to stop you getting a cold', and poured the precious fluid over his feet.

© *from* COGNAC, 1973

"Of course, I only breed them for the brandy."
Punch, 13 April 1949

Cognac

MARTIN ARMSTRONG

Through centuries unnumbered men of old
Broke stubborn Earth and taught the trailing Vine
And trod the bubbling Press and drank the Wine
Contented with the Ruby and the Gold;
Till some one of a subtler Essence dreamed
And poured the Wine into a copper Still
And set a gradual Fire beneath, until
Eddies of odorous mist arose and steamed
Along a curling Pipe, condensed, and streamed
In trickling drops into a Chamber cool
And mounted slowly in a luscious pool
In whose eye a sullen topaz gleamed,
Then in an oaken cask of portly shape
He stored the subtle spirit and darkly smiled,

Knowing that he had craftily beguiled
The Essence of the Essence of the Grape.

"You needn't smell it, Mr. Barker – it's quite fresh."

Punch, 8 April 1953

Honey for Hangovers

M. F. K. FISHER

Misery treads on the heels of joy;
anguish rides swift after pleasure
Donald Grant Mitchell

Sometimes it is impossible to tell when a preventive is only that and not a cure as well, for ailing man or beast. This is not the case with hang-overs, at least.

There is one and only one positive and infallible preventive for this ancient and universal physical hazard: abstention.

Its cures, most of them of small value but enormous social interest, are almost as many as there are people to invent them. They cover every conceivable procedure, and range from the somber to the silly. One man who spent much of his lifetime studying the problem through his own reactions to it insisted, long before he was knocked down and killed when cold sober by an enormous dog, that the only real cure was sudden death. This assertion was even more macabre to his friends because he had always professed, and backed it by practice, that two aspirins and 'a hair of the dog that had bit him' were of great help the morning after the night before...

It is interesting that most hang-over cures seem to involve more alcohol, even indirectly, as in a peculiar one still used occasionally in sporting circles. It is at least as old as *The Beggar's Opera*, and from the same social level as Macheath and Suky Tawdry.

It evolved, probably, from the basic fact that most black eyes are suffered by brawlers too drunk to duck, and that a basic cure for black eyes in those rough days, as even now, was to bleed them with leeches.

Leeches are, however, capable of being surprisingly fastidious, and most of them do not like alcohol in their drink. Occasionally one turns up, however, which loves booze as fiercely as any habitual tosspot, and which will suck from his fellow drunkard until he is, leech-wise, roaring.

Naturally such alcoholic jewels are rare, and when once found in the circles that most need them, in tough London a few centuries ago and in tough New York in 1890, they have been handed tenderly from one 'physician' to another until, I assume, they have died an alcoholic death.

It is difficult to imagine how to tell a drunken leech from a sober one, and I feel willing to let the whole peculiar question rest on hearsay, in this case from a well-read old man who had tried to earn his way through medical college and ended as a rubber in a rundown gymnasium for pugilists.

It is a relief to come upon a nonalcoholic remedy for a hang-over, and here is one as innocent as a new-born butterfly. It was given to me by a devout and therefore teetotaling Methodist, who recommended it from her own experience for fatigue or an upset stomach, but confessed that her pop, before he Heard the Call, often ate great quantities of it after his weekly trips into town from the Kansas farm:

> Mix one tablespoonful of cornstarch in one cup of good buttermilk, and heat but do not boil. Eat while hot like soup, with salt and pepper, or let cool and eat frequently, with plenty of honey for flavoring.

I have tried this, not from necessity but from curiosity, and cold it is a pleasantly refreshing bowl, somewhat like yoghurt. I can imagine that it would prove a balm to the outraged innards of anyone who had drunk too much, or suffered from some other kind of poisoning.

I asked my friend from Kansas why she put 'plenty of honey' in the recipe she copied for me from her old book, and she did not rightly know, but reminded me that 'honey never hurt *any*body.' This may not be completely so, but a current vogue for curing hang-overs with large regulated doses of it would bear her out in that it never hurt an otherwise healthy drunkard.

According to a Vermont doctor who has observed local folk medicine for a long time and written successfully about some of his simple conclusions, over-indulgence in hard liquor is caused by a lack of potassium in the human system. Honey, he says, is one of the best natural supplies of this alkaline, and will not only soothe a body drowned in alcoholic acids but will help kill a craving for them.

Vermonters, especially as interpreted by scientists, are practical, hard-headed people. Those of us who are less so may prefer to think that an urge to go on a spree is more the fault of a faithless lover or a carefree friend than of a potassium deficiency, but no matter what the cause of a night or even a week of sousing, two pounds of honey and twenty-four hours of rest are almost a sure cure, not only for the temporary ungodliness of the hang-over but for the first desire, too.

Dr. Jarvis's Honey Cure

18 teaspoonfuls of honey, to be given 6 at a time, 20 minutes apart. Then repeat in 3 hours. Let patient drink whiskey left by bed if he wishes. Next morning repeat 40-minute honey-routine, follow with soft-boiled egg, and then in 10 minutes give 6 more teaspoonsful of honey. For lunch give 4 t. honey, then glass of tomato juice, medium piece of chopped beef, and for dessert 4 more t. honey. Leave whiskey on table toward normal evening meal, but it will probably not be drunk.

I have never known anyone to follow this cure for such a serious hang-over as the one reported in the book about Vermont folk medicine, when the patient had been drinking for some two weeks and was 'paralyzed drunk' (although apparently still able to swallow!) when the honey treatment began. But I know several people who have sobered themselves by sipping honey and milk, preferably in a dark quiet room, for a few hours after they or their protective friends have realized that alcohol was in command. Even without regarding the fine word potassium, their bodies have recognized the need to counteract the acids gnawing at them, and like animals or children they have welcomed the sweet balm.

© *from* A CORDIALL WATER, 1963

[353]

This Bread I Break

DYLAN THOMAS

This bread I break was once the oat,
This wine upon a foreign tree
Plunged in its fruit;
Man in the day or wind at night
Laid the crops low, broke the grape's joy.

Once in this wind the summer blood
Knocked in the flesh that decked the vine,
Once in this bread
The oat was merry in the wind;
Man broke the sun, pulled the wind down.

This flesh you break, this blood you let
Make desolation in the vein,
Were oat and grape
Born of the sensual root and sap;
My wine and drink, my bread you snap.

Acknowledgements

FIRST FALTERING STEPS	Reprinted by permission of A.D. Peters & Co. Ltd
BUZZINGS OF A FAR-FLUNG BAR FLY	By kind permission of James Cameron
TO CYNTHIA	© The Executors of the Estate of P.M. Hubbard
IN MODERATION	By kind permission of Angus Wilson
BOTTLE DOGGEREL	By kind permission of The Wine and Food Society (Spring 1957)
ST COBDEN AND ST CRIPPS	© The Executors of the Estate of R. Postgate
BOTTLING THE BOOKIES	By kind permission of Brian St Pierre
A GOOD APPETITE	From *Between Meals*, courtesy of A.J. Liebling and Laurence Pollinger Ltd
ONE FOR THE HIGH ROAD	© Lady Glenavy
CLARET COUNTRY: FIVE POEMS ON THE MÉDOC	By kind permission of Peter Dickinson
MANKIND'S MYSTERIOUS FRIEND	By kind permission of Lady Diana Cooper
THE CASE OF YQUEM	© *The Wine Magazine, Sunday Times*
ARKETALL	By kind permission of Nigel Nicolson
FOR A WINE FESTIVAL	By kind permission of Mrs Gwen Watkins
THE EXPENSE OF SPIRITS IS A CRYING SHAME	*From Strugnell's Sonnets* by Wendy Cope (Quarto)
THE PLAINT OF A FRENCHWOMAN IN AN ENGLISH HOSPITAL	© The International Wine & Food Society
VIVANDIÈRE	Courtesy of David Higham Associates Ltd
NOT THE REAL THING . . .	© *Observer*
NORTH OF SAN FRANCISCO	By kind permission of Peter Dickinson
GRANDMOTHER CLATTERWICK AND MR MCGUFFOG	By kind permission of Michael Gilbert (May and June 1970)
THE SIREN'S GIFT TO MEN	By kind permission of Secker & Warburg
OLD BROMPTON ROAD PUB	© *Spectator* (5 July 1963)
A RUDE WORD IN CRETE	© *Observer*
TO THEA, AT THE YEAR'S END	© The Executors of the Estate of P.M. Hubbard

THE GROWTH OF MARIE-LOUISE	© le Carré Productions, by kind permission of the author and John Farquharson Ltd
THE SENTINEL'S STORY, 1805	First published in Collected Poems (Macmillan), courtesy of Charles Causley and David Higham Associates Ltd
'VERY GOOD FOR THE KIDNEYS'	© The Executors of the Estate of W. Somerset-Maugham and William Heinemann Limited
LET'S PARLER FRANGLAIS	Reproduced by permission of *Punch*
THE KERNEL OF TRUTH	© P. and M. Youngman Carter, reprinted by permission of Curtis Brown Ltd, London
REMEMBRANCE OF MEALS PAST: A GLANCE AT FOOD AND WINE IN PROUST	By kind permission of Anthony Powell
THE CHAMPAGNE CAMPAIGN	By kind permission of Wynford Vaughan-Thomas
NO WINE FOR A LADY?	Reprinted by permission of A.D. Peters & Co. Ltd
WISDEN AND WINE	By kind permission of Terence Prittie
VINTAGE DRESS AND VINTAGE DRINKING	Originally published in *The Compleat Imbiber*, courtesy of James Laver
SARDINES AND SAUTERNE	By kind permission of Mrs Thelma Holland
IMBIBER BEWARE!	By kind permission of Julian Jeffs
DEFEAT OF A DRINKING MAN	By kind permission of Alan Brien
NO . . . ER CREME DE MENTHE: A DESPERATE CONVERSATION WITH EVELYN WAUGH	By kind permission of Oliver Knox
WINE, WOMEN, FOOD, AND SONG	By kind permission of Peter Dickinson
VINTAGE FFOLKES	Reproduced by courtesy of *Punch*
HOW TO TASTE	By kind permission of J.M. Scott OBE
'YES, I THINK SO . . .'	Reprinted by permission of A.D. Peters & Co. Ltd
COGNAC	© The International Wine & Food Society
HONEY FOR HANGOVERS	By kind permission of M.F.K. Fisher and Chatto & Windus
THIS BREAD I BREAK	By Dylan Thomas from *Collected Poems* (J.M. Dent), courtesy of David Higham Associates Ltd

Index